Trekking the Nepal Himalaya

Stan Armington

Trekking in the Nepal Himalaya

5th edition

Published by
Lonely Planet Publications Pty Ltd (ACN 005 607 983)
PO Box 617, Hawthorn, Vic 3122, Australia
Lonely Planet Publications, Inc
PO Box 2001A, Berkeley, CA 94702, USA

Printed by
Colorcraft Ltd, Hong Kong

Photographs by

Greg Alford (GA)	Stan Armington (SA)
Glen Beanland (GB)	Sonia Berto (SB)
James Lyon (JL)	Ralph Roob (RR)
Kalyan Singh (KS)	Paul Steel (PS)
Tony Wheeler (TW)	

Front cover: Nuptse from Lobuje (SB)
Back cover: Family trekking (TW)

First Published
April 1979

This Edition
July 1991

Although the authors and publisher have tried to make the information as
accurate as possible, they accept no responsibility for any loss, injury or
inconvenience sustained by any person using this book.

National Library of Australia Cataloguing in Publication Data

Armington, Stan
Trekking in the Nepal Himalaya

5th ed.
Includes index.
ISBN 0 86442 051 X.

1. Hiking – Himalaya Mountains – Guide-books. 2. Nepal – Description and travel – Guide-books.
3. Himalaya Mountains – Description and travel – Guide-books.
I. Title.

915.49604

text © Stan Armington
maps © Lonely Planet 1991
photos © photographers as indicated 1991
illustrations © Nawang Chuldim Sherpa & Lonely Planet 1991

Stan Armington

Stan has been organising and leading treks in Nepal since 1971. A graduate engineer, he has also worked for the US National Park Service in the Yellowstone and Olympic parks, as well as serving as a guide on Mt Hood in Oregon. Stan is a fellow of the Royal Geographical Society, a member of the American Alpine Club, the Explorers Club, and the Alpine Stomach Club. He lives in Kathmandu where he spends his time opening new bars and trekking companies.

From the Author

A word of thanks to the many people who encouraged and assisted me with writing this material. Sushil Upadhyay, Shannan Miller, Bob Pierce, Chuck McDougal, Yangdu Gombu, Bruce Klepinger, Gil Roberts, Erica Stone, Bill Jones, Dana Keil, Harka Gurung, Jim Williams, Lindsay Swope and Hugh Swift's constant companion, K Garney, provided great help. They provided me with information about recent changes, places I had not been, or things I did not understand, and they checked my version of facts for accuracy. Hundreds of trekkers have helped me by asking questions that I would never have thought of otherwise; I have tried to answer most of them here.

This book could never have been written without the help of the many sherpas who led me up and down hills and patiently answered all my foolish questions about what we were seeing. Passang Geljen, Dawa Lama, Pemba, Ang Mingma, Tsering Wangdi and Nawang Chuldim helped with this edition. David Shlim's medical chapter gives a first-class analysis of the medical problems of a trek.

Once again, thanks to Tony and Maureen Wheeler, who pushed me to tackle this project and continue to provide suggestions on how to improve it.

Thanks to Cambridge University Press for permission to quote four lines from *Nepal Himalaya* by H W Tilman.

From the Publisher

This edition of *Trekking in the Nepal Himalaya* was edited by James Lyon, with copy editing by

Gillian Cumming and Greg Alford. Greg Herriman was responsible for the design, cover design, layout and mapping. Thanks also to Ann Jeffree for additional mapping work, Michelle de Kretser for proofreading, Sharon Wertheim for indexing and Sue Mitra for editorial guidance.

Thanks also to these trekkers who have written to us with new information and helpful suggestions: Sebastian Anstruther (UK), David Brown, James Earl and Stewart Johnson (all from Australia). Many other readers' contributions are acknowledged in Lonely Planet's *Nepal – a travel survival kit*.

Warning & Request

Things change, prices go up, schedules change, good places go bad and bad ones go bankrupt – nothing stays the same. So, if you find things better or worse, recently opened or long since closed, please tell us. Write to Lonely Planet, or to the author, c/o Malla Treks, PO Box 787, Kathmandu, Nepal.

Between editions, when it is possible, we'll publish the most interesting letters and important information in a Stop Press section at the back of the book. All information is greatly appreciated, and the best letters will receive a free copy of the next edition, or any Lonely Planet book of your choice.

Contents

MAP LEGEND

BOUNDARIES

- ·—·—·—·— ....International Boundaries
- ··—··—··—·· ....Internal Boundaries
- ·—··—··— ....National Parks, Reserves
- --------- ....The Equator
- ....The Tropics

SYMBOLS

- ◉ NEW DELHI ....National Capital
- ● BOMBAY ....Provincial or State Capital
- ● Pune ....Major Town
- ● Borsi ....Minor Town
- ▲ ....Post Office
- ✈ ....Airport
- ℹ ....Tourist Information
- ⊖ ....Bus Station, Terminal
- 66 ....Highway Route Number
- ⸙ ☦ ⸸ ....Mosque, Church, Cathedral
- ∴ ....Temple, Ruin or Archaeological Site
- ▲ ....Hostel
- ✚ ....Hospital
- ※ ....Lookout
- ⚑ ....Camping Areas
- ⊓ ....Picnic Areas
- ⌂ ....Hut or Chalet
- ▲ ....Mountain
- ₊₊▀₊₊ ....Railway Station
- ⫽ ....Road Bridge
- ₊₊▥₊₊ ....Road Rail Bridge
- ⊃ ⊂ ....Road Tunnel
- ⊅) (⊂ ....Railway Tunnel
- ⌢⌒ ....Escarpment or Cliff
- ⌐ ....Pass
- ⌣ ....Ridge Line

ROUTES

- ————— ....Major Roads and Highways
- --------- ....Unsealed Major Roads
- ——— ....Sealed Roads
- --------- ....Unsealed Roads, Tracks
- ═══ ....City Streets
- +++++++++++++ ....Railways
- ▬▬◉▬▬ ....Subways
- ················ ....Walking Tracks
- -·-·-·-·-·- ....Ferry Routes
- —╫—╫—╫—╫— ....Cable Car or Chair Lift

HYDROGRAPHIC FEATURES

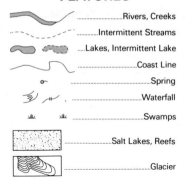

- ....Rivers, Creeks
- ....Intermittent Streams
- ....Lakes, Intermittent Lake
- ....Coast Line
- ....Spring
- ....Waterfall
- ....Swamps
- ....Salt Lakes, Reefs
- ....Glacier

OTHER FEATURES

- Parks, Gardens and ....National Parks
- ....Built Up Area
- Market Place and ....Pedestrian Mall
- ....Plaza and Town Square
- ....Cemetery

Note: Not all the symbols displayed above will necessarily appear in this book

Preface

To travel in the remote areas of Nepal today offers much more than superb mountain scenery. It provides an opportunity to step back in time and meet people who, like our ancestors many centuries ago, lived free of complications, social, economic and political, which beset the developed countries. To the Nepal peasant, his life revolves around his homestead, his fields and, above all, his family and neighbours in the little village perched high on a Himalayan mountainside. Here we can see the meaning of community, free of the drive of competition. We see human happiness despite – or because of – the absence of amenities furnished by our modern civilisation.

Change will come to the Nepalese way of life, but it behoves travellers from the modernised countries to understand and respect the values and virtues of life today in rural Nepal. They have much to teach us about how to live.

John Hunt

Lord Hunt was the leader of the 1953 Mt Everest expedition when Sir Edmund Hillary and Tenzing Norgay Sherpa scaled the peak for the first time.

Introduction

The Himalaya, the 'abode of snows', extends from Assam in eastern India west to Afghanistan. It is a chain of the highest and youngest mountains on earth and it encompasses a region of deep religious and cultural traditions and an amazing diversity of people. Nowhere is this diversity more apparent and the culture more varied and complex than in Nepal. This book concentrates on trekking in Nepal – not quite the same experience as trekking in the Himalaya of India, Pakistan and China, even though the traditions may be similar.

A trek in Nepal is a special and rewarding mountain holiday. Do not lose sight of this as you read about the problems you may encounter and the formalities you must cope with to arrange a trek. These sound worse than they really are.

If you trek on your own, remember that

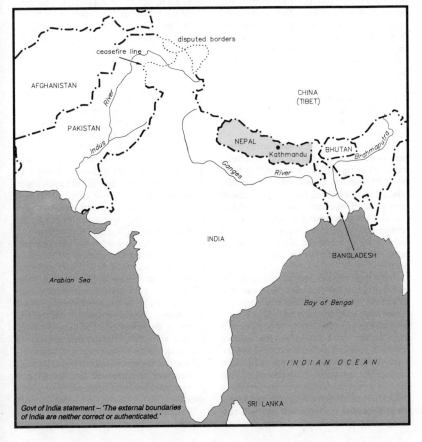

Govt of India statement – 'The external boundaries of India are neither correct or authenticated.'

9

you will be far from civilisation as you know it (including medical care, communication facilities and transport), no matter how many local hotels or other facilities may exist. It is only prudent to take the same precautions during a trek in Nepal as you would take on a major hiking or climbing trip at home, and carry a basic medical kit. There will often be nobody but your own companions to help you if you are sick or injured. Dr Shlim's excellent medical chapter will help you prepare for many possible problems.

Tourism is Nepal's major industry and one of the largest sources of the foreign exchange necessary for the continued economic development of the country. The government encourages tourists to visit Nepal because they spend money. The people in the hills expect to gain a bit of income from every traveller. Even the poorest porter in the hills buys an occasional cup of tea from local inns and purchases rice from villagers. I have made a few suggestions on how to arrange a trek in a manner that is economically beneficial to both you and Nepal, with a minimum of hassle.

The information here is based on my experiences in trekking, leading and organising treks and living in Nepal since 1970. A lot of my own opinions have crept in, especially relating to trekking equipment and cultural interaction. If you have done a lot of hiking, you will certainly have developed your own preferences for equipment and the gear you need to be comfortable. Read my suggestions about equipment, then make your own decisions.

People of various means and temperaments read and use this book. Be aware that others are not like you and that there are many ways to approach a trek. If you have booked a group trek, it may amaze you that there is any need to discuss the relative merits of carrying a sleeping bag. However, a budget trekker may find this discussion useful, but consider it preposterous that anyone would pay US$75 per day or more to trek. There is room for both attitudes (and a lot in between) in Nepal and you will certainly meet 'the other half' during your trek.

This book is your introduction to these diverse opinions and styles.

I have tried to avoid preaching about how to behave on a trek. Obviously, you should pay for what you eat and drink, bury your faeces, minimise the amount of firewood that you use, respect local customs and attitudes and try to interact gently with Nepal. Some trekkers do not do this, and it is unlikely that anything I write will change that. In rare cases, an innkeeper might overcharge you, abuse you, refuse food or accommodation or insult you. Filthy hotels, camp sites and latrines may disgust you along some popular trekking routes. If this happens, it is because someone (probably the person who stayed there last night) contributed to the problem. You have the choice of continuing to escalate the mess or doing your own small part to make Nepal more pleasant for those who follow.

WHY TREK IN NEPAL?

Just as New York is not representative of the USA, so Kathmandu is not representative of Nepal. If you have the time and energy to trek, don't miss the opportunity to leave Kathmandu and see the spectacular beauty and the unique culture of Nepal. Fortunately for the visitor, there are still only a few roads extending deeply into the hills, so the only way to truly visit the remote regions of the kingdom is in the slowest and most intimate manner – walking. It requires more time and effort, but the rewards are also greater. Instead of zipping down a freeway, racing to the next 'point of interest', each step provides new and intriguing viewpoints. You will perceive your day as an entity rather than a few highlights strung together by a ribbon of concrete. For the romanticist, each step is a step in the footsteps of Hillary, Tenzing, Herzog and other Himalayan explorers. If you have neither the patience nor the physical stamina to visit the hills of Nepal on foot, aircraft and helicopter are available. These provide an expensive and unsatisfactory substitute.

Trekking in Nepal will take you through a country that has captured the imagination of mountaineers and explorers for more than 100 years. You will meet people in remote mountain villages whose lifestyle has not changed in generations. Most people trust foreigners. Nepal is one of only a handful of countries that has never been ruled by a foreign power.

Many of the values associated with a hiking trip at home do not have the same importance during a trek in Nepal. Isolation is traditionally a crucial element of any wilderness experience but in Nepal it is impossible to get completely away from people, except for short times or at extremely high elevations. Environmental concerns must include the effects of conservation measures on rural people and the economic effects of tourism on indigenous populations. Even traditional national park management must be adapted because there are significant population centres within Sagarmatha (Mt Everest) and Langtang national parks.

Trekking does not mean mountain climbing. While the ascent of a Himalayan peak may be an attraction for some, you need not have such a goal to enjoy a trek. Throughout this book, trekking always refers to walking on trails.

While trekking you will see the great diversity of Nepal. Villages embrace many ethnic groups and cultures. The terrain changes from tropical jungle to high glaciated peaks in only 150 km. From the start, the towering peaks of the Himalaya provide one of the highlights of a trek. As your plane approaches Kathmandu these peaks appear to be small clouds on the horizon. The mountains become more definable and seem to reach impossible heights as you get closer and finally land at Kathmandu's Tribhuvan Airport.

During a trek, the Himalaya disappears behind Nepal's continual hills, but dominates the northern skyline at each pass. Annapurna, Manaslu, Langtang, Gauri Shankar and Everest will become familiar names. Finally, after weeks of walking, you will arrive at the foot of the mountains themselves – astonishing heights from which gigantic avalanches tumble earthwards in apparent slow motion, dwarfed by their surroundings. Your conception of the Himalaya alters as you turn from peaks famed only for their height to gaze on far more picturesque summits that you may never have heard of – Kantega, Ama Dablam, Machhapuchhare and Khumbakarna.

The beauty and attraction of the Nepal Himalaya emanates not only from the mountains themselves, but also from their surroundings. Nepal is a country of friendly people, picturesque villages and a great variety of cultures and traditions that seem to exemplify many of the attributes we have lost in our headlong rush for development and progress in the West.

Facts about the Country

HISTORY

What is now Nepal was once a collection of feudal principalities sandwiched between Moghul India and Tibet. You can see the palaces of these ancient rulers as you trek through Nepal at places such as Sinja near Jumla, Lamjung near Dumre, Lo Montang, Gorkha and, of course, the Kathmandu Valley. Many of these small kingdoms had little or no contact with Kathmandu. The early history of the Kathmandu Valley, with its Licchivi Dynasty from the 3rd to 13th centuries and the Malla reign from the 13th to 18th centuries, had little effect on the remote hill regions.

In 1769, Prithvi Narayan Shah, the ruler of the House of Gorkha, succeeded in unifying these diverse kingdoms and established the present borders of Nepal. He also founded the Shah Dynasty. The present king of Nepal, King Birendra Bir Bikram Shah Dev, is a direct descendant of Prithvi Narayan Shah.

Rana Prime Ministers

In 1846, the Prime Minister, Jung Bahadur Rana, conspired with the Queen Regent to gain control of the country. He invited all the top political and military leaders to a party and ambushed them in what is known in Nepalese history as the Kot Massacre. The site of the massacre, the Kot, still stands near Hanuman Dhoka in Durbar Square. Following the massacre, Jung Bahadur decreed that the post of prime minister was to be hereditary, taking the precaution to ensure that the title passed to a younger brother if the ruler had no qualified son. The Ranas adopted the title Maharaja and ruled the country for 104 years. Jung Bahadur visited England and France and was received with all the honours due a head of state.

Despite Jung Bahadur's refusal to adopt European practices which conflicted with his Hindu beliefs, he was fascinated with European architecture. The profusion of white stucco neo-classical palaces in Kathmandu was inspired by this journey.

The maharajas kept Nepal isolated and allowed almost no foreign visitors. After losing a fierce war with imperial India, they conceded most of their territory, which now comprises the northern areas of the Indian states of Kashmir, Himachal Pradesh, West Bengal, Bihar and Uttar Pradesh. They also agreed to allow a British 'resident' in Nepal, but he was not permitted to leave the Kathmandu Valley.

Re-Emergence of the Monarchy

In 1950, King Tribhuvan, assisted by the Indian Embassy in Kathmandu, fled to India. The rule of the Shah kings was reinstated through an armed people's revolution led by the Nepali Congress Party. King Tribhuvan instituted political reforms and, before the 1990 revolution, was credited with being the father of democracy in Nepal.

During a period of political squabbling, the number of political parties in Nepal grew to more than 60. In 1960 King Tribhuvan's son, King Mahendra, engineered a bloodless palace coup, declared a new constitution, jailed all the leaders of the then government and announced a ban on political parties. He established a partyless Panchayat (five councils) system that was answerable only to the monarch.

The political system was described as 'partyless Panchayat democracy' and allowed direct election of local leaders and representatives to the Rastrya Panchayat, the national assembly. Although the council of ministers was constituted from members of the Rastrya Panchayat, the king retained the right to appoint a quota of legislators, effectively retaining control.

King Birendra succeeded to the throne in 1971. After a period of political unrest, he declared that a national referendum would decide whether the country would adopt a multiparty system or retain the Panchayat system 'with suitable reforms'. The 1980 referendum endorsed the Panchayat system by a narrow margin and was thereafter cited as the will of the people.

The 1990 Revolution

Being a landlocked country, Nepal depends on its neighbour, India, for most of its manufactured goods and for access to the sea. In March 1989, the Trade & Transit Treaty between Nepal and India expired. Pride and protocol prevented the two countries from reaching any agreement on an extension. The issue was further complicated by Nepal's recent purchase of hundreds of truckloads of military supplies from China. India reduced the number of entry points into Nepal to the minimum required by international law, raised tariffs on Nepalese goods and severely limited the supply of petroleum products. Nepal's economy and quality of life declined and there was considerable popular unrest with the government's inability to resolve the issue.

This unrest reached a crescendo in the spring of 1990 when the 'illegal, banned' political parties began to severely criticise the Panchayat system for corruption, human rights violations and incompetence. The various opposition factions coalesced into a united force, bent on the restoration of democracy in Nepal under the leadership of Nepal's new 'father of democracy', Ganesh Man Singh. The government replied with a show of force that escalated from arrests to public beatings and shootings. After the resignation of several ministers forced the issue, the king reconstituted the cabinet and promised that grievances would be reviewed and appropriate changes made.

But the people were not mollified. In a spectacular display of unity, more than 200,000 people took to the streets of Kathmandu on 6 April 1990, chanting pro-democracy slogans. After exercising restraint throughout most of the day, the police attacked the demonstrators, first with bamboo staves and then with guns. Hundreds of people were killed or wounded. The army took control of the city. During a tense weekend curfew, the king negotiated with opposition leaders, then late in the evening of 8 April proclaimed that the ban on political parties was lifted.

The next day the country erupted in an outpouring of joy. If you happen to be in Kathmandu on this anniversary, you will probably witness massive revelry as well as ceremonies honouring those martyrs killed during the revolution.

The interim council of ministers appointed in the aftermath of the revolution included leaders of various parties, many of whom had spent time in jail as political prisoners. The reforms are far from complete and there are signs of stress within the system. Most Nepalese, however, are generally optimistic about the future.

One of the major accomplishments of the new government has been the restoration of better relations with India. Thus there is hope that imports of Indian goods, especially fuel, and the export of Nepalese goods to India will help Nepal's economy to recover.

HISTORY OF TREKKING

The first trekker in Nepal was Bill Tilman, who somehow wrangled permission from the maharaja in 1949 to make several treks, including the Kali Gandaki, Helambu and Everest. His exploits are described in *Nepal Himalaya*, reprinted by the Seattle Mountaineers as part of a Tilman collection. Another early visitor was Maurice Herzog, who led a French expedition to Annapurna in 1950.

During King Tribhuvan's visits to India, the king met Boris Lissannivich, a Russian ballet dancer who was running a club in Calcutta. Boris convinced the king that people would like to visit Nepal and would actually pay for the experience. Soon a few well-heeled ladies flew from Patna to Kathmandu's Gaucher ('cowfield') Airport in an Indian Airlines Dakota. Boris accommodated them in his new establishment, the Royal Hotel. The women were charmed by Boris and the exotic kingdom of Nepal. Thus Nepalese tourism was born. The Royal Hotel and its Yak & Yeti bar became the meeting

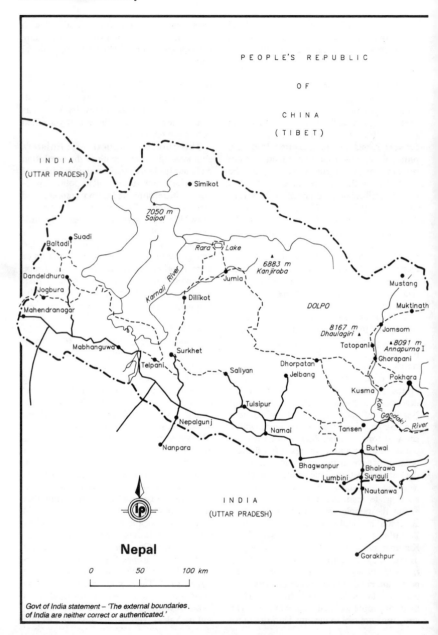

Nepal

0   50   100 km

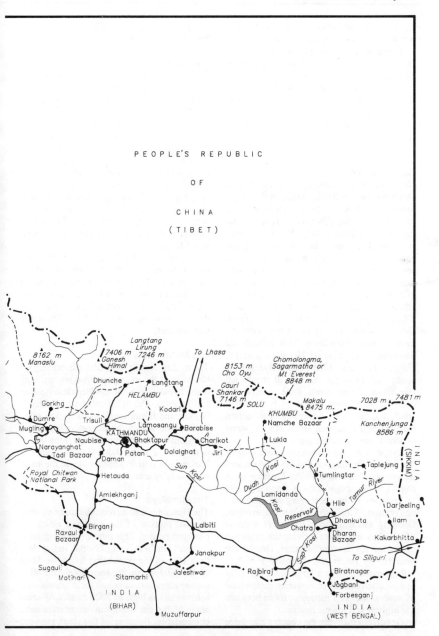

place for climbers from the 1950s until 1971 when the Royal hotel was closed.

The father of trekking in Nepal is Colonel James O M Roberts, who accompanied Tilman on his first trek and had spent years in Nepal attached to the British residency. In 1965 he took a group of ladies up the Kali Gandaki and founded Mountain Travel, the first of the mushrooming number of adventure travel companies worldwide.

GEOGRAPHY
Nepal is a small landlocked country which is 800 km long and 200 km wide. In the longitudinal 200 km, the terrain changes from glaciers along the Tibetan border to the flat jungles of the Terai, barely 150 metres above sea level. The country does not ascend gradually from the plains. Rather, it rises in several chains of hills that lie in an east-west direction, finally terminating in the highest hills in the world – the Himalaya. Beyond the Himalaya is the 5000 metre high plateau of Tibet. Despite the height of the Himalayan mountains, they are not a continental divide. Several rivers flow from Tibet through the mountains and hills of Nepal to join the Ganges in India. Many other rivers flow southward from the glaciers of the Nepal Himalaya. These rivers have scarred the country with great gorges in both north-south and east-west directions. This action has created a continual series of hills, some of which are incredibly steep.

Despite the steepness of the country, there is extensive farming on thousands of ancient terraces carved into the hills. Pressure from the increasing population is forcing people to bring even the most marginal land into cultivation. This has resulted in erosion, flooding and landslides. Extensive systems of trenches and canals provide the irrigation necessary for food production. Houses are near family fields and a typical Nepalese village extends over a large area. The hilly terrain often creates an elevation differential of several hundred metres or more between the highest and lowest homes.

Geographers divide the country into three regions: the Terai, the middle hills and the Himalaya.

The Terai
The Terai is the southernmost region of Nepal and is an extension of the Gangetic plains of India. Until 1950 this was a malarial jungle inhabited primarily by rhinoceros, tiger, leopard, wild boar and deer. Now, with malaria controlled, farming and industrial communities cover the Terai. The region holds about 45% of Nepal's population and the majority of the country's cultivable land. The Terai includes the big cities of Nepalgunj, Birganj, Janakpur and Biratnagar, but most of the region is dotted with small villages – clusters of 40 or 50 houses in the centre of a large area of cultivated fields.

Just north of the Terai is the first major east-west chain of hills, the Siwalik and the Mahabharat ranges. In some parts of Nepal only farmers live in these hills, but in other parts they are the sites of large and well-developed villages such as Ilam, Dhankuta and Surkhet.

The Middle Hills
The midlands or middle hills, a band only 60 km wide, is the most populated region. This is the home of the ancient Nepalese people. Kathmandu, Patan, Bhadgaon, Pokhara, Gorkha and Jumla are all in the middle hills. Kathmandu lies in the largest valley of the kingdom and according to legend the valley was once a huge lake. Other than the Kathmandu and Pokhara valleys, the midlands is hilly and steep.

The Himalaya
The Himalaya and its foothills make up only a small portion of the kingdom along the northern border. This inhospitable region is the least inhabited part of Nepal. In fact, less than 10% of the population live here. Most of the villages sit between 3000 and 4000 metres elevation, although there are summer settlements as high as 5000 metres. Winters are cold, but the warm sun makes most days comfortable. Because of the short growing

season, crops are few and usually small, consisting mostly of potatoes, barley and a few vegetables. The primary means of support is trading and the herding of sheep, cattle and yaks. Part of this region, Solu-Khumbu, is the home of the Sherpas. Mountaineering expeditions and trekking have a large influence on the economy of this area.

East to West

From east to west, the division of the kingdom is less clearly defined, except for the political division. Nepal is divided into 14 zones, several of which extend across the country from the Terai to the Tibetan border.

The primary difference between eastern and western Nepal is that the influence of the monsoon is less in the west. In the east the climate is damp and ideal for tea growing, the conditions being similar to Darjeeling in India. In the far west the climate is quite dry, even during the monsoon season.

Another influence on the east-west division is the large rivers that flow southward in deep canyons. These rivers often limit east-west travel as they wash away bridges during the monsoon. For this reason the major trade routes are south to north, from Indian border towns to Nepalese hill villages.

Roads

From Kathmandu, narrow mountain roads run north to China and south to India to connect the valley to the outside world. However, Nepal is undertaking a major road building programme and extensive construction is under way everywhere. An east-west highway that runs near the Indian border is nearing completion and many roads now wind their way a long distance into the hills.

Roads planned for the 1990s include a road from Surkhet to Jumla in west Nepal and on to Mugu and Humla. Thus these presently closed regions may soon be opened to tourists. The west Nepal road will also provide access to a border crossing into the Mansorovar and Kailash areas of Tibet.

Another road on the drawing board is a major east-west road in the middle hills, connecting Dipayal and Silgadi in the far west to Jajakot and Musikot, then to Beni and Pokhara. The eastern part of the route leaves the Jiri road and heads south to Ramechhap, then heads east to Okhaldunga with a spur to Salleri near Phaplu, then continues east to Bhojpur and Taplejung. The new trekking opportunities that this road presents are endless.

When trekking in the Annapurna region, you will cross the new road, presently under construction, from Pokhara to the Kali Gandaki Valley. The master plan is for this Chinese-financed road to extend all the way to Lo Montang in Mustang and on to Tibet. Depending on your outlook, this may either enhance or destroy the trek to Jomsom.

The oldest road into Kathmandu, the Tribhuvan Rajpath, is almost redundant. Most vehicles coming to Kathmandu use the east-west highway and a road along the Narayani River from Mugling to Narayanghat. Once the roads end, all travel is on a system of trails that climb the steep hills of Nepal as no road possibly can.

CLIMATE

Nepal has four distinct seasons. Spring, from March to May, is warm and dusty with rain showers. Summer, from June to August, is the monsoon season when the hills turn lush and green. Autumn, from September to November, is cool with clear skies, and is the main trekking season. In winter, from December to February, it is cold at night and can be foggy in the early morning, but afternoons are usually clear and pleasant, though therte is occasional snow in the mountains.

Because Nepal is quite far south (at the same latitude as Miami and Cairo) the weather is warmer and winter is much milder at lower elevations, including Kathmandu at 1400 metres. It rarely snows below 2000 metres.

The monsoon in the Bay of Bengal governs the weather pattern. The monsoon creates a rainy season from the middle of June to the middle of September. It is hot during the monsoon and it rains almost every day, but it is a considerate rain, limiting itself mostly to the night. During this season, trekking is difficult and uncomfortable. Clouds usually hide the mountains and the trails are muddy and infested with leeches.

It usually does not rain for more than one or two days during the entire autumn season from mid-October to mid-December. During winter and spring there may be a week or so of rainy evenings and occasional thunderstorms. The Himalaya makes its own localised weather, which varies significantly over a distance of a few km. Despite the sanguine assurances of Radio Nepal that the weather will be '...mainly fair throughout the kingdom', always expect clouds in the afternoon and be prepared for occasional rain.

Most of the precipitation in the Himalaya occurs during the summer monsoon. There is less snow on the mountains and on the high trails during winter. Everest itself is black rock during the trekking season, becoming snow-covered only during summer. There are always exceptions to this weather pattern, so be prepared for extremes. Winter snowstorms in December and January may make an early spring pass crossing difficult and can present an avalanche danger, especially on the approach to the Annapurna Sanctuary.

In Kathmandu, spring and autumn days are comfortable and the evenings are cool, usually requiring a light jacket or pullover. Winter in Kathmandu brings cold foggy mornings and clear evenings, but pleasant day temperatures with brilliant sunshine most days after the morning fog has lifted. It never snows in Kathmandu, though there is frost on cold nights in January and February. The hottest month is May, just before the rains start.

ECONOMY

Except for a few manufacturing centres, agriculture dominates the economy. In the hill regions people have cultivated every possible piece of land except where the hillsides are too steep or rocky to carve out even the smallest terrace.

POPULATION

Nepal's population of more than 19 million is growing at an alarming rate. Only 800,000 people live in the Kathmandu Valley while the majority live in the Terai or in small hill villages.

Population Density

Trekking in Nepal is not a wilderness experience. Most people live in the tiny villages that blanket the hills. Even in the high mountains, small settlements of stone houses and yak pastures dot every possible flat space. Much of the fascination of a trek is the opportunity to observe and participate in the life of these villages. People truly live off the land, using only a few manufactured items such as soap, kerosene, paper and matches, all of which are imported in bamboo baskets carried by barefoot porters.

It is difficult for most Westerners to comprehend this aspect of Nepal until they actually visit the kingdom. Our preconception of a roadless area is strongly influenced by the places we backpack or hike to at home – true wilderness, usually protected as a national park or forest. In the roadless areas of Nepal there is little wilderness up to an elevation of 4000 metres. The average population density in Nepal is more than 122 people per sq km. Only about 17% of the country is classified as cultivable land. If we alter this statistic to eliminate all the mountainous places, the average rises to an incredible 709 or more people per sq km of cultivated land. The size and type of rural settlements varies widely, but most villages have from 15 to 75 houses, a population of 200 to 1000 and cover an area of several sq km.

Rather than detracting from the enjoyment of a trek, the hill people, particularly their traditional hospitality and fascinating culture, make a trek in Nepal a special kind of mountain holiday unlike any other in the world.

PEOPLE

Anthropologists divide the people of Nepal into about 50 'ethnic groups'. This is a convenient term to encompass the various categories of tribe, clan, caste and race. Each ethnic group has its own culture and traditions. Everyone is proud of their heritage and there is no need for embarrassment when asking someone about their ethnicity (*jaat* or *thar* in Nepali). Often it's not even necessary to ask, as many people use the name of their ethnic group, caste or clan as a surname.

While some groups are found only in specific regions, many groups are spread throughout the country. Nepal has historically been a nation of traders, acting as intermediaries for transactions between India and Tibet, so there is a history of extensive travel and resettlement.

The caste system has many 'occupational castes' and these groups have also spread throughout the country. Potters (*kumahli*), butchers (*kasain*), blacksmiths (*kami*), tailors (*damai*), cobblers (*sarki*), goldsmiths (*sunar*), clothes washers (*dhobi*) and others have travelled Nepal to ply their trade.

Many ethnic groups have their own language, but almost everyone speaks Nepali – the *lingua franca* or trade language of the country – as a second language.

As the hill population has increased, many hill and even Himalayan people have migrated to lower elevations and the Terai in order to improve their lot. The following regional classification is, therefore, a bit artificial, but it does represent the traditional environment of each group.

Groups Found Throughout Nepal

Brahmins The Brahmins (Bahuns in Nepali) are the traditional Hindu priest caste and speak Nepali as their first language. They are distributed throughout the country in both the Terai and middle hills. Many Brahmins are influential businesspeople, landowners, moneylenders and government workers. They are very conscious of the concept of *jutho* or ritual pollution of their home and food. Always ask permission before entering a Brahmin house and never enter a Brahmin kitchen. Brahmins traditionally do not drink alcohol.

Chhetris The other major Hindu caste is Chhetri. In villages they are farmers, but they are also known for being outstanding soldiers. The Chhetri clans include the Ranas and the ruling family of Nepal, the Shahs. Thakuris are a group of Chhetris descended from the Rajputs in India and have the highest social, political and ritual status.

Newars The original inhabitants of the Kathmandu Valley are the Newars. To this day they remain concentrated in the valley in the cities of Kathmandu, Patan, Bhaktapur, Kirtipur and in smaller towns. Newars have a rich cultural heritage and are skilled artisans; a lot of the traditional art of Nepal is Newar crafted. There are both Buddhist and Hindu Newars. In the hills you are likely to meet Newars as government officers and merchants.

Musalman Nepal's Muslim population is known as Musalman. They live in the Kathmandu Valley, the eastern Terai and throughout the western hills. They migrated to Nepal from India, predominantly from Kashmir and Ladakh. Musalman are traditionally traders and dominate Kathmandu's trade in handicrafts, souvenirs, shoes and bangles.

Tibetans Tibetans are found mostly in Kathmandu at Bodhanath and Jawlakhel and in the Himalayan border regions. Often called by the derogatory term Bhotia, this group includes both recent migrants and Tibetans who settled here long ago. The Sherpas, Dolpo people and other groups were originally from Tibet, but settled in Nepal so long ago that they have built up their own traditions and culture. There are significant Tibetan settlements in the hills at Solu Khumbu, Jumla, Dolpo, Hile and Pokhara.

People of the Middle Hills

Tamangs You will encounter Tamangs, one of the most important groups in the hills, on almost every major trek. Tamangs believe they originally came from Tibet and speak a

Tibeto-Burman language among themselves. They practise a form of Tibetan Buddhism and there are Buddhist temples in many Tamang villages. Tamangs are farmers and usually live at slightly higher elevations than their Hindu neighbours, but there is a lot of overlap. The women wear gold decorations in their noses and the men traditionally wear a *bakkhu*, a sleeveless woollen jacket. The rough black and white blankets that you see in homes in the hills and in Kathmandu shops are a Tamang speciality.

Rais Like the Tamangs and Sherpas, Rais speak a Tibeto-Burman language of their own and are basically of Mongoloid stock. They have a very unusual culture and practise an indigenous religion that is neither Buddhist nor Hindu, although it has a fair amount of Hindu influence. Rais have very characteristic Mongoloid features which make them easy to recognise.

Some Rai villages are extremely large and boast 200 to 300 households. Typically, Rai villages are spread out over the hillside with trails leading in every direction. Finding the right route in these villages is always a challenge.

Rai people are very independent and individualistic. The 200,000 or so Rais in the eastern hills speak at least 15 different languages which, although seemingly closely related, are mutually unintelligible. When Rais of different areas meet they must converse in Nepali.

Rais (along with Limbus, Magars and Gurungs) are one of the ethnic groups which supply a large proportion of the recruits for the well-known Gurkha regiments of the British and Indian armies.

An unusual sight, to Western eyes, in regions of Rai influence is the *dhami*, shamans who are diviners, spirit mediums and medicine men. Occasionally you will see them in villages, but more often you will encounter them on remote trails, dressed in elegant regalia and headdresses of pheasant feathers. The rhythmic sound of the drums that a dhami continually beats while walking

Rai Woman

echoes throughout the hills. Most Rais live between the Dudh Kosi and Arun valleys. You will meet them on the Everest trek and the trek from Khumbu to Dharan.

Limbus The Rais and Limbus are known collectively as the Kiranti. The Kiranti are the earliest known population of Nepal's eastern hills where they have lived for at least 2000 years. Early Hindu epics such as the *Mahabharata* refer to the warlike Kirantis of the eastern Himalaya. From the 7th century AD, the Arun Valley was the site of fierce fighting between Tibetan and Assamese warlords. The Kirantis only joined the Gurkhali kingdom in 1774.

Many Limbus have adopted Subba as a surname and many men serve either in Gurkha regiments or in the Royal Nepal Army. Limbus are the inventors of *tongba*, a tasty, but very potent, millet beer that is sipped through a bamboo straw. Their religion is a mixture of Buddhism and shamanism and they have their own dhamis. Most Limbu people live in the region east of the Arun River. You will be in Limbu country during the entire Kanchenjunga trek.

Gurungs Gurungs often serve in the Royal Nepal Army and the Nepalese police, as well as in the Gurkha regiments of both the British and Indian armies. It is not unusual to meet ex-soldiers on the trail who have served in Malaysia, Singapore, Hong Kong and the UK. The stories of their exploits, told in excellent British-accented English, provide fascinating trailside conversation. An important source of income in most Gurung villages is the salaries and pensions of those in military service. The remaining income is from herding, particularly sheep, and agriculture – rice, wheat, corn, millet and potatoes. Access to many high pastures, including the Annapurna Sanctuary, is possible because of trails built by Gurung sheep herders.

Gurungs are Mongoloid in feature. It is easy to identify the men by their traditional clothing of a short blouse tied across the front and a short skirt of white cotton material, or often a towel, wrapped around their waist and held by a wide belt. In the Ghandruk area near the Annapurna Sanctuary, Gurung men fashion a backpack out of a piece of coarse cotton looped across the shoulders.

The Gurung funeral traditions and dance performances (the latter staged at the slightest excuse) are particularly exotic, and it is often possible to witness such aspects of Gurung life during a trek in this region. An elderly English-speaking ex-Gurkha captain often will explain the rituals and regale trekkers with long, involved stories of his WW I and WW II campaigns in France, Germany, Italy and North Africa. You will find Gurungs throughout the Annapurna region as well as at major settlements in the east, including Rumjatar, south of Jiri.

Magars You will find Magars throughout Nepal, generally living south of their Gurung neighbours. Traditionally they are farmers and stonemasons, but many Magars serve as soldiers in Gurkha regiments and in the Royal Nepal Army. Magars can be either Hindu or Buddhist. Hindu Magars practise the same religion as the Brahmins and Chhetris and employ Brahmins as priests. Magar women often wear necklaces of Indian silver coins. You will encounter Magars on most treks in Nepal. They are often integrated into villages dominated by other groups.

Sunwars One of the dominant groups in the region east of Kathmandu is the Sunwar, particularly in the villages of Ramechhap, Charikot and Okhaldunga. The women wear gold ornaments in their nose and ears and the men often join the Royal Nepal Army. They live in whitewashed stone houses with black window frames. They worship their own gods, but employ Brahmins as priests. You will be in Sunwar country on the Everest trek during the drive from Lamosangu to Jiri.

Jirels A small subgroup of the Sunwars that live in and near Jiri are known as Jirels. Unlike the Sunwars, they use Buddhist lamas as their priests.

Thakalis The Thakalis originally came from the Kali Gandaki (Thak Khola) Valley, but they have migrated wherever business opportunities have led. They are traditionally excellent businesspeople and hoteliers and have created hotels, inns and other businesses throughout Nepal. Their religion is a mixture of Buddhism, Hinduism and ancient shamanistic and animistic cults, but they claim to be more Hindu than Buddhist. Despite their history of trade with Tibet, the Thakalis are not of Tibetan ancestry. They are related to the Tamangs, Gurungs and Magars.

Himalayan People
Sherpas The most famous of Nepal's ethnic groups is the Sherpas, even though they form only a tiny part of the total population and live in a small and inhospitable region of the kingdom. Sherpas first came into prominence when the 1921 Mt Everest reconnaissance team hired them. The expedition started from Darjeeling in India and

travelled into Tibet. Because many Sherpas lived in Darjeeling, it was not necessary to travel into 'forbidden' Nepal to hire them.

The Sherpa economy has become highly dependent on tourism and many Sherpas have developed Western tastes and values. This Western influence has made wages and other costs higher and non-negotiable in areas of Sherpa influence. It has given Sherpas the reputation among many independent trekkers for being rather grasping and difficult to deal with. Once fees and conditions are agreed to, or a trekking agent or shop is negotiating for you, you will probably find them charming and helpful. Sherpa-run hotels usually have fixed prices and do not entertain bargaining.

Sherpas frequently name their children after the day of the week on which they were born. Sunday is Nima and the following days are Dawa, Mingma, Lakpa, Phurba, Passang and Pemba. They often add the prefix 'Ang' to the name (similar to the English suffix 'son' or abbreviation 'Jr'). You would call Ang Nima 'Nima' for short, but never 'Ang'.

Manangis Manang, the region north of Annapurna, is the home of the Manangis. A decree by King Rana Bahadur Shah in 1784 gave them special trading privileges which they continue to enjoy. These privileges originally included passport and import and export concessions not available to the general population of Nepal. Beginning long ago with the export of live dogs, goat and sheepskins, yaks' tails, herbs and musk, the trade has now expanded into the large-scale import of electronic goods, cameras, watches, silk, clothing, gems and other high-value items in exchange for gold, silver, turquoise and other resources available in Manang.

The trade network of the Manang people extends throughout South-East Asia and as far away as Korea. It is not uncommon to see large groups of Manang people jetting to Bangkok, Singapore and Hong Kong. Manangis call themselves Nye-shang, but many Manang people adopt the surname Gurung on passports and travel documents, though they are more closely related to Tibetans than to Gurungs.

Dolpo People The isolation of the Dolpo people in the remote region north of Dhaulagiri has made them one of the most undeveloped yet picturesque groups in the kingdom. They are traders, specialising in the exchange of sheep, yaks and salt between Nepal and Tibet. You will meet them in Dolpo, especially in Tarap and Ringmo villages. Dolpo people have a reputation for staying continuously occupied, particularly with spinning wool by hand as they walk.

Lo-Pa The people of Lo live in the fabled and forbidden region of Mustang. They compete with the Thakalis for trade in salt and wool, keep yaks, donkeys, mules and herds of sheep and have close ties with Tibet. The region was once ruled by the Raja of Mustang, but since 1952 his position has been only honorary. He has the rank of lieutenant colonel in the Royal Nepal Army.

Baragaunle The upper Kali Gandaki, including Kagbeni and Muktinath, is the traditional home of the Baragaunle – the people of '12 villages'. They are of Tibetan ancestry and practise a kind of Tibetan Buddhism that has been influenced by ancient animistic and pre-Buddhist Bon-po rituals. The elegantly dressed women you will see near Muktinath are from this group.

People of the Terai

Tharus The largest and probably the oldest group in the Terai is the Tharus. Now mostly peasant farmers, they once lived in small settlements of single-storey thatched huts within the jungle, which gained them the reputation for being immune to malaria. They have their own tribal religion based on Hinduism. Tharu women have a special dignity, and play a large role in their society. You will meet Tharus in Biratnagar,

Nepalgunj and in Royal Chitwan National Park.

Dhanwar, Majhi & Darai These three related groups live along the Terai's river valleys and are among the poorest and least educated of Nepal's ethnic groups. Majhi traditionally live by fishing and operate dugout canoe ferries throughout the country.

Other Groups The Satar, Dhangar, Rajbansi, Koche and Tajpuri are other Terai groups. You are not likely to meet these people during a trek.

Sherpa Guides, Gurkhas & Sahibs

These three nonethnic groups are particularly conspicuous in Nepal and you will certainly meet all of them on a trek.

Sherpa Guides Since the first expedition to Mt Everest in 1921, Sherpas have been employed on treks and mountaineering expeditions. Their performance at high altitude and their selfless devotion to their jobs impressed members of early expeditions. Later expeditions continued the tradition of hiring Sherpas as high altitude porters. Most of the hiring was done in Darjeeling or by messages sent through friends and relatives into the Solu Khumbu region of Nepal (where most Sherpas live).

The practice continues to the present day, with trekking organisations hiring Sherpas either as permanent employees or on a per trek basis. The emphasis shifted from Darjeeling to Kathmandu and to the Solu Khumbu region itself as these areas became accessible to foreigners.

It is confusing to discuss the role of Sherpas on an expedition or a trek as 'sherpa' can refer both to an ethnic group and to a function or job on a trek. Sherpa with a capital 'S' refers to members of that ethnic group, while on a trek or expedition a sherpa (lower-case 's') usually fulfils the role of trek guide or mountaineer. Traditionally, sherpas are Sherpas, but there are many exceptions. In this book, 'Sherpa' always refers to members of that ethnic group. I have also used the words sherpa and guide interchangeably.

Generally a sherpa is reasonably experienced in dealing and communicating with Westerners and can speak some English. The job of sherpa comprises several roles: *sirdar*, cook, kitchen boy, guide or high altitude porter. The head sherpa on a trek or expedition is the sirdar and he is responsible for all purchases and for hiring porters. In the lowlands, a sherpa acts as a trekking guide, asking directions from the locals, if necessary, to find the best trail to a destination. Cooks and kitchen boys can produce amazing trailside meals. The term 'kitchen boy' is used for an assistant cook or kitchen hand, but women and men of all ages can fill the position.

The term 'sherpa' does not imply a high degree of technical mountaineering skill. Although they live near the high Himalayan peaks, Sherpas usually did not set foot on them, except to cross high passes on trade routes. This changed when the British introduced them to the sport of mountaineering. Many trekking sherpas have served as high altitude porters on mountaineering expeditions, carrying loads along routes already set up by technically proficient mountaineers. The Nepal Mountaineering Association school in Manang now provides mountaineering training to Nepalese guides. If you need an experienced mountaineering sherpa, be sure that he has attended this course.

Sherpas are not the only high altitude climbers. Sambhu Tamang reached the summit of Everest with the Italian expedition in 1973, becoming the first non-Sherpa Nepalese to reach the summit of a major Himalayan peak. Numerous other Nepalese of many ethnic groups have now climbed peaks throughout the country.

Porters carry loads, and their job finishes once that load reaches camp. Once the group is in camp, the job of the sherpa begins. A porter may be a member of any ethnic group. Many Rais, Tamangs and Magars spend almost their entire lives on the trails serving as porters. They carry loads, not only for trekkers, but also to bring supplies to remote hill villages. Expeditions use either the term 'high altitude porter' or 'sherpa' to denote those who carry loads to high camps on the mountain.

Gurkhas Nepalese who enlisted in the British and Indian armies became known as Gurkhas. The name is derived from the ancient town of Gorkha which was the home of Prithvi Narayan Shah, the founder king of Nepal. The British Army applied the name Gurkha to all Nepalese and coined the name Gurkhali for the Nepali language.

In the old British Army there were 10 Gurkha rifle regiments, but when India gained independence in 1947 it took six of the regiments and the UK retained four. The UK still maintains Gurkha recruiting centres at Pokhara and near Jawlakhel in Kathmandu. Most Gurkhas are Rais, Limbus, Gurungs and Magars in roughly equal number, though the Gurkha regiments also accept recruits from other ethnic groups.

Sahibs Nepalese in the hills tend to call Western (or Japanese) men *sahib* (pronounced like 'sob'). A Western woman is a *memsahib* and a porter is a *coolie*. These terms no longer hold the derogatory implications that they did during the British Raj. In a peculiar turnabout, the locals call a trekker on his own a 'tourist' and someone with a trekking group a 'member'.

CULTURE

Nepalese are traditionally warm and friendly and treat foreigners with a mixture of curiosity and respect. *'Namaste'* ('Hello, how are you?') is a universal greeting. Most Nepalese speak at least some English, though smiles and gestures work well where language is a barrier.

Always double-check when asking for information or directions. As Nepalese hate to say 'no', they will give you their individual versions whether they know the answer or not. Their intention is not to mislead you; it is only to make you happy that you received an answer.

When trekking you will have a chance to meet and become acquainted with Sherpas and members of other Nepalese ethnic groups. The background of these people is completely different from what you are familiar with in the West. Treks are a fascinating cultural experience, but are most rewarding when you make some concessions to the customs and habits of Nepal.

Nepal is a Hindu country, although the Sherpas and most other high mountain people are Buddhists. In Kathmandu, you will be refused entry to a Hindu temple if you are wearing leather shoes or a leather belt. There are other temples that you will not be allowed to visit at all. Buddhist temples or *gompas* are less restrictive, but you should still ask permission to enter and remove your shoes when you do – and definitely ask permission before photographing religious festivals, cremation grounds and the inside of temples.

During a trek you will have many opportunities to photograph local people. Some people, however, will not want you to photograph them. Always ask before photographing women. There are always cases of shyness that you can overcome with a smile, a joke or using a telephoto lens, but don't pay people for taking their picture. Some people are afraid that a camera might 'steal their soul', but more often it is too much contact with photographers and cameras that causes the problem. Many photographs of hill people in Nepal, especially Sherpas, have been printed in books, magazines and brochures. The Sherpas, in particular the women, are afraid that a photo of them will be reproduced in quantity and eventually burned, thrown away or even used as toilet paper. This is a major reason that many local people will refuse photographs, and it is probably legitimate.

Nepal represents a culture far older and in many ways more sophisticated than our own, but you are not visiting a museum. Rather, you are visiting a country that is vibrantly alive, where many people live more comfortably and, in many cases, more happily than we do. The more you listen and observe, the more you will learn and the more people will accept you. If you must try to teach Nepalese hill people something, try teaching them English. English is a key to upward mobility for employment in, or the running of, any business that deals with foreigners. This is the one element of our culture that everyone desires – our language. Spending your time conversing with a sherpa or porter in English as you stroll the trail together will be a good start towards a lasting friendship.

A few other suggestions and considerations that will make your trek more enriching:

- Don't pollute. Pick up papers, film wrappers and other junk.

- Use locally made toilets *(charpi)* whenever available, no matter how revolting they might be.

- Burn all your toilet paper and bury your faeces.

- Don't pass out balloons, candy and money to village children as it encourages them to beg. Trekkers are responsible for the continual cries of children for *mithai* (candy), *paisaa* (money) and 'boom boom' (balloon). Well-intentioned trekkers thought they were doing a service by passing out pens for use in school, so clever kids now ask for pens.

- Don't tempt people into thievery by leaving cameras, watches and other valuable items around a hotel or trekking camp. Keep all your personal belongings in your hotel room or tent. This also means that you should not leave laundry hanging outside at night.

- Don't make campfires, as wood is scarce in Nepal.

- Don't touch food or eating utensils that local people will use. Most Hindus cannot eat food that a (non-Hindu) foreigner has touched. This problem does not apply to Sherpas, however.

- Don't throw anything into the fire in any house – Buddhist or Hindu. In most cultures the household gods live in the hearth.

- Nudity is completely unacceptable and brief shorts are not appreciated.

- Public displays of affection are frowned upon.

- Most Nepalese eat with their hands. In many places you will not be offered a spoon, but one is often available if you ask. The Nepalese use only their right hand for eating. If you eat with your hand, manners dictate that you wash it before and after eating. A jug of water is always available in restaurants for this purpose.

- Nepalese will not step over your feet or legs. If your outstretched legs are across a doorway or path, pull them in when someone wants to pass. Similarly, do not step over the legs of a Nepalese.

- The place of honour in a Sherpa home is the seat closest to the fire. Do not sit in this seat unless you are specifically invited to do so.

Life in the Hills

Most rural Nepalese families are self-sufficient in their food supply, raising all of it themselves and selling any excess in the few places, such as Kathmandu and Pokhara, that do not have a strictly agricultural economy. In return, the villagers buy mostly nonfood items that they cannot raise or produce themselves. These include sugar, soap, cigarettes, tea, salt, cloth and jewellery.

Throughout Nepal this exchange of goods creates a significant amount of traffic between remote villages and larger population and manufacturing centres. In the roadless hill areas, porters transport goods in bamboo baskets which are carried with a tumpline across their foreheads. During the many days they travel, porters either camp alongside the trail and eat food that they have brought from home or purchase food and shelter from homes along the trail. There are occasional tea shops, called *bhattis*, but porters rarely patronise them for more than an occasional cup of tea. Prices in bhattis are much higher than sharing an already prepared meal with a family. Often porters travel in groups and take turns cooking food that they carry themselves.

Second in importance to the transportation of goods is the flow of people between the warmer climates of the Terai and the colder Himalayan regions. Some of the movement is caused by seasonal migrations, but many people move permanently because of the pressures of increasing population in the hills. People also travel extensively in connection with weddings, funerals, festivals, school and government or military business.

Several of the hundreds of festivals that occur annually in Nepal require people to visit the homes of their relatives. Of particular importance is the Dasain festival in October, during which time thousands of people from a wide variety of economic and social backgrounds travel from urban centres to hill villages in a style that befits their standing. Their mode of travel may range from trailside camps, similar to those of porters, to service by an entire household staff. It is certainly rare, but still possible, to see porters carrying a woman in a sedan chair or basket.

Men who were born in hill villages and served in a Gurkha regiment in the British or Indian Army return home to their villages on leave or upon retirement. They often have a huge retinue of porters to carry items they have collected during their assignments in Singapore, Hong Kong, Brunei or the UK.

Therefore, a wide variety of modes of travel exists on the trails of Nepal. Whatever their means of travel and whatever their economic status, travellers make a direct contribution to the economy of most villages through which they pass. In some cases, it is through the purchase of food; in others it is the buying of necessary goods or services; and in yet others it is the hiring of local people to serve as porters for a few days. The inhabitants of villages along major trails have come to expect and depend on this economic contribution – in much the same way as our cafes, roadhouses, motels and petrol stations rely on highway travellers of all sorts to provide their income.

Another phenomenon in the hills is that people come into continual personal contact with others. There are no trail signs, few hotel signs and no maps available locally. So no matter how shy a person may be, travel-

Interior of a Sherpa house

lers must continually ask for directions or help in finding food and other items. They must also ask for information about places to stay, how far it is to the next village, etc. Many Westerners seem to have lost this ability, and rely on the isolation of a car to insulate them from strangers. They rarely need to ask directions because of the abundance of road signs and maps. The passing scene becomes merely another picture, framed by a car window.

Because Nepalese are constantly talking and exchanging important information, conversation often develops into long exchanges of pure chitchat or useless information. When trekking, you will hear the most commonly learned English phrases: 'What time is it?' and 'Where are you going?'. A traveller may spend an hour or two discussing trail conditions, where they have been, politics, the weather, crop conditions, the price of rice in a neighbouring village, who has just married (and who isn't, but should be), who died recently or hundreds of other topics – all with a complete stranger whom they may never meet again. This is an important part of life in the hills as there are no telephones, newspapers, TVs and few radios. Most news comes from travellers. It certainly is more stimulating to hear first-hand experiences than a radio news broadcast. Once a family has planted the crops for the season, there isn't much to do beyond the day-to-day activities of house cleaning, cooking and taking care of children, until harvest time. Besides their economic importance, travellers offer a valuable diversion, a source of information and a glimpse into a new and different world.

RELIGION

In Nepal, Hinduism and Buddhism are mingled into a complex blend which is often impossible to separate. The Buddha was actually born in Nepal but the Buddhist religion first arrived in the country around 250 BC, introduced, so it is said, by the great Indian Buddhist emperor Ashoka himself. Later Buddhism gave way to Hinduism, but

from around the 8th century AD the Tantric form of Buddhism practised in Tibet also began to make its way across the Himalaya into Nepal. Today Buddhism is mainly practised by the people of the high Himalaya, like the Sherpas, and also by Tibetans who have settled in Nepal. Several ethnic groups, like the Tamangs and Gurungs in the middle hills and the Newars in the Kathmandu Valley, practise both Buddhism and Hinduism.

Officially Nepal is a Hindu country, but in practice the religion is a strange blend of Hindu and Tantric Buddhist beliefs, with a pantheon of Tantric deities tagged onto the list of Hindu gods or, in many cases, inextricably blended with them. Thus Avalokitesvara, the prime Bodhisattva of this Buddhist era, becomes Lokesvara, a manifestation of the Hindu god Shiva, and then appears as Machhendranath, one of the most popular gods of the Kathmandu Valley. Is he Hindu or Buddhist? Nobody can tell.

The vast majority of the population is Hindu, and Buddhists make up most of the balance. There are also small groups of Muslims and a few Christians. The Muslims are mainly found close to the border with India, and in the odd isolated village. Some ethnic groups, such as the Tharus and the Rais, have their own form of religion and worship the sun, moon and trees, though their practices retain many Buddhist and Hindu influences.

Hinduism

India, the Indonesian island of Bali, the Indian Ocean island of Mauritius, and possibly Fiji, are the only places apart from Nepal where Hindus predominate, but it is the largest religion in Asia in terms of the number of adherents. Hinduism is one of the oldest extant religions with firm roots extending back to beyond 1000 BC.

The Indus Valley civilisation developed a religion which shows a close relationship to Hinduism in many ways. Later, it further developed on the subcontinent through the combined religious practices of the Dravidians and the Aryan invaders who arrived in the

Shiva, Pavarti & Ganesh

north of India around 1500 BC. Around 1000 BC, the Vedic scriptures were introduced and gave the first loose framework to the religion.

Hinduism today has a number of holy books, the most important being the four *Vedas*, or 'Divine Knowledge', which are the foundation of Hindu philosophy. The *Upanishads* are contained within the *Vedas* and delve into the metaphysical nature of the universe and soul. The *Mahabharata* is an epic poem describing in over 220,000 lines the battles between the Kauravas and Pandavas. It contains the story of Rama, and it is probable that the most famous Hindu epic, the *Ramayana*, was based on this. The *Bhagavad Gita* is a famous episode of the *Mahabharata* where Krishna relates his philosophies to Arjuna.

Hinduism postulates that we will all go through a series of rebirths or reincarnations that eventually lead to *moksha*, the spiritual salvation which frees one from the cycle of rebirths. With each rebirth you can move closer to or further from eventual moksha; the deciding factor is your karma, which is literally a law of cause and effect. Bad actions during your life result in bad karma, which ends in a lower reincarnation. Conversely, if your deeds and actions have been good you will reincarnate on a higher level and be a step closer to eventual freedom from rebirth.

Dharma is the natural law which defines the total social, ethical and spiritual harmony of your life. There are three categories of dharma, the first being the eternal harmony which involves the whole universe. The second category is the dharma that controls castes and the relations between castes. The third dharma is the moral code which an individual should follow.

The Hindu religion has three basic practices. They are *puja* or worship, the cremation of the dead, and the rules and regulations of the caste system. There are four main castes: the Brahmin, or priest caste; the Chhetris, or soldiers and governors; the Vaisyas, or tradespeople and farmers; and the Sudras or menial workers and craftspeople. These basic castes are then subdivided, although this is not taken to the same extent in Nepal as in India. Beneath all the castes are the Harijans, or untouchables, the lowest, casteless class for whom all the most menial and degrading tasks are reserved. Westerners and other non-Hindus are outside the caste system, and are therefore unclean. Westerners are not allowed to enter Hindu temples. Any food that is touched by a Westerner, or put on their plate, becomes polluted and must be discarded.

Westerners have trouble understanding Hinduism principally because of its vast pantheon of gods. In fact you can look upon all these different gods simply as pictorial representations of the many attributes of a god. The one omnipresent god usually has three physical representations. Brahma is the creator, Vishnu is the preserver and Shiva is the destroyer and reproducer. All three gods are usually shown with four arms, but Brahma has the added advantage of four heads.

Each god has an associated animal known as the 'vehicle' on which they ride, as well as a consort with certain attributes and abilities. Generally each god also holds symbols; you can often pick out which god is represented by the vehicle or symbols. Most temples are dedicated to one or other of the gods, but most Hindus profess to be either Vaishnavites (followers of Vishnu) or Shaivites (followers of Shiva). A variety of lesser gods and goddesses also crowd the scene. The cow is, of course, the holy animal of Hinduism.

Hinduism is not a proselytising religion since you cannot be converted. You're either born a Hindu or you are not; you can never become one. Similarly, once you are a Hindu you cannot change your caste – you're born into it and are stuck with it for the rest of that lifetime. Nevertheless Hinduism has a great attraction for many Westerners and India's 'export gurus' are numerous and successful. Because proselytising and conversion are not part of Hindu tradition, Nepalese law prohibits these practices, so Nepal has been spared the influence of missionaries and evangelists.

A guru is not so much a teacher as a spiritual guide, somebody who by example or simply by their presence indicates what path you should follow. In a spiritual search one always needs a guru. A sadhu is an individual on a spiritual search. They're an easily recognised group, usually wandering around half-naked, smeared in dust with their hair and beard matted. Sadhus most often follow Shiva and generally carry his symbol, the trident.

Sadhus are often people who have decided that their business and family life have reached their natural conclusions and that it is time to throw everything aside and go out on a spiritual search. They may previously have been the village postal worker, or a business person. Sadhus perform various feats of self-mutilation, and wander all over the subcontinent, occasionally coming together in great pilgrimages and other religious gatherings. Important pilgrimage sites for sadhus are Pashupatinath in Katmandu, and the sacred sites of Gosainkund and Muktinath. Many sadhus are, of course,

simply beggars following a more sophisticated approach to gathering in the paisa, but others are completely genuine in their search.

Buddhism

Strictly speaking Buddhism is not a religion, since it is not centred on a god, but a system of philosophy and a code of morality. Buddhism was founded in northern India about 500 BC when Siddhartha Gautama, born a prince, achieved enlightenment. Gautama Buddha was not the first Buddha but the fourth, and is not expected to be the last 'enlightened one'. Buddhists believe that the achievement of enlightenment is the goal of every being so eventually we will all reach Buddhahood.

The Buddha never wrote down his dharma or teachings, and a schism later developed so that today there are two major Buddhist

Buddha

schools. The Theravada or Hinayana, 'doctrine of the elders' or 'small vehicle' holds that the path to nirvana, the eventual aim of all Buddhists, is an individual pursuit. In contrast, the Mahayana or 'large vehicle' school holds that the combined belief of its followers will eventually be great enough to encompass all of humanity and bear it to salvation. To some the less austere and ascetic Mahayana school is a 'soft option'. Today it is chiefly practised in Vietnam, Japan and China, while the Hinayana school is followed in Sri Lanka, Burma (Myanmar) and Thailand, and by the Buddhist Newars in the Katmandu Valley. There are other, sometimes more esoteric, divisions of Buddhism including the Hindu-Tantric Buddhism of Tibet which is the version found in the Himalayan regions of Nepal. Tibetan Buddhism was influenced by the ancient animistic Bonpo tradition, and there are a few pockets of Bonpo remaining in Nepal, especially in Dolpo.

The Buddha renounced his material life to search for enlightenment but, unlike other prophets, found that starvation did not lead to discovery. Therefore he developed his rule of the 'middle way', moderation in everything. The Buddha taught that all life is suffering, but that suffering comes from our sensual desires and the illusion that they are important. By following the 'eight-fold path' these desires will be extinguished and a state of nirvana, where they are extinct and we are free from their delusions, will be reached. Following this process requires going through a series of rebirths until the goal is eventually reached and no more rebirths into the world of suffering are necessary. The path that takes you through this cycle of births is karma, but this is not simply fate. Karma is a law of cause and effect; your actions in one life determine the role you will play and what you will have to go through in your next life.

In India Buddhism developed rapidly when it was embraced by the great emperor Ashoka. As his empire extended over much of the subcontinent, so Buddhism was carried forth. Later, however, Buddhism began to contract in India because it had never really taken a hold on the great mass of people. As Hinduism revived, Buddhism in India was gradually reabsorbed into the older religion.

Buddhism is more tolerant of outsiders than is Hinduism; you will be welcome at most Buddhist temples and ceremonies. In Katmandu and in the hills there are Buddhist monasteries which are willing to provide spiritual training and advice to Westerners. Buddhism prohibits any form of killing, a contrast to Hinduism which requires animal sacrifices to appease the goddess Kali.

LANGUAGE
Nepali is the working tongue of Nepal and is understood by almost everyone in the country. Newars, Tamangs, Rais, Sherpas and many other ethnic groups have their own language which they speak among themselves, but they use Nepali outside their own region. Nepali is the first language of the Brahmins, Chhetris and Thakurs – the highest castes in Nepal. It belongs to the Indo-Aryan family of languages, derived from Sanskrit. Its nearest relative today is Kumaoni, spoken in a region of north-west India. Nepali has much in common with Hindi, the official language of India, which has the same origins. It has also taken many words from Persian, through Hindi.

It's not difficult to learn a bit of the language, and it can add greatly to your enjoyment of trekking. Nepalese aren't fussy about the language and will appreciate an effort to learn it. You'll find a little Nepali can go a long way.

Since Nepali, like Hindi, uses the Devanagari script, for English speakers it must be transliterated to Roman script. There are many systems of transliteration, but the one used here is from Meerendonk's *Basic Gurkhali* dictionary. To make it easier to see the difference in pronunciation, I have used 'aa' where he uses 'ā'.

Lonely Planet's *Nepal Phrasebook* also provides a handy introduction to the language.

Pronunciation

a	as in	*u*p
aa	as in	f*a*ther
e	as in	caf*é*
i	as in	r*i*m
o	as in	g*o*
u	as in	f*u*ll
ai	as in	*ai*sle

A big key to the correct pronunciation of Nepali is the 'a' and 'aa' sound. The sound represented here by a single 'a' is like the 'u' sound in 'up' and the sound of 'aa' is a true 'a' sound as in 'car' or 'far'. For example, *chhang* is pronounced like 'bung' or 'rung', not like 'clang' or 'bang'.

Another difficulty is the 'h' sound. In Nepali the 'h' almost vanishes in pronunciation, particularly when it follows a consonant. Ask a Nepali to pronounce *dhungaa* (stone) and *dungaa* (boat); they will probably sound the same to you, as will *ghari* (wristwatch) and *gaari* (automobile). To a Westerner, *mahango* (expensive) sounds like 'mungo', but a Nepali would include (and hear) the 'h' sound. In the transliteration used here, 'ch' is pronounced as in the English 'chin', while 'chh' sounds like a combination of 'ch' plus 'h'. The letter 'r' is rolled and is pronounced almost like 'dr'; some transliteration systems replace the 'r' with a 'd' or combine them as 'dr'.

Why isn't the language written as it sounds? Each of these sounds is a different letter or character in the Devanagari script used to write Nepali, and in Nepali they are distinct letters and sounds – even if they sound the same to Westerners. Nepali has more vowels than English, so English letters must be combined to represent these sounds.

In Nepali, the verb is placed at the end of a sentence. Grammatically, questions are identical to statements. The differentiation is made by the intonation pattern of the voice. For example:

Thik chha? (with a rising tone)
 (Are you) OK?
Thik chha!
 (Yes, I'm) OK!

Greetings & Civilities

Hello/Goodbye.
 namaste
Thank you.
 dhanyabaad (not commonly used)
Where are you going?
 tapain kahan jaane?
What is your name?
 tapainko naam ke ho?
My name is...
 mero naam...ho
How are you?
 tapailai kasto chha?
I am well.
 sanchai chha
What is this?
 yo ke ho?
It is cold today.
 aaja jaaro chha
It is raining.
 paani parchha
That's OK.
 thik chha
I know.
 thaahaa chha
I don't know.
 thaahaa chhaina

Trekking

house	*ghar*
shop	*pasal*
latrine	*charpi*
steep uphill	*ukaalo*
steep downhill	*oraalo*
left	*baayaan*
right	*daahine*
straight ahead	*sidha*
tired	*thaakyo*
cold (weather)	*jaaro*
warm (weather)	*garam*

This river is cold.
 yo kholaa chiso chha
Which trail goes to...?
 kun baato...jaanchha?
Is the trail steep?
 baato ukaalo chha?
Where is my tent?
 mero tent kahaan chha?

What is the name of this village?
yo gaaunko naam ke ho?
Where is a shop?
pasal kahaan chha?

Food

local inn	*bhatti*
beer (local)	*chhang* or *jaanr*
whisky (local)	*rakshi*
tea	*chiyaa*
water	*paani*
hot water	*taato paani*
cold water	*chiso paani*
boiled water	*umaleko paani*
meat	*maasu*
chicken (meat)	*kukhoroko maasu*
bread	*roti*
egg	*phul*
food	*khaanaa*
vegetable	*saag*
cooked vegetable	*tarkaari*
rice (cooked) (also food in general)	*bhaat*
hot	*taato*
hot (spicy)	*piro*
tasty	*mitho*

Please give me a cup of tea.
ek cup chiyaa dinuhos
Do you have food (rice) now?
aile bhaat chha?
It is enough.
pugchha
Is the food good?
khaana mitho chha?

Useful Words

happy	*khushi*
enough	*pugyo*
yes (it is...)	*ho*
no (it is not...)	*hoina*
this	*yo*
that	*tyo*
mine	*mero*
yours	*timro*
his, hers	*unko*
expensive	*mahango*
cheap	*sasto*
big	*thulo*
small	*sano*

good	*ramro*
not good	*naraamro*
maybe	*hola*
clean	*saaph* or *saphaa*
dirty	*mailo*
heavy	*gahrungo*
here	*yahaan*
there	*tyahaan*
where	*kahaan*
which	*kun*

Family

mother	*aamaa*
father	*baabu*
son	*chhoro*
daughter	*chhori*
elder brother	*daai*
younger brother	*bhaai*
elder sister	*didi*
younger sister	*bahini*
friend	*saathi*

Animals

cow	*gaai*
dog	*kukur*
horse	*ghoraa*
pig	*sungur*
bird	*charo*
chicken	*kukhoro*
water buffalo	*bhainsi*
male yak	*yak*
female yak	*nak*

Crops

barley	*jau*
buckwheat	*paapad*
cabbage	*banda kobi*
cauliflower	*kauli* or *phul kobi*
chilli	*khorsaani*
corn	*makai*
lentils	*daal*
millet	*kodo*
mustard	*tori*
oats	*jau*
potatoes	*aalu*
radish	*mula*
field rice	*dhaan*
husked rice	*chaamal*
cooked rice	*bhaat*
spinach	*saag*

soybeans	*baatamaas*
tobacco	*surti*
turnips	*gyante mula*
wheat	*gahun*
yams	*sutaani*

Geographical Features

hill/mountain	*daanda*
snowy mountains	*himal*
hills	*lekh*
the plains	*terai*
landing place, ferry	*ghat*
alpine pasture	*kharka*
alpine hut	*goth*
river	*kholaa*
major river	*kosi*
small stream	*naalaa*
stream (in Hindi)	*nadi*
lake	*kund, pokhari, taal*
trail	*baato*
mountain pass:	
Nepalese	*bhanjyang*
Tibetan	*la*
western Nepal	*laagna*

Temples & Villages

village	*gaon*
resting place	*chautaara*
Buddhist monument	*chorten*
arch-shaped chorten	*kani*
Tibetan Buddhist temple	*gompa*
Hindu temple	*mandir*
wall or stone carved with prayers	*maani*

Time & Dates

day	*din*
morning	*bihaana*
night	*raat*
today	*aaja*
yesterday	*hijo*
tomorrow	*bholi*
day after tomorrow	*parsi*
sometime	*bholi-parsi*

What time is it (now)?
  (aile) kati bajyo?
Five o'clock.
  paanch bajyo

Numbers

1	*ek*
2	*dui*
3	*tin*
4	*chaar*
5	*paanch*
6	*chha* (some people say *chhe*)
7	*saat*
8	*aath*
9	*nau*
10	*das*
11	*eghaara*
12	*baahra*
13	*tehra*
14	*chaudha*
15	*pandhra*
16	*sohra*
17	*satra*
18	*athaara*
19	*unnaais*
20	*bis*
25	*pachchis*
30	*tis*
40	*chaalis*
50	*pachaas*
60	*saathi*
70	*sattari*
80	*ashi*
90	*nabbe*
100	*ek say*
1000	*ek hajaar*

Facts for the Trekker

General Information

VISAS & EMBASSIES

Nepal's immigration rules are complex and cumbersome. If you plan to stay in Nepal for more than one month, you will require a visa extension. To trek, you will need from the immigration office a permit specifying the time and route of your trek.

A 15 day visa is available when you arrive in Kathmandu. You must fill in an application form and theoretically you should have a photograph available. You must pay either US$10 in cash or wait in a long currency exchange queue to change money to pay for the visa.

You can stay in Nepal for a maximum of three months on a tourist visa, although there is a special facility that allows a fourth month in certain circumstances. The major complication of a visa extension is the requirement that you must produce a bank certificate proving that you have officially exchanged US$10 into Nepalese rupees for each day your visa is extended.

Once you have stayed in Nepal more than one month, you must stay out of Nepal for at least one month before you can return. If you have been granted the special fourth month extension, it may be accompanied by a stamp in your passport saying you may not return to Nepal for six months or a year. The general practice is that you must stay out of the country for as long as you have been in Nepal, and that you may stay in Nepal a maximum of six months per year on a tourist visa. Don't overstay a visa. Airport officials often refuse to allow passengers to board a flight if their visa has expired, even for a single day.

Nepalese embassies and consulates issue one month visas. The cost is usually the local equivalent of US$10, though British subjects are charged a higher fee. You can enter Nepal without a visa, but it takes a bit of time when you arrive and the visa is initially valid for only 15 days. The immigration office will extend an airport visa for another 15 days for free, but you must make a trip to the immigration office and produce US$150 of exchange receipts. If you are arriving by road it will save time if you have a visa in advance, but you can still get a visa at a road border. A Nepal visa is valid for entry for three months from the date of issue. Do not apply too soon or it will not be valid when you arrive in Kathmandu.

Nepalese Embassies & Consulates

Australia
> Suite 23, 2nd floor, 18-20 Bank Place, Melbourne, Vic 3000 (tel 6021271)
> 3rd level, 377 Sussex St, Sydney, NSW 2000 (tel 2647197)
> 4th floor, Airways House, 195 Adelaide Terrace, Perth, WA 6004 (tel 2211207)
> PO Box 1097, Toowong, Brisbane, Qld 4066 (tel 3780124)

China
> Norbulingka Rd 13, Lhasa, Tibet (tel 22880)

Hong Kong
> Prince of Wales Building (in the gate of HMS *Tamar*) (tel 8633255)

India
> Barakhamba Rd, New Delhi 110001 (tel 3329969, 3327361)
> 19 Woodlands, Sterndale Rd, Alipore, Calcutta 700 027 (tel 452024, 452493)

Thailand
> 189 Soi 71, Sukhumvit Rd, Bangkok (tel 3917240)

UK
> 12A Kensington Palace Gardens, London W8 4QU (tel 2296231, 2291594)

USA
> 2131 Leroy Place, Washington DC 20008 (tel (202) 6674550)
> 820 Second Ave, Suite 202, New York, NY 10017 (tel (212) 3704188)

Visa Extensions & Trekking Permits

To get a visa extension or trekking permit, go to the central immigration office (tel 418573) in Kathmandu, near the Royal

Palace on Tridevi Marg at the entrance to Thamel. The office accepts applications Sunday to Thursday from 10 am to 2 pm and on Friday from 10 am to noon. The office is closed on Saturdays and holidays. Visa extensions and trekking permits are sometimes available the same day, but during the busy season you should allow up to three working days for an extension to be approved. At peak times the queues are long and the formalities are tedious.

Large signs at the entrance to the immigration office detail the latest rules and regulations. Trekking and travel agencies can assist with the visa extension process and save you the time and tedium of queuing.

Every visa extension or trekking permit requires your passport, money, photos, an application form and bank receipts. Collect all these documents before you start waiting in the queue. There are several instant photo shops near the immigration office, but Polaroid photos are expensive. If you plan ahead, there are many photographers who will provide passport photos within a day. Kathmandu is a good, inexpensive place to stock up on extra photos of yourself for future travels. There is also a bank in the immigration office if you need to top up your collection of exchange certificates.

For more details about trekking permits, see the Trekking Information section later in this chapter.

One week extensions and two week trekking permits are also available in Pokhara.

Re-Entry Permits

If you are travelling from Nepal to India or Tibet and returning to Kathmandu within a week or two you must get a re-entry permit before you leave Nepal. This is an easy process at the immigration office. Don't overlook it or you will be obliged to remain out of the country for a month.

Visa Fees

The visa issue fee is US$10 for a one month visa or re-entry permit. A visa extension costs Rs 150 per week for the second month and Rs 300 per week for the third month.

Visa extensions are free with trekking permits, but you are supposed to get your trekking permit stamped at police check posts during your trek. It would be judicious to get your trekking permit endorsed by any official you come across in order to prove that you actually did go trekking. This will help if you plan to get a second trekking permit or a further visa extension.

CUSTOMS
Arrival

Nepal customs formalities are among the most thorough in the world. Customs officials at Kathmandu Airport open most bags and inspect them. If you arouse suspicion, you may even be subjected to a body search.

The duty-free allowance includes 200 cigarettes, 20 cigars and one bottle of liquor. There is a duty-free shop in the arrival hall of Kathmandu Airport. Personal effects, including trekking equipment, are permitted free entry. Excessive amounts of film, 16 mm movie equipment, firearms or food and gear for mountaineering expeditions are subject to special restrictions.

Nepal prohibits the import and export of gold and a substantial part of the efforts of customs inspectors is to detect smuggled gold. Some items of obvious use to tourists, such as video cameras and laptop computers, are allowed, but customs officials write the details of the equipment in your passport to ensure that you take it out of the country when you leave. Other so-called luxuries, such as video players and televisions, require an import licence. If you are carrying such items they will be impounded and kept in customs bond until you depart.

You may not import Nepalese currency and only Nepalese and Indian nationals may import Indian currency. There is no restriction on bringing in either cash or travellers' cheques, but the amount taken out at departure should not exceed the amount brought in. You are supposed to declare cash or travellers' cheques in excess of US$2000.

Departure

Baggage is also inspected on departure from

Nepal. Nepal prohibits the export of antiques. Items that look old should have a certificate from the Department of Archaeology. Other prohibited exports are gold, silver, precious stones, wild animals and their skins and horns and all nonprescription drugs, whether processed or in their natural state.

Warning

There is considerable money to be made by smuggling gold, drugs and foreign currency into or out of Nepal. Nepalese may approach you in Kathmandu or Hong Kong offering you money, free air tickets or other incentives to carry goods for them. The penalties are severe, informants are everywhere and the jails in Nepal are dreary. Forget it!

TRAVEL INSURANCE

Trekking and travel agents can offer a traveller's insurance policy. Coverage varies from policy to policy, but will probably include loss of baggage, sickness and accidental injury or death. Most policies also cover the reimbursement of cancellation fees and other costs if you must cancel your trip because of accident or illness, or the illness or death of a family member. It's probably worth purchasing this inexpensive protection, especially if you are travelling on nonrefundable advance purchase plane tickets.

Insurance may also cover helicopter evacuation and other emergency services in Nepal. Be sure that the policy does not exclude mountaineering or alpinism or you may have a difficult time settling a claim. Although you will not engage in such activities, you may never be able to convince a flatland insurance company of this fact. It would be prudent to check the policy to be sure that it specifically covers helicopter evacuation.

If you purchase insurance and have a loss, you must submit proof of this loss when you make an insurance claim. If you have a medical problem, you should save all your bills and get a physician's certificate stating that you were sick. If you lose something

covered by insurance, you must file a police report, no matter how remote the location. No insurance company considers a claim without such documentation. Police check posts in Nepal will provide a police report if there is a major theft. They are all familiar with this bit of bureaucracy.

There is no rescue insurance available in Nepal. You should organise this before you come if you want this protection.

Helicopter Evacuation

If you are injured and unable to travel, you can ask for a rescue helicopter or charter flight from a remote airstrip only if you have some definite proof that you can pay for it. It costs more than US$1500 for a helicopter evacuation from 4000 metres near Mt Everest. Helicopters have saved the lives of several people who left Nepal without paying the bill for the rescue flight. The Royal Nepal Army, which operates the service, now refuses to send a chopper unless they have cash in hand. All trek organisers have an agreement in Kathmandu that guarantees payment for helicopter evacuations, though they will bill you later for the service.

MONEY

The Nepal Rastra Bank (the National Bank of Nepal) determines the value of the Nepal rupee (Rs) against a 'basket of currencies' and fixes exchange rates against several currencies. Radio Nepal, Nepal Television, Nepali and English newspapers all announce the rates every morning. In March 1991 the exchange rates were:

US$1	= Rs 32
A$1	= Rs 25
UK£1	= Rs 61
Indian Rs 1 =	Rs 1.7

There are 100 paisa (p) in a rupee. In the hills, shopkeepers often do their calculations in units of 50 paisa, called a mohar – Rs 1.50 equals three mohar. In Kathmandu, virtually everything is rounded to the next higher rupee.

You can change money officially at banks and exchange counters authorised by the Nepal Rastra Bank. Hotels in Kathmandu and Pokhara are also licensed to change foreign currency; rates are almost the same as the bank. When you change money, be sure to get a receipt with the stamp of the bank or hotel. They don't always volunteer to give you this, but any money you exchange officially counts towards the mandatory US$10 per day. Insist on a receipt.

Currencies & Credit Cards

You can carry either cash or travellers' cheques for your expenses in Nepal. Both American Express and Visa have refund facilities in Kathmandu. US dollars are the most acceptable. Banks are also happy with pounds sterling, Australian dollars and most European currencies, although Scandinavian money is sometimes difficult to change.

Credit cards are slowly gaining acceptance in Kathmandu, but are worthless in the

hills. If you are an American Express card holder, you can get US dollar travellers' cheques with a personal cheque at the American Express office. Nepal Grindlays Bank can provide a cash advance in Nepalese rupees or US$ travellers' cheques against a Visa card, and the Nepal Arab Bank provides facilities for Mastercard.

Prices for hotel accommodation and airline tickets are quoted in US dollars and you are required to pay for these in foreign currency. You must pay for tickets on domestic flights in foreign cash or travellers' cheques; Royal Nepal Airlines does not accept credit cards. If you plan to fly back from Lukla, Pokhara or Jomsom at the end of a trek, be sure you have enough foreign currency to purchase a plane ticket (if you did not buy a ticket in advance). You should carry enough cash on a trek to buy a plane ticket in case you need one in an emergency.

If you will be trekking on your own, you should carry enough money in rupees to cover all your expenses on the trek. It is usually not possible to change foreign currency or travellers' cheques except in Kathmandu or Pokhara.

Black Market

Because of Nepal's foreign exchange restrictions, the black market is so sophisticated that rates can change hourly depending on conditions in Hong Kong and the Middle East. The government makes occasional efforts to curb this trade, which is centred around Thamel in Kathmandu. Rates and availability can change rapidly, though you can often obtain a 20% to 30% premium over the official rate. The emphasis on foreign exchange receipts for visa extensions and trekking permits is an effort to encourage you to change money legally.

Costs

If you stay in hotels as you trek, estimate your costs at Rs 100 to Rs 150 per day for food and from Rs 20 to Rs 40 per day for lodging. Add 50% or 60% to these costs when you trek above 3500 metres. Estimate US$40 to US$60 per day per person if you plan to hire porters, sherpas and all the trappings.

The money you take on the trek should be in notes of from Rs 1 to Rs 100. There are banknotes of Rs 500 and Rs 1000, but it may be difficult to find change for these in the hills. If you have big notes, you may find change at banks in Namche, Chame, Jomsom and Pokhara. If you are going to a particularly remote area such as the Arun River or far west Nepal, you should carry stacks of Rs 1, Rs 5 and Rs 10, but this is not necessary on the more popular routes. Consider yourself lucky that paper money is now accepted throughout Nepal. The 1953 Everest expedition had to carry all its money in coins. The money alone took 30 porter loads!

Tipping

Waiters expect tips of Rs 5 to Rs 10 in smaller restaurants and from 5% to 10% in hotels. Bellhops and maids are happy to receive about Rs 10. Trek and travel guides expect substantially more. Taxi drivers don't expect tips, but it is OK to leave them loose change.

Trekking lodges, generally being owner operated, do not solicit tips, but they certainly do not refuse them. Sherpas and porters on group treks expect a generous tip, called *baksheesh*, at the conclusion of a trek. It is difficult to offer prudent guidelines about such tipping, but a tip of between 10% and 40% of the total wage is the norm.

WHEN TO GO

To avoid the monsoon, most trekkers travel during autumn. In the mountains the nights are cold, but the bright sun makes for pleasant day temperatures – in the high 20s°C, falling to 5°C at night, between 1000 metres and 3500 metres. At higher altitudes temperatures range from about 20°C down to -10°C. Mornings are usually clear with clouds building up during the afternoon, disappearing at night to reveal spectacular starry skies. During winter it is about 10 degrees colder.

During the high tourist seasons in October and November, flights and hotels are fully booked and the trails are alive with trekkers. Early December usually has a lull, but this is also a good trekking season. The Christmas period is cold, but this is the holiday season in Japan and Australia and these nationalities dominate flights and hotels. February is still cold, warming to the spring trekking season of March and April. Trekking tapers off in the heat of May except in the high elevations. The monsoon is a good time to visit Kathmandu, but there are few trekkers among those who come. A monsoon trek is worthwhile if you are willing to put up with the rain, leaches, slippery trails and lousy mountain views.

WHAT TO BRING

I place considerable emphasis on the selection of equipment for a trek, but in fact you can get by with a minimal kit if you can handle rough conditions and do not plan to go above 4000 metres. The task of selecting proper gear can almost overpower some people, but it is not a complex or difficult undertaking. Preparing for a trek is no more complicated than equipping yourself for a weekend backpacking trip. In some ways it is simpler. There is no food to worry about and no eating utensils or cooking pots to organise. There are no tents to stow and less overall concern with weight and bulk.

I've seen people trekking with almost nothing – a jumper (sweater) and a hash pipe. When the weather is good, when hotels are not full and you have no health problems, this arrangement can work, though innkeepers and police frown on the hash pipe. But the mountains are not always kind and you may not find warm bedding or space in a hotel. If you do head out totally unprepared, you will be on your own. Few people, either locals or other trekkers, will give up their own clothing or sleeping bag to help you when you run into trouble.

You probably already have most of the equipment needed for the trek if you hike much in cold weather. A trek is a good place to destroy clothing that is outdated or nearly worn out. A long trek, five weeks or so, is just about the maximum useful life for some clothing items. If your clothing wears out during the trek, you have repairs done at village tailor shops – they use hand-operated sewing machines.

If you follow my suggestions for equipment, you can have many happy hours – planning the trek, sorting gear, packing and repacking. It is a fine way to spend boring evenings. It will impress your friends when they find down jackets strewn over your living room floor in mid-summer. If you don't have lots of time, you can probably gather most of the items you need in a single visit to an outdoor equipment shop.

It is helpful to have all your gear – particularly shoes and socks – before you leave home, but some very good used equipment is available in Nepal. (See the section on Things to Get in Kathmandu.) Most of it is at lower prices than elsewhere. You cannot depend on getting the proper size of boots and running shoes, and socks are hard to find, but otherwise you can fully outfit yourself if you have two or three days. If you are on a prearranged trek, it is better to have your entire kit organised in advance, otherwise you might spend the night before the trek scouring all over Kathmandu for a particular item.

Equipment Checklist

The following equipment checklist is based on the experience of many trekkers over the years, I use it myself when preparing to trek, to be sure that I don't forget some important item. Everything on the list is useful, and most of it necessary, on a long trek. You can omit many items if your trek does not exceed three weeks in duration or ascend above 4000 metres. All of this gear (except the sleeping bag) will pack into a duffel bag that weighs less than 15 kg.

Some gear will not be necessary on your particular trek. You might be lucky enough to trek during a warm spell and never need a down jacket. It might be so cold and rainy that you never wear short pants. These are, however, unusual situations, and it is still important to prepare yourself for both extremes. As you read the checklist, be sure to evaluate whether or not you need a particular item of equipment. Do not rush out to an equipment shop and buy everything on this list. It works for me and has worked for many other trekkers, but you may decide that many items in this list are unnecessary.

Footwear
    boots or running shoes
    camp shoes or thongs
    socks – nylon thermal
    *boots
    *socks, high for plus fours
    *socks, light cotton for under plus fours
    *down booties (optional)
Clothing
    down or fibre-filled jacket
    woollen shirt, jumper or acrylic pile jacket
    hiking shorts or skirt
    poncho or umbrella
    sun hat
    underwear
    swimwear (optional)
    cotton or corduroy pants (optional)
    cotton T-shirts or blouses
    *down-filled pants or ski warm-up pants
    *nylon windbreaker
    *nylon wind pants
    *plus fours (knickers)
    *long underwear
    *woollen hat (or balaclava)
    *gloves
    *gaiters
Other Equipment
    backpack
    sleeping bag
    water bottle
    torch (flashlight), batteries & bulbs
Miscellaneous Items
    toilet articles
    toilet paper & matches
    sunblock, SPF 15-plus
    towel
    laundry soap
    medical & first-aid kit
    pre-moistened towelettes
    sewing kit
    small knife
    bandanna
    *goggles or sunglasses
    *sun block for lips
Optional Equipment
    camera & lenses
    lens cleansing equipment
    film, about 20 rolls
    *altimeter
    *thermometer
    *compass
    *binoculars

* Add these items if you're trekking to higher altitudes.

If you have a porter, you will need a large duffel bag with a padlock, and some stuff bags. A small duffel bag or suitcase to leave your city clothes in is also useful.

Footwear
Boots or Running Shoes Proper footwear is the most important item you will bring. Your choice of footwear will depend on the length of the trek and whether or not you will be walking in snow. Tennis or running shoes are good trekking footwear, even for long treks, if there is no snow. However, boots provide ankle protection and have stiffer soles. If you have done most of your previous hiking in boots, you may experience some discomfort in lighter and softer shoes. The trails are often rocky and rough. If the soles of your shoes are thin and soft, the rocks can bruise your feet and walking will be painful. There are several lightweight trekking shoes patterned after running shoes that have stiffer lug soles and are available in both low and high-top models.

Wherever there is snow (possible anywhere above 4000 metres), boots can become an absolute necessity. If you are travelling with porters, you have the luxury of carrying two sets of shoes and swapping then from time to time. If you are carrying everything yourself, you may have to settle for one or the other.

You should try out the shoes you plan to wear on the trek during several hikes (particularly up and down hills) before you come to Nepal. Be sure your shoes provide enough room for your toes. There are many long and steep descents during which short boots can painfully jam your toes (causing the loss of toenails).

Camp Shoes Tennis shoes are comfortable to change into for the evening. These can also serve as trail shoes in an emergency.

Rubber thongs or shower shoes make a comfortable change at camp during warm weather. You can buy these in Kathmandu and along most trails. They are called *chhapals* in Nepal. I always carry a pair of these in my backpack. I wear the thongs at lunch and in camp and put my shoes and socks in the sun to dry. I'm sure this has saved me a lot of foot troubles.

Socks Good socks are at a premium in Kathmandu, so bring these with you. There are some heavy scratchy Tibetan woollen socks available in Kathmandu and Namche Bazaar.

Thermal ski socks, a nylon-wool combination, are the best choice. Also look for the new polypropylene hiking socks. You will wash your socks several times during a long trek and pure wool socks dry slowly. Nylon-wool socks dry in a few hours in the sun – often during a single lunch stop. Most people can wear these without an inner sock, but a thin cotton liner sock is usually necessary with heavy woollen rag socks. Try on a pair on your next local hike and see whether you need an inner sock. Three pairs should be enough unless you are a real procrastinator about washing clothes.

If you bring plus fours, you will need a pair of high woollen socks and two pairs of thin cotton or nylon inner socks. Most treks do not spend enough time at high altitudes to require more than one pair of high woollen socks.

Footwear – high altitude
Down Booties Many people consider these excess baggage, but they are great to have and not very heavy. If they have a thick sole, preferably with ensolite insulation, they can serve as camp shoes at high elevations. Down booties make a cold night seem a little warmer – somehow your feet seem to feel the more than anything else. They're also good for midnight trips outside into the cold.

Clothing
Down-Filled or Fibre-Filled Jacket Down clothing has the advantage of being light and compressible. It will stuff into a small space when packed, yet bulk up when you wear it. You should bring a good jacket on a trek. Most ski jackets are not warm enough and most so-called expedition parkas are too heavy and bulky. The secret is to choose one that will be warm enough even at the coldest expected temperatures, but also comfortable when it is warmer. Don't bring both a heavy and light down jacket; choose one that will serve both purposes. If your jacket has a hood, you can dispense with a woollen hat.

Your down jacket can serve many functions on the trek. It will become a pillow at night and will protect fragile items in your backpack or duffel bag. If you are extremely cold at high altitude, wear your down jacket to bed inside your sleeping bag. You probably will not wear down gear to walk in as it rarely gets that cold even at 5000 metres. Most trekkers leave their down clothing in their duffel bag at lower elevations and only use it during the evening. At higher elevations, carry your jacket and put it on at rest or lunch stops.

Artificial fibre jackets (filled with Polargard, Thinsulate or Fibrefill) are a good substitute for down and are much less expensive. You can rent a jacket in Kathmandu, Pokhara or Namche Bazaar.

Woollen Shirt, Jumper or Acrylic Pile Jacket Two light layers of clothing are better than a single heavy layer. One or two light jumpers or shirts are superior to a heavy woollen jacket. Most of the time you will need only a single light garment in the morning and will shed it as soon as you start walking. A long sleeved shirt or jumper will suffice. A shirt has the advantage that you can open the front for ventilation without stopping to remove the entire garment.

Acrylic pile jackets and jumpers come in a variety of styles and thicknesses. Helly Hansen in Norway and Patagonia in California are two major manufacturers of pile jackets. They are light, warm (even when wet) and easy to clean. They are a little cheaper, much lighter and dry a lot faster than woollen garments. It is usually possible to rent pile jackets in Kathmandu. Tibetan woollen jumpers are also for sale in Kathmandu, but they are bulky and scratchy.

Hiking Shorts or Skirts It will often be hot and humid, the trails steep and the wind calm. Long pants pull at the knees and are hot. For hiking at lower elevations, the sherpas usually switch to shorts. It's a good idea. Either 'cutoffs' or fancy hiking shorts with big pockets are fine, but only for men. Skimpy track shorts are culturally unacceptable throughout Nepal.

Villagers can be shocked by the sight of women in shorts, so it's better to wear a skirt. Many women who have worn skirts on treks are enthusiastic about them. The most obvious reason is the ease in relieving oneself along the trail. There are long stretches where there is little chance to drop out of sight, and a skirt solves the problem. Skirts are also useful when the only place to wash is in a stream crowded with trekkers, villagers and porters. A wrap-around skirt is easy to put on and take off in a tent. Long 'granny' skirts are not good because you will be walking through too much mud to make them practical.

Poncho or Umbrella There is really no way to keep dry while hiking in the rain, however, a poncho – a large, often hooded, tarp with a hole in the centre for your head – is a good solution. The weather is likely to be warm, even while raining, and a poncho has good air circulation. The condensation inside a waterproof jacket can make you even wetter than standing out in the rain. An inexpensive plastic poncho is often as good as more expensive coated nylon gear. The plastic one is completely waterproof at a fraction of the cost. Nylon ponchos are manufactured in Kathmandu.

The most practical way of keeping dry is an umbrella. This is an excellent substitute for a poncho (except on windy days). An umbrella can serve as a sunshade, a walking stick, an emergency toilet shelter and a dog deterrent. Umbrellas with bamboo handles are available in Kathmandu for about US$2,

but these are bulky and leak black dye over you when they get wet. Collapsible umbrellas are an excellent compromise, although they cannot serve as walking sticks. Imported collapsible umbrellas are available in shops on New Rd and in the supermarket in Kathmandu. An umbrella is necessary in October, April and May and optional for treks in other months.

Sun Hat A hat to keep the sun off your head is an important item, but its design is not critical. Obviously, a hat with a wide brim affords greater protection. Fix a strap that fits under your chin to the hat so it does not blow away in a wind gust. The Nepal Cap House in the shopping centre at the entrance to Thamel has an amazing assortment of hats to choose from.

Swimwear Almost nobody older than eight goes without clothing in Nepal or India. You will upset sherpas, porters and an entire village if you skinny dip in a river, stream or hot spring, even to wash. There are many places to swim, although most are ridiculously cold – except along the Arun River in eastern Nepal, where there are some fine swimming holes. There are hot springs in Manang and in Tatopani (literally hot water) on the Jomsom trek. Either bring along swimwear or plan to swim in shorts or a skirt and be prepared to wear them till they dry.

Clothing – high altitude
Insulated Pants Most stores do not carry down-filled pants, but they are a real asset on a trek that goes above 4000 metres. You do not hike in down pants. Put them on over your hiking shorts or under a skirt when you stop for the night. Some down pants have snaps or a zipper down the inside seam of each leg. This feature allows you to use them as a half bag for an emergency bivouac and also lets you put them on without taking off your boots. As a half bag they add insulation to your sleeping bag when the nights become particularly cold.

Often you will arrive at your camp or hotel at 3 pm and will not dine until 6 pm, so unless you choose to do some exploring, there will be about 3 hours of sitting around before dinner. There is rarely a chance to sit by a fire to keep warm, even in hotels. In cold weather, down pants make these times much more comfortable. Ski warm-up pants are a good substitute, are much cheaper and are available at all ski shops. Down pants and sometimes ski warm-up pants are available for rent in trekking shops in Kathmandu and Namche.

Nylon Windbreaker Strong winds are rare in the places visited by most treks, but a windbreaker is helpful in light wind, light rain and drizzle, when a poncho is really not necessary. Be sure that your windbreaker breathes, otherwise perspiration cannot evaporate and you will become soaked. A windbreaker is more in the line of emergency gear. If there is a strong wind, you must have it, otherwise you will probably not use it.

Nylon Wind Pants Many people use these often. The temperature will often be approaching 30°C and most people prefer to hike in shorts except in the early morning when it is chilly. Wind pants provide the best of both worlds. Wear them over your shorts or under your skirt in the morning, then remove them to hike in lighter gear during the day. Most wind pants have special cuffs that allow you to remove them without taking off your shoes.

You can substitute ski warm-up pants, or even cotton jogging pants, for both wind pants and down-filled pants. The cost will be lower and there is hardly any sacrifice in versatility or comfort.

Plus Fours (Knee-Length Pants) The prime rule of selecting equipment for any hiking trip is to make each piece of gear serve at least two purposes. The great advantage of plus fours is that, combined with long woollen socks, they provide both short and long pants, simply by rolling the socks up or down.

If you are going to high elevations, you will truly be 'in the mountains' for several days. Here the weather can change quickly and sometimes dramatically. Although it will often be warm, it can cloud up and become cold and windy very fast – a potential disaster if you happen to be wearing shorts. With plus fours you can wear the socks rolled up on cold mornings before the sun rises (which, since high peaks surround you, is about 10 am). As exercise and the heat of the sun warm you, roll the socks down to your ankles. Because of this versatility, plus fours are better than long pants. Plus fours may be available in Kathmandu, but are usually for sale, not for rent.

Long Underwear Long johns are a useful addition to your equipment. A complete set makes a good warm pair of pyjamas and is also useful during late night emergency trips outside your tent or hotel. Unless the weather is especially horrible, you will not need them to walk in during the day. You can bring only the bottoms and use a woollen shirt for a pyjama top. Cotton underwear is OK, though wool is much warmer. If wool is too scratchy, duo-fold underwear (wool lined with cotton) is an excellent compromise.

Woollen Hat or Balaclava A balaclava is ideal because it can serve as a warm hat or you can roll it down to cover most of your face and neck. You may even need to wear it to bed on cold nights. Because much of your body heat is lost through your head, a warm hat helps keep your entire body warmer.

Gloves Warm ski gloves are suitable for a trek. You might consider taking along a pair of woollen mittens also, just in case your gloves get wet.

Gaiters If your trek visits high elevations, there is a chance of snow and also an opportunity to do some scrambling off the trails. A pair of high gaiters will help to keep your boots and socks cleaner and drier in rough conditions.

Equipment
Backpack A backpack should have a light

internal frame to stiffen the bag and a padded waistband to keep it from bouncing around and to take some weight off your shoulders. There are many advantages to keeping your pack small. Its small size will prevent you from trying to carry too much during the day. It is a good piece of luggage to carry on a plane. A small backpack will fit inside your tent at night without crowding and will not be cumbersome when you duck through low doorways into houses and temples.

If you don't plan to take a porter, you will need a larger pack. This can be either a frame (Kelty type) pack or a large expedition backpack, although a soft pack is more versatile. If you do eventually hand your pack over to a porter, he will certainly stuff it into a bamboo basket called a *doko* and carry it with a tumpline. A frame pack is difficult for a porter to carry because they will refuse to use the shoulder straps. There is a wide assortment of day packs and backpacks available for rent in Kathmandu.

Sleeping Bag This is one item that you might consider bringing from home. Sleeping bags are readily available for rent in Kathmandu, but the dry cleaning facilities in Nepal are pretty strange and bags lose their loft quickly during the process. The choice is usually between a clean (old and worn) bag, a dirty (warm) one or a new (expensive) sleeping bag. Most sleeping bags available in Kathmandu are mummy-style expedition bags that rent for less than US$2 a day. It is cold from November to March, even in the lowlands, so a warm sleeping bag is important at these times. A warm sleeping bag is a must at altitudes over 3300 metres, no matter what the season.

Water Bottle Because you must drink only treated or boiled water, bring a one litre plastic water bottle that does not leak. During the day your bottle provides the only completely safe source of cold drinking water. If you use iodine, fill your water bottle from streams or water spouts, add the iodine and have cold safe water half an hour later.

Fill your water bottle with boiled water at

night and take it to bed with you as a hot water bottle on cold nights – very luxurious. By morning the water will be cool for your use during the day. Many people require two litres of water during the day. If you are one of those, consider a second water bottle. Good water bottles are sometimes hard to find in Kathmandu, but you can always find (leaky) plastic Indian bottles or empty mineral water bottles that will do at a pinch.

Torch (Flashlight) Almost any torch will do; a headlight is usually not necessary. You can get spare batteries almost anywhere in the hills of Nepal if you bring a torch that uses 'D' cells. Larger batteries also perform better in the cold than small pen light 'AA' cells, but of course they are heavier. Indian and Chinese torches and exotic torches left over from expeditions are available in Nepal.

Duffel Bag If you travel with porters, protect your gear with a duffel bag. Several companies make good duffel bags that have a zipper along the side for ease of entry. This is not an item to economise on; get a bag that is durable and has a strong zipper. A duffel 35 cm in diameter and about 75 cm long is large enough to carry your gear and will usually meet the weight limit of porters and domestic flights – typically 15 kg. Army surplus duffel bags are cheaper, but they are inconvenient because they only open from the end, although there is no zipper to jam or break.

If you have porters, they will carry most of your equipment. During the day, you will carry your camera, water bottle, extra clothing and a small first-aid kit in your backpack. Do not overload the backpack, especially on the first day of the trek.

It is impossible to describe how your duffel bag will look after a month on a trek. To find out how it is treated, load a duffel bag with your equipment, take it to the second storey of a building and toss it out a window. Pick it up and shake the contents, then put it in the dirt and stomp on it a few times. Get the idea?

When it rains, your duffel bag will get wet. When it's raining, porters will leave their loads outside tea shops while they go inside to keep dry. You should pack your duffel bag in a way that important items stay dry during rainstorms. A waterproof duffel bag and waterproof nylon or plastic bags inside your bag are both necessary.

Use a small padlock that will fit through the zipper pull and fasten to a ring sewn to the bag. The lock will protect the contents from pilferage during the flight to and from Nepal and will help protect the contents on your trek. It also prevents kids, curious villagers and your porter from opening the bag and picking up something they think you won't miss. Duffel bags are hard to buy or rent in Kathmandu.

Extra Duffel Bag or Suitcase When starting a trek, you will leave your city clothes and other items in the storeroom of your hotel in Kathmandu. Bring a small suitcase or extra duffel bag with a lock to use for this purpose.

Stuff Bags It is unlikely that you will be able to find a completely waterproof duffel bag or backpack. Using coated nylon stuff bags helps you to separate your gear, thereby lending an element of organisation to the daily chaos in your tent or hotel. Stuff sacks also provide additional protection in case of rain. If you get stuff bags with drawstrings, the addition of spring-loaded clamps will save a lot of frustration trying to untie the knots you tied in too much haste in the morning. You can also use plastic bags, but these are much more fragile. A plastic bag inside each stuff sack is a good bet during the rainy season.

Sunglasses or Goggles The sun reflects brilliantly off snow, making good goggles or sunglasses with side protection essential. At high altitude they are so essential that you should have an extra pair in case of breakage or loss. A pair of regular sunglasses can serve as a spare if you rig a side shield. The lenses should be as dark as possible. At 5000 metres, the sun is intense both visually and nonvisually and ultraviolet rays can severely

damage unprotected eyes. Store your goggles in a metal case as, even in your backpack, it is easy to crush them.

Sun Block Because most treks are during autumn when the sun is low in the sky, sunburn is not a concern for most people. However, during April and May and at high altitudes, sunburn can be severe. Use a protective sun block; those with more sensitive skin need a total sun block such as zinc oxide cream. Beware of the hazard of snow glare at high altitude; you'll need a good sun block. Sun block is hard to find in Nepal.

To protect your lips at high altitude you need a total sun block such as Labiosan.

Additional Items
There is not much to say about soap, scissors and the like, but a few ideas may help. If there are two people travelling, divide a lot of this material to save weight and bulk.

Laundry soap in bars is available in Kathmandu and along most trails. This avoids an explosion of liquid or powdered soap in your luggage.

Pre-moistened towelettes are great for a last-minute hand wash before dinner. You can avoid many stomach problems by washing frequently.

A pair of scissors on your pocket knife is useful. Also bring a sewing kit and some safety pins – lots of uses.

Be sure all your medicines and toiletries are in plastic bottles with screw on lids. If in doubt, re-read the section on the treatment duffel bags receive.

The most visible sign of Western culture in the hills of Nepal is streams of toilet paper littering every camp site. Bring a cigarette lighter or matches so you can burn your used toilet paper.

You might also bring a small shovel or trowel to dig a toilet hole when you get caught in the woods with no toilet nearby.

Optional Equipment The equipment checklist suggests several items that you might bring on a trek. Do not carry all of them as you will overload your backpack.

Cameras People have brought cameras ranging from tiny instamatics to heavy Hasselblads. While most trekkers do bring a camera, it is equally enjoyable to trek without one.

A trek is long and dusty. Be sure you have lens caps, lens tissue and a brush to clean the camera and lenses as frequently as possible.

Three lenses: a wide angle (28 mm or 35 mm), a standard lens (50 mm or 55 mm) and a telephoto lens (135 mm or 200 mm) are useful if you wish to take advantage of all the photographic opportunities during the trek, but lenses are heavy. Since you will probably carry them in your backpack day after day, you may want to limit your selection. If you must make a choice, you will find a telephoto (or zoom) lens is more useful than a wide angle, because it will allow you close-up pictures of mountains and portraits of shy people. Be sure to bring a polarising filter. Don't overburden yourself with lots of heavy camera equipment; an ostentatious display of expensive gear invites theft. Insure your camera equipment.

THINGS TO GET IN KATHMANDU

What you carry in addition to your own clothing will depend on the style of trekking you choose and, if you have arranged a trek through an agency, what they provide.

If you come straight to Nepal, you can bring all your trekking clothes and equipment with you from home, but if you're in the middle of a longer trip through Asia, you might need to buy or hire some trekking equipment in Kathmandu. If you plan to carry food and kitchen gear on a trek, you should also plan to buy this in Kathmandu.

Trekking Shops

The best trekking equipment shops are in Thamel and Basantapur (Freak St). They specialise in rental of equipment, but they will also sell almost anything in the shop. Nepal's import policies do not allow the large-scale import of trekking and climbing equipment. Most gear that is available in Kathmandu was brought into the country by mountaineering expeditions so almost everything available in shops is secondhand. Any new gear is equipment that an expedition imported and never used. The other source of equipment for trekking shops is trekkers who sell off their sleeping bags and other cold weather gear before they head off to the warmer climate of South-East Asia.

Because equipment is imported in such a haphazard way, the trekking gear available in Kathmandu tends to be either high-tech mountaineering equipment or low quality, travel worn castoffs. For trekking, you want a middle ground. A down parka suitable for the top of Everest isn't very practical for a trek to Tatopani, and a sleeping bag that has spent a month on the beaches of Goa isn't going to do the job at Everest base camp. There is neither a reliable stock of any particular item nor a complete range of clothing sizes. In order to find what you need, you will have to spend time going from shop to shop looking for the right size, quality and price.

Kitchen Equipment

If you have hired a full crew, you will need a portable kitchen. Pots and pans, plates and eating utensils are available throughout the Kathmandu bazaar. If you do buy this equipment, beware that your cook does not buy lots of extra items that catch his eye. A kerosene pressure lantern is a useful but troublesome addition to the kitchen gear. It helps to extend the day by allowing you to prepare breakfast early and end your dinner late.

Stoves & Fuel

The national park rules prohibit the use of firewood in all mountain national parks. If you have a cook and are trekking in a national park, arrange for a stove. Indian kerosene stoves are expensive and delicate, so if you plan for only a short stay in a national park you might consider having meals in hotels. Theoretically, the entrance station personnel will check to see that you have a stove and kerosene if you enter the park with a group.

The use of kerosene is also required in the Annapurna Sanctuary. Kerosene is for sale at

Chhomrong at the entrance to the Annapurna Sanctuary and stoves and jerry cans are available for rent.

Hiring Equipment

It is possible to hire everything that you need for a trek – from clothing to sleeping bags, tents and cooking pots. Large sizes of shoes are often difficult to find as are gas cartridges, freeze-dried food (sometimes) and good socks. Otherwise, you can arrange everything you need in Kathmandu, though it will probably take a day or two of shopping.

If you plan to rent gear, remember that all shops require a deposit to ensure that you return the equipment in good condition. This can cause complications if you don't want to change money to pay the deposit. You might leave signed travellers' cheques or a passport with the shop, but neither of these is a good idea. Cash dollars can solve the problem, so carry some if you plan to rent equipment. A guide that the shopkeeper knows can occasionally make a personal guarantee that you will return the gear, thus saving the hassle of a deposit. Be sure to check the bill and receipt carefully before you leave the rental shop.

Some trekking companies will also rent tents, sleeping bags, mattresses and cooking pots. If you hire a guide from the same company, he can certainly serve as a guarantee and avoid the deposit problem. If you are hiring a cook, it may be worth making a deal with a trekking company to rent kitchen equipment. New kitchen equipment can cost upwards of Rs 300 per trekker and is difficult to sell at the end of the trek.

A limited supply of equipment is available for sale and rent in Pokhara, Lukla, Namche Bazaar and a few private homes in the Everest region. Namche Bazaar has fantastic trekking equipment shops because many expeditions jettison their gear here. If you are trekking around Annapurna, you need high altitude equipment only for the two or three days it takes to cross the pass. There is a need for equipment in Manang and Muktinath so it is likely that some enterprising person will arrange to have gear available on both sides

of the Thorung La before too long. Other than these places, you probably won't find any gear for rent or sale in the hills except by blind luck (a mountaineering expedition returning home, for example).

Equipment Costs in Kathmandu

The following table of costs applied for the hire or purchase of trekking equipment during autumn, 1989. Expect to pay more during the high season. In the off season, especially during the monsoon, you can probably do better than the costs I have here.

	Rs per day	Rs to buy
gloves or mittens	2-5	150-600
sleeping bag		
down-filled	30-50	3000-5000
fibre-filled	20-30	2000-4000
parka		
down-filled	7-15	1000-2500
fibre-filled	5-10	1000-1600
duffel bag*	3-5	150-300
daypack or backpack	10-15	200-500
water bottle	2	100-150
torch (flashlight)	NA	20-30 (new)
boots (big sizes scarce)	6-10	300-1500
hat, with brim	NA	25-50
hat, woollen	NA	50-90
sunglasses or goggles	2	150-300
socks (thick woollen)	NA	50-150
jumper	NA	100-250
rainwear (poncho)	4-5	400-600
umbrella	NA	50-200

* – duffel bags are hard to find in Kathmandu
NA – not available

BUSINESS HOURS & HOLIDAYS

Saturday is the weekly holiday. The working week is Sunday to Friday, though many offices work only a half day on Fridays. Most offices open at 10 am and close at 5 pm (4 pm in winter when the days are short). Shops usually remain open from 9.30 am to 7.30 or 8 pm. Banks, offices and most shopping areas are closed on Saturdays and most festival days and religious holidays.

Punctuality is not a Nepalese habit, but if you are dealing with a government office or a diplomatic functionary you should try to arrive within five to 10 minutes of the appointed time.

CULTURAL EVENTS

It is said that there are more festivals in Nepal than there are days in the year. Most Nepalese festivals are celebrated in homes and there is often little to see or photograph. Festivals complicate treks because government offices close, so you cannot get a trekking permit, and porters disappear home, occasionally leaving you at the side of the trail with your baggage.

Festivals are scheduled in accordance with the Nepalese calendar and the phase of the moon and can vary over a period of almost a month with respect to the Gregorian (Western) calendar. Nepalese months overlap Western months. The annual festival cycle through the Nepalese year is:

Baisakh – April to May

Naya Barsa The Nepalese New Year always falls in mid-April. The people of Bhaktapur celebrate the Bisket Jatra (Death of the Snake Demons Festival) on this day. Two chariots are drawn pell-mell through the narrow alleyways of the town and a mighty tug of war ensues. The winners draw the chariots to their locale. A huge lingam pole is erected in the middle of the town by drunken revellers.

Mata Tirtha Aunsi Mother's Day is the day when children offer gifts, money and sweets to their mother and literally look at their mother's face. Those whose mother is dead make a ritual pilgrimage to Mata Tirtha Aunsi near Thankot.

Rato Machhindra Nath Jatra Red Machhindra festival, also known as Bhota Jatra, the Festival of the Vest, is held annually in Patan just before the monsoon on a date decided by astrologers. Both Hindus and Buddhists celebrate the festival. The idol of Lord Machhindra is brought from Bungmati village to Pulchowk and paraded on a huge tottering chariot through the alleys of Patan to Jawalakhel. On an auspicious day, the King and Queen of Nepal, along with top government officials and thousands of devotees, descend upon Jawalakhel to catch a glimpse of the jewel-encrusted Bhoto that Machhindra has been safeguarding for centuries.

Buddha Jayanti The main festival celebrating the full moon of Buddha's birth is held in Lumbini, the birthplace of Buddha. Similar festivals are held at Swayambhunath and Boudhanath. Processions carry Buddha's image. All through the night, glowing butter lamps and blazing electric lights celebrate Buddha's birth.

Shrawan – July to August

Ghanta Karna or Ghatemangal On the 'Night of the Witch', street urchins set up barricades all over the city and solicit donations from motorists, bikers and even pedestrians. A mock funeral procession is held later in the day, followed by a feast. Effigies of the devil, made of bamboo poles and leaves, are erected on every crossroad of the city.

Nag Panchami On the day of the snake god, Brahmin priests are hired by all households to cleanse their houses by pasting a picture of the Nag over their doorways. Pujas are performed and offerings of milk and honey are left for the snake gods. The Nags are pacified through prayers and their protection and blessings are sought.

Gokarna Aunsi Father's Day is similar to Mother's Day. People offer sweets, money and gifts to their fathers and look at their father's face. Those without fathers go to the Bagmati River at Gokarna to bathe and have their father's soul blessed.

Janai Purnima The festival of the sacred thread is also known as Raksha Bhandhan and is celebrated on the full moon day of August. Higher caste Hindu men change the sacred thread they wear around their chests. In the hills of Nepal, devotees descend upon

Top: Mani Rimdu, Tengpoche (SA)
Left: Sadhu (GB)
Right: Mani Rimdu, Tengpoche (SA)

SA
    GB
JL
SB SA

Shiva temples with a *jhankri* (medicine man) leading the throngs from each village.

Gai Jatra During the festival of the sacred cows, children and adults dressed as cows pass through the city streets to honour the souls of their relatives who have recently died. It is also the day on which newspapers are legally allowed to defame and slander any and all persons.

Bhadra – August to September

Krishna Jayanti Lord Krishna's birthday is celebrated with a huge festival at the stone temple of Krishna in Patan Durbar Square. Hymns and religious songs are sung all night by devotees. The King and Queen of Nepal pay their respects to Lord Krishna at the Krishna Mandir.

Tij Brata On the day of fasting for wives, all Nepalese wives fast from sun up to midnight of that day to ensure that their husbands have good fortune and a long life. Heavily bejewelled women wearing red saris descend upon Pashupatinath to dance and sing the day away. Colourfully attired hill women trek down to Kathmandu for this festival.

Indra Jatra The festival of the king of gods is an eight day festival at Kathmandu Durbar Square. The purpose of the festival is to ask Lord Indra for post-monsoon showers for the harvest of the rice crop. This is the day the Living Goddess, or *Kumari*, of Kathmandu presides over a colourful ceremony attended by the King and Queen, government officials and foreign diplomats.

Kartik – October to November

Dasain (Durga Puja) The 10 day festival of Dasain, celebrating Durga's triumph over evil, is the biggest festival in Nepal. All creeds and castes participate. People visit their families all over the country to rejoice over Goddess Durga's triumph. Banks and government offices are closed and most of the country comes to a standstill for the duration of this festival. It is difficult to start a trek during Dasain because buses and

planes are jammed and porters are totally unavailable.

Tihar (Diwali) During the Goddess Laxmi's festival of lights the people pay homage to Laxmi, the Goddess of Wealth. Houses are given new coats of paint, hundreds of oil lamps and candles are lit, firecrackers are recklessly tossed into the streets and most households are packed with men gambling the night away. The Goddess of Wealth blesses gamblers who have made her happy.

Poush – December to January

Seto Machhindranath Snan The White Machhindra is Kathmandu's version of Patan's Red Machhindra. The chariot of Machhindra is built on Durbar Marg and dragged to Ratna Park. On the day deemed auspicious by astrologers, the Living Goddess presides over a function where Machhindra is bathed by priests.

Magh – January to February

Maghey Sankranti The first day of the Nepalese month of Magh, marking the end of winter, is an important festival all over the country. The Sankhamul Ghat in Patan is alive with devotees taking ritual baths in the Bagmati River, even though this is one of the coldest days of the year!

Falgun – February to March

Losar A two week festival of drunken revelry commemorates the Tibetan New Year in February. Though strictly a Buddhist affair, it is participated in by Hindus (like Tamangs) who believe in both religions. The Sherpas are likely to be in a drunken stupor for two weeks, so treks tend to be difficult to arrange at this time.

Shiva Ratri On the sacred night dedicated to Lord Shiva, thousands of Hindu pilgrims descend upon Pashupatinath, the holiest Hindu temple in the world – the abode of Lord Shiva. Bonfires burn throughout the night to seek Shiva's blessings. All wood that is not nailed down is stolen by urchins who then spend all night basking in Shiva's glorious bonfires.

Holi Nepal's water throwing festival is a merry affair at which people douse each other with buckets of scarlet liquid and daub red powder on their faces. The youngsters nowadays use acrylic paint and sewer water to enjoy themselves. Hashish cakes and *bhaang* (a cannabis flavoured drink) are legally sold on this day.

Chaitra – March to April
Ghoda Jatra The Royal Nepal Army takes over the Tundikhel parade ground in Kathmandu on horse racing day to display its skills in warfare, acrobatics, motorcycle stunts and horse racing. Legend has it that the horses are raced to trample devils who may rise out of the ground to create havoc.

Balaju Jatra Thousands of pilgrims keep an all night vigil at the Swayambhunath Temple. The following day they trek to the 22 waterspouts at Balaju for a ritual bath.

POST & TELECOMMUNICATIONS
The GPO is at Sundhara (The Golden Tap) in Kathmandu. It is open Sunday to Friday from 10 am to 5 pm.

The Foreign Post Office sends and receives parcels and is next to the GPO. Parcels sent to Nepal must be cleared through customs. This can be a tedious, complicated and disappointing process. Do not allow anyone to send a package to you in Nepal and think twice before sending any Nepalese a package larger than an envelope.

There is a postal service throughout the hills of Nepal. You will find post offices and letter boxes in many remote villages. It can be fun to mail postcards and letters from these facilities, but don't be disappointed if they don't reach their destination.

Sending Mail
As with all mail in Asia, you should personally take outgoing letters to the post office and watch the postal clerk cancel the stamps. The post office can be chaotic. Unless you are collecting letters from poste restante, it's better to employ someone to mail letters for you. Most hotels will mail letters for you and

Pilgrims Book Shop in Thamel offers a mailing service for a reasonable fee.

The only practical way to send letters to Nepal is by airmail. Surface mail (by sea via Calcutta) takes months. The mail service to and from Nepal is not particularly reliable, so send important letters by registered mail. Never send cheques through the mail. If someone is sending you money, it should be done through a bank.

Receiving Mail

Poste restante at the GPO will want to see your passport when you collect letters. A more reliable way to collect mail is to arrange to have it sent to a company that has a post office box. Many embassies will receive mail on your behalf. American Express has an office in Kathmandu that handles client mail.

Telephone, Fax, Telex & Telegraph

International telephone calls, telex and telegrams are coordinated through the Central Telegraph Office, about two blocks south of the GPO. The international telephone and telegraph counter is open around the clock. Hotels will book overseas calls and send telexes for a service charge.

Sabha-Doot, in an upstairs office near KC's restaurant in the Thamel area of Kathmandu, is run by the owners of the Kathmandu Guest House and offers a full range of telex, fax, mail, photocopy and telephone services around the clock.

Nepal has a sophisticated new international communications system and is within easy reach of almost any place on the international direct dialling system. Nepal's IDD code is 977 and its telex code is 891. For outgoing IDD calls the international access number is 00 followed by the country code.

Fax has virtually replaced telex in Nepal. Most hotels, travel agencies and trekking companies have fax facilities.

There are few public telephone booths, but most small shops will allow you to use their phone for a rupee or two.

There is a direct dial service within Nepal to Pokhara and most cities in the Terai. In the hills there is no telephone service, but if you have patience you can send domestic telegrams.

TIME

Nepal has one time zone which is 5 hours and 45 minutes ahead of GMT. When it is noon in Kathmandu, standard time is 6.15 am in London, 4.15 pm in Sydney, 1.15 am in New York and 10.15 pm the previous night in San Francisco.

If you drive or fly to Tibet, the time change can be fun. Tibet is on Beijing time, so when you cross the border at Kodari, set your watch ahead 2 hours and 15 minutes in winter or 3 hours and 15 minutes in summer.

During winter the days are short – first light is about 6 am and it gets dark at about 6 pm. Nepal has no summer time, but by March the days are about 2 hours longer, so you could trek from 5 am to 7 pm if you wished.

ELECTRICITY

Nepal's electricity is nominally 220 volts, 50 cycles, but fluctuations are severe and unpredictable. You must use a voltage stabiliser to protect all sensitive electronic equipment.

WEIGHTS & MEASURES

Nepal has adopted the metric system, though in the hills shopkeepers often use an ancient system of weights and measures. In the hill system there are eight *maanas* to a *paathi*, a unit of volume equivalent to about 4½ litres. The old unit of weight is the *dharni*, about 2.4 kg, which is divided into 12 *pau*. Often, however, the unit of measurement is whatever container is most convenient. Kerosene and cooking oil is usually sold by the bottle – a 650 ml beer bottle. A 'tin' usually refers to a 19 litre mustard oil tin, but I have seen sherpas flummoxed by a shopkeeper who used a fruit tin that held only about five potatoes.

While counting and talking figures, the words *lakh* (100,000) and *crore* (10 million) are commonly used. You may often see figures written using this system: 1,02,00,000 equals one crore and two lakhs.

BOOKS

There are hundreds of books about Nepal, Tibet and the Himalaya, some dating back to the 1800s. A trip to your local library will provide you with an armload of fascinating books. The following list includes publications that are historically important and describe important aspects of trekking in Nepal. Most are recent enough to be available in large libraries. You can buy many of these books and others not available in the West in Kathmandu.

Another good source of material about Nepal is the (American) *National Geographic* magazine. Over the years, about 10 issues have had some material on Nepal and the Himalaya. Also look for copies of the *Himalayan Journal*, an annual publication of the Himalayan Club in Bombay, India.

Kathmandu has some of the best and least expensive bookshops in Asia. In addition to a huge variety of books about Nepal and Tibet, there are thousands of new and used paperbacks available at moderate prices. A paperback book is very useful on a trek, both to relieve boredom while waiting for meals, buses and planes, and as a source of emergency toilet paper.

Two good shops for books about Nepal are Pilgrims in Thamel and Himalayan Booksellers, which has branches in Thamel and on Durbar Marg near the clock tower. Paperbacks are available from bookshops everywhere.

Geography

Nepal – the Kingdom in the Himalayas by Toni Hagen (Kummerly & Frey, Bern, 1980) is still the definitive documentation of the geology and people of Nepal, with many fine photos.

Mount Everest, the Formation, Population & Exploration of the Everest Region by Toni Hagen, G O Dyhrenfurth, C Von Fürer Haimendorf & Erwin Schneider (Oxford University Press, London, 1963) is a shortened version of material in Hagen's book, combined with other works describing the Solu Khumbu region in detail. The maps are good.

Karnali under Stress by Barry C Bishop (University of Chicago, Chicago, 1990) is a study of the geography and trading patterns of western Nepal.

People & Society

The Sherpas of Nepal by C Von Fürer Haimendorf (John Murray, London, 1964) is a rather dry anthropological study of the Sherpas of the Solu Khumbu region. The sequel is titled *The Sherpas Transformed*.

Himalayan Traders by C Von Fürer Haimendorf (John Murray, London, 1975) studies the change in trading patterns and culture among Himalayan peoples throughout Nepal.

Mustang – a Lost Tibetan Kingdom by Michel Peissel (Collins & Harvill Press, London, 1968) is still the best available description of the restricted Lo Mantang region of Mustang, north of Jomsom.

People of Nepal by Dor Bahadur Bista (Ratna Pustak Bhandar, Kathmandu, 1967) gives an excellent overview of the various ethnic groups in Nepal. Bista is Nepal's foremost anthropologist.

The Festivals of Nepal by Mary M Anderson (George Allen & Unwin, London, 1971) describes the important festivals of Nepal and provides a lot of background information on the Hindu religion.

The Kulunge Rai by Charles McDougal (Ratna Pustak Bhandar, Kathmandu, 1979) is an anthropological study of the Rais in the Hongu Valley, especially the village of Bung.

Vignettes of Nepal by Harka Bahadur Gurung (Sajha Prakashan, Kathmandu, 1980) provides personal accounts of treks throughout Nepal. The book includes good historical and geological background information and many maps.

High in the Thin Cold Air by Edmund Hillary & Desmond Doig (Doubleday, New York, 1962) describes many of the projects undertaken by the Himalayan trust. It also contains the story of the scientific examination of the Khumjung yeti skull.

Schoolhouse in the Clouds by Edmund Hillary (Penguin, London, 1968) describes the construction of Khumjung school and other projects in Khumbu. This provides good background information on where all those bridges, hospitals and schools came from.

Mani Rimdu, Nepal by Mario Fantini (Toppan Co, Singapore, 1976) contains colour photos and descriptions of the dances of the Mani Rimdu festival at Tengpoche Monastery.

Natural History

Birds of Nepal by Robert L Fleming, Sr, Robert L Fleming, Jr & Lain Bangdel (published by the authors, Kathmandu, 1976) is the definitive work on the hundreds of species of birds in Nepal. It contains many outstanding colour paintings of birds.

Discovering Trees in Nepal by Adrian & Jimmie Storrs (Sahayogi Press, Kathmandu, 1984) gives good information about the trees of Nepal, including their economic and cultural significance.

Flowers of the Himalaya by Oleg Polunin & Adam Stainton (Oxford University Press, London, 1984) is highly technical and very detailed.

The Arun by Edward W Cronin, Jr (Houghton Mifflin Company, Boston, 1979) is a natural history of the Arun River valley.

Stones of Silence by George B Schaller (Viking Press, New York, 1980) is a naturalist's view of travels in Dolpo.

Himalayan Flowers & Trees by Dorothy Mierow & Tirtha Bahadur Shrestha (Sahayogi Press, Kathmandu, 1978) is the recognised field guide to the plants of Nepal.

Sagarmatha, Mother of the Universe by Margaret Jefferies (Cobb/Horwood Publications, Auckland, 1985) is a detailed description of the Mt Everest National Park.

Trekking & Mountaineering

Nepal Himalaya by H W Tilman (Cambridge University Press, London, 1952) is one of my favourites. It's a delightful book filled with Tilman's dry wit and describes the first treks in Nepal in 1949 and 1950. The book

is out of print and hard to find, but it is part of a Tilman anthology published by the Seattle Mountaineers.

Round Kanchenjunga by Douglas W Freshfield (Ratna Pustak Bhandar, Kathmandu, 1979) is a reprint of the most definitive book about the Kanchenjunga region. Originally published in 1903, it describes a circuit of the mountain in 1899.

The Kanchenjunga Adventure by F S Smythe (Victor Gollancz, London, 1930) is another account of the early exploration of eastern Nepal.

Americans on Everest by James Ramsey Ullman (J B Lippincott, Philadelphia, 1964) is the official account of the 1963 American expedition.

The Moated Mountain by Showell Styles (Hurt & Blackett, London, 1955) is a very readable book about an expedition to Baudha Peak. Styles makes poignant cultural observations as he treks to the mountain.

Forerunners to Everest by Rene Dittert, Gabriel Chevalley & Raymond Lambert, translated by Malcolm Barnes (Harper & Row, York, 1954) is a description of the two Swiss expeditions to Everest in 1952. It includes a fine description of the old expedition approach march.

Annapurna by Maurice Herzog (Jonathan Cape, London, 1952) is a mountaineering classic that describes the first conquest of an 8000 metre peak. There is a good description of the Annapurna region, including Manang, and a visit to the Rana court of Kathmandu in 1950.

Annapurna South Face by Christian Bonnington (Cassell, London, 1971) describes the beginning of a new standard of mountaineering in Nepal and provides an excellent description of the problems of organising an expedition.

Faces of Everest by Major H P S Ahluwalia (Vikas, New Delhi, 1977) is an illustrated history of Everest by a summiter of the 1965 Indian expedition.

Everest by Walt Unsworth (Allen Lane, London, 1981) gives a detailed history of mountaineering on Everest.

The Ascent of Rum Doodle by W E

Bowman (Dark Peak, Sheffield, 1979) is the classic spoof of mountaineering books. It's a good diversion after reading a few expedition accounts that take themselves too seriously.

Language

Nepal Phrasebook (Lonely Planet, Melbourne, 1984) is a handy phrasebook with a particular emphasis on trekking.

Basic Gurkhali Grammar by M Meerendonk (Singapore, 1964) is a good introductory text on Nepali, which the British Army calls Gurkhali. It was written for the army, so it teaches a slightly weird military vocabulary.

Basic Gurkhali Dictionary by M Meerendonk (Singapore, 1960) is a pocket-sized dictionary of the Nepali language. It is quite useful once you understand the rudiments of the grammar.

Trekkers Pocket Pal compiled by the Summer Institute of Linguistics (Avalok, Kathmandu, 1977) is yet another phrasebook for trekkers.

Sherpa Nepali English by Phinjo Sherpa (Nepal Lithographing, Kathmandu, 1989) is the first Sherpa phrasebook.

Tibet

Tibet by Thubten Jigme Norbu & Colin Turnbull contains an excellent account of the culture and religion of Tibet by the brother of the Dalai Lama.

The Secret War in Tibet by Michel Peissel is a one-sided description of the resistance of Khampa warriors against the Chinese in Tibet. It was published in England as *Cavaliers of Kham*.

Seven Years in Tibet by Heinrich Harrer is a best selling book describing Harrer's adventures in Tibet before the Chinese occupation. It also contains commentary on Harrer's discussions with the Dalai Lama.

Travel Guides

Nepal – a travel survival kit by Tony Wheeler & Richard Everist (Lonely Planet, Melbourne, 1990) is a complete guidebook to Nepal.

Nepal Namaste by Robert Rieffel (Sahayogi Press, Kathmandu, 1987) is a good general guidebook written by a long-term resident of Kathmandu.

A Guide to Trekking in Nepal by Stephen Bezruchka (The Mountaineers, Seattle, 1985) has detailed information about how to organise a backpacking or tea house trek. There are many route descriptions.

Trekking in Nepal, West Tibet & Bhutan by Hugh Swift (San Francisco, Sierra Club Books, 1989) has route descriptions that are not as detailed, but it covers a larger area than other books.

Treks on the Kathmandu Valley Rim by Alton C Byers III (Sahayogi Press, Kathmandu, 1982) describes one day and overnight treks near Kathmandu.

Trekking in the Himalayas by Tomoya Iozawa (Allied Publishers, Bombay, 1980) is a well illustrated trekking guidebook with lots of hand drawn maps and sketches.

Nepal Trekking by Christian Kleinert (Bergverlag Rudolf Rother, Munich, 1975) is a set of route descriptions in a fancy plastic cover that you can carry while trekking. The book suggests some very ambitious routes and schedules.

The Trekking Peaks of Nepal by Bill O'Connor (Crowood Press, Ramsbuty, England, 1989) is an essential reference for anyone thinking about doing any climbing in Nepal.

Health

Medicine for Mountaineering by James A Wilkerson (The Mountaineers, Seattle, 1985) is an outstanding reference book for the layperson. It describes many of the medical problems typically encountered in Nepal. One copy of this book should accompany every trekking party.

Mountain Medicine by Michael Ward (Crosby, Lockwood, Staples, London, 1975) is good background reading on the subject of cold and high altitude problems.

Where There is No Doctor by David Werner (The Hesperian Foundation, Palo Alto, California, 1977) is also a good layperson's medical guide with lots of application to Nepal.

Altitude Sickness by Peter Hackett (American Alpine Club, New York, 1979) is required reading for anyone who treks above 4000 metres.

MAPS

The best series of maps of Nepal is the 1:50,000 series produced by Erwin Schneider for Research Scheme Nepal Himalaya and printed in Vienna. They cover the Everest region from Jiri to the Hongu Valley, Kathmandu Valley and Langtang. They're available from many map shops overseas and at many bookshops in Kathmandu. The fantastically coloured maps are also fantastically expensive – about US$8 a sheet, but if you are doing any serious trekking they are worth it. If you are planning a climb, they are absolutely necessary.

The excellent Ground Survey of India series (an inch equals a mile) are restricted and hard to obtain because in India maps are secret documents. The US Army Map Service produced a set of maps (Series U502 at 1:250,000) based on the Ground Survey of India maps. Prepared in the 1950s, they are outdated, but the topography is quite accurate. Stamfords bookshop in London has reprinted the entire series.

Other maps are available as blueprints of traced maps produced in Nepal. They aren't really very accurate, but they will give you some idea of where you are going. The Police Adventure Foundation has also produced a series of maps. A few other printed maps, including an excellent series by Dr Harka Bahadur Gurung, formerly Nepal's minister of tourism, are available in Kathmandu. Both the Royal Geographical Society and the National Geographic Society have made special maps of the Everest region.

Most of these maps are available at bookshops in Kathmandu.

MEDIA
Newspapers & Magazines
The Rising Nepal is the daily English language newspaper. There are numerous other daily and weekly papers in both English and Nepali. Since the 1990 revolution, the prime minister has emphasised total freedom of the press. Consequently, these publications now actually carry some news.

Nepal Traveller is a monthly magazine that is distributed free to all passengers on arrival at the airport. It has an excellent Kathmandu city map, a description of the current festivals and usually contains good advice about trekking.

Radio & TV
Radio Nepal broadcasts from 6 am until 11 pm and uses short wave frequencies to reach the remote hill areas. Frequencies are 5005, 7165 and 792 kHz in Kathmandu and 684 KHz in Pokhara. It broadcasts the news in English at 8 am and 8 pm. During the climbing season a special mountaineering weather report follows the English news.

Even without a radio, you should have no problem listening to Radio Nepal in the hills. As a gesture of generosity, most Nepalese people try to entertain the entire village by playing the radio at high volume.

Nepal Television broadcasts in Kathmandu, Pokhara and several Terai towns. In 1985 Nepal became one of the last countries in the world to begin television broadcasts. The news is broadcast in English at 9.40 pm.

DANGERS & ANNOYANCES
Personal Safety & Theft
In 1974 I wrote 'there is virtually nothing to fear in Nepal from thieves, hijackings or the other horrors of our urban civilisation'. Unfortunately, this has changed and it pays to be cautious about your companions – whether fellow trekkers or porters – and your belongings, especially when you camp. There are frequent reports of items being stolen from the tents and hotel rooms of trekkers, even in the most remote villages. There have even been incidents of violent crime, something previously unheard of in Nepal.

There is at least one roving gang of thieves

who watch trekkers and go after those who display valuable items or who have large amounts of cash. Most thefts have been from those who had things we would recognise as worth stealing – with the possible exception of boots. Boots are high on the list of desirable items (along with money and cameras). Don't leave your boots near the door of your tent or outside a hotel room. The most frequent thefts occur in Naudanda, Ghandruk, Dhampus and Hyangja on the Annapurna trek. Another danger spot is near Seopuri at the beginning of the Helambu trek, but it pays to be cautious everywhere. Always be especially cautious within two or three days of a road on which buses might offer a quick getaway.

The US Embassy in Kathmandu makes the following suggestions:

While Nepalese are generally friendly and present no threat to trekkers, the number of violent incidents in recent years against trekkers has unfortunately increased. Crime, while still low by Western standards, does exist on the trails. Westerners have been the victims of murder and violent assaults. All the victims have been travelling alone or as a couple. The general motive seems to have been robbery, even though the possessions of some of the victims were insignificant by American standards. To help you enjoy your trek and to minimise the risk of unpleasant incidents, the embassy recommends that you take the following precautions:

Register with the consular section, giving the trek itinerary and dates of the trek.

Do not travel alone. Join up with other Westerners going along the same trail if you are alone in Nepal. Do take a porter or guide. Backpacking by yourself may seem the noble thing to do but it is dangerous. You will also be doing a disservice to Nepal by not contributing to the local economy.

Arrange for porters and guides through a reputable trekking agency, friends or the embassy so that they can be traced if you have trouble. Do not just pick up a porter or guide off the street, no matter how friendly he may appear.

Do not make ostentatious displays of your cash or possessions. Store all valuable items in Kathmandu at your hotel or lodge. Be sure to obtain a detailed receipt of your items from the hotel or lodge.

If possible, camp at night near other trekkers. Do not walk along trails after dark.

Don't leave your passport as collateral for renting trekking equipment. You may need it in an emergency.

Be sure to register at all the police and immigration posts along the trail and go only on the route prescribed in your trekking permit.

If you encounter problems along the trail, report them to the nearest police or immigration post. When you return to Kathmandu, report any unresolved problems to the appropriate trekking agency or hotel as well as the police and the Ministry of Tourism.

The embassy recommends that you do not take night buses in Nepal. There have been serious problems recently with bandits holding up these buses.

Despite this caution, you will find most Nepalese to be friendly, helpful and honest. It is, however, essential that you travel with a well-chosen companion – either another Westerner or a guide – for your own safety. The chance of theft is still remote, but a sprained ankle, debilitating illness or other misfortune can occur at any time. It is only common sense, applicable to a hiking trip anywhere, that you should not travel alone in the mountains.

FILM & PHOTOGRAPHY

Film is available in Kathmandu, but it is quite expensive and it may have been through an airport x-ray machine before reaching Nepal. Make certain you have enough film. On a two or three week trek, 20 rolls of 36 exposure film is not too much.

Nepal has regulations governing commercial filming. If you plan to make a 16 mm movie, you will certainly need the help of a trekking agent in Nepal, although eight mm movies and videos are not subject to any restrictions.

There are many colour print processing facilities in Kathmandu. Lotus Studio, Das Photo, Nepal Photo and Photo Concern are all reliable and can handle colour prints and Ektachrome slides. Colour enlargements are produced in Kathmandu at reasonable prices.

Photo Concern on New Rd is the best place to go for camera repairs. You can also buy a second-hand camera from many photo shops. Some surprisingly high quality cameras show up on their shelves at bargain prices (read the section on theft if you are wondering where they come from).

You can buy blank VHS video cassettes at shops on New Rd, but it is hard to find blank tapes in other formats. It is almost impossible to rent video cameras in Nepal.

ACCOMMODATION
Kathmandu

Hotels in Kathmandu range from the luxurious to downright depressing. The Hotel Association of Nepal has a reservation desk at the airport and touts from small hotels meet every arriving flight, often offering free transportation to their hotel. Except at the budget end, Kathmandu hotel rates are expensive. If you are trekking with an organised group, your trek will probably include accommodation at one of the more expensive hotels. Hotels are booked solid during the trekking season, so you may have to do a bit of shopping, or take advantage of the airport touts, if you arrive without a reservation.

Kathmandu's budget accommodation is centred around the Thamel area. Hotels include the famous *Kathmandu Guest House* and the lesser known but adequate *Tibet Guest House, Star, Garuda, Shakti* and *Potala Guest House*. Costs are in the US$5 per night range. When you choose a hotel, check the room for street noise. Nepalese drivers use their horn more than their brakes, so street-side rooms tend to be intolerable.

Ecotel Nepal offers a booking service for budget hotels in Thamel. Contact them by calling 414432, 416650 or 417308, fax (977)-1-411933, or telex 2766 ECOTEL NP.

Bottom End – US$10 to US$20
Hotel Nook Kantipath, (tel 213627)
Hotel Blue Diamond Jyatha, (tel 226392, 226320)

Hotel Manaslu Lazimpat, (tel 413470)
Tara Gaon Hotel Boudhanath
Hotel Gauri Shanker Sallaghari, Thamel
Hotel Vajra Bijeshwori, Swyambhu, (tel 224719, 224545)
Hotel Marshyangdi Thamel, (tel 412129, 414105)
Hotel Ambassador Lazimpat, (tel 414432, 410432)

Middle – US$30 to US$60
Hotel Yellow Pagoda Kantipath, (tel 220338, 220337, telex 2268 PAGODA NP)
Hotel Blue Star Tripureshwore, (tel 211473, 211472, telex 2322 BLUSTR NP)
Hotel Woodlands Durbar Marg, (tel 222683 , 220123)

Top End – US$70 to US$100
Hotel Malla Lekhnath Marg, (tel 418385, telex 2238 MALLA)
Hotel Shangri La Lazimpat, (tel 412999, telex 2276 HOSANG NP)
Hotel Narayani Pulchowk, (tel 521442, 521711)
Hotel Shanker Lazimpat, (tel 410154, 410153, telex 2230 SANKER NP)
Kathmandu Hotel Maharajganj, (tel 412103, 413082, telex 2256 HOKAT NP)
Hotel Sherpa Durbar Marg, (tel 228898, 222585, telex 2223 NEPCOM NP)

Top End – US$100 Plus
Hotel Yak & Yeti Durbar Marg, (tel 413999, telex 2237 YKNYTI NP)
Hotel Soaltee Oberoi Tahachal, (tel 214211, 211211, telex 2203 SOALTE NP)
Hotel Everest International Naya Baneshwore, (tel 220614, 220567, telex 2260 HOTEVS NP)
Hotel de l'Annapurna Durbar Marg, (tel 221711, telex 2205 AAPU NP)

Hotels in the Hills

Local inns or bhattis have existed for centuries in the hills. A bhatti is usually a wooden or maybe even a bamboo structure close to the trail, with the large house of the owners situated some distance away. It usually has a simple mud stove with a pot of milk and another pot of hot water to make tea. There is usually a jug or two of *chhang* or *rakshi* in the back room to provide a bit of alcoholic diversion for the village elders and the few overnight guests who happen along. Where trekking has not developed, these reasonably primitive establishments are still the only hotel facilities available.

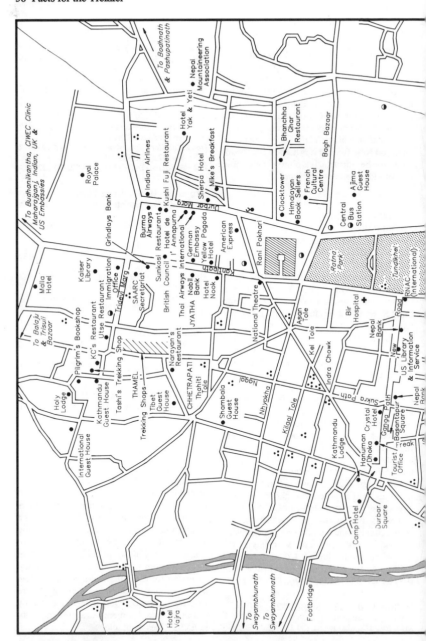

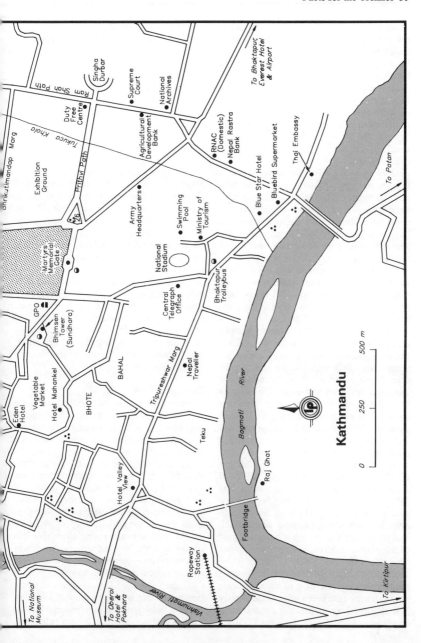

Kathmandu

As trekking increased and as Nepalese travellers began to have a bit more money, facilities have improved and the tiny inns have expanded into the extensive system of hotels that now serves major trekking routes. Most hotels in the hills are family run affairs that started in the living room. Some have separate quarters for guests, but most are still living room affairs at which the family that operates the inn eats and sleeps in the same building, and often the same room, that they offer to guests.

Only since the mid-1970s have trekkers become an important source of income in the hills, so most of the hotels that cater to trekkers opened after 1979 or 1980. Some of these have obtained government loans and have become quite grand. Several inns on the Jomsom trek even have sidewalk cafés where you can enjoy a meal in the sun. These establishments are popular with trekkers and have English language signboards. Some hotels offer private rooms, but many have only dormitory accommodation or the communal living space available.

Often the husband of the house is away trading or working as a porter or trekking guide. Usually the wife manages things, but sometimes hotels are left in the care of children. Some pretty weird meals and service can result when a six or eight year old tries to deal with customers. In remote areas that trekkers do not frequent, the 'hotel' may exist only in the mind of the proprietor and will consist of sharing the eating and living accommodation with a family.

The primary incentive for operating a hotel in the hills is to turn locally produced food, labour and firewood into cash. The hills of Nepal are increasingly becoming a cash oriented society. There are few ways to earn this cash, other than operating a hotel, that allow people to remain at home and tend to the house, children, livestock and crops. The prices at most hotels in the hills are artificially cheap for this reason. Intense competition and the lack of an alternative way to secure cash keeps prices ridiculously low. It certainly is not profitable to sell a cup of tea with sugar for Rs 1 (about US$0.03 cents) when sugar is Rs 8 per kg, tea is Rs 18 per 250 gram packet and it takes a full day to fetch a load of firewood. There is a movement in the major trekking areas to standardise rates for food and accommodation, so that most hotels in a particular village charge the same.

FOOD
Nepalese Food
The most common meal in Nepal is *dhal bhaat* – rice (bhaat) with a soup made of lentils (dhal) poured over it. Hill people subsist on dhal bhaat and a thick paste called *dhindo*. This is coarse ground corn or millet, often mixed with a few hot chillies. In the northern regions people call this dish *tsampa* and make it from roasted and ground barley. Sherpas and other Himalayan people often mix tsampa with buttered and salted Tibetan tea.

The local diet rarely includes meat or eggs, so dhal provides the primary source of protein. *Roti* (unleavened bread) or *chappati* is another frequent addition to a meal and often substitutes for rice. Other items may supplement a meal, usually a curry made from potatoes or whatever vegetables are available locally.

Food on a Trek
Although some hotels in the hills can conjure up fantastic meals, the standard hotel diet is dhal bhaat, or at higher elevations, potatoes. Dal bhaat twice a day for a month presents a boring prospect to the Western palate. On major trek routes, restaurants vary in standard from primitive to luxurious, and beer, Coke and other soft drinks are available at high prices. The menus are often attractive and extensive, but too often the menu represents the innkeeper's fantasy of what he would like to serve, not what's available. No matter what the hotel advertises, the choice almost always comes back to rice, dhal, potatoes, pancakes and instant noodles.

Thirty years ago, Tilman observed that a person can live off the country in a sombre fashion, but Nepal was no place in which to make a gastronomic tour. It hasn't changed.

In Kathmandu, a city of half a million people, it takes a lot of imagination to provide the variety in diet that Westerners expect. In remote regions, it is almost impossible to provide this variety, unless you bring the food with you. Most people can adapt to a Nepalese diet, but try it for a few days at home so you know what to expect. Boiled rice with a thick split pea soup poured over it is the closest approximation to dhal bhaat. This experiment might help convince you to fill the remote corners of your backpack with spices, trail snacks and other goodies.

Kathmandu Restaurants

Trekkers attach great importance to their stomachs. Kathmandu's restaurants have responded by offering some of the most varied menus in Asia. In Thamel, try *KC's*, the original budget traveller's restaurant, *La Dolce Vita* for Italian food and *Him Thai* for Thai food. There are many other restaurants and pie shops, particularly in Thamel, that serve meals in the Rs 50 to Rs 100 range. Monday is pizza night at *Mike's Breakfast*, behind the Hotel Sherpa. You can find dhal bhaat at street corner restaurants, but for safety, stick to the *Sun Kosi*, *Bhancha Ghar* or the *Nanglo Pub* if you want Nepalese food.

For a big splurge, head for the hotels for good Indian, Chinese and continental food. Indian food at the *Ghar E Kabab* in the Hotel Annapurna and the *Far Pavilions* in the Everest International is expensive. The *Kabab Corner* in the Hotel Gautam is cheaper. *Mountain City* in the Malla has Sichuan food and the *Chimney Room* in the Hotel Yak & Yeti is the last incarnation of Boris' legendary restaurant.

DRINKS

Soft Drinks & Bottled Water

Nepal has all the international brands of soft drinks. All are sold in bottles, not cans. The bottle deposits are more than the cost of the drink, so leave the bottle behind when you quaff a Coke at a trailside stall. So-called mineral water is available throughout Nepal

and the plastic bottles make emergency trekking water bottles.

Alcohol

For a small country, Nepal has a thriving beer industry. The local brands, Star, Golden Eagle, Iceberg and Leo come in 650 ml bottles. Tuborg and San Miguel also brew in Nepal and distribute in cans if you want to carry them on your trek.

Despite the traditional Brahmin abstinence, a lot of alcohol is consumed in Nepal. The local potions are chhang and rakshi, which can be quite tasty and potent, but there are also numerous Western-style liquors available. The notorious Kukhri Rum makes a fine after-trek drink on cold nights. Snow Lands Gin advertises its roots in London, Glasgow and Kathmandu.

Drinks on a Trek

Don't drink tap water or stream water anywhere. Instead, stick to soft drinks, bottled water, beer, or water you have purified yourself. It can be difficult to get boiled water on a trek. Ask an innkeeper if the water is boiled and he will assure you that it is, even if it has just been taken from the river. This response illustrates several unusual facets of Nepalese culture and personality. Most hill people do not understand germs. They accept good naturedly the desire of Westerners that their drinking water be boiled, but few people understand why. They often believe that Westerners like only hot water. Another consideration is that Nepalese like to please others and dislike answering any question negatively. So, you get a 'yes' answer to almost every question, particularly 'Is this water boiled?'. Hotels also do not like to prepare boiled water because it uses fuel and takes up space on the stove – and they can't charge for the service.

There are two easy solutions that ensure that you have safe drinking water: good tea must be made from boiling water, so a cup of tea will always be made with boiled water; and treating water with iodine solves the boiled water problem in a way that does not consume scarce fuel. See the discussion of this technique in the Health & First Aid chapter.

If you decide to sample chhang and rakshi, remember that chhang is made from water straight from the river, not boiled water.

THINGS TO BUY

Bring enough money to buy whatever souvenirs, incredible bargains or art objects you may find. In Kathmandu there are Tibetan carpets (US$90 to US$150), woollen jumpers and jackets (US$5 to US$25). Some genuine Tibetan art pieces (US$20 plus) and semiprecious stones (US$15 to US$25) are also available. On the trek you may find objects from Tibet (prayer wheels, *thankas*, butter lamps and bells) or Sherpa household articles (chhang bottles, boots, aprons, carpets and cups) at prices from US$1 to more than US$100.

Most Tibetan jewellery, statues and handicrafts were historically and traditionally made by Newar craftspeople in Nepal. You can often buy modern reproductions of Tibetan antiques that are as authentic as antiques smuggled in from Tibet.

If you plan to make a major purchase in Nepal, first visit an importer at home and find out what is available at what price. Especially note the quality, so that you will have a basis for comparison in Nepal. Many pieces exported from India and Nepal may be available in your locale at prices lower than in retail shops in Kathmandu because of large volume discounts. Tibetan carpets made in Nepal are for sale in San Francisco, for example, for less than it would cost to buy one in Nepal and ship it home.

Other bargains in Kathmandu include extra visa photos, climbing gear, woollen socks and cotton clothing. You can also buy embroidered T-shirts in a variety of standard patterns or with your own special design.

Trekking Information

ABOUT TREKKING

In Nepal there are numerous ways to arrange a trek because of two major factors. Firstly, inexpensive (by Western standards) professional and nonprofessional labour is available to carry loads and to work as guides and camp staff. Secondly, you can almost always find supplies and accommodation locally because there are people living in even the most remote trekking areas.

I have classified the many possible ways of trekking into four approaches: backpacking, tea house treks, self-arranged treks and treks with a trekking company. There is a lot of overlap among these, because many aspects of each trekking style spill over into the next. A backpacking trek that stays a few nights in hotels has many of the attributes of a tea house trek. A tea house trek with porters starts to become a self-arranged trek. A self-arranged trek that uses the services of a trekking agency in Nepal is similar to the trekking company approach.

Backpacking

The backpacking approach of a light pack, stove, freeze-dried food and a tent really is not an appropriate way to trek in Nepal. So much food is available in hill villages that it doesn't make much sense to try to be totally self-sufficient while trekking. This is true throughout Nepal except in the high mountains and the far west, near Jumla, where food is scarce. Backpackers violate two cardinal rules for travellers in Nepal. Because they are self sufficient, they do not contribute to the village economy. Also, they must do so many camp chores that they do not have the time or energy to entertain villagers.

At higher altitudes, however, the backpacking approach works. Depending on the terrain and local weather conditions, villages are found up to 4000 metres, but above this there isn't much accommodation available except in tourist areas such as Annapurna Sanctuary and Everest. It is also difficult to arrange to hire porters who have the proper clothing and footwear for travelling in cold and snow. If you plan to visit these regions, you may wish to alter your trekking style and utilise a backpacking or mountaineering approach to reach high passes or the foot of remote glaciers.

A good solution is to leave much of your gear behind at a temporary 'base camp' in the care of a hotel or trustworthy sherpa. You can then spend a few days carrying a reduced load of food and equipment on your own. This will provide you with the best of both worlds: an enriching cultural experience that conforms to the standards and traditions of the country in the lowlands, and a wilderness or mountaineering experience in the high mountains.

Tea House Treks

The Nepali word bhatti translates well as 'tea house'. It is a bit pretentious to call some of these village establishments a hotel, but the Nepalese use of English translates restaurant or eating place as 'hotel'. Since the word hotel has, therefore, been pre-empted, Nepalese use the word 'lodge' for sleeping place or hotel. Thus a 'hotel' has food, but may not provide a place to sleep, while a 'lodge' offers accommodation. Many innkeepers specify the services they provide by calling their establishments 'Hotel & Lodge'. To avoid all this semantic confusion, I have used hotel, lodge and tea house interchangeably. In reality you can almost always find both accommodation and food at any trailside establishment.

The most popular way to trek in Nepal for both Nepalese and Westerners is to travel from tea house to tea house. Hotel accommodation is most readily available in the Khumbu (Everest) region, the Langtang area and the entire Annapurna region. In these areas you can operate with a bare minimum of equipment and rely on tea houses for food and shelter. In this manner, it will cost from US$3 to US$10 a day, depending on where you are and how simply you can live and eat. It becomes much more expensive at high altitude and in very remote areas.

Most Thakali inns (found along the Pokhara-Jomsom route) have bedding available – usually a cotton-filled quilt. Sometimes the bedding has the added attraction of lice and other bed companions. Bring

along your own sheet or sleeping bag to provide some protection against these bugs. During the busy trekking seasons in October to November and March to April, it may be difficult to find bedding every night on the Jomsom trek. Bedding is not usually available at hotels on the Everest trek or around Annapurna, so on these treks you should carry your own sleeping bag.

Although many hotels in the hills are reasonably comfortable, the accommodation in some places may be a dirty, often smokey, home. Chimneys are rare, so a room on the 2nd floor of a house can turn into an intolerable smokehouse as soon as someone lights the cooking fire in the kitchen below. Often it is possible to sleep on porches of houses, but your gear is then less secure. The most common complaint among trekkers who rely on local facilities is about smokey accommodation.

By arranging your food and accommodation locally, you can move at your own pace and set your own schedule. You can move faster or slower than others and make side trips not possible with a large group. You can spend a day photographing mountains, flowers or people – or you can simply lie around for a day. Hotels provide a special meeting place for trekkers from throughout the world in a unique situation where both of you are out of place. You are free (within the limits imposed by your trekking permit) to alter your route and change your plans to visit other out of the way places as you learn about them. You will have a good opportunity to see how the people in the hills of Nepal live, work and eat and will probably develop at least a rudimentary knowledge of the Nepali language.

You are, however, dependent on facilities in villages or in heavily trekked regions. Therefore you must trek in inhabited areas and on the better known routes. You may need to alter your schedule to reach a certain hotel for lunch or dinner. You can miss a meal if there is no hotel when you need one or if the hotel you are counting on is closed. A few packets of biscuits in your backpack are good insurance against these rough spots.

Most of the major routes are well documented, but they are also well travelled. A hotel can be out of food if there are many other trekkers or if you arrive late. You may have to change your planned destination for the day when you discover that the lunch you ordered at an inn will take a very long time to prepare. You will usually make this discovery only after you have already waited an hour or so. It is wise to be aware of these kinds of problems and to prepare yourself to deal with them.

If you deviate from popular routes, be prepared to fend for yourself at times. If, however, you carry food, cooking pots and a tent to use even one night, you have already escalated beyond the tea house approach into a more complex form of trekking with different problems.

Making your own Arrangements

A third style of trekking is to gather sherpas, porters, food and equipment and take off on a trek with all the comforts and facilities of an organised trek. On such a trek you camp in tents, porters carry your gear, sherpas set up camp and cook and serve meals. You carry a backpack with only a water bottle, camera and jacket.

Trekkers who opt for this approach, particularly with a small group of friends, often have a rewarding, enriching and enjoyable trip. You can use a trekking company in Nepal to make some or all of the arrangements, though you may have to shop for an agency that suits you. Some Nepal trekking companies offer equipment for hire, some will arrange a single sherpa or porter and some will undertake only the entire arrangements for a trek.

If you want to have everything organised in advance, you can contact a Nepal trekking company by mail or fax and ask them to make arrangements for your trek. There are more than 100 trekking companies in Kathmandu that will organise treks for a fee and provide all sherpas, porters and, if necessary, equipment. Unless you have a good idea of what you want, it will require a huge volume of correspondence to provide you with the information you require, to determine your specific needs, to define your precise route and itinerary and to negotiate a price that both parties understand. Mail takes up to three weeks each way to and from Australia, the Americas or Europe. It's better to use a telex or fax machine. Be specific in your communications and be sure that the trekking company understands exactly who will provide what equipment. It is most embarrassing to discover on the first night that someone forgot the sleeping bags.

One solution is to go to Nepal and simply sort out the details in an hour or two of face to face negotiations with a trekking company. You should be prepared to spend a week or so (less, if you are lucky) in Kathmandu settling these details. An alternative to endless correspondence with Nepal is to use the services of the overseas agent of a Nepalese trekking company. These agents should have someone who can give you the information you require, and they should have a regular system of communication with Nepal. Dealing with an agent usually involves paying them a fee to make all the arrangements. This then becomes the 'trekking company' approach.

Trekking with a Trekking Company

Companies specialising in trekking can organise both individual and group treks from the USA, Germany, UK, Japan, Switzerland, France, Australia, New Zealand and Scandinavia. Each overseas trekking agent works through a particular trekking company in Nepal. Some agents have agreements for the exclusive representation of a Nepalese company in their own country. I have listed the names and addresses of some of the major trekking agencies in the Getting There chapter.

A usual condition of an arranged trek is that the group must stick to its prearranged route and, within limits, must meet a specific schedule. This means that you may have to forego an appealing side trip or festival and, if you are sick, you will probably have to keep moving with the rest of the group. You also may not agree with a leader's decisions

Tibetan Gompa

if the schedule must be adjusted because of weather, health, political or logistical considerations.

You will be trekking with people you have not met before. Although some strong relationships may develop, there may be some in the party you would much rather not have met. For some people, this prospect alone rules out their participation in a group trek. The major drawback, however, will probably be the cost. Organised treks usually start at about US$100 per person per day of the trek. On the positive side, by fixing the destination and schedule in advance, all members of the group will have prepared themselves for the trip and should have proper equipment and a clear understanding of the schedule and terrain. Read the brochures and other material prepared by the agent to see if it is likely to attract the type of people you'd get along with.

Most prearranged treks cater for people to whom time is more important (within limits) than money. For many, the most difficult part of planning a trek is having the time to do so. These people are willing to pay more to avoid wasting a week of their limited vacation sitting around in Kathmandu making arrangements or waiting along the way for a spare seat on a plane. A trekking agent usually tries to cram as many days in the hills as is possible into a given time span. Trekking agents make reservations for hotels and domestic flights well in advance. Thus, theoretically these hassles are also eliminated.

Because the group carries its own food for the entire trek, a variety of meals is possible. This may include canned goods from Kathmandu and imported food bought from expeditions or other exotic sources. A skilled cook can prepare an abundant variety of tasty Western-style food. The meals a good sherpa cook can prepare in an hour over a kerosene stove would put many Western cafés to shame.

A group trek carries tents for the trekkers.

This convenience gives you a place to spread out your gear without fear that someone will pick it up, and probably means that you will have a quiet night. In addition, a tent also gives you the freedom to go to bed when you choose. You can retire immediately after dinner to read or sleep, or sit up and watch the moon rise as you discuss the day's outing.

Money and staff hassles rarely surface on an arranged trek. The sirdar is responsible for making minor purchases along the way and ensures a full complement of porters every day. Unless you are particularly interested, or quite watchful, you may never be aware that these negotiations are taking place.

A group trek follows a tradition and routine that trekkers and mountaineers have developed and refined for more than 50 years. You can travel in much the same manner as the approach marches described in *The Ascent of Everest*, *Annapurna* and *Americans on Everest*, a feature not possible with other styles. If your interest in the Himalaya was kindled through such books, you still have the opportunity to experience this delightful way to travel. There are many reasons why these expeditions went to all the trouble and expense to travel as they did.

It is an altogether refreshing experience to have all the camp and logistics problems removed from your responsibility so you are free to enjoy fully the land and the people which have attracted mountaineers for a century.

A Trek is Not a Climbing Trip

Whether you begin your trek at a road head or fly into a remote mountain airstrip, a large part of your trek will be in the middle hills region at elevations between 500 and 3000 metres. In this region, there are always well-developed trails through villages and across mountain passes. Even at high altitudes there are intermittent settlements used during summer by herders, so the trails, though often indistinct, are always there. You can easily travel on any trail without the aid of ropes or mountaineering skills. There are rare occasions when there is snow on the trail, and on some high passes it might be

necessary to place a safety line for your companions or porters if there is deep snow. Still, alpine techniques are almost never used on a traditional trek. Anyone who has walked extensively in the mountains has all the skills necessary for an extended trek in Nepal.

Though some treks venture near glaciers, and even cross the foot of them, most treks do not allow the fulfilment of any Himalayan mountaineering ambitions. Nepal's mountaineering regulations allow trekkers to climb 18 specified peaks with a minimum of formality, but you must still make a few advance arrangements for such climbs. Many agents offer so-called climbing treks which include the ascent of one of these peaks as a feature of the trek. There are a few peaks that, under ideal conditions, are within the resources of individual trekkers. A climb can be arranged in Kathmandu if conditions are right, but a climb of one of the more difficult peaks should be planned well in advance. The section on climbing, in the last chapter of this book, describes these processes in more detail.

A Trek Requires Physical Effort

A trek is physically demanding because of its length and the almost unbelievable changes in elevation. During the 300 km trek to and from the Everest base camp, for example, the trail gains and loses more than 9000 metres of elevation during many steep ascents and descents. On most treks, the daily gain is less than 800 metres in about 15 km, though ascents of as much as 1200 metres are typical of some days. You can always take plenty of time during the day to cover this distance, so the physical exertion, though quite strenuous at times, is not sustained. You can always take plenty of time for rest.

Probably the only physical problem that may make a trek impossible is a history of knee problems on descents. In Nepal the descents are long, steep and unrelenting. There is hardly a level stretch of trail in the entire country. If you are an experienced walker and often hike 15 km a day with a pack, a trek should prove no difficulty. You will be pleasantly surprised at how easy the hiking can be if you only carry a light back-pack and do not have to worry about meal preparation.

Previous experience in hiking and living outdoors is, however, helpful as you make plans for your trek. The first night of a month long trip is too late to discover that you do not like to sleep in a sleeping bag. Mountaineering experience is not necessary, but you must enjoy walking.

PREPARATIONS IN NEPAL
Trekking Permits
A Nepalese visa is valid only for the Kathmandu Valley, Pokhara and Chitwan National Park in the Terai. To travel outside these regions you need a trekking permit. The permit specifies the places you may visit and the duration of your trek. Long ago, trekking permits cost Rs 1 and were basically a translation of your passport into Nepali. Now the fees have increased, there is no Nepali at all on the permit and the issuance of trekking permits has become a large scale industry. Theoretically you can leave your passport in a hotel safe during a trek, because a trekking permit is sufficient documentation to travel throughout Nepal.

Trekking permits are issued by the immigration office. The procedure is similar to getting a visa extension and involves a lot of queuing and waiting. There are preprinted trekking permit application forms, each a different colour, so you only need to state 'Everest', 'Annapurna', 'Kanchenjunga' or 'Langtang' on the application if you are headed to one of these areas. Be sure you fill in the right application form, otherwise you will wait in a long queue, only to be sent back for another form if the colour is incorrect. Once you have filled in the application, waited in a queue, presented all the necessary documents and paid the fee, you will be told to come back after 5 pm and queue again to pick up the completed document.

The preprinted forms allow all the possible routes in each region. For less usual destinations, you should include on the application an extensive list of village or district names. If you are headed for an unusual locale, check that the immigration office writes these destinations correctly on your trekking permit. Only the immigration offices in Kathmandu or Pokhara can alter the permit.

It is not necessary, as it once was, to have a trekking company arrange a trekking permit for you, although a trekking company can usually get a permit faster than you can. Kanchenjunga permits are issued only to organised groups arranged by a trekking company; other areas are open to individual trekkers.

You must have a trekking permit. Police check posts are abundant on every trekking route and you will be endlessly hassled if you do not have proper documentation. Rangers at entrance stations to national parks and the Annapurna Conservation Area Project (ACAP) check post at Chhomrong also conscientiously check permits and collect park fees.

A trekking permit costs Rs 90 per week for the first month of trekking and Rs 112.50 per week during the second and third month. Permits for Dolpo and Kanchenjunga treks cost US$10 per week for the first four weeks and US$15 per week thereafter. Visa extensions are free with trekking permits, but you still must produce exchange certificates of US$10 for each day of trekking. You are limited to 90 days of trekking in a year.

Conservation Fees If you trek in the Annapurna region, you will enter the ACAP area and must pay a conservation fee of Rs 200. This is collected at the same time you pay for the trekking permit and a special stamp is stuck on your permit as a receipt.

Restricted Areas There are many parts of Nepal that foreigners are not allowed to visit. Many treks that may be suggested on a map are in restricted areas and you cannot get a trekking permit for those regions. Some areas specifically closed to foreigners are: Mustang (north of Kagbeni), Dolpo (north of Phoksumdo Lake), Humla, Walunchung Gola, Rolwaling and the route to Nangpa La in Khumbu. When planning your trek, assume that these areas will remain closed. Don't count on a last minute change in the rules. Police check posts are numerous in the hills and police will turn you back if you try to trek into a restricted area.

There are many reasons why the restricted areas exist. In some cases, it is a hangover from a time when the border with China was more sensitive than it is now, but environmental groups, particularly the Nepal Nature Conservation Society, are pressuring the government to keep some places closed for ecological reasons to avoid both cultural and environmental degradation. Because trekkers require assistance when something goes wrong (accident, illness or theft), the government restricts some areas because it doubts that it could provide the security that trekkers would require. There are also political reasons for some restrictions. In the 1970s, for example, the Jomsom trek was closed because a major foreign aided military operation had been mounted there in support of the Khampas in Tibet.

There are many influences on the decision to open or close certain parts of Nepal to foreigners. Recent changes have liberalised both trekking and climbing, and there is considerable pressure to open more areas to trekkers. There are continual (and still seemingly unfounded) reports that Mustang will be opened soon, but this rumour has been circulating for more than 15 years. The trek around Manaslu is supposed to open any time. You should check with a trekking agent or the central immigration office before planning any unusual trek, but you can assume that new regulations will not affect the treks listed here.

Trekking Companies

In addition to normal travel agencies, Nepal has a special group of travel agencies that are licensed as trekking companies. In theory, a trekking company arranges treks and does not handle air tickets and transportation, while a travel agency does handle transportation but does not arrange for sherpas, porters and food for treks. In practice, either kind of company manages to furnish all the

facilities that are needed for any aspect of travel and trekking.

There are more than 100 trekking agencies in Nepal, ranging from large companies that operate in cooperation with major overseas agents to small operations that support a single family. The following is an arbitrary list of agents who have a reliable history and are likely to reply to correspondence and faxes from overseas. The list includes the biggest and best trekking companies, those that have office staff and can deal with correspondence and a few small ones that have made a name for themselves.

A complete list of trekking companies is available from the Department of Tourism or from TAAN (Trekking Agents Association of Nepal), PO Box 3612, Kantipath, Kathmandu.

A walk through the bazaars of Kathmandu will uncover many trekking company offices that are not on this list or even the list prepared by TAAN. Many of these are reliable and easy to deal with in person once you arrive in Nepal, and some can handle inquiries by mail or fax.

You can get a lot of advice from trekking companies, but remember that they are trying to sell you their services. You will be more welcome and get more comprehensive information if you choose one company and work with them to plan your trek and then buy your air tickets and rent equipment through them.

Adventure Nepal Trekking
   Tridevi Marg, Thamel, PO Box 915, Kathmandu, (tel 412508, fax 977-1-222026)
Ama Dablam Trekking
   Lazimpat, PO Box 3035, Kathmandu, (tel 410219, 415372, 415373, telex 2460 AMDBTRK, fax 977-1-222026)
Annapurna Mountaineering & Trekking
   Durbar Marg, PO Box 795, Kathmandu, (tel 222999, telex 2204 YETI)
Asian Trekking
   Tridevi Marg, Thamel, PO Box 3022, Kathmandu, (tel 412821, telex 2276 HOSANG, fax 977-1-411878)
Guides For All Seasons
   Gharidhara, PO Box 3776, Kathmandu, (tel 415841, 419035, 416047, telex 2558 NEPEX)

Great Himalayan Adventure
Kantipath, PO Box 1033, Kathmandu, (tel 216144, fax 977-1-419614)

International Trekkers
Narayanhity Marg, PO Box 1275, Kathmandu, (tel 418561, 418594, 412942, telex 2353 INTREK)

Journeys Mountaineering & Trekking
Kantipath, PO Box 2034, Kathmandu, (tel 225969, 226639, telex 2375 PEACE, fax 977-1-226567)

Lama Excursions
Durbar Marg, PO Box 2485, Kathmandu, (tel 220186, 226706, telex 2237 LAMEX, fax 977-1-227292)

Lamjung Trekking & Expeditions
Kantipath, PO Box 1436, Kathmandu, (tel 220598, 522964, 521057, telex 2291 PACMOV, fax 977-1-226820)

Malla Treks
Lekhnath Marg, PO Box 787, Kathmandu, (tel 418389, 418387, telex 2238 MALLA NP, fax 977-1-418382)

Mountain Travel Nepal
PO Box 170, Kathmandu, (tel 414508, 411562, telex 2216 TIGTOP, fax 977-1-419126)

Natraj Trekkings
Kantipath, PO Box 495, Kathmandu, (tel 226644, telex 2270 NATRAJ, fax 977-1-227372)

Nepal Himal Treks
Baluwatar, PO Box 4528, Kathmandu, (tel 419796, telex 2244 ATTOUR)

Nepal Treks & Natural History Expeditions
Gangapath, PO Box 459, Kathmandu, (tel 212511, 224536, 222985, telex 2239 KTT, fax 977-1-225131)

Overseas Adventure Trekking
Thamel, PO Box 1017, Kathmandu, (tel 411045, telex 2558 NEPEX)

Rover Treks & Expeditions
Naxal, Nag Pokhari, PO Box 1081, Kathmandu, (tel 412667, telex 2321 BASS)

Sherpa Co-operative Trekking
Durbar Marg, PO Box 1338, Kathmandu, (tel 224058, telex 2558 NEPEX)

Sherpa Society
Chabahil, Chuchepati, PO Box 1566, Kathmandu, (tel 470361, telex 2731 SSTREK, fax 977-1-470153)

Sherpa Trekking Service
Kamaladi, PO Box 500, Kathmandu, (tel 220423, 222489, telex 2419 STS)

Trans Himalayan Trekking
Durbar Marg, PO Box 283, Kathmandu, (tel 224854, 223871, telex 2233 THT, fax 977-1-227289)

Treks & Expeditions Service
Kamal Pokhari, PO Box 3057, Kathmandu, (tel 412231, 410895, fax 977-1-410039)

Venture Treks & Expeditions
Kantipath, PO Box 3968, Kathmandu, (tel 221585, 225780, telex 2495 METCON, fax 977-1-220178)

Yangrima Trekking & Mountaineering
Kantipath, PO Box 2951, Kathmandu, (tel 227627, 225608, telex 2474 SUMTRA, fax 977-1-227628)

Yeti Mountaineering & Trekking
Ramshah Path, PO Box 1034, Kathmandu, (tel 410899, telex 2268 PAGODA)

Himalayan Rescue Association

The best source of free advice and information about trekking is the Himalayan Rescue Association (tel 418755) which has an office within the compound of the Kathmandu Guest House in Thamel. A Western volunteer is on duty Sunday to Friday from 11 am to 5 pm. The office maintains a logbook with recent information about trekking conditions and provides information on equipment and health considerations for trekking.

The HRA was founded in 1973 and operates aid posts staffed with volunteer doctors in Pheriche on the Everest trek and Manang on the trek around Annapurna. The aid posts charge for medical services to cover their operating costs and the salaries of Nepalese staff, but otherwise the entire organisation is operated by volunteers. The HRA survives because of donations, memberships and the sale of T-shirts and patches. The organisation deserves your support.

Nepal Mountaineering Association

The NMA office is in Hatisar behind the Hotel Yak & Yeti, near the Krishna Bread Factory. It issues all permits for trekking peaks and collects reports from expeditions when they return.

Trekking Agents Association of Nepal

The TAAN office (tel 225875, 223352) is next to the Hotel Yellow Pagoda. It can provide an up-to-date list of trekking companies in Nepal and may be able to give you information about new or changed trekking regulations.

Department of Tourism

The tourist information office on New Rd near Basantapur has government publications and an information counter. Most Nepalese who have lived all their lives in Kathmandu are not well informed about life in the hills, so you will probably not get much sophisticated trekking information from the people who staff the counter.

Trekking Food

It is possible to rely entirely on hotels for meals during your trek and not carry any food at all. Most trekking hotels have supplies of tinned food, chocolate bars, biscuits, toilet paper and other essentials, but you may want to carry a small supply of goodies to use for emergencies or to relieve the boredom of dhal bhaat.

In Kathmandu, numerous food shops in Thamel and Asan Tole carry a large range of staples. The Bluebird Super Market has branches in the Blue Star Hotel and Lazimpat, and the Fresh House is near Joche Tole (near Freak St). Both have open shelves where you can wander about and choose from a wide variety of Indian and imported foods, tinned meat and fish, spices and sweets. They also carry a few imported medical supplies and useful chemicals such as potassium permanganate to sterilise vegetables and Lugol's Solution to purify drinking water. You can often find drink powders, such as Tang, which make iodine treated water more palatable.

There are several Nepalese produced packaged foods that can add variety to meals. Two brands of muesli and granola are available, and several companies produce a large variety of biscuits. Yak cheese is available in Thamel shops and at the dairy near the Hotel Malla. The Pumpernickel Bakery in Thamel can provide natural grain bread that will last for many days on the trail. Pilgrims Book House carries a variety of herbal teas that offer a respite from caffeine-based tea and coffee. Nepalese natural peanut butter will appeal to Americans, but be careful how you carry it because the oil tends to leak into your backpack.

If you are arranging a fully organised trek with a cook and porters, you will make major food purchases of canned goods, rice and other staples. All good trekking cooks can estimate how much you need for a trek, depending on the number of people, the destination and duration. There are food wholesalers that operate out of tiny shops in Asan Tole and Lazimpat that can provide amazing quantities of food in a few hours.

Hiring Guides & Porters

On the Everest, Langtang and Annapurna treks the routes are so well known by everyone that you do not need a guide to help you find the way. Still, a good guide will be useful in making your trek easier (and often cheaper) by negotiating on your behalf. Also, a guide will hopefully show you places of interest and short cuts that you might have otherwise overlooked. There are, of course, poor guides who will do nothing but complicate everything throughout the trek and make considerable money at your expense. If you travel with a sherpa to Khumbu there is the additional benefit of an invitation (almost always) to the house of your guide where you can become familiar with the Sherpa culture. You and your guide will (almost always) get drunk. In remote regions there are fewer signs that say 'Hotel', so a traveller must find accommodation and food by asking from house to house. A guide can be indispensable in such situations.

Nepal has a very structured society – a hangover from the caste system. This structure leads to people having very definite ideas, ingrained since birth, about what jobs they will or will not do. If someone considers themselves a trekking guide, they will be reluctant to carry a porter load. Porters are often reluctant to do camp chores or other duties unless they have hopes of moving up in the pecking order. If a porter agrees to do extra work, guides may discourage or even prevent the porter from doing this to maintain their own status. The ideal guide/porter combination is a rare phenomenon, though a few do exist. If you are lucky enough to find one of these people, you can probably get away with a single employee for a trek.

Hiring only a single porter or hiring several porters without a guide sounds like a good idea and is usually easy to arrange, but it is not always easy to control this sort of situation on the trail. While most porters are reliable, they usually have little education in the Western sense. They tend to be superstitious and are, of course, subject to fear, uncertainty and ill health. Porters may decide that they have gone far enough and want to return home, in which case they may just vanish. If you have a sherpa who has hired the porters for your trek, it is the sherpa's responsibility to assure their performance. Thus, if a porter vanishes you can probably persuade the sherpa to carry the load until another porter can be found. Sherpa guides are not at all happy about carrying a load, so you can be sure that he/she will find a new porter in a hurry. If you have hired the porter yourself, you must either sit alongside the trail until a replacement comes along, or carry your own heavy baggage.

Trekking with only a porter is also complicated because you must constantly be aware of where he is to protect your possessions, that is unless you have somehow managed to secure the services of someone who has already proven his reliability. Even this isn't foolproof. I've had a porter, who had already been on two treks, disappear on the third trek with two duffel bags of gear.

You can hire guides through trekking companies, trekking equipment shops or referrals from other trekkers. Trekking shops are more willing to help you if you offer a fee for their advice or hire equipment from them. Many restaurants and hotels, particularly in the Thamel area of Kathmandu and in Pokhara, have bulletin boards. These often have messages from trekkers who are looking for trekking companions or are recommending a reliable guide. Also check at the Himalayan Rescue Association office for guide, porter and companion referrals.

You can often find out of work sherpas outside the immigration office or in momo and rakshi shops on Asan Tole. Hiring a guide directly is a hit or miss situation. You might find someone brilliant or you might have endless problems. They will convince you of their ability by producing certificates and letters from past (always satisfied) customers. It is not likely that you will hit upon someone whose sole purpose was to steal from you, but such people do exist and are offering their services as guides. All embassies in Nepal suggest that you either go through a known intermediary, or check references carefully before you employ a guide.

October, November, March and April are very busy trekking months. Any sherpa who does not have a job during these months may be of questionable reliability. At other times, it is often possible to find excellent staff.

You can sometimes hire sherpas and porters in Lukla and Pokhara. Except during October and early November you will probably be successful if you fly to Lukla and try to arrange a trek without any advance preparations. However, there are no sherpas or porters available at Jomsom or Langtang.

A good trekking guide can arrange porters. Things will work much better if you tell the guide where you wish to trek and how much you are prepared to pay, after which you go off for a cup of tea to let him do all the negotiations on your behalf. On a long trek, an experienced guide will lay off porters as the party eats through porter loads of food. He will also replace porters when they get nervous because they are too far from their homes.

It is becoming difficult to suggest specific rates for porters' and guides' wages. Political and social pressures in Nepal have resulted in occasional exorbitant demands for wages and benefits. Union organisers are working to improve the lot of trekking workers and are trying to establish minimum wages and other facilities. Many guides and porters, however, are operating at a subsistence level and will work for considerably less than the union scale. Consult the HRA, TAAN or a trekking company for the latest guidelines.

Wages for porters will probably be between Rs 80 and Rs 120 per day for trekking, but demand from other trekkers and

Sherpa kitchen boy

dictates that a guide does not carry a load. Suddenly your trek transmogrifies into a 'do it yourself' trek with all its attendant bureaucratic hassles.

One important point to consider when you employ porters is the provision of warm clothing and equipment for cold and snow. If you are going into snow, you must provide goggles, shoes, shelter and clothing – porters are not expendable. Also provide plastic sheets (available in Kathmandu) so that porters can protect themselves and your baggage from rain.

In Khumbu, clothing is usually not a problem because you will probably hire Sherpas or Sherpanis (women) who have their own shoes and warm clothing – ask them to be sure. The place where most problems occur with porters is crossing Thorung La, the pass between Manang and Muktinath. From·whatever direction you approach the pass, the route starts in low tropical country and any porters that you hire will probably be from these lowland regions. When you reach the snow, the unequipped lowland porters either quit and turn back or continue foolishly without proper clothing or footwear, often resulting in frostbite, snow blindness or even death. Porters are not usually available in Manang or Muktinath, so it is really worth the extra planning and expense to buy porter equipment in Kathmandu (though occasionally such items are available in Manang) if you plan to use porters on this pass. You should also have some sort of shelter for them for the one or two nights that shelter is scarce.

When you do provide equipment for porters, be sure to make it clear whether it is a loan or a gift. In reality it will be very hard to get back equipment that you have loaned unless you are very determined and thick-skinned. The porters and sherpas have special techniques to make you feel guilty and petty when you ask for the return of equipment.

An important consideration when you decide to trek with a guide or porters is that you place yourself in the role of an employer. This means that you may have to deal with

expeditions can drive prices higher. Road building in the hills also pushes up porter wages while the construction passes through a village. Porters expect to buy their own food out of their wages, so you do not ordinarily have to carry food for them. However, unless you do provide food and shelter for porters, you will always have to camp near a village where they can buy food.

Tradition dictates that guides receive a lower salary than porters, usually Rs 70 to Rs 100 a day (in 1990), but they also receive accommodation and food. If you are staying at inns, it will amaze you how much your tiny guide can eat and drink at your expense. Set a limit on the guide's food bill before you set out or pay him a daily food allowance, though this must increase at higher elevations where food is more expensive. If you are really watching your pennies you could always carry a small amount of food and cook it yourself if you have a guide. This leads, however, to hiring a porter to carry the food and cooking pots because tradition also personnel problems including medical care, insurance, strikes, requests for time off, salary increases and all the other aspects of being a boss. Be as thorough as you can when hiring people and make it clear from the beginning what the requirements and limitations are. After that, prepare yourself for some haggling – it's almost impossible to protect against it.

Porter Insurance Trekking rules require that trekkers insure all their sherpas and porters for Rs 25,000 (about US$1000) against accidental death. So few trekkers do this that you would surprise an insurance company if you asked them to arrange insurance. There is no system for checking on whether you actually purchase insurance, though you will certainly have a major row if there is an accident and you cannot produce an insurance certificate. If you are planning to climb one of the trekking peaks, you must insure any Nepalese who go beyond base camp. There is a system for checking on insurance in this situation.

Trekking companies have a blanket policy that covers all their staff. Oriental Insurance Co and Rashtriya Bima Sansthan in Kathmandu can provide the required coverage for a fee of about US$8 per person. These companies can also provide, at a higher cost, the mandatory insurance for sherpas if you are climbing a trekking peak.

ON THE TRAIL
Accommodation
Hotels When you arrive at a hotel for the night, reach an agreement with the innkeeper on the cost for sleeping. Look around and see what facilities the hotel provides and determine the cost of meals. Some inns waive the sleeping charge if you eat meals there. In other inns the sleeping charge can be as little as Rs 5, though most charge Rs 10; it's up to Rs 20 or Rs 50 per person in more sophisticated lodges.

There are a few special hotels in the hills, particularly those that obtained government loans, and a few special facilities in Lukla and Jomsom that cater to people who are tired of trekking. These all charge US$20 or more. During times of heavy demand, such as during a flight back-up at Lukla or when snow on the pass has caused a backlog of trekkers at Manang or Muktinath, innkeepers charge what the traffic will bear. Accommodation becomes expensive and difficult to find. Most times, however, accommodation will cost from Rs 10 to Rs 20 and will be found without too much trouble.

Usually the innkeeper keeps an account of all the food and drink that you consume and collects payment for everything in the morning. It's worth keeping track yourself because other trekkers' food often makes its way onto your account when the hotel gets busy. Many hotels have menus that show all their prices, including the charges for sleeping. There rarely is any bargaining and the menu really does represent a fixed, and usually fair, price. Check the prices before you order to avoid later hassles. Strangely, the places most prone to bargaining are the fancy hotels – the US$10 per night and up variety – that have lost a lot of their business to smaller and cheaper facilities.

Meals typically take an hour or two to prepare unless there is stew or dhal bhaat already cooked, so soon after arriving you should order your meal and establish a time to eat. There are some pretty sophisticated short-order kitchens that operate in the hills, the best being at Namche, Lukla and along the Kali Gandaki. If you patronise one of these, you may get an exotic Western-style meal. More often the choice is between dhal bhaat with vegetables *(tarkari)* at Rs 20 to Rs 40 or dhal bhaat with meat *(maasu)* for Rs 20 to Rs 30 extra. Eggs *(phul* or *andaa)*, when available, cost Rs 2 to Rs 6 each.

Most hotels offer an extensive choice of bottled soft drinks, beer and bottled water. Tea or coffee will be made with milk and laden with sugar. If you want black tea or coffee, be sure to order it that way. Many hotels can also concoct exotic drinks with rum, local rakshi and fruit.

Most Nepalese do not eat breakfast and have only milk tea when they arise. They have a heavy brunch of rice and vegetables at about 10 am. When staying in a local inn, you will find it faster to operate in the same manner. If you order a large breakfast early in the morning, you will probably have a late start. Sophisticated inns are usually able to deal with short orders in the morning, though it is still better to organise this the evening before. You can also save time in the morning by carrying some cereal or muesli for breakfast. *Chiuraa* (beaten rice), available locally, makes a less tasty but satisfactory substitute. You should be able to move for a few hours on tea and biscuits, arriving at 9 or 10 am at a place that has dhal bhaat prepared.

If you want to have lunch at noon or 1 pm you will almost certainly have to wait an hour or two while the hotel cooks rice specially for you. Depending on your mood and fitness this may or may not be an attractive break in the day. If you find yourself with a long wait, accept it and use the time for a good rest rather than agitate to try to get things moving faster in the kitchen. A hotel can become chaotic when 20 people order 20 different things in a dozen diverse languages. This confuses even a Western cook who uses order slips and has a complete stock of goods. In a small hotel where the innkeeper cooks everything over a single wood fire with a limited supply of pots, it can get crazy. If you can adjust to the local schedule of tea for breakfast and a 10 am brunch, you will avoid a lot of waiting in kitchens. If you cannot adjust, you can still save yourself a lot of time and hunger by talking to other trekkers and combining your orders into two or three dishes.

At inns along the main trekking routes you can behave just as you would in any small hotel anywhere. In remote regions where the hotels cater mainly to locals, you should take special care to follow the customs of the people. Staying out of the kitchen goes a long way towards this.

At high altitudes, hotels become more expensive. Tea costs Rs 1 in the lowlands, Rs 2 in places more than three or four days from the nearest road, and Rs 3 or Rs 4 in high places such as Lobuje and Annapurna

base camp. When food and drink is expensive it is tempting to economise and eat and drink less. You must resist this temptation because a large liquid intake is one of the important aids for the prevention of altitude sickness. A low food intake can leave you weak and subject to hypothermia.

Hotels at high elevations rarely have private rooms. Instead, their dormitories have several huge beds that sleep 10 or 20 people, often in two tiers. High altitude can make people uncomfortable, sleepless, crabby and strange. In hotels there can be a lot of thrashing about and opening and closing of doors throughout the night. Ear plugs are a good investment. If you value sleep and privacy, reconsider the advantages of bringing your own tent.

During the trekking season there is a daily rush for hotels. It's quite mad to spend your holiday in competition with other trekkers racing to get a good space or a private room at the best hotel in the next village. In the Everest region, in particular, this can be dangerous because of the elevation gain and the chance of altitude sickness. If you find yourself travelling on the same schedule as a gaggle of other trekkers, relax for half a day and try to operate a half day behind them. Traditional lunch spots are often deserted in the evening and hotels that are crowded at night can be empty at lunch time.

Dealing with an inn when you have a guide is another matter. Theoretically a guide is more sophisticated than a porter and should have the ability to organise an inexpensive and trouble-free trek. This sophistication also may be a mastery of ways to make money with a minimum of work. If you have a responsible guide, the easiest approach is to have your guide arrange everything and then pay the bill yourself in the morning. Sometimes the guide will leave you with a bill for several glasses of chhang, extra food and the losses at last night's card party. In such cases, one solution is to agree on a daily rate for his subsistence. Each of you can then pay for your own food and accommodation separately. It should cost from Rs 40 to Rs 60 per day for a guide to live on a trek. If you add another Rs 20 for drinks and cigarettes you are providing a generous allowance.

Since a hotel doubles as a home, whether it has a sign that says 'Hotel' or not, you may have a difficult time sleeping until the entire household has retired. Trekkers who walk and exert themselves all day require more sleep than they normally do at home, often as much as 10 or 11 hours each night. Village people who are not exerting themselves during the day can get by with 6 to 8 hours. This presents an immediate conflict in lifestyle and sleep requirements. The conflict escalates when the inevitable booze and card party erupts in the next room or, worse yet, in your bedroom. Another universal deterrent to sleep is the ubiquitous Radio Nepal which does not stop broadcasting until 11 pm.

Staying in a Home If you are in a particularly remote region where there are no hotels, you can often arrange food and accommodation in private homes. You could also end up in a home if your guide has friends in a particular village, if someone is just opening a new lodge or in an emergency when you cannot make it to the next hotel. Though it may appear that you are a guest, the householder always expects that you will pay for your food and lodging. Prices are flexible in such a situation, but usually the owner of the house will quote a fair price in the morning when you depart – but they will be shy and you will have to ask how much.

In a private home, you will probably have to wait until everyone else decides to go to sleep before you can roll out your sleeping bag. Be sure to find out where the toilet facilities are, if they exist. Don't dispose of garbage of any kind in the cooking fire. If there is a religious statue or alter, arrange your bed so your feet do not point in that direction when you sleep.

Guides & Porters on the Trail
If you are travelling with porters, their ability to cover the required distance each day will limit your progress. Porters carrying 30 kg

up and down hills cannot move as fast as a trekker carrying a light backpack. Other factors such as weather, steepness of the trail, sickness and festivals can turn a schedule upside down. Beware especially of the Dasain festival in October when porters are almost impossible to find and tend to vanish without warning.

You will rarely experience a strike, but you may find that the evening discussion of the next day's destination has turned into a delicate negotiating session. On major trails there are certain stopping places that all the porters are familiar with, and it is difficult to alter them. I once congratulated myself on having covered three 'porter days' of walking by lunch time the third day. I looked forward to covering a good distance after lunch. An embarrassed sirdar then informed me that our lunch spot would also be our camp for the night. He explained that by definition it took three full days to reach where we were and whether it had taken us that long or not was immaterial. Nothing I could say (or pay) would entice the porters to go further until the following day when we were able to start trekking early in the morning, on schedule.

A Day with a Trekking Group
A group trekker begins the day at about 6 am with a call of 'tea sir'. A cup of tea or coffee soon appears through the tent flap. After you drink your tea or, as I do, spill it all over the tent, you pack your gear and emerge to a light breakfast of Darjeeling tea, coffee, porridge and eggs or pancakes. While you are eating, the sherpas take down the tents and pack up loads for the porters. The entire group is usually on the way by 7 am. The early start takes advantage of the cool morning to accomplish most of the day's hike. Even on a group trek, many trekkers find an opportunity to hike alone for much of the day. The porters are slower and the sherpas, especially the cook crew, race on ahead to have lunch waiting when you arrive.

There are many diversions on the trail. It is not unusual to find sherpas and fellow trekkers in shops or bhattis. Sometimes the entire group may stop to watch a festival or some other special event along the way. At a suitable spot, at about 11 am, there is a stop of an hour or two for lunch. The noon meal includes the inevitable tea, a plate of rice, potatoes or noodles, some canned or fresh meat and whatever vegetables are in season.

The afternoon trek is shorter, ending at about 3 pm when you round a bend to discover your tents already set up in a field near a village. The kitchen crew again prepares tea and coffee soon after arrival in camp. There is then an hour or two to nurse blisters, read, unpack and sort gear, wash or explore the surrounding area before dinner.

Trekking groups usually have Western food with chicken, goat, mutton or buffalo meat frequently, though not daily. The cow is sacred in regions of Hindu influence, so beef is unavailable. The cook varies the rice diet by substituting potatoes, noodles and other items. The food is tasty and plentiful, but will probably be pretty boring after two weeks or so. Even so, the meals will be taxing the imagination of the cooks, who will be providing a variety of foods which they never experience in their own meals. Most trekkers feel healthy and fit on this diet as the food is fresh and organic, with no preservatives.

The sun sets early during the trekking season, so it is dark by 6 pm. There is time to read by candlelight in tents or to sit around talking in the dark. To conserve firewood, there is never a campfire. Most trekkers are asleep by 8 or 9 pm.

On an Organised Trek

If you are on an organised trek, the sherpa sirdar's resources will include only the food, equipment, money and instructions that either you or the trekking company provide. No matter how scrupulous the arrangements and how experienced your sherpa staff, there will be some complications. A trek is organised according to a prearranged itinerary and the sherpas expect to arrive at certain points on schedule. If you are sick or slow, and do not tell this to the sherpas, you may discover that camp and dinner are waiting for

you far ahead. Be sure to communicate such problems and other desires to the staff.

Most trekking sherpas are true professionals. They will make a lot of effort to accommodate you if they understand what you want. If you do not wish to follow their daily routine, you must decide this early in the trek. A routine, once established with the sherpas, is difficult to change later.

You may buy or bring some special food 'goodies' that you are saving for high altitudes or an important occasion. If you hand these over to a cook at the outset of the trek, you are likely to find them (despite instructions to the contrary) cooked during the first few days of the trek or, worse yet, served to the sherpas. You should keep any special food in your luggage to prevent such mistakes.

Route Finding

It isn't easy to get totally lost in the hills, but finding the trail you want, particularly through a large village, can sometimes be a challenge. If you are on a major trek route, most local people know where you are going. If you see children yelling and pointing, you probably have taken a wrong turn. Watch for the lug sole footprints of other trekkers and for arrows carved into the trail by guides with trekking parties. It is always worthwhile to talk to local people and ask them about the trail to your next destination and discover what facilities you can expect to find on the way.

If you are in a less frequented area, you must ask people. Be sure to phrase the question in a way that forces them to point the way. *Kun baato Namche Bazaar jaanchha?* (Which trail goes to Namche Bazaar?) will usually do the job. If you point to a trail and ask if it goes where you want to go, most Nepalese will say yes, because they like to please you. When asking directions, ask the name of the next village. People near Jiri probably have no idea where Namche Bazaar is, but they know the trail to Shivalaya, the next village.

In particularly remote areas, be ready for confusion about destinations and times. I've seen situations where asking directions has developed into a massive argument involving 10 or more people, each having an opinion on the best route and the time involved.

Police Check Posts

There are police posts throughout the country. While the trekking rules do not specifically state that you should seek out and visit every police post along a trekking route, some police officers seem to believe this to be the case. As a general rule, if there is a sign or barrier on the trail, it would be prudent to pay a call on the local constabulary. Formalities are usually as simple as writing your name in a register, but in some places they can become cumbersome with forms to fill in and endorsements on your trekking permit. In national parks, what look like police check posts are often army posts where they will want to examine your national park entrance receipt.

SOCIAL & ENVIRONMENTAL IMPACT
A Nepalese View of Foreigners

Although Nepal has been accessible to foreigners only since 1950, there are few places in the kingdom that either trekkers, photographers, expeditions or foreign aid representatives have not visited. Foreigners, particularly light-skinned Westerners, stand out readily in Nepal. The Nepalese view foreigners according to the stereotype created by those who have preceded them. They too, will contribute to the image of the next Westerners who happen to come along.

Unfortunately, the image which has predominated is one of great wealth and a superior culture which Westerners wish to share with the Nepalese. Such traditions as passing out balloons, sweets and pens to kids are part of this, but it is on a far grander level that the real image has developed.

Mountaineering expeditions have spent seemingly limitless sums of money for porters, sherpas and equipment, including a lot of fine gear for the high altitude sherpas.

At the conclusion of an expedition, the expedition usually gives away excess food and gear rather than repacking the equipment and shipping it home. This type of extravagance, even though it is often supported by foundations and other large organisations and not by the expedition members themselves, leads many Nepalese to believe, with some justification, that Westerners have a tremendous amount of money and will simply pass it out to whoever makes the most noise.

An interesting by-product of this phenomenon is that a variety of used mountaineering gear was once for sale in Kathmandu at ridiculously low prices. This was possible because nobody in Nepal ever had to pay for it. A Nepalese received it as a gift or bought it for a very cheap price, then sold it for whatever they could get. Now, however, prices are the same or higher than they are in the West. Astute shopkeepers have seen equipment catalogues and charge according to the retail prices for new items.

The sherpas and other Nepalese who deal with trekkers and expeditions are aware of the cost of an air ticket to Nepal from the USA, Europe or Australia. For people in a country with an annual per capita income of US$170, US$1500 is an astronomical amount of money. No matter how small a trekker's budget may be, they were still able to get to Nepal. The Nepalese know this and are unwilling to accept a plea of poverty from someone who, according to their standards, has already spent the equivalent of about three years wages, or enough money to build three large houses. It is impossible to explain the difference in our relative economic positions to a Nepalese in the hills.

Many trekkers and expedition members in the past have given substantial tips to sherpas. Reports of US$100 tips are not unheard of. Compare a tip of US$40 for a six day trek to a sherpa's total salary of US$10. This type of extravagance forces up wages, resulting in higher demands on the next trekker or expedition. It also contributes to an unhealthy view of Westerners as rich, lavish and foolish. This image makes it difficult for individuals on a tight budget to convince a Nepalese person that they cannot afford outrageous salaries, tips or huge amounts of food during a trek.

Well-intentioned trekkers often overreact to the needs of porters and sherpas on treks and provide an exorbitant amount of free equipment to their staff. This is certainly kind and generous, and porters do need to be equipped with warm shoes, clothing and goggles when they are travelling into the mountains. Many trekkers overdo this, however, and it is becoming increasingly common for porters to demand fancy new equipment. They then pack it away to keep it in pristine condition to sell later. On the trek they often use their own old blankets to keep warm. Porters need protection and attention, but many trekkers have gone far beyond what is necessary. This overgenerous behaviour has created unreasonable expectations in the minds of many porters and makes it difficult and expensive to hire them, especially in the Annapurna region.

Foreign aid projects have built schools, hospitals, roads, and electricity and water projects in Nepal. These facilities are largely supported by contributions from organisations of the Western world, although there is usually an effort to require contributions of local labour and money. Nepal needs these projects and they perform a great service, but this method of financing does help sustain the preconception of Westerners as people with a lot of money from which they can readily be parted if they are approached with enough cleverness.

Many trekkers feel a strong affinity for villagers or sherpas they have met. Many have supported the education of local children or even provided free overseas trips for them. This practice is certainly worthwhile and kind, but it does encourage Nepalese people to seek such favours in their dealings with Westerners. The US Embassy has published a paper, titled *So you want to take your Sherpa to America*, that points out some of the procedures and pitfalls of this process.

The problem is not confined to the hills and the efforts of some thoughtless individuals. Many nations are eager to have a foothold in what they feel is a strategic part of the world. They spend vast sums of money on aid programmes in Nepal to strengthen their position. Such programmes might not contribute further to an unhealthy view of Westerners (and would undoubtedly do more good) if they did not also support the Westerners who work for them in lavish style. Many foreigners live in Kathmandu and other places in Nepal in conditions similar to their Western homes. They eat food flown from home at their own government's expense and are served by more servants than they could conceive of at home.

Most foreigners carry with them an astonishing array of camera gear, tape recorders and other gadgetry. It's obvious that these things are expensive, even by Western standards. Yet a surprisingly large number of people seem to have no care for this wealth. A surprising number of trekkers leave cameras behind on rocks or give their watches away at the end of a trek. Not only can Westerners afford to buy such expensive things, but they don't even take care of them. Compare this attitude to that of the porter carrying a double load of 60 kg to make more money or the sherpa kitchen boy with patched and repatched jeans, shoes and backpack.

This is the Westerner with whom the Nepalese is familiar. They may also recognise the qualities of sincerity, happiness or fun, but the primary quality they see is wealth. Many Nepalese consider it their personal obligation to separate Westerners from a share of their money. They may do this by appealing to a sense of fair play, through trickery or blackmail (a porter's strike in a remote location), through shrewdness, or even by outright thievery. Westerners retain this image, no matter what they do personally to dispel it, and an appreciation of this is very helpful in developing an understanding of local attitudes during a trek in Nepal.

Environmental Stress

The population of Nepal is growing at a furious rate. In the 16 years since this book was first published the population has increased from 12 to 19.5 million. Development is moving ahead at an even faster pace. During the 11 years from 1978 to 1989, the number of vehicles in the country increased from fewer than 7500 to almost 60,000, half of which are in the Kathmandu Valley. There are now real traffic jams in Kathmandu and the unnecessary noise and pollution caused by these vehicles is immediately noticeable. There are now few days with clear mountain views, yet 10 years ago the towering white mountains and clear blue skies framed the Kathmandu Valley. Now you can see the smog from your plane as it approaches Kathmandu.

In the hills, this growth is manifested in many ways. There was a furore 10 years ago about garbage left by trekkers and expeditions along the Everest route. This was not an important issue compared to the current problems of sanitation, overgrazing, deforestation, landslides and uncontrolled development of hotels for trekkers.

There is no systematic waste disposal system in the hills, and many hill people are acquiring more and more manufactured items from Kathmandu. A look at the stream of worn out shoes and broken toys in the streets of Namche will show that litter is not only a trekking problem. The piles of garbage and human waste at Ghorapani and on the route to Annapurna Sanctuary and the relentless clearing of rhododendron forests between Ghorapani and Ghandruk to allow even more hotel construction are, however, related to trekkers. Yet the protection afforded by a national park can lead to greater pressures. It takes a staff of more than 100 army personnel to manage and enforce the regulations of Sagarmatha National Park, which has a local population of less than 2500 people.

It is naive to think of maintaining the ecological balance of the Himalaya in a pristine state. There are simply too many people living in the hills. To accomplish this goal it would be necessary to relocate entire villages, as was done in both Lake Rara and Royal Chitwan national parks.

The primary reason for the destruction of forests throughout the Himalayan hill region is the pressure of a population that requires natural vegetation for food, fodder, fuel and even shelter. The lack of roads and other development, combined with the lack of any local deposits of fossil fuels, allows no easy alternative. About 70% of Nepal's total domestic energy consumption is wood. The inevitable result of the destruction of forests is an increase in erosion and extensive loss of topsoil.

The most dramatic result of deforestation is huge landslides that carry away fields, houses and occasionally entire villages. As you fly or trek in Nepal you can easily spot many examples of these landslides. One solution would be a massive tree planting campaign, but to hill people this is expensive and unrewarding because they must fence off the plantations to protect them from cattle and goats. Fencing is expensive and the financial returns are a long way off.

Tourists, particularly trekkers, contribute to the mess. A typical hotel burns from three to eight loads (about 25 kg each) of firewood per day and a large trekking party can consume from three to five loads a day. National park regulations that ban the use of firewood do not apply to those who use hotels, except in the Annapurna Sanctuary where firewood is forbidden to everyone. This loophole exempts individual trekkers and the porters of trekking parties from any limit on fuel consumption. More than 10,000 trekkers visit the Everest region annually and 25,000 visit the Jomsom and Annapurna Sanctuary areas. More than half of these trekkers use lodges.

Everyone should agree that the hill people have a right not only to live in their traditional home sites but also to try to improve their standard of living. Their lifestyle may be picturesque, but it is a meagre subsistence-level lifestyle that could be improved in numerous ways by many forms of development. Trekkers can contribute to this development, not only through their cash but through their example. Solutions to the energy problem, such as hydroelectric plants, biogas generators, solar energy units and the wholesale import of fossil fuels, all take time and cost money.

As solutions are developed and implemented, they will change the trekking experience – and certainly increase costs. When attempts are made in this direction, it is reasonable to support them, even when the result is a more expensive trek. It will cost more to eat at a hotel that has a new energy-efficient wood stove or a kerosene stove and a proper latrine, and it will cost more to trek with a group that uses no firewood. It is through this sort of direct economic encouragement that you can help and teach hill people.

Hoteliers have become aware that clean hotels and toilets and solar heating attract more customers. Trekkers should encourage hotels that adhere to environmentally sound practises so that hoteliers will find the means to continue their attempts. The hotel system in the hills should become something that not only turns firewood into cash, but also serves as a demonstration for all villagers of the need for, and advantages of, limiting their dependence on the forests.

One good start is to spurn the offers of hot showers. You can talk to other trekkers and try to order the same food at the same time so a hotel can do all the cooking at once instead of keeping a fire roaring throughout the day. You can purify your water with iodine instead of ordering boiled water. The process of conserving energy will take time and effort, as old habits and traditions are hard to change.

Even in Kathmandu and Pokhara, where alternatives are readily available, many homes, hotels and restaurants rely on firewood for cooking. Hundreds, perhaps thousands of loads of wood are carried into the cities, not only by porters but also by huge Mercedes trucks.

If you are interested in current events in Nepal's efforts towards environmental protection, subscribe to *Himal*, a bi-monthly magazine published in Kathmandu. An annual subscription costs US$25 and is available from:

Himal
    PO Box 42, Lalitpur, Nepal
M Basnet
    4 S Pinehurst Ave, 6A, New York, NY 10033 USA
Indra Ban
    12 Norfolk St, Paddington 2021, Sydney, Australia

Using this Book

The teacher can but point the Way,
The means to reach the Goal
Must vary with each Pilgrim.

This quotation is one of the Tibetan 'elegant sayings' attributed either to Nagarjuna, the Indian mystic who lived in the 2nd century AD, or to the Head Lama of the Sakya Monastery in Tibet in 1270 AD.

SCOPE & PURPOSE

In this book I have described the best known trekking routes in Nepal. These desciptions will give you some insight into the type of country and culture that you may encounter on specific treks. They should also help you to choose the area you wish to visit, because they give an indication of the difficulty of each trek and the number of days it will take to follow a particular route.

I've tried to include a general explanation of the lay of the land and cultural background, but these are not self-guiding trail descriptions. If you are not travelling with a Nepalese companion, you must continually ask hoteliers or other trekkers about the correct path. If you are with a guide, he or she will be asking questions as you travel. What to us may be a major trekking route is likely to be, for the people of a village, only a path from Ram's house to Bir Bahadur's house to Dawa's house. In our minds we string all these sections of trail together to form a major route to some place that village people may never go.

Most trekking routes either travel in an east-west direction or go to high mountain regions. Local people do not often follow

Top: Sete Monastery (SA)
Left: Mani stones and prayer flags, Lamjura Pass (SA)
Right: The yeti skull from Khumjung Gompa (SA)

Top: Mt Everest - 8848 metres, from Kala Pattar (SA)
Bottom: Trekkers with Ama Dablam (right), Lhotse (centre) & Mt Everest (left) (SB)

these routes because most trade routes are south to north and avoid high elevations. There is nothing more frustrating than wandering around the hills of Nepal looking for the correct trail. It is impossible, no matter how detailed the route description, to document every important trail junction. Also, trails change for a multitude of reasons. The descriptions that follow portray what you may expect if you follow the shortest available routes, but it will be all too easy to get lost if you try to walk through Nepal using only this (or any other book) as a guide. Develop the habit of talking to people and asking questions.

Just as it is impossible to document every trail junction, it is also impossible to describe every possible trek. What follows is a description of the major routes, a few optional side trips and some alternative routes that avoid backtracking. You should seriously consider backtracking, however. Often the second time over a particular trail provides insights and views that you did not see or appreciate the first time.

If you're making your first trek in Nepal, it is likely that you will choose one of these routes. They are not only the best known, but are also the most attractive. There is good reason for the fame of the Everest trek, the Jomsom trek and other well known routes. Most of the treks I have described have hotels of some sort available every night and reasonably well-defined trails. The exceptions are western Nepal, the Khumbu to Dhankuta route, the Lamidanda trek and the Barahbise to Jiri option.

You may be tempted to go to some other region where there won't be so many tourists because of stories and articles you may have read about the 'freeway' to Everest. When you listen to these discussions you should place them in their proper perspective. Even in 1989, the 'overcrowded' conditions in the Everest region consisted of 10,000 trekkers over a period of eight months. More people would stay in a typical USA national park camp ground on a single weekend night.

No matter where you trek there will be local people living and moving through the area. Getting to remote and unexplored areas has little meaning in Nepal unless you are prepared to tackle a Himalayan peak.

ROUTE DESCRIPTIONS

This book describes the following routes:

Mt Everest Region
Jiri to Everest Base Camp
To Gokyo
To Thami
The Lamidanda Escape Route
Barahbise to Jiri

Annapurna Region
Jomsom Trek
Annapurna Sanctuary
Around Annapurna
The Royal Trek

Langtang & Helambu
Langtang Trek
Across Ganja La
Helambu Circuit
Gosainkund

Eastern Nepal
Solu Khumbu to Dhankuta
Kanchenjunga Trek
North Kanchenjunga Base Camp
South Kanchenjunga Base Camp

Western Nepal
Jumla to Rara Lake
Jumla to Dolpo
To Phoksumdo Lake
Do & Tarap
Pokhara to Dunai

Other Destinations
In each section there is a brief introduction outlining some of the many other options possible in that region. There are many routes in Nepal that proceed over high passes, but I have described only two of these: Ganja La and Thorung La. These treks have the dangers of rockfall, avalanches and high altitude. All members of the party, including the sherpas and porters, must have good equipment before you attempt these

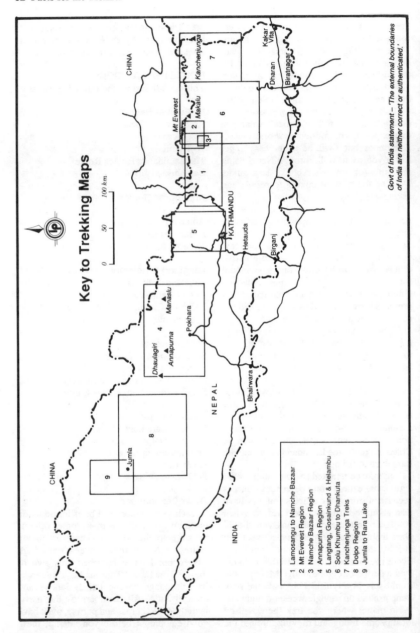

Key to Trekking Maps

1 Lamosangu to Namche Bazaar
2 Mt Everest Region
3 Namche Bazaar Region
4 Annapurna Region
5 Langtang, Gosainkund & Helambu
6 Solu Khumbu to Dhankuta
7 Kanchenjunga Treks
8 Dolpo Region
9 Jumla to Rara Lake

Govt of India statement – 'The external boundaries of India are neither correct or authenticated.'

routes. The chance of snow increases from December to April and snow on a pass may force you to turn back.

Daily Stages

I have separated the route descriptions into daily stages. This helps to make them readable and is a quick estimate of the number of days required for each trek. The suggested night stops are the ones most trekkers use. In all cases, wood, water, food for porters (and usually chhang for sherpas) and a place large enough to pitch four or five tents are available at each night stop. Food and accommodation are usually available at each suggested stop for those who are relying on local inns.

When you trek these routes, either with an organised group or alone, you may find that you are not stopping at the places listed here. Don't panic. This is not a tour itinerary that requires you to be in Namche Bazaar on Tuesday. Your actual stopping place will depend on your fitness, whether you or someone in your party is sick on a particular day, the weather, trail conditions, arrangements with the porters and whether you find some place more interesting or attractive than the village I have described. Porters can severely influence the speed at which you travel, as their heavy loads make them slow. Your trek should allow you the freedom and opportunity to move as fast or as slowly as you wish. It's a vacation, so don't take schedules and timetables too seriously where they are not necessary.

It is easy to alter the number of days suggested here. Perhaps you can cut a day or two off the time if you walk from first light to sunset each day, but since a trek is a continual experience, not simply progress to a particular destination, there is little point in rushing the trip only to get to some place that may not be as engrossing as where you are now. At high altitudes you should proceed no faster than the ascent times recommended here in order to avoid altitude sickness. You can lengthen any trek to almost any degree by side trips, rest days and further exploration of inviting looking villages.

Times & Distance

The route descriptions do not list approximate walking times. Any moderately fit trekker can accomplish the suggested daily stages in a single day. The stages do, however, tend to become more difficult in the later days of each trek, because you will get fitter as the trek progresses, as I do myself. Porters also can accomplish each stage in a single day and will accept the stages listed here.

I did try to record walking times but it is boring trying to keep track of when you stop, when you walk and when you rest. When I compared the times on a particular trip with the times for that same trek the last time I travelled it, I found unbelievable variations. This must have depended on other factors that I did not record, such as my mood, physical condition, the condition of the trail, the number of other people and cattle on the trail, how many photographs I took, and the weather. Because of these wide variations in walking times, I have not attempted to project approximate times for anyone else. Most days require from 5 to 8 hours of walking.

If you really need to know times, you can ask people on the trail. The hill Nepalese use a unit of distance called a *kos*, the distance that a person can walk in 1 hour. *Namche Bazaar kati kos laagchha?* should elicit a reply that approximates the number of hours to Namche Bazaar (as should *Namche Bazaar kati gantaa laagchha* – 'How many hours to Namche Bazaar?'). It is more fun and rewarding to try to talk to people instead of continually looking at a book and checking it against your watch.

Another statistic that is difficult to determine is distance. It is easy to judge distances from a map, but a printed map is two-dimensional. With the many gains and losses of altitude – and all the turns and twists of the trail – a map measurement of the routes becomes virtually meaningless. In researching a guidebook to Glacier National Park in the USA, a friend pushed a bicycle wheel odometer over every trail in the park to get accurate distance measurements. I have neither the ambition nor the patience for such a project and, besides, it would take most of the fun out of a trek. You gain a different perspective of travelling by discussing how many days to a particular destination rather than how many km. Most of the days listed here are 10 to 20 km of trekking, depending on the altitude and steepness of the terrain.

Maps

The maps included in this book are based on the best available maps of each region. As with everything else, they are reasonably accurate but not perfect. To make them legible, I have deleted most villages and landmarks not mentioned in the route descriptions. In some cases, even major villages and mountains have vanished from the maps. The maps do not show elevations, as these are detailed in the route descriptions.

Instead of contour lines, the maps depict only ridge lines. This is the line of the highest point on a ridge. If the trail crosses one of these brown lines, you must walk uphill. If the trail leads from a ridge line to a river, you must walk downhill. The maps show mountain peaks in their true position, but villages may not always be located accurately. The problem occurs because of the size of villages. Where does the dot go for a village that is 3 km from end to end and which has no real centre or town square? The trails and roads follow the general direction indicated on the maps, but a map this size obviously cannot show small switchbacks and twists in the trail.

Trek Profiles

These profiles indicate the altitude changes for the major treks. They are reasonably to scale, in that the horizontal axis represents days during the trek and thus gives an indication of the steepness of the trail. Most high and low points are shown for each day, therefore when there are many ups and downs in a single day, the scale becomes distorted a bit. The numbered days across the bottom relate to the days in the text; a level line means a rest day. When you compare treks looking at these profiles, look at the number

of climbs, not the height of them; the vertical scale is different on each chart. The most frightening of these profiles is the Rara Lake loop in western Nepal because it crosses several ridges each day, but all the profiles look like saw teeth because treks in Nepal go from ridgetop to river valley and back to a ridgetop.

Altitude Measurements

The elevations shown in the route descriptions are composites, based on my measurements with an altimeter and the best available maps. Most elevations correlate with the Ground Survey of India maps of the 1960s except where these are obviously wrong, a frequent occurrence in western Nepal. The Schneider map series used the Ground Survey of India maps as a starting point but refined most elevations, so I have used these elevations in the areas covered by these maps. Except for specific elevations shown on the Schneider maps, I have rounded all elevations to the nearest 10 metres. The elevations of peaks are those shown on the official mountaineering regulations of Nepal.

This uncertainty over precise elevations will cause no problems during a trek. The primary reason that you need to know the elevation is to learn whether the trail ahead goes uphill or downhill and whether it is a long ascent (or descent) or a short one. The elevations shown here fulfil that purpose. The idea of precise elevations becomes even more complicated because villages cover such large areas. What is the 'correct' elevation of a village such as Bung, which extends almost 500 vertical metres up a hillside?

Changes

In the 1980s, major new roads were opened to Jiri, Gorkha, Dhankuta and along the Narayani River from Mugling to Narayanghat. Construction of the Dumre to Besi Sahar road (at the start of the trek around Annapurna) is proceeding slowly, and there are plans to extend this road as far as Chame. The Trisuli Bazaar to Dhunche road now takes several days off the Langtang trek and the new extension to Somdang opens up a major portion of Ganesh Himal. The trek to Jomsom now starts with a drive that bypasses the old trekking haunts of Hyangja, Suikhet and Naudanda. The road leaves the Jomsom trail near Birethanti and heads south and west to Baglung, but there are plans to extend the road north up the Kali Gandaki to Jomsom and Mustang. There is also a major road planned to go up the Arun River to provide support for the construction of several dams. The road up the Indrawati Valley towards Helambu is finally being repaired and put back into service.

As a result of these road changes, every major trek in this book is two to four days shorter than it was in the previous edition, and most are five to eight days shorter than in the 1980 edition.

Roads also change the relative importance of villages. Lamosangu, for example, was a major road head from 1970 to 1981. It lost its importance and many of its facilities vanished when Jiri became the road head. The same will probably happen to Dumre when a sensible bus service begins up the Marsyandi. Roads also bring about an increase in theft. Before a road reaches a village, travel must always be on foot and nobody complains. No self-respecting Nepalese will walk when a bus is available, but the bus fares on the new roads are expensive – creating a new demand for cash. For many, the only source of easy cash is theft, and the road offers a quick getaway. Be especially watchful of your possessions within a few days walk of any road.

Trail and bridge construction is also proceeding at a furious pace in the hills. Local governments and foreign aid programmes have reconstructed or widened many trails. On the Everest trek, a new trail has changed the route significantly, bypassing some places and visiting villages that the old expedition route did not reach before. The Swiss are planning an extensive new series of bridges in the hills. Landslides and flood damage is becoming more frequent as villagers remove the forest cover and topsoil washes away. These phenomena can alter trek routes drastically as whole villages can disappear and trails can require extensive detours to cross slide areas.

The construction of small trekker hotels and the conversion of private homes into hotel facilities is proceeding at an even more frantic pace. New hotels spring up every week on the major trek routes. They also vanish when the innkeepers get bored or discover that the costs are higher than the potential returns. The competition for trekker rupees is intense, so innkeepers lower their prices to attract customers, and it becomes hard to make a hotel pay its way. There are pressures for hotels to improve the way they deal with fuel usage and sanitation, particularly toilet facilities, so this may change the number and location of hotels before long.

I have mentioned many hotels by name. When you look for these places, you may find a hotel with a different name. There is a funny system in Nepal that allows a hotelier to avoid tax by changing the name of his company. Often the Namaste Hotel becomes the New Namaste Hotel, but sometimes the new name is a lot less similar.

A trek route changes because of the season. The routes described here work during the trekking season from October to May, though some high passes, particularly in Dolpo, are open only in October and November and again in May. If you trek during the monsoon, the trails may not bear any resemblance to what I have described here. Bridges can be washed away and trails become flooded during this season. In early October, and again in April and May, rice growing in many of the terraces along most trek routes. Many camp sites that are excellent in November and December are under water in the rice growing season. Hotels in high places, particularly Gorak Shep, Annapurna Sanctuary and along the Ghorapani to Ghandruk route, often close in the coldest part of winter (December to February) and during the monsoon.

Place Names & Terminology

The route descriptions list many places that

do not correlate with names in other descriptions of the same route or with names on maps. The diversity occurs because there is no universally accepted form of transliterating Nepali and Tibetan names into English. Different authorities will spell the same place name in different ways. To make matters more complicated, a particular place may have several different names. Mt Everest, for example, is also known as *Sagarmatha* (Nepali), *Chomolungma* (Sherpa) and *Qomolangma Feng* (Chinese). The same applies for many village names.

Several years ago the Nepalese Government set up a committee to assign new Nepalese names to 31 peaks and three tourist places that had been known before only by English names. I have mentioned the new names in the text, but I have also used the old English names to avoid confusion.

Many maps produced before 1960 had very little ground control and village names had little resemblance to reality. This is particularly true of the maps prepared by the US Army Map Service that Nepalese mappers have traced and distributed as trekking maps in Kathmandu.

Proper geographical usage defines the left side of a river or glacier as that which is on the left when you face downhill in the direction of flow. This terminology often confuses me when following a river uphill – the 'left side' of the river is on your right. Fortunately, most Himalayan rivers travel either north-south or east-west, so I have tried to avoid the 'proper' usage by referring to riverbanks by points of the compass.

In the route reports that follow I have translated many names and descriptions, but to avoid a lot of repetition I have used several Nepali and Tibetan words throughout the text. These include names of the ethnic groups that populate Nepal's hills: Tamang, Chhetri, Brahmin, Rai, Sherpa, Gurung, Limbu, Newar and Magar.

You will see several Buddhist monuments during a trek. A *maani* is a single stone or stone wall carved with the Tibetan Buddhist prayer *Om Mani Padme Hum*. A *chorten* is a round stone monument; a *kaani* is an arch over a trail, usually decorated with paintings on the inside; and a Tibetan Buddhist temple or monastery is called a *gompa*. A *chautaara* is a stone resting place under a tree and usually has a shelf for porter loads.

Rivers are called, in decreasing order of size, *kosi*, *khola*, *naalaa* and sometimes *nadi* and *gaad*. A mountain pass is called *la* in Tibetan and Sherpa and *bhanjyang* or *laagna* in Nepali. Lakes are *taal* or *pokhari* and a ridge is a *daanda* or *lekh*. A high pasture is a *kharka*; during summer, herders live in a kharka in a shelter called a *goth* (pronounced like 'goat'). The flat plains of Nepal, near the Indian border is called the Terai, and the local booze is chhang and rakshi.

Throughout the text I refer to 'trekking peaks'. These are the 18 peaks that can be legally climbed by trekkers with a simple application and fee to the Nepal Mountaineering Association.

All those 'aa' words look strange, so I have lexiconically misspelt several frequently used words including *tal*, *danda*, *mani*, *kani*, *nala*, *lagna*.

Health & First Aid

The medical information in this chapter was prepared and written by David R Shlim MD, medical director of the CIWEC Clinic and medical director of the Himalayan Rescue Association.

When a person returns from a trip to Nepal, he or she is usually greeted by two questions: 'Did you have a good time?' and 'Did you get sick?' The answer to both questions is likely to be 'Yes', but only a very small percentage of travellers become so ill that they alter their plans significantly. This chapter outlines the preparations to make before you leave home, makes recommendations for a first-aid kit, and describes the prevention and treatment of the health problems you are most likely to face in Nepal.

PREDEPARTURE PREPARATIONS FOR TREKKING
Physical Conditioning

Obviously, the better the shape you are in, the more you will enjoy a trek. You do not have to be an Olympic athlete, but you should be in condition for the activity you are going to do – a lot of walking.

Physical training, particularly walking up and down hills, is the best method of preparing for trekking in Nepal. If possible, make your training jaunts in the same boots you will wear on the trek. This will also give you a chance to find out whether your socks are comfortable for you and whether tennis shoes or running shoes give enough support to your feet during long walks.

Jogging helps, but does not really prepare you unless you run on hills. Weight training can help build leg strength for the relentless 2000 metre climbs that occur on some treks. It is not just aerobic conditioning that is important: you must try to condition your joints, particularly the knees, to continual up and down hill travel. The only way to do this is to walk up and down hills. Cycling builds thigh strength but doesn't condition the legs to the pounding they will get.

If you can climb a mountain to get used to high altitude, the physical conditioning will certainly help your muscles, but it does not guarantee that you will not have trouble at high elevations.

Although a trek is usually not particularly strenuous at any given time, especially as staff wait upon you almost to the point of embarrassment, a trek is long – probably the longest time you have ever been in the outdoors, even if you stay in hotels. The continual day-to-day grind up and down hills can be a relaxing experience or just a nightmare. Be sure you do enjoy walking and are willing to put up with the regimentation of walking each and every day. When trekking on your own you can always spend a day resting if you arrive at a place you really like; but if you are with a group, you may have to keep walking when you don't feel like it.

Medical Exam

The worst place on your adventure to discover that you have a medical problem is on the trek itself. Most trekking agents supply an examination form that is designed to outline to your doctor some of the potential problems of a trek. You want to be sure that he/she views the examination a little more seriously than a routine life insurance exam. It's sensible to list any abnormalities, chronic problems or special medicines on the form. This will help you to identify a problem in case you exhibit any symptoms along the trek. If you are trekking on your own, it's a good idea to carry a brief outline of your medical history and notes on any special problems or allergies. This will help if you do have an accident or illness in a remote region.

A routine physical examination is probably overrated as a means of predicting problems that young healthy people will have while trekking, but it is worth your while to investigate little nagging problems or any unexplained recurrent symptoms before you go, because problems have a way of escalating under the stresses of travel.

For example, haemorrhoids can become markedly worse with diarrhoea or constipation. Most developing tooth problems can be detected by a thorough dental checkup. This is highly recommended because reliable dental care is difficult to obtain in Nepal. Repeated urinary tract infections in women, ear or eye problems, abdominal problems such as gastritis or ulcer symptoms, a chronic cough or wheezing, and particularly chronic musculoskeletal problems such as tendinitis or bursitis should be investigated or treated prior to a long trip to Asia that involves trekking in remote, difficult terrain.

Older Trekkers

People over the age of 40 often worry about high altitude and potential heart problems. There is no clear data to support the opinion that high altitude is likely to bring out heart disease or heart attacks that have not previously been suspected. However, having your first heart symptoms in a remote village at 4200 metres and two weeks walk from a hospital increases the anxiety and difficulty of obtaining treatment. If an older person runs or hikes regularly on difficult terrain, there is no reason at present to think that high altitude will be an increased risk for that person. If you would like reassurance because you are not very active in your daily life, a stress electrocardiogram obtained near the time of your trip will bring you to your maximal heart rate and exertion under a controlled situation and detect any heart strain.

Immunisations & Prophylaxis

Nepal has no official vaccination requirements for entry. However, you should make an effort to protect yourself from some of the serious infectious diseases that can be prevented by vaccine or prophylactic (ie preventive) measures.

It is often said that you should consult a doctor regarding immunisation advice before travelling to Asia. In all fairness to your doctor, it is very difficult to have current or accurate information about travelling in Asia unless you have a special interest in that area. See if you can be referred to a travellers' health clinic or to a doctor who has some particular interest in the subject. You can use this chapter as a starting point for discussion with your doctor.

Cholera This vaccine may still be required to enter some countries, notably India. Health cards are not routinely checked, but can be asked for at random. A World Health Organisation meeting in April 1988 recommended that all countries drop cholera as a required vaccination for entry, but individual countries are slow to change their rules. The vaccine is not very effective at preventing cholera infection, and it often causes a significant reaction. The chances of acquiring cholera under any circumstances of travel are remote: a study has calculated the risk at less than one in 10,000 for USA travellers abroad. The incidence of tourists acquiring cholera in Nepal is zero. The dilemma of whether to obtain the vaccine or risk being held at a border and either sent back or given a less than sterile injection will remain until this vaccine requirement is dropped.

Hepatitis A Immune Serum Globulin (Gamma Globulin) is not a vaccine against hepatitis A, but a collection of blood protein containing antibodies which has been taken from other humans. Although elsewhere there is debate about its effectiveness, particularly among doctors who see very little hepatitis, there is no debate in Kathmandu. The effectiveness of gamma globulin in preventing hepatitis A is almost 100%. We recommend taking one cc for every month of travel, plus one extra. Thus, the dose would be two cc for one month, three cc for two months, four cc for three months and a maximum of five cc for four months of travel. Seek another dose of gamma globulin after four months of travel.

The rise in the number of acquired immunodeficiency syndrome (AIDS) cases in the world has led some travellers to elect not to use gamma globulin for fear of acquiring AIDS. This fear is unfounded; gamma globulin can be considered 100% safe from transmitting the AIDS virus.

The risk of acquiring hepatitis A is significant while travelling in Asia and probably increases with the length of the trip rather than decreases. Trekkers have occasionally had to be evacuated because of the disease showing up while on the trail, and two tourists have died of fulminant hepatitis A which would probably have been prevented if they had taken gamma globulin.

This injection is probably the single most important of all I have listed in terms of protecting both your health and your trip.

Malaria There is currently no vaccine against malaria. Chloroquine phosphate (Aralen) or chloroquine sulphate (Nivaquine) is recommended in a single weekly dose (500 mg) in nonresistant malaria areas, while chloroquine plus proguanil (Paludrine, 200 mg per day) is recommended where resistant falciparum malaria is found in the Indian subcontinent. In South-East Asia, malaria is mainly limited to rural areas, but the resistance to medication is high in these areas. Ideas about the best malaria prophylaxis in South-East Asia keep changing, so it would be good to consult a travel clinic if you plan to go to these areas.

Malaria exists in Nepal in the lowland area near the Indian border (the Terai), although the risk of transmission during a short visit is very low. There is no risk of malaria in the rest of the country, which includes all the main trekking trails. I have never seen anyone acquire malaria while trekking in Nepal, but I have seen several treks ruined by adverse reactions to antimalaria drugs which were not needed in the first place.

Meningitis An epidemic of meningococcal meningitis occurred in the Kathmandu Valley in the spring of 1983. In the ensuing two years, six foreigners contracted meningococcal meningitis and two died. In March 1985, the Centres for Disease Control in the USA issued an alert to travellers to be vaccinated against meningococcal meningitis before travelling to Nepal. Since that time there have still been sporadic cases of meningitis in travellers to Nepal. The advice to be vaccinated against meningococcal meningitis is still sound. The vaccine is free of serious side effects, is not painful and a single injection provides good protection for three years or more. Unlike most of the other vaccine-preventable diseases, meningococcal meningitis can rapidly become fatal if it occurs away from medical care. It is worthwhile being vaccinated against this disease for travel in India too. You should get this vaccination before you leave home, but it is available in Kathmandu; try the CIWEC Clinic where it costs US$15.

Polio The current generation is no longer afraid of polio because vaccination has made it rare in the West. In fact, the disease is rising in the USA because some parents are irrationally more afraid of the vaccine than the disease. However, no such eradication of the disease has taken place in Asia; thus a booster for people who have been previously immunised is recommended before travelling to Nepal. If you have been immunised in childhood, one booster as an adult is all that is needed for the rest of your life. If you grew up without being immunised, you should complete a series of immunisations before heading to Asia. If you have never had polio vaccine in any form, do not use the oral polio vaccine as an adult. You can use the oral vaccine as a booster if you have been previously immunised by any method.

Rabies The modern rabies vaccine is now a highly purified substance with high effectiveness and few side effects. The drawback is that it is relatively expensive. Rabies is a severe brain infection caused by a virus transmitted by animal bites, mainly dogs and occasionally monkeys in Nepal. The disease is uniformly fatal once the symptoms are manifest. Therefore, all efforts must be made to avoid getting the disease once you have been exposed.

Two strategies are employed with the

rabies vaccine. One is called pre-exposure immunisation and consists of three injections spaced over one month. These injections prime your immune system against rabies so if you are bitten by an infected animal you just need two more shots, three days apart, as a booster. If you don't take the pre-exposure immunisation and you are bitten by a potentially rabid animal, you will need the full postexposure immunoprophylaxis which consists of five injections spaced over one month, and a single injection of rabies antibodies called rabies immune globulin. The rabies immune globulin is often very hard to obtain (it is available only at the CIWEC Clinic in Nepal), and it is very expensive (from US$350 to US$650 for the injection, depending on your body weight).

A recent study we conducted in Nepal calculated that only one out of 6000 visitors is bitten by a suspect animal. If you are planning to come to Nepal for only one or two months, I think that the pre-exposure series is not necessary. If you are planning to travel in Asia for three months or more, and are going to remote areas where the rabies vaccine is going to be hard to obtain (and rabies immune globulin impossible to obtain), you should consider having the pre-exposure series. Once you have the series, a booster should be obtained every two or three years. Remember that a bite must still be followed by post-exposure treatment, even if you take this series.

Smallpox Thanks to an incredible worldwide effort at eradication, smallpox no longer exists as a disease. The vaccination is therefore neither required nor available.

Tetanus & Diphtheria Most people from Western countries receive these vaccines in childhood. The tetanus and diphtheria germs are worldwide, so overseas travel is a good opportunity to catch up on your immunity. You should take a booster if it has been longer than 10 years since your last one.

Typhoid This disease is highly prevalent in Nepal. A CIWEC Clinic study has shown that the normal typhoid vaccine offered 95% protection against typhoid fever and 70% protection against paratyphoid fever. The new oral typhoid vaccine (Berne Ty 21a) has not demonstrated good protection for travellers (who avoid injections), so I don't recommend it for travellers to Nepal. A third vaccine, called the capsular polysaccharide typhoid vaccine, may be available soon and potentially has greater efficacy and fewer side effects than the older injectable typhoid vaccine. Its efficacy with travellers remains to be proven.

FIRST-AID KIT
The question of what to bring with you as a medical kit for trekking arises so commonly that I have included a rather detailed discussion of such a kit. Because trekking in Nepal can place you one or two weeks from outside medical help, the kit contains the medication that you would ordinarily need to treat most trail problems. The list of contents is to help you assemble the supplies and medications for your first-aid kit. The kit listed is designed to treat up to four people for two weeks. You should adjust the amounts of medicine and supplies you take to meet specific needs.

The medicines are mainly listed by generic (chemical) names, but certain combination medicines, with cumbersome ingredients, are listed by their most familiar brand names. Generic equivalents are always acceptable. Almost all of these medications are available from pharmacies in Kathmandu without prescription. Most cost much less than they do overseas, with the following exceptions: suppositories are not available; and the quality of the supplies (tape, dressings, band-aids, etc) is poor in Nepal, so these items should be imported if possible.

A discussion of each of the medications listed (and some extra ones), with details of its use, dosage and major side effects, is included under the heading Use of Medication, later in this chapter.

If a doctor is accompanying your trip, he or she may elect to bring additional, more sophisticated supplies including urinary catheters, oral airways, injectible medications and syringes, and suturing materials. These types of additions can be quite useful if someone in the group knows how to use them.

Supplies

1 thermometer (low reading preferred)
1 pair of scissors
1 pair of tweezers
1 tape (25 mm adhesive or paper)
1 sewing needle
10 100 mm x 100 mm gauze pads
1 large sterile dressing
2 100 mm rolled cotton bandages (kling)
1 75 mm rolled cotton bandage (kling)
20 25 mm band-aids
1 muslin triangular bandage for sling
1 bottle Betadine antiseptic (Piodin)
1 100 mm ace bandage
1 Steri-Strips pack
  moleskin

Supplies (Optional)

1 100 mm x 450 mm wire mesh splint or
  SAM splint
5 safety pins
  pencil & pad of paper

Medication

30 Acetamenopehen (Paracetamol) 500 mg
15 Acetazolamide 250 mg
20 Actifed
40 Amoxicillin (250 mg tablets)
20 antacid tablets
30 Acetamenophen with codeine 30 mg or
60 codeine (15 mg)
10 Bisacodyl 10 mg
40 Cephalexin 250 mg
1 tube Clotrimazole 1% cream
10 Dexamethasone 4 mg
10 Diphenhydramine 50 mg
40 Erythromycin 250 mg (If allergic to
  penicillin)
1 tube Hydrocortisone 1% cream
20 Lomotil or Imodium
14 Mycostatin vaginal tablets
10 Nifedipine 10 mg

24 Norfloxacin 400 mg or Ciprofloxacin
  500 mg
12 throat lozenges (Strepsils)
12 Tinidazole (500 mg)
  oral rehydration solution packets
  Promethazine 50 mg suppositories
  bottle Sulamyd 10% eye drops

Injectable Medication (Optional)

Promethazine 50 mg/1 cc
Meperidine 50 mg/1 cc
Adrenaline 1:1000
syringes and needles
alcohol swabs

HYGIENE ON THE TREK

As perverse as it sounds, the germs that cause diarrhoea are acquired mainly from ingesting someone else's faeces through the water supply. One of the major medical advances of Western countries was to develop a sure way of keeping faeces out of the water supply. This problem has not been solved in Nepal, so all water must be viewed as being potentially contaminated. While there is no consensus on the best method of purifying water in all circumstances, here are some considerations.

All faeces pathogens (disease producers) are killed by boiling water. The recommended length of time for which water must be boiled varies from five to 20 minutes, depending on which authority you read. A consensus paper by the Wilderness Medical Society in the USA has confirmed that just bringing water to the boil is sufficient to kill all potential disease-causing organisms, even at high altitude. As an alternative to boiling, chemicals can be added to water to kill the pathogens. Iodine preparations and chlorine preparations are equally effective in killing the germs, but iodine is a bit more reliable in the field.

Iodine Treatment of Drinking Water

There are three practical ways to carry iodine on a trek: tetraglycine hydroperiodide tablets; Lugol's solution; and iodine crystals.

Tetraglycine hydroperiodide tablets are

not available in Nepal and can deteriorate in as little as six months in their original containers. If you can find a fresh bottle of these tablets, they are convenient to use and non-messy to carry. One bottle contains 50 tablets, enough to purify 50 litres of water.

Lugol's solution is a water-based iodine concentrate, of which eight drops per litre of water is sufficient to purify reasonably clean, cool water. It is available in Kathmandu at many pharmacies, especially the larger ones on New Rd.

To use iodine crystals, place four or five grams of crystals in a 30 ml glass bottle (do not use a plastic bottle as the iodine eats it). Iodine is available from some pharmacies in Kathmandu and this small amount will treat an almost limitless amount of water. Fill the bottle with water and wait 30 minutes. The resulting concentrated solution, not the crystals, may be added to your water bottle to purify the water for drinking. Add between 15 and 30 cc of the solution and wait for 30 minutes before drinking. Refill the glass bottle at the same time and after 30 minutes it will be ready to use again. Be particularly careful not to ingest an iodine crystal as this can be fatal.

In general, with any of these methods, the cleaner the water appears and the warmer it is, the less iodine is necessary. If you don't like the iodine taste, use a smaller amount of iodine and allow the bottle to sit for a longer time before drinking it. It will be just as safe and will taste better. A rough rule is to double the waiting time if you cut the iodine amount in half. No evidence has been presented that says using iodine to purify water, even for long periods of time, causes any harm.

Filtration of Drinking Water
Filtering devices for field use have become popular in recent years. There is debate as to whether the filters can eliminate viruses that cause diarrhoea or hepatitis (some say the viruses stick to larger particles and can be filtered that way; in fact, the viruses are in fact smaller than the smallest holes in all commercial filters). The filters can be expensive (up to US$180 or more). A 0.2 micron

filter is necessary to filter harmful bacteria (a filter this size would also trap amoeba and giardia cysts, which are much larger). Filtering can eliminate suspended particles that might hamper the effects of iodine, allowing you to use a smaller dose. Some filters incorporate a pentaiodine resin which iodises the water as it filters it. This would seem to be an adequate method if the filter is not old and has no cracks.

Other Precautions
Unfortunately, just treating your water carefully will not eliminate the chances of ingesting someone else's faeces. Throughout Nepal there is very little use of sewers to dispose of human waste. Thus, faeces is present throughout the environment and finds its way into your food. Contamination of food from people's hands remains a major source of infection. Also, vegetables and fruits can be contaminated from the soil they are grown in and by handling along the way. The general rule is to not eat any vegetables that cannot be peeled or freshly cooked, unless you are certain of the methods that have been used to soak them. Many restaurants in Kathmandu now soak their vegetables in an acceptable manner to make them safe, but if you are not sure, don't eat them. The locally brewed chhang, a fermented brew made from corn, rice or millet, is reconstituted with untreated water and is a source of infection for unwary travellers. However, since the drinking of chhang is so tied up in social custom, many travellers are forced to put aside their judgement so as not to offend generous hosts.

Making a point of washing your own hands frequently can also help prevent illness. The tiny amounts of water that might cling to dishes and glasses washed in untreated water are not likely to make you sick, and drying the dishes can eliminate this problem. In general, the likelihood of getting sick is related to the amount of contamination you ingest. Try to avoid eating foods that are cooked early in the morning and then reheated (perhaps inadequately) when you place your order (foods such as lasagne and casseroles). These types of foods can incubate bacterial growth throughout the day. You should always do your best to avoid known sources of contamination, but don't worry excessively about those areas in which you have no control.

One area you can control is the disposal of toilet paper. The trails of pink and white toilet paper in popular trekking areas are disgusting and are growing every year. There are three acceptable ways to deal with used toilet paper: carry it away in a plastic bag for later disposal; bury it (carry a little plastic shovel, they're available in many backpacking stores); or burn it on the spot (put matches or a cigarette lighter in with your toilet paper for the purpose). To successfully burn toilet paper after use, pull it open before lighting. Urine soaked paper is harder to burn. There is no excuse for leaving toilet paper exposed along the trail!

HEALTH PROBLEMS & TREATMENT
Diarrhoea
Diarrhoea remains the novice Asian traveller's biggest fear. The incidence of diarrhoea among tourists to Nepal has not been calculated, but if you stay long enough in Nepal, you will get it. However, travellers on guided treks, where cooking conditions can be controlled, can return home without ever having diarrhoea. Since diarrhoea is so easy to acquire in Nepal, it is important to know its causes and its treatments. Most cases of acute diarrhoea can be rapidly cured if the right treatment is used.

Almost all diarrhoea in travellers is caused by eating or drinking something that is contaminated. You must make up your mind to be conscientious about what and how you eat, and never to drink untreated water. With prolonged travel, one can develop some immunity to some of the causes of diarrhoea in travellers. However, it seems that much of this immunity is lost when you return home for a long time.

The intestines of normal people harbour trillions of microorganisms of many different types. These generally live in harmony with each other and their host, and the body produces a consistent amount of formed stools without abdominal discomfort. When certain other organisms are accidentally ingested they can irritate the bowels either through the production of a toxin or by directly invading the wall of the bowel. The bowel reacts to the toxin by secreting extra fluid, causing a watery diarrhoea. The bowel reacts to invading organisms by crampy pain and frequent loose stools. The process of fighting off foreign germs in the intestine is remarkably successful and almost all viral or bacterial diarrhoeas in previously healthy people are self-limited, meaning that they will cure themselves without having to take medication. In the case of bacterial infection, however, antibiotic treatment will greatly shorten the length of the illness. Certain other parasites, notably giardia and some species of amoeba, are harder for the body to combat and infection can go on for months if not treated.

The loss of fluid from diarrhoea and/or vomiting can produce dehydration, which in its mild form causes slight weakness, and in its moderate form dizziness and fatigue, and in its severe form the inability to stand at all without passing out. You must remember to drink more fluids when you have a diarrhoeal illness, particularly if it began with vomiting, if you have a fever or if the weather is hot. Any fluid (except alcohol) will do initially, but oral re-hydration solutions (Jeevan Jal is the brand in Nepal) are more rapidly absorbed in the intestines.

Many travellers believe that fasting will cure a mild stomach upset, but there is no scientific evidence that fasting or any special diet will shorten the course of a diarrhoeal illness. However, diarrhoea exagerates the normal reflex by which the bowel contracts when food reaches the stomach, and this can make you feel that eating makes your diarrhoea worse. The general rule is to eat if you're hungry, but don't force yourself.

This section was written to help you to treat yourself for diarrhoea when you're away from medical help. Stool tests may be useful to determine the cause of your diarrhoea, but some local laboratories in Nepal are not completely reliable. They can tend to detect amoebic dysentery even when it's not present, and this can lead to to the use of the wrong medication, and a longer period of illness than necesary. If you are in Kathmandu, a medical consultation and a stool test at a reliable clinic is the quickest way to be sure of the right diagnosis and treatment.

The CIWEC Clinic has studied travellers' diarrhoea in Nepal for nine years. We have learned that there are three causes which account for almost all instances of the problem. Bacteria cause about 85% of cases, Giardia causes 14%, and amoebic infection is a factor in only 1%.

Bacterial Diarrhoea This common illness is characterised by an abrupt onset, often in the middle of the night. The sufferer gets abdominal cramps, frequent loose stools, and sometimes nausea, vomiting and fever. Blood can occasionally be seen in the stool, but this is no cause for great alarm. If there is vomiting and fever, these usually last no longer than 24 hours, but the diarrhoea may continue. The infection can clear itself without treatment in a few days, but it can also last for two weeks or more at times.

In Nepal, bacterial diarrhoeas seem to be more severe and long-lasting than in other developing countries. Most people want to take medication to shorten the illness as much as possible. We have found that early antibiotic treatment is highly successful in curing the symptoms within one or two days.

Studies have shown that taking antibiotics prophylactically while travelling in developing countries can prevent many cases of travellers' diarrhoea. The benefits and risks of taking antibiotics in this fashion have not been clearly established. The first pill tested, doxycycline, is quite expensive, can cause nausea on an empty stomach and can sensitise the skin to the sun, producing a painful rash. It did offer significant protection against some kinds of bacterial diarrhoea, but there are no studies published which show whether the protective effect can be continued for several months, or what the negative effects of taking full doses of antibiotics for a long time might be. Other antibiotics have been tested in the same way and found to be effective also. Some non-antibiotic preparations, such as bismuth subsalicalate (Pepto-Bismol) have also been effective in preventing bacterial diarrhoeas in short term travel.

Researchers who were concerned about masses of travellers taking antibiotics daily for extended periods tested the effectiveness of taking an antibiotic as soon as the traveller developed symptoms, but not before. They found that this method significantly shortened the time that the person was bothered by the diarrhoea. This method has obvious advantages over taking medication daily throughout a long trip.

These studies were aimed at people who had been in a new country for a short time. In the first week or two of travel in a developing country, the abrupt onset of diarrhoea will almost always be bacterial and presumptive treatment can be taken. When a person has been travelling for a number of weeks or months in an area of risk, the development of diarrhoea can be due to other organisms as well, and one has to weigh the symptoms more carefully to choose treatment.

In general, the abrupt onset of bacterial diarrhoea differs from diarrhoea caused by protozoal parasites (amoeba and giardia), which have a more gradual onset, and it often takes a few days to realise that the mild diarrhoea you have is not going away. The antibiotic that used to be prescribed most often for bacterial diarrhoea in Nepal was trimethoprim-sulfamethoxasole (Bactrim). Our studies have shown that from 10% to 50% of bacteria are now resistant to this antibiotic. Our current drug of choice is either norfloxacin or ciprofloxacin. The dosage of norfloxacin is 400 mg every 12 hours for three days. The dosage of ciprofloxacin is 500 mg every 12 hours for three days. One of these drugs should be in your first-aid kit if you are trekking away from medical care.

Giardia This organism is thought by tourists

to be the most common cause of diarrhoea in Nepal, but this is not so. It is present however, and can cause a chronic, relatively low-grade diarrhoeal illness. The organism is a protozoa, a single-celled animal that inhabits the upper intestine, just after the stomach. They are oval, and propel themselves with a tail inside the host. When they decide it's time to move to another host, they secrete a sturdy shell and become a nonactive cyst. The cysts are strong enough to survive in mountain streams and dust, and to pass through the intense stomach acid of a new host. Cysts in water can be killed by boiling or by adding iodine.

Once ingested they begin causing symptoms after one or two weeks, not the next day after a suspect meal. Upper abdominal discomfort, 'churning intestines', foul-smelling burps and farts, and on-and-off diarrhoea are the main characteristics of giardiasis. Often people have symptoms for a week to a month or more before deciding to seek treatment because it is not very severe each day and they hope it will go away. Sometimes the only symptoms are one to three urgent loose bowel movements in the morning followed by a symptom-free day and night, repeated day after day. Because the organisms live in the upper part of the intestine, they don't consistently show up in stool examinations. If a giardia infection is suspected, and a stool examination is either unavailable or negative, it is often reasonable to treat yourself anyway. If you have guessed right, the relief of symptoms is often dramatic.

In Nepal, the drug of choice is tinidazole (brand name Tiniba). The dose is two grams all at once, one time only (four 500 mg tablets). This single dose is 95% effective in curing a giardia infection. The medication can cause a bad taste in the mouth, headache, loss of appetite and nausea, and must never be taken with alcohol. However, these side effects rarely last more than a day.

Amoebic Dysentery The term 'amoebic dysentery' still strikes fear into the heart of the Asian traveller, even though this form of an amoebic infection is very rare in travel-lers. Amoebas are shapeless protozoans that live in the large intestine. There are many different species, but only a few can cause symptoms. Occasionally, amoeba can migrate through the blood stream to the liver and cause a serious abscess characterised by fever and pain in the liver. Infection with E histolytica amoeba can produce a relatively low-grade daily diarrhoea, with vague abdominal pain. Diarrhoea occurs for a few days and then you feel better, sometimes going without a bowel movement for a day or so, only to begin having diarrhoea again. This cycle can go on for weeks or months. Weight loss and chronic fatigue can accompany long standing infections.

Rarely, amoebic infections can cause very frequent production of small amounts of bloody stool. This is the dysenteric form and is potentially dangerous. It would be best to start treatment immediately if these symptoms are present, although it can be confused with a bacterial infection, which is much more common.

The treatment of amoebic infections is also tinidazole, two grams taken as a single daily dose repeated on three consecutive days. Ideally the three days of tinidazole should be followed by 500 mg of Furamide (diloxanide furoate), three times per day for 10 days to rid the intestines completely of the organism. Furamide has no significant side effects and can be taken with alcohol. It's very unlikely that you'll need this drug on a trek, so it's not included in the firs-aid kit. If necesary, you could obtain it when you return to Kathmandu or Pokhara.

Other Intestinal Disorders

There are other causes of acute intestinal upset which cannot be treated with antibiotics. Fortunately, they all go away by themselves, given time. These conditions include:

Food Poisoning Some bacteria, if deposited on food that is conducive to their growth, produce a very potent poison as they grow. If you eat this contaminated portion of food, you can become violently ill within 4 to 8 hours, typified by the sudden onset of nausea, vomiting, fever and profuse watery diarrhoea. Fortunately, most victims are well on the way to recovery by the time they are strong enough to leave their rooms and seek help, usually within 12 to 24 hours. In these cases the body is reacting to the poison, not the germs themselves and therefore no antibiotics are necessary. Attempting to drink as much as possible to prevent dehydration is the only therapy necessary. If diarrhoea persists after the vomiting and fever are finished, you may have a bacterial infection (see previous sections).

Gastrointestinal Viruses Viruses are the smallest of all germs and the hardest to treat with medication. There are several kinds of viruses which can cause diarrhoea, and in some parts of the world they are a common cause of travellers' diarrhoea. However, in Nepal, gastrointestinal viruses were found to cause only about 2% of travellers' diarrhoea, and this was mainly in the colder months. Therefore, it is a mistake most of the time to attribute acute diarrhoea to a virus. Viruses cause diarrhoea for from one to several days. Occasionally nausea is very prominent.

Worms These intestinal parasites are never the cause of diarrhoea and rarely the cause of any symptoms. They can occasionally be associated with mild abdominal discomfort. It takes seven weeks or so for a worm egg, once ingested, to grow into an adult worm, so worms are not a hazard to short-term travel. Studies have shown that approximately 95% of Nepalese have worm eggs in their faeces. Despite these overwhelming figures, worm infestation in foreigners is relatively rare. Even among US Peace Corps volunteers living for two years in remote villages, the rate of worm infestation was less than 5%. Whether or not it is important to take worm medicine at the end of an Asian trip is hard to say. However, the medicine is quite free from side effects, thus it is not a major decision if you want to be sure you are not carrying worms home. The medicine is

mebendazole (Wormin in Nepal). Take one pill twice a day for three days.

Cryptosporidium This organism was first found in Nepal in a CIWEC study in 1987. It was present in about 6% of the stool samples. However, wider screening has shown it to be rarely a cause of diarrhoea in CIWEC patients. It can cause the abrupt onset of diarrhoea, which can sometimes last from several days to a few weeks. At present, there is no antibiotic treatment readily available. The organism is not routinely looked for in local laboratories because it requires a special stain in order to be seen. When we find it, most patients are relieved at least to have a diagnosis, and to know that the illness will eventually go away by itself.

Altitude Sickness (AMS)

The Himalayan Rescue Association has a saying that 'the Himalaya begins where other mountain ranges leave off'. This refers to the fact that even if you trek to the height of 5500 metres, you are still only at the base of most mountains. The exposure, over a period ranging from days to weeks, to these altitudes requires some adjustment by your body, a process called acclimatisation. If you move up in altitude too quickly, a syndrome known as Acute Mountain Sickness (AMS) can develop.

In the early '70s, when trekking was just becoming popular in Nepal, many groups had the shock of watching someone become ill with what seemed like the flu or a chest infection and then die within a day or two. As many as five to 10 people a year died in the Everest region alone out of a total of only 500 trekkers annually. In the past 10 years, there has been only one mountain sickness death per year in tourists, despite a four-fold increase in trekking to almost 50,000 people per year.

However, in the autumn of 1989, two Japanese trekkers died of acute mountain sickness in one trekking group in the Gokyo Valley. Many of the new trekkers in Nepal are not experienced mountain hikers and are unaware of the hazards of going to a remote area and high altitude. At a time when everything that is needed to be known to prevent deaths from mountain sickness is known, it is terribly tragic to still see mountain sickness deaths among trekkers in Nepal. If you follow the simple advice outlined in this section, you will not have to worry about dying from mountain sickness.

AMS occurs as the result of failure to adapt to higher altitudes. Fluid accumulates in between the cells in the body and eventually collects where, unfortunately, it can do the most harm – in the lungs and brain. As fluid collects in the lungs, you become breathless more easily while walking and eventually more breathless at rest. A cough begins, initially dry and irritative, but progressing, in its most severe form, to the production of pink, frothy sputum. The person ultimately drowns in this fluid if he/she doesn't descend. This syndrome is referred to as High Altitude Pulmonary Edema (HAPE). When fluid collects in the brain, you develop a headache, loss of appetite, nausea and sometimes vomiting. You become increasingly tired and want to lay down and do nothing. As you progress, you develop a problem with your balance and coordination (ataxia). Eventually you lie down and slip into coma. Death is inevitable if you don't descend. This syndrome is called High Altitude Cerebral Edema (HACE). HAPE and HACE can occur singly or in combination.

Awareness of these syndromes has caused some trekkers to be unnecessarily anxious as they trek. The progression of symptoms is usually quite slow, but steady if symptoms are ignored, taking 24 to 48 hours or more. The onset of early symptoms, particularly headache or breathlessness, should be a warning that you have reached your limit of acclimatisation for now and not to ascend further until the symptoms have cleared, usually in one or two days. If you continue upwards with symptoms, they will inevitably become worse. If symptoms don't clear within 24 to 48 hours, or you are steadily getting worse, then you should descend at

least to the last altitude at which you felt well. When you feel well it is safe to continue back up. However, if you have become quite ill before you descend, requiring someone else to help you down, you should not try to re-ascend on that particular trek.

AMS has been reported at any altitude over 1800 metres, although it occurs more commonly and more severely at higher altitudes. In general you should not ascend more than 300 metres per day above 3000 to 4000 metres. Instead of walking for short distances, most people spend an extra day at, for example, 3700 metres before moving up to 4300 metres, thus averaging 300 metres per day. But no schedule will guarantee the individual trekker that they will not have symptoms.

People who elect to trek with organised groups have the problem of sticking to a group schedule. If they fail to acclimatise on a given day they often have to be left behind. Trekkers arranging their own treks have the luxury of being able to take an extra day at will if they don't feel well, so take advantage of this when necessary. Trekkers tend to be very goal oriented, and ambition can lead you to want to deny your symptoms. Over the years people have come to me with AMS symptoms which they explain away as being due to the sun, dehydration, hitting their head on a low doorway, sleeping in smoky tea houses, medicine they have taken, bronchitis, the flu, in fact anything except mountain sickness. None of these substitute conditions can be fatal; ignored AMS can be consistently so.

If you feel ill at a certain altitude and you are not sure why, assume it is AMS and react accordingly. Guessing incorrectly can have serious consequences. The Himalayan Rescue Association aid posts in Pheriche and Manang can give you helpful advice, but if you are on your own, be cautious. All of the fatalities in recent years have been people who persisted in ascending despite symptoms that should have been recognised as AMS. AMS rarely strikes a trekker without warning. Relax and enjoy your trek if you are feeling well and be prepared to rest an extra day or so if you are not. Remember the three basic rules to avoid dying of AMS:

- Learn the early symptoms of mountain sickness and recognise when you have them.
- *Never* ascend to sleep at a new altitude with any symptoms of acute mountain sickness.
- Descend if your symptoms are getting worse while resting at the same altitude.

Trekking at higher altitude should be a very safe activity. It will be if you pay attention to your body and to the behaviour of your friends and allow time to adjust to the extreme altitudes that seem deceptively low because of the height of the surrounding peaks. The fact that 5000 tourists a year rather than 500 now trek to Kala Pattar does not make it a safer altitude.

Treatment The treatment of AMS is firstly not to ascend with symptoms, and if symptoms are more severe, to descend. Descent will always bring improvement and in serious cases should not be delayed in order to try some other form of therapy.

Three medications have proven useful as an adjunct to treating acute mountain sickness. Acetazolamide (Diamox) can prevent mild symptoms of AMS if taken prior to ascent. However, the HRA does not recommend its routine use in the Himalaya since treks often last for a month and most people will not need any drug. It is useful in treating the headache and nausea associated with mild AMS, and it also can improve your sleep if you are disturbed by the irregular breathing and breathlessness that can occur normally in sleeping people at high altitudes. My recommendation regarding Diamox is to carry it with you, use it to treat mild symptoms and use it prophylactically only if you have had experience before with AMS on a certain schedule. The usual dose is 250 mg every 12 hours as needed. Recent evidence has shown that 125 mg (half a tablet) every 12 hours may be just as effective, with fewer side effects. Mild tingling of hands and feet

is common after taking Diamox and is not an indication to stop its use. Some people fear that Diamox can somehow 'mask' the symptoms of AMS, but there is no basis for this fear. If you take Diamox and improve, you have improved. If you don't improve, consider descent.

Dexamethasone (Decadron) is a potent steroid drug which improves the symptoms of HACE through an unknown mechanism, but apparently without improving acclimatisation. It is an important drug to carry for emergency use, but it should never be taken prophylactically to prevent AMS. People with severe headache and loss of balance can be improved enough with this drug to allow them to avoid a night descent, or to convert them from a stretcher case to being able to walk. Once the drug is started, the person should refrain from going to a higher altitude while still taking the drug. If you are able to go off the drug for 24 hours, and have no further symptoms, you may continue your ascent.

Nifedipine is a drug that is ordinarily used to treat heart problems and high blood pressure. However, it has been shown to reduce the pressure in the blood vessels in the lungs, dramatically improving severe high altitude pulmonary edema. For this reason, nifedipine should be included in trekking first-aid kits. It has a liquid centre and the initial dose can be given by poking a hole in the capsule, or biting it, and letting the liquid be absorbed under the tongue. The dose can then be continued by swallowing a 10 mg capsule every 8 hours, starting 1 hour after the first dose. Further ascent should not be made while taking the drug.

Hyperbaric Treatment This new form of treatment for altitude sickness is, in a sense, the oldest – descent. Igor Gamow constructed a portable, inflatable pressure chamber which has been dubbed 'the Gamow bag'. He has sold his idea to DuPont Corporation in the USA, which is currently marketing the bag for about US$2500. The bag has been in use at the HRA aid posts in Pheriche and Manang since 1988.

The bag is about 60 cm in diameter by 2.5 metres long when inflated. It is entered through a strong, airtight zipper. A standard rafting foot pump is used to inflate the bag, and two pressure relief valves automatically open when the pressure has been increased two pounds per square inch. This increase in pressure effectively mimics descent and increases the amount of oxygen breathed in each breath. The ideal lengths of treatment for various severities of AMS have not been calculated. However, based on our preliminary work at the HRA aid posts, and other reports from around the world, it seems that a one hour treatment in the bag is very effective in improving the mild to moderate symptoms of acute mountain sickness. Also, this improvement may continue, even after coming out of the bag.

Severe cases of mountain sickness (HACE and HAPE) are improved in the bag, but this improvement tends to deteriorate after coming out of the bag, requiring repeat treatment or prolonged time (4 to 6 hours) in the bag. The pump needs to be pumped eight to 10 times a minute to keep the bag inflated and to replenish oxygen and remove carbon dioxide. Fifty kg of pressure are needed to depress the rafting pump when the bag is inflated, and some Nepalese are not large enough to be able to help with the pumping.

The Gamow bag may replace oxygen as the last resort treatment of acute mountain sickness. However, it is not foolproof (the escape valves can jam; the bag could develop a leak) and it should not be relied on as a way of pushing the limits of AMS in rapid ascents. Unlike oxygen, the bag does not 'run out' and has the distinct advantage of being able to treat as many people as require it, for prolonged periods of time (given enough healthy pumpers).

Frostbite

Frostbite is not a big concern on the majority of trekking trails on most days. However, from October through April, storms can occur which may dump a metre or more of snow on the high passes. The two most popular treks, to Kala Pattar and around Annapurna, take people above 5000 metres in altitude. The combination of high altitude and snow can produce frostbite very easily in unwary or unprepared trekkers.

On the Annapurna circuit, most of the walking is at low to moderate altitude on easy trails. Therefore, the temptation is great to wear either running shoes or lightweight cloth and leather hiking boots. The heavy boots that would be necessary to cross the Thorung La in snow seem too great a burden to carry for the one or two days they might be needed. But if snow catches trekkers at the pass and they try to push on in their light shoes, frostbite can result. Altitude plays a deceptive role in inducing frostbite, making tissue more susceptible to cold injury due to lack of oxygen to protect the skin cells. Several frostbitten people have told me that they were very surprised to see that they were frostbitten because they had felt colder in other settings without getting any cold injury.

What is frostbite? Frostbite is the injury resulting from frozen skin tissue. The circulation of warm blood to the extremities ordinarily can prevent them from freezing in cold weather if the extremities are protected enough from the environment. When hands or feet get cold they first feel cold, then numb, and then they begin to freeze. In extreme cold, touching a piece of metal or spilling petrol on your hands can induce instant freezing of skin, but in the Himalaya one almost always goes through the progression of cold to numb to frozen.

The key to prevention is to notice when your feet or hands have become numb and to stop right away to warm them. Once they are numb, you have no control over whether they are starting to freeze, since you can't feel it. To warm numb feet you must stop walking, get out of the wind if possible, avoid sitting directly on the snow if possible, take off your boots and place your feet against someone's abdomen or under their arms. The return of feeling is often painful for a short time. Put on dry socks if your socks are wet. Be prepared to stop and warm your feet every time they become numb. If your whole body is cold, then increasing your layers, adding a hat, getting out of the wind and drinking hot drinks is important, if this is possible.

If you are not vigilant enough, you may notice that the skin on your toes or fingers has frozen. The digits will be numb and feel hard and waxy, with a whitish appearance. The one acceptable way to warm frozen extremities is by a process of rapid rewarming, which may be hard to perform if you are not carrying stoves and large pots. The technique is to heat enough water to submerge the frozen extremity. The water should be at a temperature of about 34°C to 37°C. The extremity is placed in the water until it warms and a red flush of circulation returns. This process can be very painful. Blisters may form and the foot will have to be protected from further trauma.

Most of the time (every trekker case that I have been involved with), the frostbite is not noticed until the person reaches their next destination and the foot has already rewarmed during the descent. The person takes off their shoes and notices that blisters have formed. If a disaster has occurred, such as getting lost on a pass and spending one or two nights out, the toes may appear blackened and shrivelled, without the formation of blisters. This is a sign of freezing and thawing and refreezing and means that deeper damage has taken place.

There is no accepted treatment for frostbite. Drugs to reduce inflammation or restore circulation might be useful in limiting the damage after freezing has occurred, but the main aspect of treatment is to prevent further trauma and to prevent infection. It is not necessary to start taking antibiotics. If there are blisters or open skin, the afflicted area should be washed in a sterile fashion and a sterile dressing applied. If there are only deep blisters, with hard skin over them, or blackened skin, dressings may not be necessary. Walking should be abandoned or kept to a minimum. Evacuation by horse, yak or helicopter may be necessary, depending on the degree of injury.

There are only a handful of people who get frostbite injuries each year, but like altitude sickness, these injuries are all preventable. Even relatively minor frostbite ends the trip and forces a return to your home country, since healing can take several months. If you are going above 4000 metres, be prepared for walking in snow.

Fever

Fever means an elevation in body temperature above normal, which is usually 37°C. Fever almost always means that you have acquired some kind of infectious disease. By itself, it does not tell you the cause, but by evaluating the associated symptoms and the travel history, it's often possible to make a good guess, even while trekking in a remote area. Some febrile illnesses go away without treatment (the flu), while others will require treatment (typhoid fever). The purpose of trying to guess the cause of a fever is to determine whether specific treatment will be of benefit and whether the trek should be abandoned.

If specific symptoms are associated with a fever, the cause can usually be determined. If you have the onset of severe diarrhoea and fever, a bacterial dysentery can be suspected. If there is a thick or colourful nasal discharge, sinus pain and a fever, sinusitis may be present. Fever with a severe cough may be bronchitis or pneumonia. A large abscess in the skin can cause a fever.

Sometimes a fever occurs with only a vague feeling of being unwell, such as headache, fatigue, loss of appetite or nausea. In the first few days of such an illness it is difficult to determine the cause of the fever. We have found, however, that there are five main diseases which account for almost all the presentations of fever and headache and malaise in Nepal. By taking a careful history and noticing key aspects of the fever and headache, a presumptive diagnosis can often be made. The five diseases are:

Viral Syndromes The circumstances of travel mean exposure to many more viruses than one would encounter at home. The influenza viruses and others can be passed through respiratory droplets, which means they can be inhaled in aeroplanes, buses and crowded restaurants. The disease usually has an abrupt onset of fever, often very high (40°C) on the first day. Headache is often present and is typically very motion sensitive, which means it hurts to turn the head suddenly or to step down hard. The illness usually lasts two to four days and goes away without specific treatment. It usually ends abruptly, the fever and headache staying about the same for the duration of the illness. The key hints that you may have a virus are the abrupt onset, the characteristic motion-sensitive headache and the fact that it goes away just about the time that you are getting worried that it might not.

Enteric Fever Enteric fever is an infection with one of two specific bacteria, salmonella typhi (typhoid fever) or salmonella paratyphi (paratyphoid fever). The two illnesses are identical, which is why it is convenient to refer to them as enteric fever. The bacteria are passed in the stools of infected people. Nepal has a very high rate of enteric fever in the local population. The same precautions taken to prevent diarrhoea will help to prevent enteric fever. A vaccine to help prevent the disease was shown to be 90% effective in preventing both types of enteric fever in travellers in Nepal, according to a study in the CIWEC Clinic.

The illness starts with the gradual onset of fever and headache and fatigue. On the first few days the fever is often low, and it is hard to tell if you are really getting sick or not. After three or four days, the fever rises to 40°C or more, and fatigue begins to be profound, although some people have milder cases. The headache is typically dull and not motion sensitive. Loss of appetite, nausea and even vomiting can develop. Thinking can become slightly cloudy, which is typical of this illness. Overall, after four or five days, the patient feels very weak, moves slowly and doesn't want to eat. The disease can be distinguished from the viral illnesses by its gradual onset, the dull character of the headache and the fact that the person is getting

worse at a time when the viral patient should be getting better.

Enteric fever is one of the treatable causes of prolonged fever. If suspected, treatment should be started on trek, since the person will remain sick for up to a month without treatment, and complications can result. The treatment of choice for adults is 500 mg of ciprofloxacin every 12 hours for 10 days. Other treatments that might be encountered include chloramphenicol, 500 mg, four times a day for 10 days, although this potentially has more side effects. Trimethoprim-sulfamethoxasole (Bactrim) can be effective, but was erratic when we used it in the CIWEC Clinic.

In children under 18, the drug of choice is high doses of amoxicillin, 50 mg per kg per day in three divided doses. For a 40 kg child, this would be 50 x 40 = 2000 mg per day divided by three, or 667 mg every 8 hours. This can be safely rounded down to 500 mg every 8 hours.

The response to treatment is slow but steady, with the fever persisting for another two to five days. You can tell that the treatment is working because the patient starts to feel better and the height of the fever is a little bit lower each day until it is gone. The infected person is only contagious through his or her faeces, and does not need to be isolated from the group. Since the disease produces such profound fatigue and malaise, the person almost always has to abandon their trek.

Hepatitis

Hepatitis A is a viral infection of the liver which is acquired by eating something contaminated with faeces from an infected person. There are three main viruses which can cause hepatitis in Nepal: hepatitis A, hepatitis B and enterically transmitted nonA-nonB (ETNANB). In a CIWEC Clinic study, all the cases of hepatitis in tourists were due to hepatitis A. Hepatitis A can be almost completely prevented by taking immune serum globulin (gamma globulin) every four months while travelling (see the Immunisations & Prophylaxis section). If you have taken gamma globulin appropriately and you become sick with a fever and headache and nausea, you can practically rule out hepatitis as the cause.

The incubation period of hepatitis is usually four weeks. Shorter periods have occurred, but they are unusual. So if you have just come to Nepal within the past two weeks, you can't have hepatitis. If you have travelled for a few months and have not taken gamma globulin, then you could have hepatitis A. Hepatitis A presents with the relatively gradual onset of fever, headache, nausea and loss of appetite. The nausea and loss of appetite are often more pronounced than in the other illnesses. The headache is slightly motion sensitive, but is usually dull. These symptoms go on for four or five days. At that point the urine turns a dark tea colour and the whites of the eyes appear yellow (this colour change is called jaundice). The fever ends at this point; nausea, fatigue and loss of appetite are now the main symptoms and can go on for from two weeks to a month. There is no specific treatment to shorten the illness. The trek is finished at this point (and usually the whole vacation). The person should be encouraged to drink (but not alcohol) to prevent dehydration and to eat whatever he or she can stomach to avoid profound weight loss. The bright side is that a bout of hepatitis A confers life-long immunity to the disease.

The main clues to hepatitis A infection are at least a month of travel in Asia, no history of taking gamma globulin, the relatively gradual onset of fever and nausea and loss of appetite, and the abrupt end of fever when the jaundice becomes apparent.

Malaria

Malaria is a protozoan parasite which is transmitted between humans by a certain species of mosquito. There are four types of malaria, but two types, falciparum malaria and vivax malaria, account for 90% of all cases worldwide. In the Asian subcontinent, vivax malaria is the most common. Falciparum malaria is the only type which has become resistant to choloroquine and other drugs. Malaria can be prevented in

most cases by taking certain prophylactic drugs (see the Immunisations & Prophylaxis section).

Malaria presents with fever and headache, along with muscle aches and a feeling of having the chills. The symptoms last for one or two days and then go away, at which point you may feel quite well. Then after one or two days, the symptoms return. However, sometimes malaria presents as a steady fever lasting several days without a break. The first thing to do when trying to decide if someone has malaria is to take a careful travel history. If the person has not been in a malaria area, malaria is thereby ruled out. The incubation period is usually a minimum of two weeks, but it can stretch to several months or a year or more in the case of vivax malaria, so you should extend your questions to cover some time period past (the person may have visited Africa a year before).

If the person has been travelling in northern India, and has not taken malaria prophylaxis, then they are a candidate for malaria, and it is almost always vivax malaria. The southern portion of Nepal (the Terai) has malaria, but it is very rare for travellers to get infected there. Overall, there are only about half a dozen cases of malaria diagnosed in travellers in Nepal each year. Travellers from remote sections of Indonesia, Malaysia and Thailand are at theoretical risk of malaria, including falciparum, but in practice, cases from these areas are almost never seen in Nepal.

If a person has a fever for two days, then no fever for a day and then fever again, malaria is suspected and presumptive therapy can be tried. However, vivax malaria is not associated with severe illness or death, in contrast to falciparum malaria, and the need to treat immediately is lessened. We have seen only one case of falciparum malaria in a traveller in Nepal in the past seven years.

The treatment of vivax malaria is chloroquine phosphate or chloroquine sulphate: 1000 mg to begin, then 500 mg 6 hours later, 500 mg 24 hours later and another 500 mg 48 hours later. Improvement is almost immediate and the trek could be continued if the fever goes away and stays away. If you presume that a fever is malarial and treat it with chloroquine, and it seems to work, you should have a follow-up treatment when you reach medical care. A two-week course of the drug primaquine is recommended to rid the liver completely of the vivax parasites.

The clues to a malaria infection are travel in an endemic area without taking prophylaxis (or in a falciparum area that might be resistant), fever and headache and chills that go away for a day or so, leaving the person feeling remarkably well between episodes, and then a return of the symptoms. Steady fever can be a presentation, and a blood test might eventually be necessary to make the diagnosis. If you are ill in an area where a blood test is available, by all means have the test before starting self-treatment.

Dengue Fever

Dengue fever is caused by a virus carried by a mosquito which tends to favour urban environments. It is endemic in northern India, particularly the Delhi-Agra-Jaipur triangle, and also in Thailand. Autumn seems to be the time of highest risk. The disease is not present in Nepal; all the cases that we see there are imported from India or Thailand.

The disease has a very predictable incubation period, from five to 10 days. Thus, if the person has not been in an endemic area within the past 10 days, the disease is not possible. Exposure to the virus while in transit in Delhi or Bangkok, however, can put you at risk to the disease.

There is a very typical presentation which can allow the diagnosis to be made presumptively in most cases. The onset is very abrupt, with high fever on the first day. Headache is almost always present, centred mainly behind the eyes, with movement of the eyes exacerbating the pain. Muscle aches and backaches are more prominent than in the other diseases discussed here. The nickname for the disease is 'breakbone fever'. Nausea and vomiting can be present. A characteristic rash is almost always present, but this is not

seen unless looked for. The rash is a continuous faint reddening of the skin on the trunk, which resembles a light sunburn. If you press your hand flat against the patient's stomach or back for a few seconds, and then remove it, the skin will lose colour from the pressure, and preserve the imprint of the hand for a few seconds. This blanching effect lasts only half a second or so on normal skin.

There is no treatment for the disease, but a diagnosis will forestall the start of treatment for some other disease and help you not to panic. The fever lasts from three to six days, then goes away suddenly, along with all the other symptoms. The person feels weak for an additional one to two weeks, but some people recover quite quickly.

The clues to dengue infection are travel within the past five to 10 days in an endemic area, the abrupt onset of symptoms including a headache behind the eyes, a lot of muscle aching, and the characteristic rash.

Sexually Transmitted Diseases

These diseases are spread by sexual contact with an infected partner. As at home, abstinence is the only 100% preventative, though using condoms is also effective. When travelling, people may be more likely to have sex with a new partner, so the need for safe sex should be remembered. Either a local person or another traveller could be a source of sexually transmitted disease, including AIDS.

I have treated many male travellers for gonorrhoea or chlamydia urethritis following sexual contact with prostitutes in Asia. I have also seen women who contracted genital herpes from casual relationships with male travellers. The prospect of acquiring AIDS from this source is a very real concern. If you have sexual intercourse with a new partner, always use a condom.

AIDS Apart from sexual transmission, AIDS can be be spread by infected needles and by blood transfusions. Try to insist on brand-new needles and syringes for injections. These can be purchased from local pharmacies. Screening of blood supplies for the

AIDS virus is being introduced in many Asian countries, but can't always be done in an emergency. Try to avoid blood transfusion unless it is absolutely necessary. If transfusion is essential, you may be able to arrange for a friend, or another person you know, of the same blood group to donate blood for you.

Other Illness
Even when things are going well, travel is stressful. Stress can make your body more susceptible to illness, particularly the new strains of viruses that you will be encountering for the first time. The crossing of time zones; all-night train, plane and bus rides; tropical heat and Himalayan cold; noise and dust; and culture shock – these all combine occasionally to bring the most hardened traveller to his or her knees. Most illnesses acquired in this manner are short-lived and minor, and in the course of a long trip are barely remembered, although they seem devastating while they are happening. On shorter trips they can interfere with tight schedules, but other than being aware of stress and taking what steps you can to reduce it, there is little you can do to prevent occasional illness while travelling.

Colds Upper respiratory infections caused by viruses account for 20% of the visits to the CIWEC Clinic, second only to diarrhoea (at 30%). Colds often make people feel miserable, leading to postponements of treks and bus rides. Symptomatic relief is all that is available in the first few days of a cold. In Nepal, many colds go on to cause either acute ear infections, sinusitis or bronchitis, which require antibiotic treatment. If your cold is getting worse instead of better after a week, see a doctor or consider taking antibiotics if you are on trek (see first-aid kit list of medications).

Skin Diseases Skin problems are also very common in travellers. A diffuse rash, covering most of the body, may be due to a drug allergy, since travellers are often taking new medications for the first time, including anti-

malarials. A round red patch (lesion), clearing in the centre and advancing at its edges is usually a fungus and can be treated with an antifungal cream. These lesions can also occur in the groin and in the armpits. Painful red swellings, which may burst to reveal pus, are due to staphyloccal skin infections, and antibiotics are necessary. This type of skin infection can move from one spot to another over several weeks if not treated. Small very itchy red spots, usually seen in clusters or in small straight lines suggest an infestation with a tiny skin mite, causing a disease called scabies. This is relatively common in travellers and is treated by a skin cream rubbed onto the whole body and left on for one day.

WOMEN'S HEALTH
Gynaecological Problems
It is not clear whether or not travel in Asia increases the risk of contracting vaginitis. It can, however, be most uncomfortable, and even frightening, if you have not had it before, or you are not carrying any treatment for it. Yeast vaginitis is by far the most common, and can be triggered by the use of oral antibiotics. The symptoms are vaginal itching, which progresses to burning and more severe discomfort. There is often increased vaginal discharge. A number of non-medical douches and other treatments can work, but the definitive treatment is with an antifungal tablet, such as Micostatin, inserted morning and night for seven days. If the symptoms don't clear up promptly, you may have another vaginal infection, and you should try to see a doctor if you can.

Some women find that their periods stop, or become irregular, when they travel. It is not known why travel interferes with the menstrual cycle, but it does appear to be any cause for concern.

Pregnancy
The decision to trek in Nepal while pregnant should not be taken lightly. Little is known about the effects of of altitude on a developing fetus, but almost all authorities recommend against travelling above 3650 metres while pregnant. There is also the risk

of getting ill and not being able to take medication which would relieve the symptoms or the illness itself. Though there is no evidence that travel increases the risk of miscarriage, it should be noted that one in five pregnancies ends in miscarriage in any case. This can be accompanied by heavy bleeding or other complications which might require emergency treatment.

Even normal pregnancies can make a woman feel nauseated and tired for the first three months. She may have food repulsions and cravings which can't be satisfied by dhal bhat in Nepal. In the second three months, general feelings improve but fatigue can still be a constant factor. In the final three months the size of the baby can make it uncomfortable to move around, and there is the danger of complications following what would otherwise be a minor accident.

Most vaccinations can be given safely during pregnancy, but there are some whose effects on pregnant women, or their unborn babies, are not known. Chloroquine can be taken safely during pregnancy, but mefloquine definitely cannot.

USE OF MEDICATION

All medications are potentially harmful and ideally should be used only after consultation with a doctor. If, because of an urgent problem in an isolated area, you have to use any of the medications listed here without medical advice. You should be aware of the general precautions for using medications, the specific information given here for each type of medication, and the instructions given by the manufacturer.

This section includes information on some medications not listed in the first-aid kit. The chances of needing these on a trek are very small, but they may be needed by travellers who spend several months in Asia before or after their trek.

Some medications have rare but serious side effects (eg penicillin), while others have very common but not serious side effects (eg Tiniba). Every decision to use a medication must weigh the risk versus the benefit. The medications listed here are generally safe to

use, if the patient has no history of allergies to the drug. If you have a history of drug allergy, you must adjust the list so that it will be of use to yourself in the field.

In general, there are two types of medicines: symptomatic medicines relieve the ill effects of a disease without treating the cause; therapeutic medicines treat the underlying cause and so relieve the symptoms. Symptomatic drugs can be used as needed. Therapeutic drugs should be given as a course. The following list states which kind a medicine is, the usual doses and the potential side effects.

Drug nomenclature can be confusing. Some drugs are best known by their proprietary brand name; others by their generic name. I have chosen to use the generic name most of the time except for a few combination drugs that are best known by their brand names. The ingredients of these drugs are given in parenthesis.

There are still only a few small children who go trekking with their parents. If you are trekking with children, it is best to check with a doctor concerning the liquid preparations and dosages which you should include in your first-aid kit.

Acetamenophen

(Symptomatic) For relief of mild pain and to help reduce a fever.
Side Effects: None
Dose: Two tablets every 4 hours as needed.

Acetamenophen 325 mg with Codeine 30 mg

(Symptomatic) Combines the pain-relieving and fever-reducing effect of acetamenophen with the narcotic codeine. Used for the relief of severe pain. Codeine is also an effective cough suppressant. Codeine tablets can also be taken alone if the combination drug is not available.
Side Effects: Nausea, vomiting, stomach pain, rash, sedation, constipation.
Dose: Two every 4 hours as needed.

Acetazolamide (Diamox)

(Therapeutic) A mild diuretic that acidifies

the blood, stimulating respiration at high altitude. For the treatment of mild symptoms of acute mountain sickness. *Not to be taken by people allergic to sulfa drugs.*

Side Effects: Tingling of fingers and toes. This is common and does not mean you should stop taking the medicine.

Dose: 125 to 250 mg every 12 hours.

Actifed (Triprolidine HCL with Pseudoephedrine HCL)

(Symptomatic) A decongestant for the relief of discomfort due to colds, sinus infection or internal ear infection.

Side Effects: Jitteriness, sedation.

Dose: One tablet every 8 hours as needed.

Adrenaline (Epinephrine)

(Symptomatic & Therapeutic) Injectable For the treatment of severe or life-threatening allergic reactions.

Side Effects: Tachycardia, nervousness.

Dose: Adults – 0.5 cc injected subcutaneously and may be repeated in 1 hour if needed. Children – 0.01 cc per kg of body weight; not to exceed adult dose.

Amoxicillin

(Therapeutic) Antibiotic for treatment of suspected internal ear infections, sinusitis, bronchitis, pneumonia, urinary tract infection. It is related to penicillin and *must not be given to people allergic to penicillin.*

Side Effects: Rash, diarrhoea.

Dose: 250 mg every 8 hours. For severe infection 500 mg every 8 hours. Usual course is seven to 10 days.

Antacid Tablets

(Symptomatic & Therapeutic) For the treatment of burning stomach pain due to gastritis or suspected ulcer.

Side Effects: Essentially none.

Dose: Two or three tablets every hour as needed.

Bisacodyl (Dulcolax)

(Therapeutic) A relatively strong laxative for the relief of constipation.

Side Effects: Abdominal cramps, diarrhoea.

Dose: One or two at night and 12 hours later if no relief.

Cephalexin

(Therapeutic) An antibiotic particularly effective against staphylococcal skin infections which can be resistant to other drugs. A relative of penicillin and must *not* be given to people allergic to penicillin. Can also be used to treat ear infections, sinusitis, bronchitis or urinary tract infection.

Side Effects: Severe allergic reactions and rash are both rare.

Dose: 250 mg every 6 hours for seven to 10 days; 500 mg every 6 hours for severe infections.

Ciprofloxacin

(Therapeutic) A potent antibiotic for the treatment of bacterial diarrhoea or enteric (typhoid) fever. Also good for treating urinary tract infections. It is not very good respiratory and skin infections, although it is promoted for these problems.

Side Effects: Nausea, vomiting.

Dose: 500 mg every 12 hours: three days for diarrhoea, seven days for urinary tract infections, 10 days for enteric (typhoid) fever.

Clotrimazole Cream

(Therapeutic) An antifungal skin preparation for suspected fungal infections. Fungal infections are most common in the groin and armpit, but can occur as isolated lesions anywhere.

Side Effects: Possible local allergic reaction.

Dose: Apply to rash three to four times per day until rash is gone.

Dexamethasone (Decadron)

(Symptomatic) For treatment of severe acute mountain sickness, particularly high altitude cerebral edema. Can buy time if descent is not immediately possible. Should not be taken to aid further ascent. See discussion on mountain sickness in this chapter before using this medicine.

Side Effects: Euphoria, depression on withdrawal.

Dose: Four mg every 6 hours.

Diphenhydramine

(Symptomatic) For the relief of severe itching due to allergic reactions. Can also be used as a mild sedative for sleeping.
Side Effects: Sedation.
Dose: 50 mg every 6 hours as needed.

Erythromycin

(Therapeutic) An antibiotic for the treatment of skin infections, bronchitis, suspected strep throat. An alternative to cephalexin for persons allergic to penicillin.
Side Effects: Abdominal pain, nausea, rash.
Dose: 250 mg every 6 hours for seven to 10 days.

Hydrocortisone 1% Cream

(Symptomatic) A steroid skin cream for the relief of itching insect bites or other rashes.
Side Effects: Essentially none unless used for more than a month.
Dose: Apply to lesions as needed.

Oral Rehydration Solution (Jeevan Jal in Nepal)

(Symptomatic & Therapeutic) A balanced electrolyte powder for mixing with boiled water to replace salts and fluid lost through vomiting and/or diarrhoea.
Side Effects: None.
Dose: Should be encouraged in anyone suspected of becoming dehydrated.

Lomotil (Diphenoxylate HCL with Atropine Sulfate)

(Symptomatic) A medication derived from a narcotic which paralyses the bowel for the symptomatic relief of diarrhoea. Should not be used casually. Imodium (loperamide) is used in exactly the same dosage.
Side Effects: Constipation
Dose: Two to start, then one after each loose stool until relief, then one every 4 to 6 hours to maintain. Do not exceed eight in 24 hours.
NB: Paralysing the bowel may allow infections to get worse and prolong the illness. Do not use if the patient has fever or bloody stools.

Meperidine

(Symptomatic) Injectable. A potent narcotic pain reliever for the relief of severe pain.
Side Effects: Respiratory depression, nausea and vomiting, rash, dizziness, sedation.
Dose: Five to 75 mg intramuscularly every 3 to 4 hours as needed.

Mycostatin Vaginal Tablets (Miconazole)

(Therapeutic) For treatment of yeast vaginitis. The condition can develop quite suddenly and is quite uncomfortable, but easily treated. Yeast infections can follow the use of some antibiotics.
Side Effects: Essentially none.
Dose: One in the morning and one at night for seven days.

Nifedipine

(Therapeutic) For treatment of high altitude pulmonary edema. Works specifically on the lungs and is not useful for other forms of altitude sickness. Can also be used in the early days after frostbite has occurred. Works very well to improve circulation in people suffering from Raynaud's phenomenon.
Side Effects: Dizziness, flushing, headache.
Dose: 10 mg every 8 hours.

Norfloxacin

(Therapeutic) A very good drug for treating bacterial diarrhoea. Also very good for urinary tract infections. Should not be used to treat enteric (typhoid) fever.
Side Effects: Nausea, vomiting.
Dose: 400 mg every 12 hours for three days for diarrhoea; 400mg every 12 hours for urinary tract infections.

Promethazine Suppositories

(Symptomatic) An antinausea medication for the symptomatic relief of nausea and vomiting to help prevent dehydration. Suppositories are inserted rectally and are useful when vomiting prevents the taking of oral medication.
Side Effects: Sedation.
Dose: One in rectum every 8 hours as needed.

Promethazine (Injectable)

(Symptomatic) Injectable medication to relieve vomiting. Like a suppository, it can be given when vomiting prevents the taking of oral medication.

Dose: 25 to 50 mg intramuscularly every 6 hours as needed.

Sulamyd 10% Eye Drops

(Therapeutic) An antibiotic solution for the treatment of bacterial conjunctivitis (eye infections).

Side Effects: Possibly local allergy.

Dose: One to two drops every 3 hours for three to five days.

Throat Lozenges (Strepsils in Nepal)

(Symptomatic) Soluble lozenges for soothing inflamed throats.

Side Effects: None.

Dose: Suck one slowly every half-hour as needed.

Tinidazole (Tiniba in Nepal)

(Therapeutic) An antibiotic for the treatment of the intestinal parasites, giardia and amoeba.

Side Effects: Predictable nausea, headache, metallic taste on tongue, weakness. Must *not* be taken with alcohol.

Dose: Two grams once only for the treatment of giardia; two grams each day all at once for three days for the treatment of amoebiasis.

TREATING NEPALESE IN THE HILLS

Almost every trekker will encounter a situation where he or she is asked to give medical treatment to a sick Nepalese. The potential patient may just have a headache or may be covered with severe burns from which he or she will most likely die. The moral dilemma that the trekker is occasionally faced with can remain with the person long after the trek. There is no simple answer, but I will offer some guidelines to help you think about the problem before you encounter it.

The Nepalese government is attempting to establish and maintain health posts in remote areas. So far, this has not brought medical care to the majority of the people. The local people often have their own healers, beliefs and practices regarding health. Either when these prove ineffective or out of growing curiosity, the local people may consult passing trekkers, whether they are doctors or not. In many areas there is no understanding at all of the basis of Western medical practice. Ideas that we take for granted, such as the relationship of germs to infection, have no meaning to these villagers. A pill can be seen as a form of magic – the shape, size and colour often having more meaning than an attempted explanation that the medicine will kill the germs.

Thus, some of the medical interactions are based on the desire of villagers to get closer to a form of Western magic. This has created a form of medical begging, whereby it is not clear whether the person is indeed ill at the time of the encounter. It is fair and advisable under these circumstances to say that you have no medicine. Otherwise the pills are indiscriminately given out at later times, possibly doing someone some harm.

The Nepalese who is clearly suffering from a problem presents another level of dilemma. If you can clearly recognise the problem and know that your treatment will be effective, and have a way of explaining this to the people involved, there is no reason to withhold this treatment from someone who can clearly benefit. If you do not know what is going on, or are not sure of the right treatment, you may do more harm than good. Also, the treatment failure may lead the villagers away from seeking appropriate Western medical care at a health post in the future.

The fact that you are trekking through at that moment does not mean that you suddenly have to take on the continuing insoluble problems of remote village life. The feelings of compassion and wanting to help are natural, but if you see that you truly can't offer anything that is likely to improve the situation, don't feel obligated to 'do something'. The fact that there are large populations in the world that can't call an ambulance and be rushed to a hospital with a serious illness is a reality that catches the

Western trekker emotionally unprepared. The discovery of these feelings and the processing of your reactions are part of the reason for trekking.

In summary, the problem remains a difficult one. Try to be aware of, and refer to, local health posts whenever possible (the Kunde Hospital in the Khumbu is a good example). If this is not possible, determine whether you can definitively help someone and then do so if your resources allow. If you are not sure what to do, express your concern but admit that you don't have anything to offer. The Nepalese can usually accept this gracefully.

RESCUE

If you walk from Kathmandu into the mountains for two weeks, you are two weeks walk from Kathmandu. This fact often does not impress itself on trekkers until they become sick or injured on the trail and the desire to return to Kathmandu arises. Radios are few and far between in Nepal, and roads are just beginning to be extended into the hills. The Himalayan Rescue Association provides medical clinics and doctors in Pheriche near Mt Everest, and in Manang on the Annapurna circuit, and there are a few other health posts. But in general, once you head into the hills, it will be up to you to get yourself out. Here are some hints to accomplish this.

Firstly, don't panic. If someone falls, take some time to assess the situation. Suspected broken bones may only be bruises and a dazed person may wake up and be quite all right in an hour or two. If the problem is severe diarrhoea, try to follow the guidelines in the Diarrhoea section. If it is severe mountain sickness, descend with the victim; do not wait for help. If the illness is severe, but not diagnosable, evaluate your options. In most areas of Nepal, some type of animal will be available to help transport a sick or injured trekker. In the west of Nepal, ponies are common; in the mountains, yaks are usually available. As extraordinary as it may seem, many Nepalese are both willing and capable of carrying Westerners on their backs for

long distances. An Australian woman who broke her leg by slipping on ice on Poon Hill above Ghorapani was carried for three days by a series of porters and later became tearful as she recalled how kind and thoughtful they had been, demonstrating concern for her comfort while they were struggling under a 60 kg load.

Sometimes either the seriousness of the injuries or the urgency of getting care will make land evacuation impractical. The next best option is to try to get to one of the STOL airfields that have regular flights by either Twin Otter or Pilatus Porter aircraft. By negotiation, space can usually be found for a seriously injured or ill trekker, or a charter flight might be arranged, but the airport officials are quite unsympathetic to trekkers who are merely demoralised by the unexpected hardships of trail life and hope to jump the queue to get out sooner. If there is no nearby airfield, or if you know the flights are only once a week and just went yesterday, then the only alternative is to request a helicopter rescue flight. Before using this option, be aware of the following facts that govern rescue flights in Nepal.

The helicopters used for rescue are operated through the VIP section at Tribuvan Airport (tel 414670). When these helicopters are not available, the Royal Nepal Army will supply them. There are six small Alouette choppers and three large Pumas. The Alouettes are used for most rescues and cost the victim US$600 per hour of flight time. A typical rescue flight will cost between US$1500 and US$2000. Once a request is sent, and a helicopter actually leaves Kathmandu, you must pay for it, whether or not you still need or want rescue or the helicopter is unable to find you.

The helicopter will not leave Kathmandu until someone in Kathmandu has paid cash in advance for the flight. In practice, this is usually a trekking agency, if the victim has been trekking with an agency, or the victim's embassy. Depending on the rules of the embassy, sometimes the victim's parents or family must be contacted in their home country to guarantee payment before the embassy will front the money. Registering with your embassy on arrival in Kathmandu can greatly expedite the rescue process.

Arranging a rescue usually takes one day, although if the weather permits, helicopters can sometimes leave the same day the message is received. Most of the time, if the message arrives in Kathmandu in the afternoon, the helicopter will leave early the next morning. Given that it usually takes at least a day to have someone hike to a radio post or send a message out of an airstrip, it can take one or two days for a helicopter to arrive once a decision has been made that it is necessary. Rarely, a helicopter will not be available at all due to mechanical troubles or prior commitments or because the message cannot be passed due to a religious festival.

Flying on rescue flights has made me familiar with some of the difficulties involved. One of the most important pitfalls is the rescue request itself. Give details! Try to assess the patient's condition and detail the degree of urgency. If he/she has frostbite injuries and can't walk, but is otherwise stable, say this. If he/she is unconscious and has an apparent broken hip, send this in the message. On the basis of your rescue request alone, the pilots and the doctors involved will have to decide whether to take a chance and fly through bad weather or wait for the usually better weather in the morning. The army pilots do not receive extra pay for rescue flights and are often forced to take unusual chances while trying to perform rescues. Don't risk other lives needlessly with unnecessary flights or inadequate information.

Place names in Nepal are often confusing and rescue requests sometimes mistakenly give the name of a district rather than a village, forcing rescuers to comb large tracts in sometimes unsuccessful efforts to find someone. Once a request is sent, stay put for at least two days or make it clear in the message where and how you will be travelling. If you see the helicopter, make elaborate efforts to signal it. It is very difficult to pick out people on the ground from a helicopter moving at 140 km an hour when you are unsure where to look. Try to locate a field large enough to land a helicopter safely, but do not mark the centre of the field with cloth, as this can fly up and wreck the rotors on landing. If you are a trekker who has not sent for a helicopter, do not wave at a low-flying helicopter! We have made a number of unnecessary and occasionally dangerous landings only to find that the people had nothing to do with a victim and were just waving.

When I was working at the Pheriche aid post near Mt Everest, the sight of a rescue helicopter in a desperate situation was the sweetest thing I can ever remember seeing. If you are ever rescued in Nepal, make a point of thanking the pilots and doctors who are often risking their lives to help you out of a tight spot. If there are alternatives for getting out of that tight spot, don't ask others to risk their lives for you. In the past few years there has been a disturbing trend of trying to charter helicopters out of the mountains because the trekker has become tired or simply finds that he or she doesn't like trekking. Don't contribute to this unfortunate practice, which sometimes makes helicopters unavailable for real rescues.

The helicopters cannot land above 5500 metres. There is currently no way to expect to be rescued from trekking or mountaineering peaks.

Getting There

AIR

To/From Asia

The most reasonable connections to Kathmandu are via Bangkok, Hong Kong and Singapore. There are reduced inclusive tour (IT) fares on all these sectors. Bangkok flights are heavily booked in October, November, April and early May, but it's sometimes worth hanging around the airport looking for a standby seat to Kathmandu.

From India the fares are high, flights are fully booked and reservation procedures are chaotic. The only concessional fares are for students. There are flights to Kathmandu from Delhi, Calcutta, Patna and Varanasi.

Kathmandu has some other interesting airline connections. China Southwest Airlines, part of the Civil Aviation Administration of China (CAAC) group, operates a flight from Lhasa to Kathmandu on Saturdays. This spectacular 1 hour flight costs US$190 and is supposed to operate from April to December. You can also fly from Paro in Bhutan on Druk Air, or from Yangon (formerly Rangoon, Burma) and Dhaka (Bangladesh).

To/From Europe & the Middle East

Royal Nepal Airlines Corporation (RNAC) operates two flights per week to London via Dubai. Contact its agent in London for cheap excursion fares. RNAC's London flight operates through Frankfurt, and both RNAC and Lufthansa have direct Frankfurt-Kathmandu flights. German bucket shops can produce special deals on these. Pakistan International and Bangladesh Biman both have a one airline service from Europe to Kathmandu, though both require a connection in either Dhaka or Karachi. Also try charter companies; Condor operates a weekly flight from Munich to Kathmandu during winter.

To/From North America

North America is halfway around the world from Nepal, so you have a choice of crossing either the Atlantic or Pacific oceans. If you are flying via the Atlantic, you will probably be happier connecting to a direct flight to Kathmandu from London or Frankfurt. Avoid flights via India as the Delhi to Kathmandu fare is high and transit facilities at Delhi Airport are tedious. Pacific routeings usually require an overnight stay in Bangkok or Hong Kong, but there are frequent flights and most airlines have APEX fares of about US$600 one way from the West Coast to Kathmandu.

To/From Australia

Look for routeings via Singapore, Hong Kong or Bangkok. Kathmandu is not on any airline routeings for 'round the world' (RTW) tickets, and is usually charged as an extra segment on an Australia to London routeing. If you are travelling to the UK, you might find a cheap fare on RNAC from either Bangkok or Singapore, via Kathmandu, to London.

ORGANISED TREKS

If you arrange a trek through an overseas trekking company, they should be able to either recommend a group flight or arrange air transportation, hopefully at a reasonable rate, on space that it has prebooked. In October, early November and late December these may be the only seats available to Nepal.

Trekking Agents

I have used the term 'trekking agent' to describe the company, travel agent or individual that is organising the trek. If you are trekking on your own, you are the trekking agent. If you are arranging the trip yourself, you can skip many advance preparations because you can only deal with them after you arrive in Kathmandu.

If you are trekking through a trekking

agent, be aware that various organisers of treks provide different equipment and facilities. Be sure to read the material provided by your trekking agent. They may provide some of the equipment or services that I have suggested you arrange yourself. Similarly, be sure that they do not expect you to bring something that I have not suggested.

It becomes difficult to prepare an up-to-date list of all trekking agents throughout the world because new agents spring up (and disappear) every season. The following list includes a number of established agents who have specialised in Nepalese trekking for many years. It makes no pretence of being a complete list of every trekking agent in the world.

The huge number of agents now selling trekking trips makes it difficult to make any judgement about the quality of service you may expect. From each agent you should be able to get any additional information you need about Nepal and trekking; most have staff who have trekked in Nepal. All these agents offer a variety of treks and several choices of dates. Most of them can also arrange your plane tickets to and from Nepal if you wish. Most will also allow you to book your trek and flights through your own travel agent.

Australia & New Zealand

Ausventure
        Suite 1, 860 Military Rd, Mosman, NSW 2088, (fax (02) 9691463)
Peregrine Adventures
        258 Lonsdale St, Melbourne, Vic 3000, (fax (03) 6638618)
Venture Treks
        71 Evwlyn Rd, Howick, Auckland, New Zealand, (tel (9) 799855)
World Expeditions
        3rd floor, 441 Kent St, Sydney, NSW 2000, (tel 2643366, fax (02) 2611974)

USA & Canada

Adventure Centre
        1311 63rd St, Suite 200, Emeryville, California 94608, (fax (415) 6544200)
Himalayan Travel
        PO Box 481, Greenwich, Connecticut 06830, (fax (203) 6220084)

Inner Asia
        2627 Lombard St, San Francisco, California 94123, (fax (415) 3465535)
Journeys International
        4011 Jackson Rd, Ann Arbor, Michigan 48103, (fax (313) 6652945)
Mountain Travel
        6420 Fairmount Ave, El Cerrito, California 94530, (fax (415) 5257710)
Mountain Travel Canada
        101-511 West 14th Avenue, Vancouver, BC V5Z 1P5, (fax (604) 8764354)
Nature Expeditions International
        PO Box 11496, Eugene, Oregon 97440, (fax (503) 3453286)
Sobek Expeditions
        PO Box 1089, Angels Camp, California 95222, (fax (209) 7362646)
Wilderness Travel
        801 Allston Way, Berkeley, California 94710, (fax (415) 5480347)

UK

Exodus Expeditions
        All Saints Passage, 100 Wandsworth High St, London SW18 4LE
ExplorAsia
        Blenheim House, Burnsall St, London SW3 5XS
Explore Worldwide
        1 Frederick St, Aldershot, Hants GU11 1LQ, (fax (0252) 343170)
Sherpa Expeditions
        131A Heston Rd, Hounslow, Middlesex, TW5 0RD, (fax (081) 5729788)
WEXAS International
        45 Brompton Rd, Knightsbridge, London SW3 1DE, (fax (071) 5898418)

France

Delta Voyages
        54 Rue des Ecoles, 75005 Paris
Explorator
        16 Place de la Madeleine, 75008 Paris, (fax 42-66-53-89)
Nouvelles Frontières
        37 Rue Violet, 75015 Paris

Germany

Dav Berg-und-Skischule
        Furstenfelderstrasse 7, D 8000 München 2
Hauser Exkursionen
        Neuhauserstrasse 1, 8000 München 2
Sporthaus Schuster
        Rosenstrasse, 8000 München 2

Top: Annapurna South - 7273 metres (SB)
Bottom: The final climb from Muktinath to Thorung Pass (SA)

Top: Phewa Tal, near Pokhara (TW)
Bottom: Chhetri homes near Pokhara (KS)

Other European Countries

Arca Tour
Bahnhofstrasse 23, CH-6300 Zug, Switzerland, (fax (042) 223406)

ARTOU
8 Rue de Rive, CH-1204 Genève, Switzerland, (fax (022) 7812058)

Intertrek
Nollisweid 16, CH-9050 Apenzell, Switzerland, (fax (071) 872423)

Trekking International
Via Giafrancesco Re, 78-10146 Torino, Italy

Ulf Prytz Adventure Travel
PO Box 7573, Skillebaek, Oslo 2, Norway

Asia

Alpine Tour Service
7F Kawashima Building, 2-2-2 Shimbashi, Minato-ku, Tokyo 105, (fax (03) 5082529)

Himalaya Kanko Kaihatsu
5F Kaikei Building, 3-26-3, Shimbashi, Minato-ku, Tokyo

Mera Travel
Room 1307-9, Argyle Centre, Phase 1, 688 Nathan Rd, Kowloon, Hong Kong, (fax 7891649)

Saiyu Riyok
1-1-17 Kouraku Bunkiyoku, Tokyo

LEAVING NEPAL

Reconfirming Reservations

Airline reservations out of Kathmandu are difficult to get at any time, but are particularly hard to obtain during the trekking season in Nepal. You must always reconfirm reservations or the airline will cancel them. This is not an idle threat, as it often happens. Take the time before your trek to reconfirm your flight out of Nepal. A bit of planning can save a last-minute drama at the airport. All airlines have fully booked their flights out of Kathmandu from mid-October to the end of November, and during January and April. If you don't have a reservation, make a booking before you start your trek. By booking three to five weeks ahead, you may get a seat. If you wait until you finish your trek to book a seat, you will certainly have to wait a week or two for a flight. Be sure to allow a four or five day buffer if you are flying out of Lukla or Jomsom.

Airport Tax

The airport tax on departure is Rs 450. Other airport taxes in the region are:

from Bangkok, Thailand,
200 Baht
from India,
Rs 50 to Nepal,
Rs 100 to destinations outside the Indian subcontinent;
from Lhasa, Tibet,
Yuan 20
from Hong Kong,
HK$100

Getting Around

AIR

The national carrier, Royal Nepal Airlines Corporation (RNAC), operates all flights within Nepal. RNAC's domestic fleet includes 19-passenger Twin Otter and six-passenger Pilatus Porter aircraft that fly regularly to some of the highest, remotest and most spectacular airstrips in the world. Both these planes are STOL (Short Take Off & Landing) aircraft to enable them to negotiate short grass airstrips at Jomsom, Lukla, Dolpo, Shyangboche, Manang, Langtang and Taplejung.

The approaches to these airstrips are difficult. Many are on mountainsides surrounded by high peaks. Therefore, if there are clouds or high winds, the pilot cannot land. The classic remark by one RNAC captain explains the picture perfectly: 'We don't fly through clouds because in Nepal the clouds have rocks in them.' RNAC is famous for delaying or cancelling flights to remote regions because of bad weather.

If your trek involves a flight in or out of a remote airstrip, you will probably experience a delay of several hours or, more often, several days. Delays are the price you pay for the timesaving and convenience of flights in Nepal. Pack a good book into your hand luggage to make the inevitable waiting at airports a little more tolerable.

Reservations

It may seem a bit silly to describe how to buy an air ticket, but RNAC has so many complicated and strange rules and regulations that it's worth some discussion.

In Kathmandu RNAC's domestic booking office is in Thapathali, across from the Rotary Club, near the Blue Star Hotel. It is best to go there in person because the airline will confirm seats only after you pay the fare and it has actually issued the ticket. You must pay for tickets in foreign currency. RNAC doesn't take credit cards, so bring cash or

travellers' cheques – and exact change, if possible. If you are using a trekking company or travel agency, they can make the flight booking for you and expedite the payment process. Local people pay a lower fare than foreigners on most flights.

Lukla and Pokhara are domestic flights, but they are labelled 'tourist sectors' and reservations are controlled by the head office. For tickets to these destinations, go to the international reservation office on New Rd, not the domestic office.

There are many obstacles to booking a seat on a domestic flight, but the most common problem is 'no seats'. Agents book seats to Lukla, Jomsom and Pokhara up to two years in advance for their groups. There is a lot of seat swapping among local agencies in Kathmandu, so when RNAC has no seats you may still find one by checking with a few travel or trekking agencies. Seats can also mysteriously become available at the last minute, so it's always worth a trip to the RNAC office to ask for a reservation.

In an Outlying Station There are no airline computers or telexes in the hills. RNAC operates a manual system with handwritten reservation lists for outlying stations. The Kathmandu office cannot confirm a flight back to Kathmandu after the reservations list is sent to the remote airstrip, as once the list leaves Kathmandu, only the outlying station can confirm a seat. The Kathmandu office usually sends the list a week ahead of the flight, but the time varies for each destination.

If you are planning to fly out from Lukla, it would be prudent to confirm your flight back to Kathmandu before starting the trek. The trouble is that you must then buy a ticket. If your flight does not operate and you decide to walk out, you can only obtain a refund for the ticket in Kathmandu. Having a ticket can be useful, however. Sometimes there is such a crowd in Lukla that the airline just stops selling tickets.

Another Lukla peculiarity is that when a passenger backlog occurs, RNAC often enforces the rule that they will only accept tickets with confirmed reservations. They can declare 'open' and 'request' tickets void, and require you to walk to Kathmandu or to buy a new ticket.

Cancellation of Reservations

On domestic flights there is always a cancellation charge. If you do not fly, be sure to cancel your reservation on time and have it recorded on your ticket as proof. If you cancel a reservation more than 24 hours before the flight there is a Rs 20 cancellation charge. If you cancel less than 24 hours before the flight, the charge is one-third of the ticket cost. For 'no shows' there is no refund at all. An interesting loophole is that if a flight is delayed by more than 1 hour, there is no cancellation charge if you decide not to fly.

Flight Check-in

Once you have a ticket and a confirmed seat, the fun is just beginning. If you are lucky, your flight will exist when you get to the airport, your name will still be on the seating chart, your baggage will be accepted, the flight will depart and it will land at the destination. This sometimes happens, but often something goes wrong. Bad weather or other complications frequently force the delay or cancellation of flights.

Check-in for domestic flights begins an hour before the flight. It is wise to be in line when the counter opens in case of some snag. In the morning, there are often Sherpa businesspeople at the airport trying to send cargo to Lukla and other remote destinations. These people often offer to assist you with checking in so that they can use your unused baggage allowance. It's usually safe to accept their offer and also let them try to solve any glitches that occur.

If you have a lot of trekking gear, try to have someone with you who can send it later if it is off-loaded from the flight. The allowance on Lukla flights is nominally 25 kg, but sometimes this limit is arbitrarily reduced. On other domestic flights the limit is 15 kg. Sometimes space is at such a premium that extra baggage cannot be accommodated, even if you agree to pay the excess charge.

Both checked luggage and hand luggage are subject to a security check. Be sure you put your pocket knife in your checked baggage so that airport security does not confiscate it. Theoretically you will get the knife back on arrival, but it's one more delay.

Flight Cancellations

When this happens, start again. Having a confirmed seat on a flight that did not operate usually does not gain you any priority for the next flight. In Lukla you will go from having a boarding pass in hand to the bottom of the waiting list. If you are lucky, and your plane does come, you will go ahead of those who may have been waiting a week or more. In Kathmandu there is no such system, but RNAC operates a complex programme of 'delayed schedule', 'nonschedule' and 'charter' flights. You can often find a seat if you are willing to spend some time at the RNAC office, but it's almost like starting from the beginning again. An agent can be helpful in such situations.

BUS

Booking a bus ticket is easier than buying a plane ticket. Several companies operate on each bus route, so the competition forces them into a bit of efficiency, at least in the sales department. The government fixes bus rates, but these vary with the class of service. The Nepalese people build buses for Nepalese who average 175 cm in height and 65 kg in weight. If you are larger than this, you should make an effort to get one of the few large seats so you don't start your trek looking like a pretzel.

The agent assigns seats when you buy your ticket. If you are large, look for a seat in the front or near the door. Seating charts are rare and there is no assurance that the bus that travels will have seats that match the chart. It is worthwhile to go to the bus station a day or two ahead and see the buses that each company operates and find out which seats have a bit of room.

One solution is a night bus. These operate on several long distance routes and are usually more comfortable than express buses. Look for companies that advertise '2x2 folding seats'. These are almost Western-size reclining seats, and theoretically they only sell as many seats as they have and do not stop en route to take on extra passengers. If you visit the bus station at about 6 pm you can see the difference between the day and night buses.

Long distance buses leave from two places: the bus terminal behind the Electric Corporation near Bagh Bazaar (just across from Ratna Park) and from Sundhara, the area near the General Post Office. You can buy tickets a day ahead at either of these places; there are many ticket outlets and touts at both. Most bus companies print their tickets in Nepali script. Be sure to ask the ticket seller to translate it and tell you where the bus leaves from, and when.

When budgeting your expenses, include the extra charges for luggage. Large pieces of baggage go on the roof. You must either drag it up the ladder on the back of the bus or pay a rupee or two to have someone do it for you. The baggage charge is often negotiable with the conductor and is higher for the so-called express and deluxe services. If you have a lot of gear, the baggage costs can add up to more than the cost of the bus seat.

An 'express' bus is anything but express, but it certainly beats a local bus. Local buses can take twice (or more) as long as an express. An express bus, in turn, takes about twice as long as a private vehicle. Pokhara is served by many companies. In addition to the express busses designed for local people, there are several companies that run express busses for foreigners. Student Travels, Memoire Travels, Arun Travels and the famous Swiss Bus all provide more comfortable seats than their competitors.

Unlike aeroplanes, which depart with a minimum of ceremony, buses in Nepal make a great drama out of their departure. Honking horns, racing engines, last minute baggage loading, and an attempt to cram a few extra passengers, chickens and goats on board make for a huge production that can often delay departures. Bring a book to read.

Occasionally it is possible to sit on the roof of the bus after it leaves Kathmandu. This is often an attractive spot if the weather is warm and it gets you out of the smoke filled bus. The roof is either a more or a less dangerous place to be in case of an accident, depending on the circumstances. Buses have a nasty habit of rolling over, driving off steep embankments or colliding head-on. One place on the bus is probably as safe as another.

Buses stop for a multitude of reasons – breakdowns (mostly), police check posts, road tolls, tea breaks, meal stops and chats with drivers of buses headed in the opposite direction.

Mugling, the lunch stop on the Pokhara road, is a well organised fast-food operation serving dhal bhaat with a curried meat side dish. Other meal stops patronised by buses can be a bit rough. The bus driver gets a free meal by stopping at a particular restaurant, so look up and down the road for a place that is less crowded and might have better food than the one that the driver chose. In any case, get your meal organised before you do any wandering around; once the driver decides it's time to go, everyone immediately piles into the bus.

CAR & TAXI
Rental

It's expensive to hire a car or Land Rover to get to the start of a trek, but it's much more comfortable and can save a lot of time over public transport.

You can rent a car in Nepal, but even Hertz and Avis usually supply a driver – free. Traffic can be chaotic and an accident puts the driver in jail until the situation is resolved, so it's not a good idea to drive in Nepal unless you are familiar with the country and are used to dodging the cows, chickens, kids, bicycles and rickshaws that pop up out of nowhere. Traffic is supposed to stay on the left side of the road, though this is not obvious when you watch vehicle movements.

Land Rovers, that will undertake either long or short distance trips, can be found in front of the Mt Makalu Hotel, near New Rd. Rates are negotiable with the driver.

Taxi

Most travel agencies can arrange cars or you can negotiate with one of the private taxis that hang out behind Mike's Breakfast, just off Durbar Marg.

LOCAL TRANSPORT
To/From Airport

Taxis are usually available at the airport, but fares vary according to demand. Drivers should use a meter. A trip to a Thamel hotel should cost Rs 40 or so. When taxis are in short supply, drivers cover their meters with a dirty rag and prices double or triple. There are blue public buses that operate on a fixed route to several hotels, including those at Thamel, for Rs 15.

Bus

Blue Isuzu and Mitsubishi buses and private minibuses cover the entire valley on various routes. During rush hours they resemble sardine cans, but at other times Rs 1 or Rs 2 gets you around in relative comfort.

Taxi

Metered taxis are inexpensive and abundant during the day. However, they are hard to find after 8 pm, and those that are available will quote you their own 'take it or leave it' rates. If you are stuck out late without a taxi, try a large hotel or call the night taxi service on 224374. Three-wheeled scooters are also metered and are slightly cheaper than taxis, but a ride in one of these is a bone-rattling adventure.

Rickshaw

Rickshaws are available in some parts of the city. They can be fun, but be sure to negotiate the price beforehand.

Motorbikes & Bicycles

It costs Rs 5 per hour or Rs 20 per day to rent a Chinese or Indian single-speed bicycle. Mountain bikes are available in Thamel for Rs 80 to Rs 100 per day. Be careful of cars when you are on a bicycle, especially vehicles making nonstop left turns at red lights.

With a driving licence, you can rent motorbikes for Rs 60 per hour or Rs 300 per day.

Tempos

There is a system of jitneys that operates on fixed routes throughout Kathmandu using tiny Indian scooters called tempos. These are not for Western foreigners, who generally are too big and heavy to fit inside the vehicles.

Mt Everest Region

The Everest or Solu Khumbu region is the second most popular trekking area in Nepal. It would probably be the most popular destination, but it is more difficult to get to Solu Khumbu than to the Annapurna area. To get near Everest, you must either walk for 10 days or fly to Lukla, a remote and notoriously unreliable mountain airstrip.

Solu Khumbu is justifiably famous, not only for its proximity to the world's highest mountain (8848 metres), but also for its Sherpa villages and monasteries. The primary goal of an Everest trek is the Everest base camp at an elevation of about 5340 metres. But you cannot see Everest from the base camp, so most trekkers climb Kala Pattar, an unassuming 5545 metre bump on the southern flank of Pumori (7161 metres).

Other than the problem of access, the other major complication to an Everest trek is the high likelihood of Acute Mountain Sickness (AMS). This potentially deadly disease, commonly known as altitude sickness, is caused by climbing too quickly to a high elevation. Be sure to read the section on mountain sickness in the Health & First Aid chapter if you are planning an Everest trek. If you suffer symptoms of altitude sickness and cannot go to base camp, you can still make a worthwhile trek to less ambitious destinations such as Namche Bazaar, the administrative headquarters of the Khumbu region; Khumjung or Thami, more typical Sherpa villages; or Tengpoche Monastery. From Tengpoche you will have an excellent view of Everest and its more spectacular neighbour Ama Dablam (6856 metres).

INFORMATION

There is almost too much information available about Everest. In addition to the books I have listed, there are at least 100 more books and thousands of magazine articles about the Sherpas and Mt Everest. Whether your interest is in mountaineering, Buddhism, anthropology or the environment, you can probably find literature about the Everest region that you can relate to.

Maps

The Everest area has also been mapped to death; there are more detailed maps of this area than any other part of Nepal. Many locally produced maps are available in Kathmandu. The Schneider maps are:

Khumbu Himal – Namche Bazaar to Mt Everest
Shorong/Hinku – Solu and the Hongu Valley
Dudh Kosi – Lamidanda to Lukla
Tamba Kosi/Likhu Khola – Jiri to Junbesi
Rolwaling Himal
Lepchi Kang

A map titled the *Mount Everest Region*, published in the UK, covers about the same region as the map of the same name in this book in the section on the Everest trek. The UK map is available by mail from the Royal Geographical Society, 1 Kensington Gore, London SW7, at a cost of £5 per copy.

The November 1988 issue of *National Geographic* contained a 1:50,000 computer enhanced topographic map of the Everest area. This map does not cover much of the trekking route, but is a fascinating document to study. Copies are available in Kathmandu bookshops.

The Army Map Service sheet, 45-2 *Mount Everest*, isn't worth carrying because there are so many better maps of the region.

Place Names Maps and route descriptions for the Everest trek become confusing because of conflicting names for the same place. Most villages have both Sherpa names and Nepali names. I have used the Nepali names because these are on all official maps and records. The Sherpa names for villages along the route appear in parenthesis after the more common Nepali name.

FESTIVALS

In addition to the February celebration of the Tibetan New Year or *Losar*, there are two uniquely Sherpa festivals that you may come across in Solu Khumbu.

Mani Rimdu

This festival is celebrated at the monasteries of Tengpoche, Thami and Chiwang. The lamas wear elaborate masks and costumes and through a series of ritualistic dances, dramatise the triumph of Buddhism over Bon, the ancient animistic religion of Tibet. The first day of Mani Rimdu involves prayers by the lamas in the monastery courtyard. The second day is the colourful lama dancing, wearing brocade gowns and wonderfully painted paper mache masks. Hundreds of local people attend the performance; it is an important social occasion as well as an entertaining spectacle. Along with the serious and intricate dances the lamas also stage two absurd comic sequences that make the entire performance a grand and amusing event. On the final evening of Mani Rimdu all the local people join in an all night Sherpa dance.

The Tengpoche celebration of Mani Rimdu is usually at the November-December full moon. Large crowds of Westerners attend this ceremony and hotel accommodation is at a premium. Even tent space is hard to come by. Prices creep up in accordance with the capitalist tradition of charging what the traffic will bear. The monastery charges for entrance tickets, usually Rs 10 per person, with a surcharge for movie cameras.

A spring celebration of the Mani Rimdu festival is held about the middle of May each year in Thami. Mani Rimdu at Thami tends to be a little more spirited (literally) than the festival in autumn at Tengpoche, because the weather is warmer in spring and the *Rimpoche*, or reincarnate lama, at Thami is a bit more liberal than the Tengpoche lama.

Mani Rimdu is also held in autumn at Chiwang Gompa in the Solu region, usually on the same day as Tengpoche's Mani Rimdu. This monastery is set high on a ridge overlooking Phaphlu and Salleri.

Dumje

Dumje is a celebration of the birth of Guru Rimpoche. It is a six day celebration that takes place in June when few tourists are in the Khumbu. Eight families sponsor the event each year. It is a heavy financial burden, so this responsibility is rotated in turn among the villagers. Separate celebrations take place in the villages of Namche Bazaar, Khumjung and Thami.

PLACES TO STAY

There are hotels of varying degrees of sophistication all the way from Jiri to Everest base camp, but there is not the profusion of hotels and bhattis that there is in the Annapurna area. Many times you will hike for 2 or 3 hours without finding any facilities, and for several days you will have to schedule your night stop according to the available accommodation.

In Namche Bazaar and Lukla the competition among hotels is intense. Some hotels are outstanding and almost all have both private rooms and dormitory accommodation. At other places the facilities may be either too primitive or too sophisticated, so you may have to walk on to the next village to find something that suits you.

Above Namche Bazaar most hotels have only dormitory facilities consisting of huge bunks that sleep eight to 10 people. One common phenomenon at high altitude is very strange dreams and even nightmares. These occurrences lend a bit of entertainment to a night in a crowded lodge on the way to Everest.

During the trekking season the hotels fill up quickly. You will probably get involved in a daily race with other trekkers to get the best, and sometimes only, accommodation. This can be dangerous at high elevations because altitude sickness is encouraged by overexertion and fast ascent. At Pheriche and Lobuje, particularly, you must be a bit aggressive in dealing with the crowds.

The Hotel Everest View, above Namche Bazaar, is a Japanese project that caters to the blue rinse set. The hotel was closed from 1982 until 1989, but it has recently been renovated and is now open – and expensive. All 12 rooms have private bathrooms with Western toilets. Rates start at US$120 per person; meals are extra. The hotel operates the flights to Shyangboche airstrip.

Sherpa Guide Lodges is a chain of lodges based on the European mountain hut system. A chain of 11 lodges covers every night stop from Jiri to Namche Bazaar. You can book a fully guided trip with prearranged accommodation in private rooms, or just book yourself into the lodge system with confirmed accommodation every night. The lodges must be prebooked as they do not accept walk-in customers, so don't be put off when you are turned away at one of their facilities. Book through the USA office (tel (415) 5278100, fax (415) 5257710).

GETTING THERE & AWAY

You can either fly or walk to the Everest region. Those who fly to Lukla miss the historic and culturally fascinating route followed by the Everest expeditions of the '50s and '60s, although the trek has changed a lot in the past 35 years.

Trailheads

Jiri This is the starting point for 'walk to Everest' treks. You should plan on a 10 day trek from the road head at Jiri, 188 km from Kathmandu. If you take the time to walk from Jiri, the hike will help to acclimatise and condition you to visit the base camp or climb Kala Pattar. You can then either fly out from Lukla or walk back by an alternative route to Kathmandu. Direct buses to Jiri depart from the Ratna Park bus station in Kathmandu. There are at least two buses daily at 6 am. The buses that serve Jiri are dilapidated, crowded and slow, so if you have the wherewithal and a group of five or six people, you might consider hiring a private Land Rover.

Barahbise Five km beyond Lamosangu and 85 km from Kathmandu, this is the starting point of an extended Everest walk-in trek. There is no express bus service to Barahbise, so you must take a funky local bus which takes 5 to 6 hours, but it's cheap – only Rs 25. You can make the trip by private car or taxi in about 2½ hours.

Dharan & Dhankuta These villages in south-east Nepal can be used as a starting or ending point for an Everest trek. See the details of how to get to these villages in the Eastern Nepal chapter.

Airports

When flying to one of the mountain airstrips near Everest, do not attempt a quick visit to the base camp because you won't have had time to acclimatise. Allow at least eight or nine days to reach the base camp region if you fly to Lukla. You can return from the base camp to Lukla in as few as four or five days, so it takes an absolute minimum of two weeks for a safe trek to the base camp. Precise scheduling is complicated because flights to Lukla often do not take off as planned. Allow a few spare days for both the flight in and the flight out.

Lukla At 2800 metres, this airstrip is served by 19-passenger Twin Otter aircraft that carry, due to the high elevation, only 14 or 15 passengers to and from Lukla. If you truly have a limited amount of time, you can fly to Lukla and spend as little as six days to visit Namche Bazaar and Tengpoche, but beware of flight delays.

Lukla is unique. A Hillary team built Lukla airstrip as part of the Khunde Hospital project in 1965, envisioning it as a makeshift strip to handle emergencies at the hospital. RNAC expanded the strip in 1977 and the Department of Civil Aviation added a control tower in 1983. It is now the second busiest airport in Nepal. The flight approach path is totally visual; there are no instruments or navigational aids of any kind. If there are clouds, no plane will come – occasionally for days at a time during periods of extended bad weather. Flight planning is complicated because while only 60% of trekkers to the Everest region fly to Lukla, 96% of them fly out of Lukla.

Situated on the side of a mountain, the

grass strip is built on a slant so that there is an elevation difference of about 60 metres between the ends of the runway. This slope slows planes and helps them stop before they run into the mountain peak that rises from the eastern end of the 450 metre long runway.

RNAC often enforces a rule at Lukla that they will honour only tickets with confirmed reservations. At such times they totally reject 'open' or 'request' tickets. If you are planning to fly out of Lukla, you should select a date, get a confirmed reservation and have the ticket issued in Kathmandu.

Shyangboche This tiny airstrip is served by a five or six passenger, single engine Pilatus Porter. Shyangboche is above Namche Bazaar at an elevation of 3565 metres. It is used by guests at the Hotel Everest View and for occasional charter flights.

RNAC has contracted the operation of Shyangboche flights to the Hotel Everest View. To buy a Shyangboche seat, go to the Trans Himalayan Tour/Hotel Everest View office on Durbar Marg (tel 224854, 223871) or to the Hotel Everest View itself above Khumjung. The cost is US$160 one way and $290 return, with a five kg baggage allowance. Excess baggage is US$2 per kg.

Phaphlu It's a four day walk from Lukla and six days from Namche Bazaar to Phaphlu (2364 metres). If you have an extra few days this may be a viable alternative for flights both to and from the Everest region. Phaphlu Airport was extended in 1986 to accommodate Twin Otter (19 passenger) aircraft. Few tourist groups use the airstrip, so there is a good chance of finding a seat at the last minute.

Lamidanda This place is about five days walk south of Lukla. It is a largely unknown alternative as either an approach to or exit from the Everest region. From Lamidanda there are flights to both Kathmandu and Biratnagar. From Biratnagar, take a bus or plane to Kathmandu.

Biratnagar This city is in the Terai, south-east of Lukla. RNAC operates an eastern Nepal hub from Biratnagar that serves Lukla, Lamidanda, Tumlingtar, Taplejung and other eastern Nepalese destinations. Because there is no morning fog in Biratnagar, early morning flights operate more regularly than in Kathmandu. Thus the Biratnagar to Lukla flight is often more reliable than the Kathmandu to Lukla flight. You pay, however, for this reliability. There is no through fare via Biratnagar, so Lukla to Kathmandu via Biratnagar costs a whopping US$143. There is a night bus service between Biratnagar and Kathmandu, so you could use this to save money if you fly via Biratnagar.

Airfares

	one way
Kathmandu-Lukla	US$83
Kathmandu-Phaphlu	US$77
Biratnagar-Lukla	US$66
Kathmandu-Biratnagar	US$77
Kathmandu-Lamidanda	US$66
Biratnagar-Lamidanda	US$50
Kathmandu-Shyangboche (charter flight)	US$160

Flight Delays

RNAC schedules three or four flights a day to Lukla but there are usually either more or less than four flights because of cancellations, extra flights, charters or delayed schedule flights.

When flights are cancelled, those who have planned to fly to Kathmandu must wait. Soon a backlog of people builds up, each person convinced that he or she must fly on the next available aircraft. The situation often becomes ludicrous, but provides a great opportunity to develop patience and to become acquainted with trekkers from all over the world as you wait together. The stories of overcrowding in the Everest area now become real. In the past, 350 or more people have waited here – especially in late October and early November each year. The problem usually solves itself within a week, but it's important to prepare yourself for a long delay for any flight to or from Lukla.

It's also possible to depart from Lukla exactly on schedule.

See the description of the trek to Lamidanda for a few horror stories and Lukla jokes, as well as some suggestions on what you can do if you find yourself stranded here.

Shyangboche flights are expensive but provide an emergency exit from Khumbu. Hotel guests receive priority on flights, so it's sometimes possible (but expensive) to check in to the Hotel Everest View for a night and move to the head of the Shyangboche waiting list.

JIRI TO EVEREST BASE CAMP

This section details a 21 day trek from Jiri to the Everest base camp. The trek I describe ends with a flight back to Kathmandu from Lukla. If you fly to Lukla, begin reading at Day 8 and spend your first night at Phakding, but be sure to take an extra day at Namche Bazaar or Tengpoche for acclimatisation. You can make an excellent 32 day trek by walking on to Dhankuta instead of flying out from Lukla. The description of this route is in the Eastern Nepal chapter.

The Everest trek involves a tremendous amount of up and down walking. A glance at the map will show the reason why. All the rivers in this part of Nepal flow south from Himalayan glaciers, but the trek route proceeds east. Therefore the trail must climb to the ridge that separates two rivers, descend to the river itself and ascend the next ridge. Even though the trek begins at an elevation of 1860 metres, on the sixth day it crosses the Dudh Kosi at only 1500 metres – after considerable uphill walking. If you total all the uphill climbing, it will come to almost 9000 metres of elevation gain from Jiri to the Everest base camp. The Jiri road saves almost 4000 metres of uphill walking over the old approach from Lamosangu.

The Road to Jiri

By bus it takes a full day to cover the 188 km from Kathmandu to Jiri. The development of roads has been a characteristic of this trek since the first Everest expedition in Nepal.

In 1953 the British Everest Expedition started from the Bhadgaon in the Kathmandu Valley. By 1963 the American Expedition could begin from Banepa, saving a day of walking over the British. The Chinese road to Kodari allowed the trek to begin from Dolalghat in 1967 and from Lamosangu in 1970. The Jiri road reached Kirantichhap in 1980 and by 1984 it was finally possible to drive all the way to Jiri. There is talk of continuing the road further, perhaps to Phaphlu or even to Namche Bazaar, but this is still only a dream and no firm plans exist.

The Swiss Association for Technical Assistance (SATA) built the Jiri road as part of the Integrated Hill Development Project, a large programme of agricultural development in this region. It employed labourers to build the road instead of using machines. This was intended to have a beneficial economic impact by employing hundreds of workers. A direct effect of this approach to road building is that it has raised porter wages and created a porter shortage.

Day 1: Kathmandu to Jiri

The first part of the drive is via the Arniko Rajmarg, the Chinese constructed Kodari Highway that links Nepal with Tibet. The road follows the Chinese trolley bus route to Bhaktapur, then passes smoke belching brick factories, finally leaving the Kathmandu Valley and passing by the old Newar towns of Banepa and Dhulikhel. If it is clear as you pass Dhulikhel, you should have an excellent panoramic view of the eastern Himalaya, including Langtang Lirung, Dorje Lakpa and Manaslu.

The road descends to Panchkal, the starting point for Helambu treks, then follows the Indrawati River to its confluence with the Sun Kosi at Dolalghat, crossing the river on a large bridge 57 km from Kathmandu. The Sun Kosi (Gold river) is one of Nepal's major rivers; it is possible to make a week long rafting expedition from Dolalghat all the way to the Terai. The road climbs over a ridge behind Dolalghat, then follows the Sun Kosi north to Lamosangu, a bustling bazaar about 50 km south of the Tibetan border.

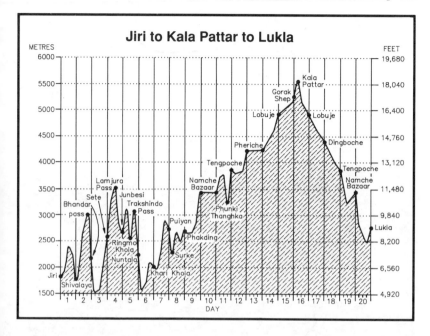

Jiri to Kala Pattar to Lukla

Close to Lamosangu is a hydroelectric power plant built with Chinese aid.

At Lamosangu the bus crosses the Sun Kosi and joins the Swiss road, climbing towards the top of the 2500 metre ridge that forms the watershed between the Sun Kosi drainage to the west and the Tamba Kosi drainage to the east. The villages in this area are of mixed ethnic and caste composition. Most of the population is either Chhetri or Brahmin (who speak Nepali as their first tongue) or Tamangs.

A new series of km posts start here. The bridge is km 0 and Jiri is km 110. After some initial switchbacks that take the road out of the Sun Kosi Valley, the road turns east and heads up a canyon towards the top of the first ridge. The first large settlement along the road is Pakhar (1980 metres). This is a predominantly Tamang village, and is the site of a Swiss vehicle and road maintenance centre. There is little mineral wealth in Nepal, but near Pakhar there is an economically viable

source of magnesite, a mineral that refractories use. Nepal Orind Magnesite Corporation has a mine here and plans to export magnesite to India and other countries using a ropeway that stretches from here to Lamosangu. From Pakhar the road climbs along the top of a ridge towards the pass. Buses often stop at Muldi (3540 metres) for tea or lunch at one of several bhattis.

After crossing the pass at 2440 metres the road makes a long sweep around the head of the valley, finally reaching Charikot at the road junction for Dolkha at km 53. Dolkha is a large and diverse bazaar a few km to the north. This is the departure point for treks to Rolwaling. There are several hotels here and it might be prudent to grab a snack if the wait is particularly long, as the police check trekking permits and record all comings and goings of vehicles and foreigners. Though buses are often late because of breakdowns, road problems or an excess of bureaucratic formalities, you rarely need to spend a night

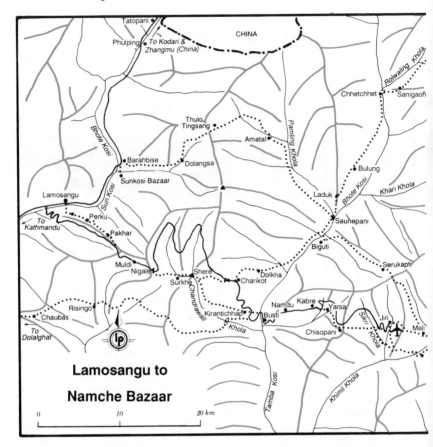

Lamosangu to

Namche Bazaar

in a hotel along the road. The buses continue their trip at night, no matter how late. The Swiss project has published a pamphlet, titled *Dolkha*, that describes several short treks and excursions in the region near Charikot.

The road descends from Charikot through a region of heavy settlement to Kirantichhap at 1300 metres, 64 km from Lamosangu. It then makes a circuitous descent from Kirantichhap into the Tamba Kosi Valley. This is a fertile area, containing a good deal of terraced land for irrigated paddy cultivation. The population is mainly Brahmins and

Chhetris, but there are also Tamangs and a few Newars. Crossing the river on a large steel bridge at 800 metres, the road makes a steep ascent to Namdu. The only part of Namdu that you can see from the road is the large school. Namdu and its neighbouring village, Kabre, are large and spread out. Reafforestation and agricultural projects, part of the Swiss development scheme, are occurring in both villages.

The road climbs above Namdu and past Mina Pokhari, one of the road project stations. This settlement is a good example of a phenomenon that takes place as road con-

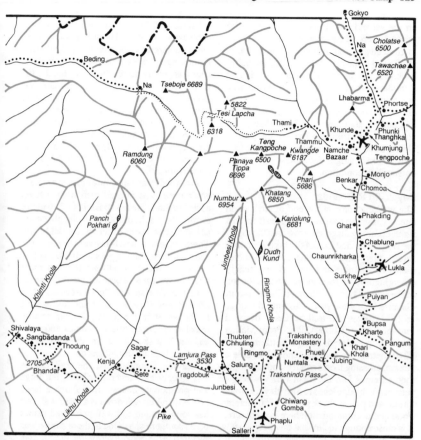

struction continues. Mina Pokhari hardly existed before SATA conceived the road. For several years the road ended here and Mina Pokhari became a boom town. When the road finally reached Jiri, Mina Pokhari lost its importance. Many villages have suffered just such a rise and fall – Dumre on the Pokhara road, Betrawati on the Langtang road and Pakhar and Kirantichhap on the Jiri road.

The road finally reaches the top of the forested ridge at 2500 metres. It remains high and contours around the head of the valley in forests above the village of Thulo Chaur,

then descends along the top of a ridge above Jiri. This is the Jiri Bazaar (2100 metres), where there are a few hotels and a weekly Saturday market. It is a short descent to the main village of Jiri (1860 metres) where the road ends at a cluster of hotels near the Swiss dairy and agricultural project. The people of Jiri and the surrounding area are Jirels, a subgroup of Sunwars whose language is related to that of the Sherpas.

You have a few choices to make as you plan your first few days of trekking. On your own, you can reach Thodung or Bhandar on the first day – it is a long hard day – and Sete on the second day, in accordance with the schedule here. If you have porters, or are not in good shape, you may have trouble reaching Bhandar the first day. You will probably have to settle for Shivalaya the first day and Bhandar on the second day. Whichever way you schedule it, plan on spending a night at either Sete or Sagar to break the long climb to Lamjura sign pass into two stages. The elevation gain from the river to the pass is almost 2000 metres – a fairly difficult climb to make in a single day unless you are in outstanding condition.

Day 2: Jiri to Bhandar

The walking starts at the end of Jiri's main street. Climb up past some houses then turn right, climbing diagonally towards the top of the ridge. The first part of the hike is in deep forests then fields, passing the tiny settlements of Bharkur and Ratmati and finally emerging into pastureland as it nears the top of the ridge. There is a bhatti at Chitre, a short distance below the pass. Crossing the ridge at 2400 metres, the trail begins to descend into the Khimti Khola Valley. From Mali, a sparsely populated Sherpa settlement at 2240 metres, the trail descends alongside a stream, crossing it on a small wooden bridge, then emerges into the main valley where a suspension bridge leads to Shivalaya, a small bazaar and police check post at 1750 metres. Food and accommodation here is mediocre; it is close enough to Jiri that few people stay here. At night you may hear the howls of jackals that live in the nearby hills.

The old trail went via Those (pronounced 'toe-say') and provides an alternative to the newer direct route. To reach Those *(Maksin)* from Jiri, follow a trail downstream along the eastern side of the Jiri Khola. The trail climbs a bit in forests, then drops to join the old route from Lamosangu. The trail descends past Kattike to the Khimti Khola then follows the river upstream to Those at 1750 metres. A good camp is just beyond the iron suspension bridge that crosses the Khimti Khola. There are several hotels in the village itself. Beware of 2nd floor rooms above smoky kitchens here.

Those is a large pleasant bazaar with a cobblestone street and whitewashed houses. Once the largest market on the trail between Lamosangu and Namche Bazaar, its importance has greatly diminished now that the Jiri road is complete. Many of the Newar shopkeepers here have closed or abandoned hotels in the village. It is possible to buy items manufactured locally from the nearby sources of low-grade iron ore. Rooster lamps are a speciality. From Those the trail leads upstream to Shivalaya where it joins the route from Jiri.

From Shivalaya the route crosses a stream and passes some houses, then starts a steep ascent towards the next pass. It's a 350 metre climb to a schoolhouse at Sangbadanda (2150 metres), where there is a small bhatti. There are several hotels between here and the pass, and more on the pass itself. Along this section of trail you will see the first mani walls on the route. These are stones covered with the Tibetan Buddhist inscription *Om Mani Padme Hum*, usually translated as 'hail to the jewel in the lotus', though its true translation is much more complex and mysterious. You should walk to the left side of these walls as the Buddhists do.

Leaving Sangbadanda, the trail climbs less steeply past several isolated, but large and prosperous houses. Just above a large house with blue windows is a mani wall that has some unique and well-preserved stones on its southern side. One of these stones was pictured in the book, *Everest, the West Ridge*. To find it, peek around each wall after you pass it on the left. There is a small tea shop at Kosaribas (2500 metres), then the trail becomes reasonably level, and even descends a bit, as it goes towards the head of the canyon.

Crossing a stream on a wooden bridge, the trail ascends steeply in forests to another tea shop, crosses another stream, this time on two logs, then makes a final climb through quince and cotoniaster forests. On the top of the pass at 2705 metres is an impressive array of long mani walls, indicative of the fact that the trek is now entering an area dominated by Tibetan culture. There is an excellent view of the Likhu Khola Valley and the village of Bhandar (Chyangma), a large Sherpa settlement, far below in a hanging valley.

You can make a side trip to Thodung either by climbing north for about 1¼ hours from the pass or by detouring from the main trail just beyond Sangbadanda. Thodung (3090 metres) is the site of the first cheese factory built by the Swiss in the 1950s. The Nepal Dairy Development Corporation now operates it. Your reward for the long hard climb to the factory is a feast of cheese, yoghurt and yak (actually nak) milk. Cheese is available year round but other fresh dairy products are available only during autumn. From Thodung you can trek down the ridge and rejoin the main trail at the top of the pass, then descend to Bhandar. Good food and accommodation is available in Thodung if you have the courage to seek out the manager in the presence of several huge Tibetan mastiff dogs.

Just below the pass is an important trail junction. After a one or two minute walk below the pass itself, take the left-hand trail to reach Bhandar. By continuing straight you would stay high on the ridge and reach the village of Roshi. This is the trail to the Solu region and crosses a pass to the south of Lamjura. Few foreigners ever use this route.

After an initially steep descent on stone steps, the trail reaches the outskirts of the large village of Bhandar and descends gradually through fields and pastures to a gompa and two imposing chortens at 2200 metres. A chorten is literally a receptacle for offerings and often holds religious relics. Each of its elements has a symbolic meaning. The square or rectangular base symbolises the solid earth. On the base is a half-spherical dome, symbolising water. On top of the dome is a rectangular tower, the four sides of which are painted with a pair of eyes, the all seeing eyes of Buddha. What appears to be a nose is actually the Sanskrit character for the number one, symbolising the absoluteness of Buddha. Above the rectangular tower is a conical or pyramidal spire (symbolising fire) with 13 steplike segments, symbolising

the 13 steps leading to Buddhahood. On top of the 13 steps is an ornament shaped like a crescent moon symbolising air, and a vertical spike symbolising ether or the sacred light of Buddha. The two chortens at Bhandar are painted frequently and are well preserved. One has a pyramidal spire and the other has a circular conical spire. A large chorten is called a *stupa*; there are stupas at Bodhanath and Swayambunath in Kathmandu

There are some hotels just below the gompa and an excellent camping spot is in a large meadow about a 15 minute walk below the village. Several hotels surround the village square in Bhandar and several others are just below these. Also, imagine this – the *Shobha Hotel* has a radio repair shop on the premises. Stop at the Medical Hall Health Centre for any last minute medical supplies.

Day 3: Bhandar to Sagar

From the hotels at Bhandar the trail descends through the lower fields of the village, then follows a small stream. It crosses the stream on a covered wooden bridge, then descends through deep forests for a while. Leaving the forests, the trail drops into a steep canyon, passing the settlement of Baranda, then finally meets the same stream, crossing it on another covered bridge at Tharo Khola. A hotel is here, but food is also available in Kenja, about 1½ hours away. The trail turns north, following the Likhu Khola, crossing the river on a suspension bridge at 1510 metres. This bridge replaces an ancient chain link bridge that collapsed under a load of 12 porters during the approach march for the American Mt Everest Expedition in 1963. You can see the remains of the abutments for the old bridge just downstream of the high suspension bridge.

As you follow the trail up the east bank of the river to Kenja, watch for grey langur monkeys in the forests. The trail continues along the east bank of the river, climbing over a spur, through the settlement of Namang Gaon, before crossing a small suspension bridge at Kenja (1580 metres), a small village inhabited by Newars and Magars. When I first came here in 1969,

Kenja was a single dingy shop. Now there are more than 15 shops, restaurants and hotels operated by Sherpas who have migrated from the village of Kyama, several km to the north. The large *Sherpa Guest House* has accommodation for more than 40 people and there is a weekly Sunday market. One speciality of Kenja is instant tailoring performed on hand operated sewing machines.

Leaving Kenja, the ascent towards the high Lamjura ridge begins. The first part of the ascent is very steep, then it becomes less severe as you gain elevation. After about 2 hours of climbing, a large house appears. This is not a hotel, but food and accommodation is sometimes available. There is also a welcome supply of water.

The house marks a trail junction; the left fork leads to the north and climbs around the hillside to the Sherpa settlement of Sagar *(Chandra)* at 2440 metres, a large village with two-storey stone houses and an ancient village gompa. It is possible to camp in the yard of the school, one of the projects of the Himalayan Trust (headed by Sir Edmund Hillary). There are no true hotels in Sagar, but this is a Sherpa village, so many people are willing to take guests into their homes. The trek is now completely in Sherpa country. With only one exception, all the remaining villages up to Namche Bazaar are inhabited by Sherpas.

If you are trekking on your own, take the right-hand fork. This is the trail to Sete (2575 metres), a small defunct monastery where there are three small hotels and a new group camp ground. There is a water shortage in Sete, especially during spring.

Day 4: Sagar to Junbesi

From Sagar or Sete it is a long, but fairly gradual, climb although in spots it gets steep – to the top of the 3530 metre Lamjura pass. The way is scenic and varied and it is one of the few parts of the trek that has no villages. The trek gets into fine, moist mountain forest, with huge, gnarled, moss covered rhododendron, magnolia, maple and birch trees. There is often snow on the trail and the mornings are usually frosty throughout the trekking season. On very rare occasions snow blocks the pass for a few days at a time, but the crossing usually presents no difficulties.

In spring the ridge is alive with blooming rhododendrons – the white, pink and red blossoms cover the entire hillside. The flowering occurs in a band of a few hundred metres of elevation that moves up the hill along with the spring weather. The first blooms start at lower elevations in mid-February and finally reach the pass in mid to late April. This day is also a delight for the bird lover. Nepal has more than 800 species of birds and many of the most colourful ones are found in this zone – sunbirds, minavets, flycatchers, tits, laughing thrushes and many others.

The trail from Sagar joins the Sete trail at a small settlement of three houses near two small ponds. The forest changes from pines to rhododendrons and the trail continues to climb to Goyem – five hotels at 3300 metres. Although Goyem is only about 2 hours from either Sagar or Sete, it is best to have lunch here because the next hotel of any consequence is at Tragdobuk, at least 3 hours away, although there is a small bhatti about 30 minutes below the pass on the other side. The trail climbs steeply up the ridge, finally reaching a mani wall. Here the trail leaves the ridge and begins to contour towards the pass on a trail that is always muddy and often covered with snow or ice.

Deep in a forest of large trees with silver bark, the trail passes three kharkas, each consisting of a goth or two and a mani wall. Herders use these in spring and summer and leave them empty from October to June. The houses have no roofs, so they cannot be used as shelter. Since you will probably be crossing the pass about noon or early afternoon, it will be cloudy, cold and windy. There is no view of Himalayan peaks from the pass, although there are glimpses of the top of some snow peaks on the way up. If you are here in the early morning, you will undoubtedly see planes crossing the pass enroute to Lukla. They fly so close to the ridge that you feel you can almost reach up and touch their wheels.

The pass is the highest point on the trek between Jiri and Namche Bazaar and is marked by a tangle of stones, twigs and prayer flags erected by devout travellers. On the eastern side of the pass the route descends steeply for about 400 metres through fragrant fir and hemlock forests to a stream and a small hotel. The trail then enters open grassy country and descends gently through fields and pastures where horses graze to the small settlement of Tragdobuk (2860 metres). There are hotels here, but they usually close on Saturdays when the owners go to the market in Salleri, about 3 hours walk to the south. The trail climbs from Tragdobuk to a huge rock at the head of the valley, then climbs over the ridge to a vantage point overlooking Junbesi *(Jun)*, a splendid Sherpa village amidst beautiful surroundings at 2675 metres. Numbur (6959 metres), known in Sherpa as *Shorong Yul Lha*, God of the Solu, towers over the large green valley above Junbesi.

This village is at the northern end of the Sherpa region known as Solu *(Shorong* in Sherpa). On the whole, the Sherpas of Solu are economically better off than their cousins in Khumbu because the fertile valley here is at a lower elevation, so they can grow a wide variety of crops. In recent years employment with expeditions and trekking parties has done much to improve the lot of both the Solu and Khumbu Sherpas.

A short distance below the ridge is a trail junction marked by a sign:

The big building in front of you is a monastery called Serlo. All are welcome to drop in. We speak some English and (real!) fruit juice are available. You might enjoy seeing the statues, taking some pictures, or asking some questions about the things we do here. We can offer food and lodging also.

If you do not visit the monastery, stay on the main trail and descend gently to Junbesi, keeping to the left of a huge mani stone, and enter the village near a small hotel. There is an abundance of hotels in Junbesi so it is worth doing a bit of investigation before settling in. Several lodges offer hot showers and other enticements. Trekking groups usually camp below the village on the banks of the river because the schoolmaster does not allow camping in the school yard. The Junbesi school is one of the largest and most active of the Hillary schools.

The region near Junbesi is well worth exploring, and a day spent here can offer a variety of alternatives. To the north of Junbesi, about 2 hours away, is the village of Phugmochhe (3100 metres), where there is a Traditional Sherpa Art Centre. Enroute to Phugmochhe, a short diversion will allow a visit to Thubten Chhuling, a huge Tibetan Buddhist monastery about 1¼ hours walk from Junbesi.

The trail to Thubten Chhuling starts in front of the Junbesi village gompa and follows the Junbesi Khola upstream, crossing it on a bridge, then makes the final climb to the monastery at 3000 metres. The central gompa is large and impressive and often has more than 450 monks chanting both inside and outside. The monastery expects an offering from any visitor, whether foreign or Sherpa. There is no accommodation or food available here. There are small cells all over the hillside that are the residences of monks and nuns. You probably won't be welcome at these because many of the inhabitants are on extended meditation programmes. The monastery was founded in the late 1960s by Tushi Rimpoche, who travelled to Nepal with many monks from Rongbuk Monastery in Tibet. It is a large, active and impressive religious community.

To rejoin the main trail without returning to Junbesi, follow a yak trail that climbs from Thubten Chhuling to the Lapcha La (3475 metres), a pass marked by a large chorten and many prayer flags. The Schneider map does not show this trail, but it shows Thubten Chhuling as Mopung. The trail is steep, tiring and confusing, so a guide is almost essential. From the monastery, continue up the hill, cross a stream and angle steeply up the side of the ridge. As you near the ridge there is a maze of trails but you should proceed generally south-east and always up. The trail down from the Lapcha La is a herders' trail that drops steeply to the Ringmo Khola, passing through the yards and fields of several houses. It requires about 3 hours of tough walking to reach Ringmo from Thubten Chhuling.

Day 5: Junbesi to Nuntala

Below Junbesi the trail crosses the Junbesi Khola on a wooden bridge at 2640 metres. Just beyond the bridge there is a trail junction. The right-hand or downhill trail leads to Phaphlu, the site of a hospital (operated by the Himalayan Trust) and an airstrip. South of Phaphlu is Salleri, the administrative centre for the Solu Khumbu district. The route to Khumbu takes the left-hand trail that leads uphill. After it has climbed high on the ridge, at about 3080 metres, there is an excellent view of Everest, Chamlang (7317 metres) and Makalu (8463 metres). This is the first view of Everest on the trek and the peak seems dwarfed by its neighbours. The trail turns north, descending through Salung (2980 metres), where there are hotels, to the Ringmo Khola at 2650 metres. This river provides one of the last opportunities to wash clothes and bathe in a large river as the next river, the Dudh Kosi, is too cold for all but the most determined.

From the river the trail ascends to Ringmo where Dorje Passang, an enterprising (and very patient) Sherpa has succeeded in raising a large orchard of apples, peaches and apricots. The fruit has become so abundant that many fruit products – including delicious apple rakshi, apple cider, dried apples and even apple pickles – are available at reasonable prices from the Apple House. At Ringmo the trail joins the 'road' from Okhaldunga to Namche Bazaar that several aid programmes rebuilt between 1980 and 1984. From here to Namche, local labourers widened and levelled the trail and rebuilt many bridges. The aid programmes paid for the work with food instead of cash. The result will probably never be a motorable road, but you can now walk side by side with your friends on the wide trail and the route

avoids many steep ascents and descents that had characterised the old expedition route.

Just beyond Ringmo the trail passes two mani walls. The second wall hides another unexpected opportunity to get lost. Go to the left of the mani wall, make a U-turn and head uphill. The straight trail heads north through unpopulated country (not even a single house), eventually reaching Ghat in the Khumbu Valley after five days. It is not a practical trekking route; several porters perished on this trail during the approach march for the 1952 Swiss Everest Expedition. Assuming you are on the correct trail, it is a short ascent from Ringmo to Trakshindo pass (3071 metres), marked by a large white chorten. A little above Ringmo is a sign advertising a 15 minute walk to the Trakshindo cheese factory. It is worth a visit. Cheese is available year round (at the time of research, the price was Rs 75 per kg), but fresh dairy products such as yoghurt *(dahi)* and milk *(dudh)* are available only in summer and early autumn. Food and accommodation is available at the cheese factory and also at the pass itself in three tiny hotels.

A few minutes below the pass, on the eastern side, the trail passes the isolated monastery of Trakshindo, a superb example of Sherpa monastic architecture. The monastery is certainly the most imposing building seen so far on the trek. Two hotels are outside the monastery grounds. The trail then descends through a conifer and rhododendron forest alive with birds. There are a few herders' huts alongside the trail, but the route is mostly in dense forest. The trail crosses several picturesque streams on wooden bridges just before it reaches Nuntala *(Manidingma)* at 2320 metres. Here there are stone-walled compounds enclosing numerous hotels that range from mediocre to crummy. There is also one small shop. The largest hotel in Nuntala is the *Sherpa Guide Lodge,* which does not normally accept walk-in guests.

Day 6: Nuntala to Khari Khola

From Nuntala the descent continues to the Dudh Kosi (milk river) – the largest river met since the Sun Kosi. Most of the trail is well graded, though it sometimes passes through terraced fields and the yards of houses, then descends steeply through forests to a chautaara overlooking the river. From here it drops on a rough and rocky trail for about 100 metres to a suspension bridge that crosses the Dudh Kosi at 1500 metres. The trail now concludes its trip eastward and turns north up the Dudh Kosi Valley. The old bridge here was destroyed by a flood in 1985. The trail on the eastern side of the river is rough as it crosses debris left by the flood. Beware of stinging nettles *(sisnu)* from here to Chaunrikharka. Local people use nettles as cattle fodder, as a vegetable (they pick them with bamboo tongs) and to make rough cloth. The nettles inflict a painful rash the instant you touch them. At the end of the bridge, turn left and climb through fields of barley, wheat and corn to the large spread out village of Jubing *(Dorakbuk)* at 1680 metres. The people of this village are Rais. Look for signs of Rai culture in this area – the garlands of marigolds that decorate the Dudh Kosi bridge and the use of traditional bamboo pipes instead of plastic hose for the village water supply.

The trail stays below the village. The *Amar Hotel* and the post office are at the northern edge of the village at 1800 metres. Beyond Jubing there is a short climb across a side valley, then a steep climb over a spur. From this ridge you can see Khari Khola *(Khati Thenga)* below you at about 2070 metres. This is predominantly a Sherpa village, though it also has a small Magar community. Descend a little on a sandy trail, then it's a pleasant walk into the main Khari Khola Bazaar. There are several hotels here. The *Quiet View Lodge* and the *River View Lodge* are the upmarket hotels while the *Milan, Annapurna, Sagarmatha* and *Mayalu* hotels are pretty much shared accommodation with the proprietors. A camp site is beyond the village just across the bridge (no camping is allowed in the school yard).

You can save a day on the trek by continuing to Bupsa today, then Ghat the following day and Namche the day after that. This is possible because the new trail has eliminated several steep climbs. If you have porters, however, you may have trouble convincing them to change the schedule because tradition dictates that the camping places should be the ones described here.

Day 7: Khari Khola to Puiyan

From Khari Khola you can see a white chorten on the ridge in Bupsa. The trail descends from Khari Khola village and crosses a stream with the same name on a suspension bridge near some water driven mills at 2010 metres, then makes a steep climb to Bupsa *(Bumshing)* at 2300 metres. There is a hotel halfway up the ridge, three hotels on the ridge and two others about 10 to 15 minutes up the trail. The Bupsa Gompa has been renovated and a lama is usually on hand if you want to visit it.

The trail then climbs steadily, but gently, through forests inhabited by monkeys. The Dudh Kosi canyon is extremely steep here and in many places you can see all the way to the river, 1000 metres below. The trail climbs to a cleft in the rock, then into another canyon before reaching a ridge at about 2900 metres overlooking Puiyan *(Chitok)*, a Sherpa settlement of about 10 houses completely surrounded by forests at 2730 metres. Much of the forest near this village was cut down in the '70s to make charcoal which many hotels and villagers used for fuel in the Khumbu region before kerosene became easily available.

From the ridge, the trail turns almost due east as it descends into the deep canyon of the Puiyan Khola. This portion of the trail is totally new and in many places it is narrow and exposed, especially where it was blasted out of a vertical rock wall. At one point there is a collection of logs and shrubbery, to give you a false sense of security as the trail crosses a rock face above a precipice. After crossing a large slide area, the trail climbs on a stone staircase, then crosses two streams on wooden bridges. All the bridges built under the trail renovation programme are identical in design, though many handrails have now been removed and burned for firewood. A

The God Khumbila & Khumjung Village

large, overhanging rock creates a cave that porters use for shelter. A few minutes beyond the cave is a small stone hotel and a camping place. The owner of this hotel, Passang Phuttar, is likely to be away, so it might be better to continue to the *Holiday Inn*, the last

house in the village, about 15 minutes up the trail.

An old trail goes directly from Khari Khola to Surkhe and avoids the long climb through Puiyan, but it is in disrepair and is subject to rock falls. There is no food or accommodation on this route and even the local people don't use it. There are conflicting reports about the future of this trail. Some people say it is 'cancelled' and others say that it will be improved. This discussion has been going on for as long as I can remember.

Day 8: Puiyan to Phakding

The trail climbs for about an hour after Puiyan to a ridge at 2800 metres then up to another ridge. You can easily recognise Lukla airstrip from here by the multitude of large hotels. You might also be able to spot the remains of one of the two planes that crashed there. The trail descends to Surkhe *(Buwa)* at 2293 metres, on a small tributary stream of the Dudh Kosi. The trail stays above the village, circling it like an expressway. There are a few tea shops near the bridge, but these cater mostly to the local porters that serve the Namche market. A trekkers' hotel is off the trail as you first enter the village. Beware of Friday and Saturday nights in Surkhe and the nearby villages. The porters to and from the Namche market start to travel at first light, and if there is a full moon, this can be at 2 am, causing an uproar in every hotel.

From Surkhe the trail climbs for about 15 minutes to a junction where a stone staircase leads off to the right. This is the trail to Lukla and it requires about an hour of steep climbing to reach the airstrip. It is not necessary to go to Lukla at this point unless you want to make a reservation for a return flight, although they can usually only put you on a waiting list at this end. The Khumbu trail goes north up the steep canyon on a route that a local contractor blasted out of the rock. The trail crosses the large stream that comes from Lukla, then climbs steeply up some wobbly stone steps past several caves to another stream where there is a small bhatti. It is then a short walk uphill through a jumble of boulders to a series of mani walls, then to two brightly painted houses at the beginning of Mushe *(Nangbug)*. Many more mani stones and walls are along this part of the trail. Mushe blends almost imperceptibly into

Chaunrikharka *(Dungde)*, a large village at 2680 metres.

The region from Khari Khola to Jorsale is called Pharak. The Sherpas in this area have slightly different traditions from their neighbours in Solu and Khumbu and have better agricultural opportunities due to the gentler climate in the Dudh Kosi Valley. Pharak villagers raise large crops of corn (maize) and potatoes in summer. They grow wheat, turnips, cauliflower and cabbage in winter and raise herds of cows and yak crossbreeds, as well as sheep and goats.

The major hotel in Chaunrikharka is the wooden building on the right of the trail just after the short steep climb from Mushe. The house just before the stone kani over the trail to the north of the hotel (which isn't much of a hotel) also offers food and accommodation. A shop of sorts is further on, around the corner near the first large chorten. There are three more chortens and some wonderful mani walls, then the trail passes through fields to Chablung *(Lomdza)*.

Here the trail from Lukla joins the route and the character of the trek changes abruptly. When flights operate, 75 to 100 trekkers fly into Lukla every day. If you have walked from Jiri, you will immediately recognise those who have stepped right off the plane – they are cleaner than you and don't smell. Hotels are grander, more frequent, crowded and expensive from here on. In the autumn of 1990 there were at least 20 hotels under construction between here and Namche Bazaar. At Chablung, the trail crosses a stream and continues past a few hotels then continues north through a brief stretch of forest. The trail descends steeply to the Kusum Kangru Khola, crossing it on a wooden bridge. A hotel is near the bridge. The peak at the head of the valley is Kusum Kangru (6367 metres).

Soon you will probably meet your first yaks, wonderful shaggy beasts that create lumbering mobile roadblocks on the trail. Technically, what you will meet are mostly *dzopchuks*, male crossbreeds of yaks and cows, but yak is easier to remember and pronounce. Though yaks are uncomfortable at low elevations, Sherpas use them to transport trekking gear between Lukla and Everest base camp. They are relatively tame and well controlled, but beware of waving horns or an out of control yak roaring down a steep hill. Yaks are all-purpose animals. In addition to their role as load carriers, their wool is woven into blankets and ropes, dung is burned as fuel and female yaks give high quality milk. Being relatives of the cow, the slaughter of yaks is prohibited in Nepal, but when one of these sure footed animals 'falls off the trail', the tasty meat makes its way into yak steaks and yakburgers in hotels throughout Khumbu.

Beyond the Kusum Kangru bridge, the trail climbs a bit, then contours around a ridge to Ghat (*Lhawa*) at 2550 metres, on the banks of the Dudh Kosi. Part of this village and much of the old trail was washed away by floods. A new trail climbs through the village to the Lama Lodge. People sleep in the funny platforms that you can see in the fields in order to chase bears away from the crops. Cross a ridge and climb a bit above the river, passing several scattered houses, then descend a steep stone staircase to a lodge and camping place. The trail climbs again to the *Namaste Lodge,* the first hotel in Phakding. There are many hotels here on both sides of the river at 2800 metres.

In September 1977, an avalanche from Ama Dablam fell into a lake near the base of the peak. This created a wave of water 10 metres high that raced down the Dudh Kosi and washed away large parts of the trail, seven bridges and part of the village of Jorsale, killing three villagers. The drama was repeated in 1985 when a glacial lake above Thami broke loose. The trail is continually undergoing repair and improvement, so portions of the trail between here and Jorsale will probably be different from this description because of recent changes to the trail. In 1990 another glacial lake began building up near Chhukung, above Dingboche. When the moraine that created this lake breaks there will be yet another flood here, so be prepared for frequent changes in this part of the route.

At Phakding the first signs of this devastation become apparent. A long wobbly wooden cantilever bridge crosses the river just beyond the village at 2650 metres. There may be a new suspension bridge south of Phakding, but the trail from this bridge climbs steeply over a ridge. No climbing is necessary if you use the old bridge. At Phakding the *Khumbu Alpine Camp* has been under construction for more than eight years. You can stay here in a reasonably comfortable hotel room for about US$10 a night.

Day 9: Phakding to Namche Bazaar
Another part of Phakding is just above the Khumbu Alpine Camp. Upper Phakding has several bhattis and group camp sites. From Phakding the trail continues north up the Dudh Kosi Valley, staying 100 metres or so above the river on its west bank. The trail crosses a small stream where a tiny hotel sits on the opposite side of the wooden bridge. Take the route straight up the hill and do not follow the old level trail that leads to the right. Climb through fields past a few hotels then past a waterfall to Benkar at 2700 metres. There are several hotels here just behind the huge mani stone in the centre of the trail. Past Benkar the trail crosses the river on another wooden bridge. The trail follows a pleasant route alongside the river then climbs to the village of Chomoa, the site of an agricultural project that was set up to serve the Hotel Everest View, and the *Hatago Lodge*, a creation of funny old Mr Hagayuki who lived here for almost 10 years without a visa and was one of the most colourful of Nepal's many strange characters. All along this part of the trail, villages are interspersed with magnificent forests – rhododendron and magnolia trees and giant firs. In both the early autumn and late spring, the flowers on this portion of the trek make it a beautiful walk. On the cliffs above the river it is possible to see musk deer and Himalayan tahr. If you sit quietly beside the Dudh Kosi you may see water rats swimming in the fast current. When I first heard of these, I assumed they were a close kin of

the legendary yeti, but they do exist in the river here and further upstream towards Thami.

From the lodge at Chomoa, the trail climbs a bit to another hotel (there are more than 100 inns and hotels in Khumbu) and a camp site, then descends steeply into a big valley below Thamserku peak. The trail crosses the stream and climbs out of the valley to Monjo. The *Monjo Hotel* (which once had a sign proclaiming itself to be the Monjo Sheraton) is up a little rise at the northern end of the settlement of only three or four houses. Beyond the hotel, the trail makes a steep rocky descent to a large farm.

Here the trek enters the Sagarmatha (Everest) National Park. There is an entrance station where rangers collect a fee of Rs 250 (about US$8) from each trekker. The rules printed on the back of the entrance ticket are:

Children below 12 years of age shall pay half the entry fee. This permit is nontransferable and good for one entry only. You enter the park on your own risk. His Majesty's Government shall bear no liability for damage, loss, injury or death. Trekking is an acceptable challenge, but please do not:
  litter, dispose it properly.
  remove anything from the park.
  disturb wildlife.
  carry arms and explosives.
  scale any mountain without proper permission.
  scale any sacred peaks of any elevation.
Please keep all the time to the main trek routes. Please be self sufficient in your fuel supply before entering the park. Buying fuel wood from local people or removing any wood materials from the forest is illegal. This will apply to your guides, cooks and porters also.
Park personnel are entitled to arrest any person in charge of having violated park regulations or search his belongings.
For further information visit Park headquarter or ask any park personnel.
National Parks Family Wishes Your Trip Pleasant.

The degree of enforcement of these regulations varies, especially about the use of firewood. It is sometimes difficult to buy kerosene to use as a fuel and almost impossible to find petrol or cooking gas. Kerosene is sometimes available in Namche at the Saturday market in 16 litre tins that are carried by porters from the road head south of Okhaldunga. The price is very negotiable depending on supply and demand. Lesser quantities are available from shopkeepers in Namche throughout the week. If you plan to use kerosene, bring along a filter. Dirt and water can mess up stoves, and both are present in most of the locally available kerosene. Trekkers on their own may eat in houses and hotels that cook over wood fires. Theoretically the national park rules will also eventually prohibit hotels from using firewood.

Lukla General Store operates a kerosene depot out of the Yeti Lodge near the RNAC check-in counter in Lukla. It supplies kerosene and stocks stoves, jerry cans, lanterns and repair parts – available for either sale or rent. It maintains a smaller supply in Namche Bazaar, but Lukla is the main source of kerosene in Khumbu. Kerosene is a nasty porter load. It sloshes around and throws people off balance; and plastic jerry cans and tins always leak and cause chemical burns and irritate the skin of the porters. The Lukla kerosene depot transports kerosene to Lukla by plane and helicopter and has been quite successful in maintaining a reliable supply. The price is high because of the exorbitant cost of the flights. In 1990 the cost was Rs 32.50 per litre in Lukla and Rs 35.50 per litre at their subdepot in Namche, compared to the official rate of Rs 8.50 per litre in Kathmandu. The price is not unreasonable, however, as it costs Rs 3 to Rs 4 per litre per day to carry kerosene from Jiri by porter. When trekking with a group, you or your sherpas will at some stage need to make a side trip to Lukla to arrange a kerosene supply.

There are two routes up the next part of the Dudh Kosi Valley. The easiest one crosses the river beyond the national park entrance station and follows the west bank of the river. A short distance up the river is Jorsale *(Thumbug)* at 2850 metres. Several hotels are packed together along the main street of Jorsale, and you usually have to detour around cows and crowds of porters hanging around the village. The trail then follows the river for a while, then recrosses the Dudh Kosi and makes a steep climb to join the trail near the new Namche bridge.

The Jorsale trail involves two bridge crossings, so it may get washed away. A high trail stays on the east bank of the river, climbing over a ridge above the Dudh Kosi. From the park entrance station there is a climb of several hundred metres, a steep descent and another steep climb, all through forests.

Both routes join above the confluence of two rivers – the Bhote Kosi from the west and the Dudh Kosi from the east. The trail crosses the Dudh Kosi on a new suspension bridge high above the river. After a long climb, the trail reaches a ridge where it joins the old (1970s) route. A welcome tea shop is at the trail junction. It's called the *Everest View*, not to be confused with the Japanese Hotel Everest View near Khumjung.

There is a view of Mt Everest, Nuptse and Lhotse. Because clouds usually obscure the peaks in the afternoon, Everest will probably not be visible when you reach this point. Leaving the hotel the trail climbs less steeply, but still steadily, through forests to a small tea shop and a defunct national park forest nursery. Just beyond the nursery is a small spring and a hydraulic ram system that pumps water to the national park and army offices on the hill. When the trail turns into a stream, take the right, upper trail to reach the main street of Namche. The left-hand trail leads to the lower pastures of the village.

Namche Bazaar *(Nauche)*, at 3440 metres, is the administrative centre for the Khumbu region and has a police check post, the headquarters for Sagarmatha National Park, a bank (you can sometimes change money here), several shops selling items of every description and a proliferation of hotels and restaurants. There is even a small bakery and several hotels with hot showers among the 100-odd houses of this prosperous village. You can stock up here on food, film, postcards and souvenirs. You can also buy or rent any trekking or climbing gear that you need.

It is probably futile trying to keep up-to-date on the latest hotel developments in Namche. Not counting the small bhattis

catering to locals and the homes that offer food and accommodation but do not have hotel signs, there are at least 11 major hotels here. The most popular is Lakpa Dorje's *Trekkers Inn*, which churns out yak steaks by the hundreds. The largest is Passang Kami's *Khumbu Lodge*, which offers private rooms for Rs 60 including the 'Jimmy Carter slept here' suite. Private rooms are also available in *Namche Hotel* (also called the *Cooperative Hotel*) which is the large low building in the centre of town. Sit in the sun at the *Tawa Lodge* and watch the village activity as you eat freshly baked cinnamon rolls. *Namche Bazaar Guest House* also has a camp ground and features Friday night slide shows. Other popular hotels are the *Thamserku*, *Kala Pattar* and the *Sherpa Hotel*. The owners of the *Khumbila Hotel*, which is near the entrance to the village, have a sister who married a Japanese, so this hotel is a bit upmarket with private rooms and other amenities. It is also the village disco.

A UNESCO sponsored project introduced electricity to Namche in October 1983. The hydroelectric plant is below Namche and uses the small stream that runs through the village. Each house has two 40 watt lights; some hotels have electric stoves that they can use during the day. All the wiring is underground. Despite technical problems caused by overloading the system, the electricity is working surprisingly well and Namche exudes a certain amount of charm in the evening. The lights go off at 10 pm. There are 125 houses with electricity, including the national park and government offices on the hill and the houses of Chhorkung, above Namche. Four hotels in Namche also have electric stoves. The electricity project is part of an effort to conserve energy and reduce environmental degradation in Khumbu. The large area fenced in by stones above Namche is a forest plantation that is part of the same effort.

There is a lot of trekking equipment available for rent in Namche. If you discover that your jacket or sleeping bag is not warm enough, you can rent one here. There are three competing clocks in Namche. The bank, police and army all sound the hour by striking an empty oxygen cylinder.

Historically, Sherpas were herders and traders. Namche Bazaar was the staging point for expeditions over the Nangpa La into Tibet with loads of manufactured goods from India. On the return trip they brought wool, yaks and salt. In the barren fields of Khumbu they raise barley, potatoes and a few vegetables, but the Sherpa economy has always relied on trading. As you walk through Khumbu you will see women excavating potatoes from the deep pits in which they store them during winter to keep them from freezing. Trekking has provided the people of Khumbu with the income to remain here despite the limited indigenous food supply.

Each Saturday there is an important weekly *hat* or market. Lowland people come to Namche to sell corn, rice, eggs, vegetables and other items not grown in Khumbu. During the trekking season, butchers usually slaughter two or more buffaloes each week, so meat is available on Saturdays and Sundays.

Porters carry their loads to Namche Bazaar from villages six to 10 days away (the buffaloes walk themselves) and sell their wares directly. It is an important social event, as well as the focus for the region's trade. Sherpas from all the neighbouring villages come to purchase food and socialise and the bazaar becomes a crowded rumpus of Sherpas, local government officials, porters and sightseers. It is totally a cash market, in which Sherpas exchange money they have received from trekking or mountaineering parties for the goods they require. The market starts early and is usually finished by noon.

The fun loving Sherpas often tell the Rais and other people who carry goods to the market that the money comes from Mt Everest, and it is not uncommon to find an unsuspecting lowland porter shivering with cold as he accompanies a trekking party to Everest base camp in search of the free money that tumbles from the highest peak on earth.

Day 10: Acclimatisation Day in Namche Bazaar

Acclimatisation is important before proceeding higher. This is the first of two specific 'acclimatisation days' that everyone should build into their trek schedule. You can spend the day by taking a day hike to Thami, by visiting Khunde or Khumjung, or by relaxing and exploring Namche Bazaar. There is a police check post in Namche where you must present your trekking permit. The police officials endorse the permit and enter the details into a register. Sometimes there is a form to fill in and often police require that trekkers sign the register. If so, you will have to go personally to the police check post, but often a trekking guide can take your permit and undertake the formalities for you. Bring both your trekking permit and national park entrance ticket for police to examine.

Above the police check post, at the top of the hill, is the Sagarmatha National Park headquarters. The visitor centre here is well worth a visit. It has displays about the people, forests, wildlife, mountaineering and the impact of tourism.

The name of the region above Namche, but below the national park headquarters, is Chhorkung. This nonvillage has grown a lot, and now has several hotels and camp sites.

Some of Namche's strangest visitors are the runners in the Everest Marathon, an annual event in late November that follows a route from Gorak Shep to Tengpoche, then to Namche and a loop out to Thammu before returning to the finishing line in Namche. Runners complete the 26 mile (42 km) run in a respectable 4½ to 5 hours, but remember that they made a slow ascent in order to acclimatise.

Day 11: Namche Bazaar to Tengpoche

There is a direct route from Namche Bazaar to Tengpoche that starts from Chhorkung. A more varied trip is via a slightly longer route visiting Khumjung, the largest village in Khumbu, and Khunde, its smaller neighbour. From Namche Bazaar it is a steep 1 hour climb to the Shyangboche airstrip (3720

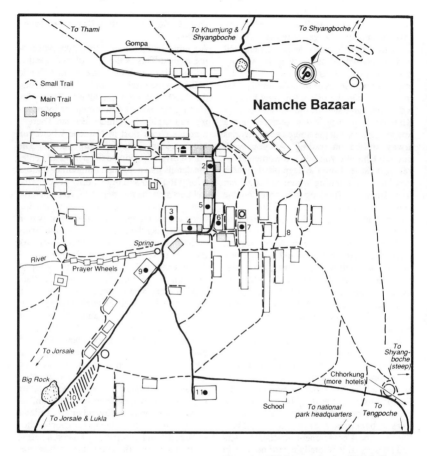

Namche Bazaar

1 Post Office
2 Bank
3 Cooperative Hotel
4 International Footrest
5 Khumbu Lodge
6 Tawa Lodge
7 Trekkers Inn
8 Namche Bazaar Guest House
9 Khumbila Hotel
10 Saturday Market
11 Police Check Post

metres), which serves the Hotel Everest View. In the early morning you might see the spectacular landing (or the more spectacular take off) of a Pilatus Porter STOL aircraft at Shyangboche. Expensive seats on the six passenger plane to Kathmandu are sometimes available at short notice.

There are a few tea shops near the airstrip, but there is a water problem here, so it isn't a good place to stay for the night. From the airstrip it is a 20 minute walk to the hotel, which provides excellent views of Everest and Ama Dablam. The hotel was closed for many years, but was refurbished in 1990.

You can get a cup of coffee or tea or an extravagant meal here. Breakfast is US$7, lunch US$10 and dinner US$18. Rooms are US$120 per night with an extra charge for oxygen or a pressurised room. Just outside the door of the posh hotel is a bhatti that offers cheaper food and lodging.

A trail descends from the hotel to Khumjung village (3790 metres) or you can walk from the airstrip directly to Khumjung. To take the direct trail from the airport, head for the chorten at the top of the hill and follow the trail down through the forest. In the morning, just follow the schoolchildren from Namche to Khumjung, at the foot of the sacred peak of Khumbila (5861 metres).

The Khumjung Gompa possesses what is said to be the skull of a yeti or abominable snowman. Sir Edmund Hillary, village headman Khunjo Chumbi, Desmond Doig and Marlin Perkins took this relic to the USA in 1960 to be examined by scientists. They said the scalp was made from the skin of a serow, a member of the antelope family, but the yeti legend still continues.

Also in Khumjung is the original Hillary school which has succeeded in providing an excellent primary education for many of the children of Khumbu. In 1983 the Himalayan Trust expanded the school to include a high school. Sherpa children no longer have to go to boarding school at Salleri, a week away, to complete their education. It is only a short detour from Khumjung to Khunde, the site of the Khunde Hospital, also built and maintained by the Himalayan Trust.

From Khumjung the trail goes down the valley, continuously passing picturesque mani walls and chortens. After a short descent it meets the main Namche Bazaar to Tengpoche trail. Beyond a few mani stones is another group of hotels. This settlement, called Kenjoma *(Sanasa)* by the locals and 'schlockmeister junction' by trek leaders, is inhabited primarily by Tibetans. There is always an extensive display of Tibetan (and made in Kathmandu) souvenirs to tempt you. Bargaining is very much in order. The trail descends gradually to Teshinga, then steeply to Phunki Thanghka, a small settlement with several water driven prayer wheels on the banks of the Dudh Kosi (3250 metres).

There is only one hotel in Khumjung, none in Khunde, only food (and lots of booze) in Kenjoma, a small hotel in Teshinga and three hotels in Phunki Thanghka.

From Phunki Thanghka the trail climbs steeply at first, then makes a gradual ascent through forests and around mani stones as it follows the side of a hill up to the saddle on which Tengpoche Monastery sits at 3870 metres, in a clearing surrounded by dwarf firs and rhododendrons. The view from this spot, seen to best advantage in the morning, is rightly deemed to be one of the most magnificent in the world. Kwangde (6187 metres), Tawachee (6542 metres), Everest (8848 metres), Nuptse (7855 metres), Lhotse (8616 metres), Ama Dablam (6856 metres), Kantega (6779 metres) and Thamserku (6608 metres) provide an inspiring panorama of Himalayan giants.

The following sign used to appear near the monastery guesthouse:

I am happy to welcome you to Tengpoche.

This is the religious centre of the whole 'Sherpa-land', in fact the entire Solu-Khumbu area.

A very modest rest house has been built on the far end of the meadow facing Chomolungma (Mt Everest).

It has been erected with the funds collected from friends and visitors who have come to this sacred and beautiful place. If you wish, you may contribute to our meagre funds to enable us to make it more comfortable when you come again, for we hope you will. Anything you wish to give will be gratefully accepted.

While you are a guest at Tengpoche, whether you stay in the rest house or in your own tents, I wish to request you to observe the few rules in observance of the Divine Dharma. Please do not kill or cause to kill any living creature in the area of this holy place. This includes domestic fowls and animals, as also wild game.

Please remember that this holy place is devoted to the worship of the Perfect One, and that nothing should be done within these sacred precincts which will offend or cause to hurt those who live here in humility and serenity. May you journey in peace and walk in delight, and may the blessings of the Perfect One be always with you.

Nawang Tenzing
The Reincarnate of T

The sign has long since disappeared and has been replaced by a fancy carved sign directing visitors to the New Zealand built *Tengpoche Trekkers Lodge*, a part of the Sagarmatha National Park development. No longer is it necessary to endure the simple lodging offered by the lamas; now you can sit around a stove burning charcoal (from Puiyan, outside the national park) and write comments in the guest book either praising or damning the lodge concept.

In addition to the national park lodge, there is a choice of other facilities at Tengpoche. The gompa owned hotel is the most popular and has two rooms of dormitory accommodation and a huge kitchen-dining room that is often the centre of social life for both foreigners and locals. It has a cosy ski lodge atmosphere and is worth visiting at least for a cup of tea or rakshi. The *Namaste Lodge* across the field is cheaper and a bit rougher, but Passang Thongdup is a personable and helpful hotelier. There is another unnamed hotel near the Namaste, but it caters primarily to locals. The gompa charges Rs 5 for each tent at Tengpoche and a lama comes around with a receipt book to be sure that you pay this fee. It is one of the few sources of revenue for the monastery, which supports about 50 or 60 monks, so it isn't reasonable to argue about this charge. Several trekking companies donate money to the monastery each year and in return receive the use of certain camping sites. The lamas won't let you camp in these places. There is also a camping place and a hotel at Devuche, about a 20 minute walk from Tengpoche. This may be a better choice when Tengpoche camp sites are filled to capacity.

Tengpoche (many older maps spell it as Thyangboche, but the preferred phonetic spelling is Tengpoche) was founded by Lama Gulu, a monk from Khumjung, on the instructions of the abbot of Rongbuk Monastery. Construction of the main temple building was completed in 1919. An earthquake destroyed the gompa in 1933, killing Lama Gulu. The temple was rebuilt a few

years later and the remains of the founding lama were buried inside the gompa. On 19 January 1989 a fire devastated the monastery. Many items of the monastery's extensive collection of books, paintings and religious relics were saved, but the entire gompa building was destroyed. The Sherpa people of Khumbu, with help from many international organisations, have raised funds for the reconstruction of the gompa building, estimated at US$500,000. Construction was begun in April 1990 and an imposing edifice is rising from the ruins.

Tengpoche is the largest and most active monastery in Khumbu, but it is not the oldest. Sherpas believe that Buddhism was introduced into Khumbu towards the end of the 17th century by Lama Sange Dorje, the fifth of the reincarnate lamas of the Rongphu (or Rongbuk) Monastery in Tibet, to the north of Mt Everest. According to legend, Lama Sange Dorje flew over the Himalaya and landed on rocks at Pangboche and Tengpoche, leaving his footprints. He is thought to have been responsible for the founding of the first gompas in Khumbu, at Pangboche and Thami.

The gompas of Khumjung and Namche Bazaar are of a later date. None of these were monasteries. Their priests were married lamas and there was no monastic community with a formal organisation and discipline. The first monasteries, at Tengpoche and Thami (at about the same time) were established as offshoots of the Nyingmapa (Red Hat) sect monastery of Rong-phu in Tibet, and young monks were sent there to study. Tengpoche's charter bears the seal of the abbot of Rong-phu. A nunnery was later founded at Devuche, just north of Tengpoche. Trakshindo was established in 1946 by a lama from Tengpoche.

A library and cultural centre behind the gompa was designed by the abbot to cater to both Tibetan scholars and trekkers. The plan is to develop an extensive library of books on religion, culture and history in several languages. A school building adjoining the gompa was also severely damaged by the fire. While a new building is being constructed, about 30 young monks continue their religious education in the homes of lamas.

Day 12: Tengpoche to Pheriche

From Tengpoche it's a short, steep and muddy descent to Devuche through a forest of birches, conifers and rhododendrons. Because of the ban on hunting at Tengpoche, you can often see almost tame blood pheasants and Nepal's national bird, the Danphe or Impeyan pheasant. This colourful bird lives only at high altitudes. The tail is reddish, it has a shiny blue back and has a metallic green tinge and pure white under its wings. It appears almost iridescent when seen in sunlight. Another common bird in this region is the snow pigeon, which swoops in great flocks above the villages of Khumjung, Namche and Pangboche. The crowlike birds that scavenge any food that you might drop (I have even seen them fly away with a full packet of biscuits that they have stolen) are red billed choughs and occasionally ravens. The Sherpas call both birds *goraks*. Near Gorak Shep you are likely to see Tibetan snow cocks racing happily down the hillside. High above you may see goshawks, Himalayan griffons, golden eagles and lammergeiers circling on the updrafts from the mountains. In the early morning and just before dusk you may see musk deer, especially in the forests below Tengpoche, leaping like kangaroos.

There is a lodge near the stream at Devuche. The few houses of Devuche and the village gompa are off in the trees to the west and the nunnery (which isn't very enthusiastic about visitors) is up the hill to the east. From Devuche the level trail passes many mani walls in a deep rhododendron forest. Watch the leaves curl up in the cold and open in the morning when the sun strikes them. After crossing the Imja Khola on a steel bridge, swaying a terrifying distance above the river at a spot where the river rushes through a narrow cleft, the route climbs past some magnificently carved mani stones to Pangboche at 3860 metres. Just before the village are two chortens, a kani

and a resting place. Just east of here is a monument where you can see the footprint of the patron saint Lama Sange Dorje preserved in stone.

Pangboche is the highest year round settlement in the valley. The Pangboche Gompa is the oldest in Khumbu and has relics which are said to be the skull and hand of a yeti. Visitors may see these artefacts for a small fee. Pangboche is actually two villages, an upper and a lower village. On the way to the Everest base camp the lower route is best, but on the return trip, use the upper trail and visit the gompa, 120 metres above the lower village. There are three hotels in lower Pangboche, one at each end of the village and one in the centre – good choices for lunch.

From Pangboche the route enters alpine meadows above the tree line. Most of the vegetation is scrub juniper, tundra and wildflowers, including edelweiss. At Showma there is a tea shop, then the trail passes several yak herders' goths as it ascends on a shelf above the river to Orsho where there is a small hotel. Beyond Orsho the trail divides. The lower, more important looking trail, leads to Dingboche while the trail to Pheriche goes up to the left, through the front yards of a few herders' huts, over a stone wall and climbs a small ridge before descending to the Khumbu Khola, crossing it on a wooden bridge. From the bridge it is a 10 minute walk, usually in the wind, to Pheriche at 4240 metres. Pheriche is windier, so it feels colder than most places in Khumbu. Be sure that you carry your warmest clothing on this day.

A trekkers' aid post is at Pheriche, supported by the Himalayan Rescue Association and Tokyo Medical College. A Western physician is usually in attendance during the trekking season. This establishment and the doctors who operate it specialise in the study and treatment of altitude sickness and strive to educate trekkers in the dangers of too fast an ascent to high altitudes. The doctors give lectures every day, usually at 3.30 pm. The aid post also rents books and sells patches, T-shirts and mani stones to raise money. Visit the clinic if you have even the slightest

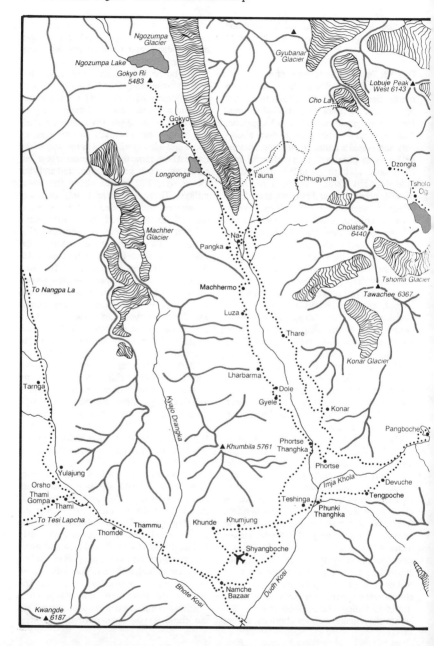

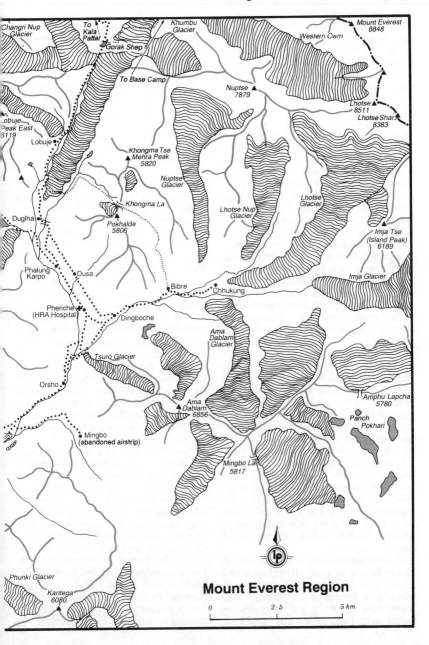

Mount Everest Region

problem with altitude. Even though the doctors are volunteers, the HRA has considerable expenses, so they charge for consultations and treatment.

Pheriche is a labyrinth of walls and pastures. There are five hotels, including the *National Park Lodge* that is an on-off affair depending on who has the contract to operate it. The biggest hotel is Nima Tsering's *Himalayan Hotel*, a two-storey place with a tin roof. Other hotels are semipermanent buildings which have evolved from sod huts with a tarp on the roof into more substantial structures that are forever expanding.

Be careful when you sit down in these crowded places – that comfortable looking cushion in the corner is likely to be a baby wrapped up in blankets. The *Snow View Hotel* has a mountaineering equipment shop. The usual jumble of new and used climbing equipment is for sale and there is often an unlikely collection of expedition food available, such as Bulgarian stews, Russian borscht, Yugoslavian halibut, French snails or American granola bars – depending on which country recently had an Everest expedition.

Day 13: Acclimatisation Day in Pheriche

The most important key to acclimatisation to high altitudes is a slow ascent. Therefore it is imperative that you spend an additional night at Pheriche to aid the acclimatisation process. This is the second of the mandatory acclimatisation days on this trek.

You may spend the day in many ways. You may wish to declare a rest day and relax in camp or you may wish to do some strenuous exploring. It is a short hike to the small Nangkartshang Gompa, a climb of about 400 metres above the village. From this vantage point there is a good view to the east of Makalu, the fifth highest mountain in the world.

A more strenuous trip is to climb the hill to Dingboche, then hike up the Imja Khola Valley past Bibre to Chhukung, a small summer settlement at 4700 metres. The views from Chhukung and further up the valley on the moraines towards Island Peak

(6189 metres) are tremendous. The great southern face of Lhotse towers above to the north and Amphu Lapcha and the immense fluted ice walls that flank it dominate the horizon to the south.

To the south-west, the eastern face of Ama Dablam provides an unusual view of this picturesque peak. This hike is one of the highlights of the trek. It is a fast trip back down the valley to Pheriche for the night. There are hotels in Chhukung and Dingboche that provide lunch.

Day 14: Pheriche to Lobuje

The trail ascends the broad, gently sloping valley from Pheriche to Phalang Karpo (4340 metres). In many places the trail crosses small streams on boulders. Look back down the valley from Phalang Karpo to see how much elevation you have gained. The views of Tawachee and Cholatse (6440 metres) are particularly good from this portion of the trail as it passes through country reported to be the habitat of the snow leopard and yeti. Ama Dablam is seen from a different aspect here and is hardly recognisable. The true top of Kantega is visible far to the left of the prominent saddle seen from Tengpoche. Beyond Phalang Karpo the trail climbs steeply onto the terminal moraine of the Khumbu Glacier then contours down to a stream, crossing it on a bridge just before the village of Duglha (4620 metres). A tea shop is near the stream and two others are a bit higher.

From Duglha the trail climbs higher on the moraine to a row of stone monuments in memory of six Sherpas who died in an avalanche during the 1970 Japanese Skiing Expedition on Everest. There are several other monuments to climbers who have perished since then. The collection has now grown to a total of 18 memorials, mostly for Sherpas. The trail then drops a bit and follows the western side of the valley to Lobuje, a summer village that boasts several hotels at 4930 metres. The New Zealand National Park advisors built a lodge at Lobuje that has 24 bed spaces and is run on contract by Karma Sherpa. The *Above the*

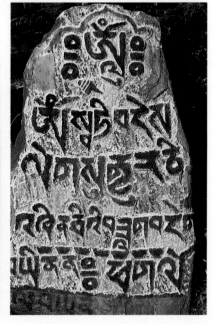

Top: Pilgrim shelters, Gosainkund Lake (SA)
Left: Glacier Dome from Manang (RR)
Right: Carved mani stone (SA)

Top: A sherpa cook packing provisions for a group trek (SA)
Left: Swimming hole below Keswa village (SA)
Right: Icefall on Kyabru (SA)

Clouds Lodge accommodates 18 and the *Kala Pattar* and *Sherpa* hotels provide a few more beds. The sherpas and porters that accompany trekking groups further crowd the hotels when they come in for tea or rakshi (which can have a dramatic effect at this elevation).

Everything is expensive in Lobuje. Tea is Rs 2 per cup and wood costs Rs 60 for a load that is one third the size of a lowland load. If you are travelling with a group, the sherpas will do the racing ahead to stake out a good camp site and get the use of one of the two herders' huts as a kitchen. You can almost always rely on finding food and accommodation (though it may be crowded) at Lobuje, but you will certainly need a warm sleeping bag – there is usually no bedding available and there is a limited supply of mattresses. The sunset on Nuptse, seen from Lobuje, is a memorable sight.

Day 15: Lobuje to Gorak Shep

The first section of the trail from Lobuje follows the western side of the broad Khumbu Valley and ascends gently through meadows beside the glacial moraine. A pyramid shaped Italian research station that looks like an invading spaceship is in the first side valley beyond Lobuje. Fortunately, you cannot see it from the trail. The ascent becomes steeper and rougher as it crosses several side moraines, although the trail is usually well defined. In places, however, an active glacier is under the moraine, so the trail is constantly changing. Route finding techniques here include looking for stone cairns as markers and watching for traces of yak dung – a sure sign of the correct trail.

After rounding a bend in the trail, the conical peak Pumori (7161 metres) comes into view. On the lower slopes of this mountain a ridge extending to the south terminates in a small peak. This peak, Kala Pattar, meaning 'black rock', is 5545 metres high and provides the best vantage point for viewing Mt Everest. Kala Pattar is actually a Hindi name. Legend has it that the late Dawa Tenzing accidentally named the peak when he accompanied the first foreigner, Jimmy

Roberts, to the top. Roberts and Dawa Tenzing communicated in Hindi, not Nepali. You can easily make the ascent of Kala Pattar from Gorak Shep in the afternoon or the following morning.

The trail makes a short descent onto the sandy flat expanse of Gorak Shep (5160 metres). This was the base camp for the 1952 Swiss Everest Expedition. In 1953 the British Everest Expedition called this 'lake camp'. Gorak Shep has a small lake that is usually frozen and several monuments to climbers who have died during various Everest expeditions. The carved stone in memory of Jake Breitenbach of the 1963 American Expedition and the monument for Indian Ambassador H Dayal who died during a visit to base camp after the 1965 Indian Expedition are to the north-east of the lake.

It is normal to reach Gorak Shep by lunch time. Most people spend the rest of the day resting, but if you are not tired by the altitude, you can climb Kala Pattar or go to the base camp in the afternoon. There are two herders' huts at Gorak Shep near the lake, but they are small and dirty and are only emergency shelter. The *Yeti Tea Shop*, run by Ang Lamu Sherpani, has a few bunks in its one room building. Ang Lamu often closes during the coldest months from December to February and returns to Khumjung, so it is best to inquire at Lobuje before counting on this facility during winter. It should be possible to find food and shelter here at most other times during the trekking season. The best plan of all is to start early in the morning and go from Lobuje to Kala Pattar via Gorak Shep and return to Lobuje for the night, avoiding the necessity of staying at Gorak Shep.

Day 16: Gorak Shep to Lobuje

It is impossible to explain the discomfort of high altitude to someone who has not experienced it. Most people have an uncomfortable, often sleepless, night at both Gorak Shep and Lobuje, despite the extra time taken for acclimatisation. By descending 300 metres to Lobuje, or better yet, to

Lama Sange Dorje & Tengpoche Gompa

Pheriche, most people experience an immediate improvement, so it is really not worth spending an additional night at 5160 metres.

Mornings are usually sparkling clear and the climb of Kala Pattar is one of the most rewarding parts of the trip. It is a steep ascent up the grassy slopes west of Gorak Shep to a shelf at the foot of Pumori. Even from this low vantage point the entire Everest south face is visible as well as the Lho La (the pass between Nepal and Tibet, from which

George Leigh Mallory looked into Nepal in 1921 and named the Western Cwm), Changtse (the northern peak of Everest) and most of the West Ridge route climbed by Unsoeld and Hornbein in 1963. Those familiar with the accounts of expeditions to the Tibetan side of Everest will be able to spot the northern ridge and the first and second steps, prominent obstacles during the attempts on the mountain in the 1920s and '30s. Continuing to the top of Kala Pattar, more of the peak of Everest itself comes into view, and a short walk north from the summit of Kala Pattar on the ridge towards Pumori will allow an unobstructed view all the way to the South Col.

The walk to base camp is about a 6 hour round trip, possibly more unless an expedition in progress has kept the ever changing trail in good condition. The route follows the Khumbu Glacier, sometimes on the moraine and sometimes on the glacier itself. The walk is especially intriguing for the views of the 15 metre high seracs of ice, a feature peculiar to Himalayan glaciers.

Everest base camp is not actually a specific site. Various expeditions have selected different locations for a semipermanent camp during their assault on the mountain. Some of the base camp sites are identifiable from debris on the glacier at 5360 metres or more. The trip to base camp, while fascinating, is not as spectacular as the ascent of Kala Pattar because there is no view of Everest itself from base camp.

It is difficult to go to both base camp and Kala Pattar in a single day. If you wish to do both, use the afternoon of the day at Gorak Shep for one trip and the next morning for the other. The exhaustion and lethargy caused by the altitude limits many people to only one of the possible options. The descent to Lobuje is easy, but seems endless because of the many uphill climbs from Gorak Shep. The night, however, will be much more comfortable than the previous one.

Day 17: Lobuje to Dingboche
To go to Dingboche, retrace your steps back down to Duglha, then go straight up the hill

from the bridge to reach an upper trail, staying high above the valley floor, past the yak pastures at Dusa to a chorten at the head of the Imja Valley. From here the views are great – you can easily recognise Island Peak because its name is an apt description. Makalu is the greenish-grey peak visible in the distance over the pass to the right of Island Peak. From the chorten descend to Dingboche at 4360 metres, following the trail as it traverses east into the valley. The high pastures in this region are sometimes referred to as 'summer villages'. Sherpas with homes lower in the valley own small stone huts in the higher regions and occupy them in summer while their herds of yaks graze in the surrounding pastures. A few crops, especially barley, are also grown in these high fields. While Dingboche does not have all the hotels and tourist facilities of Pheriche, it is a more typical summer village and the mountain scenery is outstanding. There is one real hotel in Dingboche and two houses that have hotel signboards. There are also two hotels in Chhukung, several hours up the valley.

Day 18: Dingboche to Tengpoche
The route from Dingboche descends the Imja Khola Valley, then crosses the Khumbu Khola on a wooden bridge and climbs to rejoin the upward trail. Following the trail downhill, it is easy to make a detour and visit the upper part of Pangboche and the village gompa, then continue to Tengpoche for the night. While ascents at high altitudes must be slow, you may safely descend as fast as you wish.

Day 19: Tengpoche to Namche Bazaar
The trail returns to Phunki Thanghka, then ascends the ridge towards Namche Bazaar. The direct route to Namche follows the side of the ridge and avoids a lot of climbing, but it's a long walk in and out of side valleys. An alternative route through Khumjung allows a visit to either the Hotel Everest View or Sherpa villages before the steep descent to Namche, but involves climbing an extra 200 metres. In Namche Bazaar you will have a

last opportunity to buy (mostly) phoney Tibetan jewellery from a dozen Tibetan merchants who spread their wares beside every camp site and alongside the trail at the oddest places.

Day 20: Namche Bazaar to Lukla

From Namche, the steep descent back to the Dudh Kosi at Jorsale is a bit rough on the knees, but the warmer climate offers a good opportunity to finally shed down jackets and woollen jumpers. You must be at the airport at Lukla the night before your flight to reconfirm reservations if you have these – your seats will vanish if you do not reconfirm reservations. The trail from Jorsale to Lukla follows the upward route as far as Chablung, then turns off above the village of Chaunrikharka towards Lukla.

The broad trail to Lukla climbs steadily past a few bhattis. After the steep final climb there is a collection of houses and bhattis in a new settlement far from the airport. As you approach the airstrip the houses and hotels rapidly proliferate.

High above the river on a shelf at 2800 metres, Lukla is another classic paradox in determining altitudes because the runway is on a slope and there is a difference of almost 60 metres between the lower and upper ends of the runway.

Lukla has a good choice of hotels. The upmarket *Sherpa Cooperative Hotel* halfway down the airstrip offers rooms for about US$10 a night. The hotel's Tibetan-style dining room is the centre of Lukla's social life and is also the source of all the rumours about flight operations. *Hotel Sagarmatha* near the airport check-in building is the newest, fanciest and most expensive at US$25 per night. *Buddha Lodge*, near the airport, also has private rooms, hot showers and a reasonably efficient short-order kitchen. Most other hotels offer dormitories and less extensive (but cheaper) menus.

The RNAC office is open for 1 hour in the evening – usually from 5 to 6 pm, but sometimes from 6 to 7 pm. It posts a sign announcing the office hours. You can recon-firm flights only during this period. If you are not present the night before the flight you probably will lose your seat. The radio message telling the RNAC staff how many flights are scheduled for the following day usually doesn't come until after the office closes. This adds an atmosphere of mystery and intrigue to the proceedings. In fact, the airline does not prepare the actual flight schedule for each day until about 7 pm when they know where each plane ended up for the night. Check-in begins early and can be chaotic. If your innkeeper or trekking agent offers to check you in for the flight, take advantage of this. There isn't much to do at Lukla other than wait for planes or talk about when the plane will come.

Day 21: Lukla to Kathmandu

The trek to Dhankuta becomes attractive because it avoids the pile up at Lukla and explores some unusual country unlike any that you have seen on the first portion of the trek.

The flight from Lukla to Kathmandu takes 35 minutes and is a jarring return to the noise, confusion and rush of a large city.

TO GOKYO

The trek to Gokyo offers an alternative to the traditional trek to Everest base camp. From Gokyo, more of Everest itself is visible, though from a slightly greater distance than from Kala Pattar above Gorak Shep. The mountains are more spectacular, the Ngozumpa Glacier is the largest in the Nepal Himalaya and from a ridge above Gokyo, four 8000 metre peaks (Cho Oyu, Everest, Lhotse and Makalu) are visible at once. The view of the tremendous ice ridge between Cho Oyu (8201 metres) and Gyachung Kang (7952 metres) is one of the most dramatic panoramas in Khumbu. There are many options for additional exploration and high altitude walking, including a 5400 metre high pass into Khumbu.

Day 1: Namche Bazaar

Acclimatisation is essential for this trek. It is easy to get too high too fast and succumb to

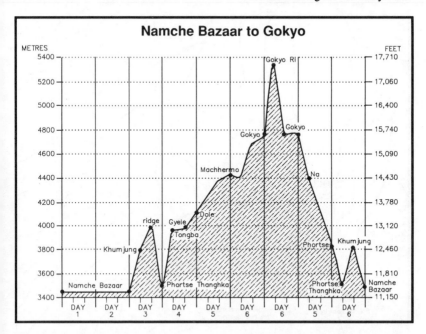

Namche Bazaar to Gokyo

altitude sickness. Only after a minimum of three days in the Namche-Khumjung region is it safe to begin this trek.

Day 2: Namche Bazaar

Don't rush. The Himalayan Rescue Association doctors have determined that you must acclimatise before you begin the Gokyo trek. There are lots of things to do here. Take a hike to Thami, visit Khumjung or eat apple pie in Namche. Hiking will help acclimatisation more than the apple pie, however.

Day 3: Namche Bazaar to Phortse Thanghka

Climb the hill to Khumjung and descend to the west of the village down the broad valley leading to the Dudh Kosi. The Gokyo route turns north, climbing above the more frequented route to Tengpoche and Everest base camp.

There is a choice of routes in the begin-

ning: the yak trail which climbs gently, but traverses a long distance around the ridge; or the steep staircase-like trail made of rocks embedded in a narrow cleft in a large boulder. The Sherpas claim that the steeper trail is better – for exercise. The two trails soon join and continue towards a large chorten on the top of a ridge at 3973 metres. This ridge descends from Khumbila (5761 metres), the abode of the patron god of the Khumbu region. Khumbila (or more correctly *Khumbu Yul Lha*, translates as Khumbu area god). On thankas and other monastery paintings this god is depicted as a white faced figure riding on a white horse. Numbur, the mountain that towers over Junbesi and the Solu region, is the protector god of that area and has the Sherpa name *Shorong Yul Lha*, Solu area god.

From the ridge, the trail descends in a series of steep switchbacks down a sandy slope to the Dudh Kosi. An excellent camping spot is at Phortse Thanghka, near

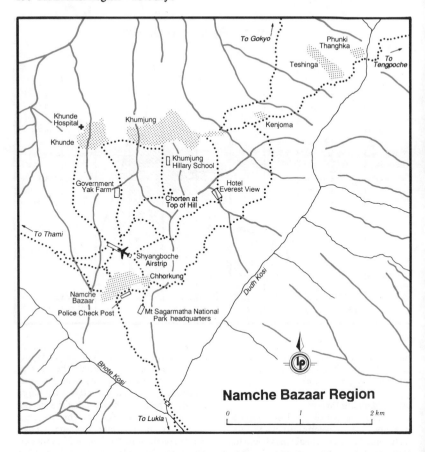

Namche Bazaar Region

the river at 3500 metres, just before the bridge that provides access to Phortse, an isolated village of about 60 houses. It is possible to go much further in a single day from Khumjung – as far as Tongba or Gyele – but it doesn't serve much purpose and it can be dangerous because of the rapid increase in elevation.

Day 4: Phortse Thanghka to Dole
You should make this another easy day to aid your acclimatisation to the altitude. The trail climbs steeply out of the valley through rhododendron forests which give way to

fragrant stands of juniper and large conifers as the elevation increases. This portion of the trek is especially beautiful in spring when the rhododendrons are blooming – late April and early May at this elevation. The trail passes through many kharkas, summer settlements used when sherpas bring herds of yaks to graze in these high pastures. Some of the villages in this valley are occupied as late as December by people grazing their herds.

We tend to oversimplify the many manifestations of the yak into this single word, yet it is only the full blooded, long haired bull that truly has the name yak. The female is called a nak. A female crossbreed between a cow and a yak is called a *dzum*. It's prized for its milk, rich in butterfat, which Sherpas use to make cheese and butter. The male crossbreed, the infertile dzopchuk, is (relatively) docile and is used to transport loads and as a plough animal. Most of the 'yaks' seen along the trails of Khumbu are in fact dzopchuks. There are numerous other names for crosses between cattle and naks and for second generation crossbreeds, but the yak, nak, dzum and dzopchuk are sufficiently confusing for this lesson in yak husbandry.

The route passes through the settlements of Tongba (3950 metres) and Gyele (3960 metres) to Dole where there are two hotels. The views of Khumbila and Tawachee (6542 metres) are tremendous throughout the day, and it is possible to climb a ridge behind Dole for an even broader view up and down the valley.

Day 5: Dole to Machhermo
From Dole the trail climbs to Lhabarma at 4220 metres and Luza at 4360 metres. The trail is steep in most places as it climbs through scrub junipers. There are kharkas wherever there is a flat spot and the slightest hint of water. In winter, some of these villages have no nearby water source. However, Luza is on the banks of a large stream and has a year round supply. People from Khumjung own all the kharkas on this side of the valley. Many families have houses in several settlements and move their herds from place to place as the grass becomes overgrazed and the snows melt.

The trail continues to climb along the side of the valley, high above the river, crossing sandy spurs to Machhermo at 4410 metres. It was in Machhermo in 1974 that a yeti killed three yaks and attacked a Sherpa woman. This is the most credible yeti incident ever reported, so be watchful as you visit this region.

There are two hotels in Machhermo.

Day 6: Machhermo to Gokyo
Beyond Machhermo the trail climbs a ridge for an excellent view both down the valley

to Kantega and up towards Cho Oyu (8153 metres). Beyond the ridge, the valley widens as the trail passes through Pangka (one hotel here) at 4390 metres, then descends to the river bank before beginning the climb on to the terminal moraine of the Ngozumpa Glacier.

It is a steep climb up the moraine, switchbacking alongside the stream to the first small lake at 4650 metres, where a family of green Braminy ducks resides. The trail now becomes almost level as it follows the valley past a second lake at 4690 metres and finally up a boulder strewn path to Gokyo at 4750 metres. Gokyo is a kharka of seven houses and walled pastures on the shores of a large lake. The setting is reminiscent of an abandoned summer resort. There are three hotels at Gokyo.

Day 7: Gokyo
The views in the Gokyo region are tremendous. For the best view, climb Gokyo Ri, the small peak above the lake. This peak of 5318 metres is sometimes called Kala Pattar. It is a 2 hour climb to the top of the peak, providing a panoramic view of Cho Oyu, Gyachung Kang, Everest, Lhotse, Makalu, Cholatse and Tawachee.

Those with more time and energy can make a trip up the valley to another lake, marked with the name Ngozumpa on the maps, or even beyond to a fifth lake. There are several small peaks in this region that offer vantage points for the surrounding peaks and even of the Nangpa La, the old trade route into Tibet.

Day 8: Gokyo to Phortse
You can descend to Phortse in a single long day, or you can spend the night at Thare or Konar on the way to make the day less strenuous. Rather than retrace the upward route, follow the eastern side of the valley on the downward route to gain different views of Khumbila and to enjoy somewhat warmer weather, as the sun stays on these slopes longer in the late afternoon.

Descending from Gokyo, the route passes the second lake. About halfway between the first and second lakes a trail leads off across the moraine to the east. This is the route to the 5420 metre Cho La (or Chhugyuma pass) into the Everest region. The pass is not difficult, but it is steep and involves a glacier crossing on the eastern side. Allow three days from Gokyo to Pheriche on this high altitude route. An ice axe, crampons and a rope are often necessary for negotiating the small icefall at the foot of the glacier on the other side of the pass, although in ideal conditions there are no technical problems and there is a trail of sorts in the rocks beside the icefall. The western approach to the pass varies in difficulty depending on the amount of snow. It can vary from a rough scramble up a scree (gravel) slope to an impossible technical ice climb. The best conditions are when there is snow soft enough for kicking steps up the slope. The pass is not possible for yaks and usually not suitable for heavily laden porters, but you can send the porters and yaks around the mountain via Phortse and they can meet you in Lobuje or Pheriche three days later. If you plan to cross the pass, spend a night at Chhugyuma and the following night at Dzongla on the other side.

The main trail follows its upward route through Pangka, then climbs to Na (4400 metres), the only year round settlement in the valley. The descent from Na along the eastern side of the Dudh Kosi Valley is straightforward, with a few ups and downs where landslides and streams have carved side valleys. The trail enters Phortse at its upper end and there are camping places in the potato fields of this large village. There are hotels in Na, Phortse and in Thare, about halfway between them.

Day 9: Phortse to Namche Bazaar

The trail descends from Phortse to the bridge and rejoins the original route from Khumjung. It is easy to reach Namche Bazaar, or even beyond to Jorsale, for the night.

An alternative route from Phortse leads up a steep, narrow and exposed trail to upper Pangboche, where it joins the trail to the Everest region. There is also a trail that descends steeply from Phortse to the Imja Khola and climbs through forests to Tengpoche.

TO THAMI

Thami lies at an elevation of 3800 metres near the foot of a large valley to the west of Namche Bazaar. The village is the departure point for crossing Tesi Lapcha, the 5755 metre high pass into the Rolwaling Valley. Only experienced, well-equipped and well-informed parties should attempt Tesi Lapcha because frequent rockfalls near the pass present a very dangerous complication.

The trail to Thami starts above the village of Namche Bazaar and leads west past a large array of prayer flags and mani stones. The carved mani stones all the way to Thami are some of the most complex and picturesque in Nepal. Contouring around the hill on a wide and almost level trail, the route passes through Gonglha and Drama before reaching the large village of Thomde. Just before Thomde, a trail leads uphill to the monastery at Mende. A few Westerners are studying here under the tutelage of an English speaking lama. At Thomde are the remains of a dam and office buildings for a hydroelectric project that was destroyed during the 1985 flood. The hydroelectric scheme is being rebuilt upstream and will someday generate electricity from the Bhote Kosi to provide lights for all the homes of Khumbu.

After a short climb followed by a descent to the river, which is crossed on a sturdy wooden bridge, the trail makes a steep ascent beside a stream to Thami, about 3 hours from Namche Bazaar. Thami is in a large valley with good views of the snow peaks of Teng Kangpoche (6500 metres) and Kwangde (6187 metres) to the south. To the north of the village is a police check post that does not allow trekkers to travel further north on the the trade route between Nepal and Tibet. It is a two day trip to Nangpa La, the 5741 metre pass that trains of yaks cross as they carry goods between the two countries.

Sherpas now use it primarily for the trade of yaks and wool.

About 150 metres above Thami is the Thami Gompa, a picturesque monastery set amongst the many homes of lamas and lay people. It's perched on the side of a hill overlooking the valley. This is the site for the spring celebration of the Mani Rimdu festival, held about the middle of May each year. During Mani Rimdu many Sherpas set up temporary hotels near the gompa and offer momos (meat-filled dumplings), *thukpa* (noodles) and endless quantities of tea, chhang and rakshi.

It is possible to make the trip to Thami and back to Namche Bazaar in a single day, but it's more worthwhile to spend a night in Thami to see the peaks in the clear morning. This side trip provides a good acclimatisation day before proceeding to higher elevations. There is a hotel in Thami and another in Thammu.

THE LAMIDANDA ESCAPE ROUTE

Occasionally the pile up of people at Lukla becomes unmanageable. Imagine 350 people vying for seats on planes that carry 15 passengers. Many people, having completed a great trek, make themselves miserable by fighting for seats out of Lukla. It's a helpless feeling to be in a place where no amount of influence or money can make the planes come, but you did come to an undeveloped country. If you expect things to operate on time (or sometimes to operate at all), you should head for the mountains of Switzerland.

Unbelievable things happen when people flip out at Lukla. I've seen the station manager chased around the airport by a tourist brandishing an ice axe. I've seen chanting mobs outside the airline office. I've seen rock fights on the airstrip. Twice I've seen planeloads of police arrive in Lukla to get things under control; and I've heard endless tales of woe from people who had to be at work the following day (they weren't). If it gets like this – usually in late October and early November, and occasionally at other unpredictable times – the only way to

maintain your composure is to be sure your name is somewhere on the reservation list. Assign one of your sherpas (or better yet, your innkeeper or the Lukla representative of your trekking company) to ensure that other names are not slipped in ahead of yours, then retire to a kettle or two of chhang to consider your alternatives.

You can wait. It might be a day (I've seen a dramatic airlift of 14 flights to Lukla in a single day) or as long as two weeks. You can walk to Jiri. At a normal pace, it's six days to Jiri where you can get a bus to Kathmandu. If you walk 10 to 12 hours a day (you save days in Nepal by walking a longer time each day, not by walking faster) you could reach Jiri in four days, perhaps even three. You can walk to the airstrip at Phaphlu, two long days (or three comfortable days) from Lukla. It is an appealing walk, but it's uncertain that it will hasten your return to Kathmandu because there are only one or two flights a week and seats are in heavy demand for government officials stationed in nearby Salleri.

You can walk from Phaphlu south to Janakpur in six days. The 10 day trek to Dhankuta described in this book is also a route to escape from Lukla. Another alternative is described here. You can walk to Lamidanda, an airstrip five days to the south. The important thing is not to make yourself, and everyone else, miserable by fighting and bemoaning your fate. Instead, do something positive. You can always go back to Namche Bazaar for a few days and wait for things to clear up, or you can climb the ridge behind Lukla, where there are some wonderful high meadows and a good view of Kariolung.

The Lamidanda escape route works in either direction. You can walk to Khumbu after a flight to Lamidanda. Although I have called it a five day trek, it can be done (if the porters agree) in four days. The opposite direction, however, will certainly require five days because of the long initial climb to Aiselukharka.

Day 1: Lukla to Bupsa
A trail leads off the end of the Lukla airstrip

and descends to join the main trail to Kathmandu. The descent continues on the main trail to Surkhe, then the trail climbs to Puiyan, crosses the pass and descends again to Bupsa. See Day 7 and 8 of the Everest trek description.

Day 2: Bupsa to Wobsa Khani

The trail descends steeply to Khari Khola (2070 metres). If you did not walk from Kathmandu, this will be your first view of extensive terracing and of Nepal's middle hills. A bazaar is held in Khari Khola on Wednesdays if you need to stock up on provisions. There is only dhal bhaat available between here and the next bazaar at Aiselukharka. The trail climbs out of Khari Khola on a trail higher than the main route to Kathmandu, then turns south about 20 minutes beyond the village. The path climbs over a ridge, then contours south, high above the village of Jubing. The route passes through scrub forests and a few cultivated fields to Jube at 2100 metres, then through forests of rhododendron and oak. The trail descends, crosses the Thana Khola, then climbs steeply out of a side valley. There are a few houses and herders' huts, but for the most part the trail is through forests and is reasonably level (for Nepal). The Rai village of Wobsa Khani is about 2 hours beyond the Thana Khola at an elevation of 1800 metres. Below Wobsa is Tamba Khani (copper mine) where you can see the smelter and buildings for the mine that gave the town its name.

Day 3: Wobsa Khani to Lokhim

Porters carry oranges and rice from here to the market at Namche Bazaar. Except for those porters, few locals or trekkers use this trail, so there are no hotels and few bhattis along the route. From Wobsa Khani the trail continues fairly level as the valley becomes wider, then it descends a bit to Waku, a Chhetri village at 1500 metres. The trail descends further through forests to Suntale at 1100 metres and drops steeply to the Hinku Khola, crossing it on an old suspension bridge at 980 metres. This is the same river (also called the Inukhu) that is crossed on Day 3 of the trek to Dhankuta.

After a steep climb on a series of steps cut into the rock, the trail reaches a ridge at 1290 metres and descends a bit to the Rai and Chhetri village of Khorde. The trail descends further through trees to the Hongu Khola, crossing it on a temporary log bridge at 900 metres. The remains of an impressive cantilever bridge are here; it looks as if this bridge collapsed years ago. There is some trade up the Hongu from this point, and people who live in villages as far away as Bung travel down the valley to Aiselukharka on bazaar days. Climbing steeply past the herders' huts of Utha, the trail reaches a ridge at 1590 metres. It may be necessary to camp in Utha, because it's another 1½ hours from Utha to Lokhim. Lokhim, a huge Rai village with beautiful stands of bamboo, is in a large side valley at about 1800 metres. This being Rai country, it is usual to encounter dhamis (shamans) walking the remote trails, or at least to hear the echoes of their drums in the distance.

Day 4: Lokhim to Ilim

Lokhim is a large village, almost 45 minutes walk from beginning to end. From the eastern end of the village the trail climbs through Chuwa towards the pass at Deorali (2400 metres). The Schneider *Dudh Kosi* map covers this part of the trek, but does not show this section of trail. The trail contours around the Dudu Khola Valley before it ascends steeply towards Deorali. A tea shop, the first since Khari Khola, is at the pass. Descending from the pass, the route travels through Harise, a Sherpa village at 2300 metres, then descends a steep stone staircase to Aiselukharka, a large town strung out along a ridge at 2100 metres. Aiselukharka has shops and government offices and a very large bazaar on Saturdays. The trail descends the ridge to the south on a wide trail to Ilim at 1450 metres.

Day 5: Ilim to Lamidanda

It is a steep descent through tropical country to the Ra Khola. A bridge is upstream at 800 metres, or you can wade the river. This is a rice growing region. The trail follows a complex and intricate route through a network of dikes and irrigation canals. It makes a steep ascent up the Pipal Danda, then contours around the valley between 1200 and 1400 metres. The route is through terraced fields and has little shade – it will probably be hot. Finally the trail passes a school and follows a ridge out towards the airport. The Schneider map does not show either this trail or Lamidanda. A hotel near the terminal building is at 1200 metres. From Lamidanda there are flights several times a week to both Kathmandu and Biratnagar.

Local people say that it is a two day walk to Bhojpur and a one day walk to Okhaldunga from here. Those timings are probably accurate. Once, however, the Lamidanda people terrified a trekking group by all agreeing that it required at least 12 days to walk to Lukla (where none of the locals had ever been). There is nothing to see or do in the Brahmin village of Lamidanda, except wait for a plane. There is a Buddhist shrine about a day's walk away that might provide some diversion if you get stuck here for a long time. Lamidanda is the air traffic control point for this part of Nepal, so the radio is in constant use here (unlike Lukla) and it is easy to find out about flight movements.

BARAHBISE TO JIRI

It takes a bit of the continuity out of the Everest trek when you drive all the way to Jiri. The following route from Barahbise to Shivalaya avoids the Jiri road entirely and visits some new country that trekkers rarely visit. Few people, including locals, follow the route I have described here, so villagers will probably not be able to point you in the right direction. A local guide (or a basic knowledge of Nepali) is almost essential for this trek. There are so many trails leading in every direction that it is impossible to document all the junctions and alternatives. This description is only a suggestion. You can modify it in many ways once you are on the trail. There are some bhattis on this route, but

none from Biguti to Mali, so you will be more comfortable if you carry food on this trek.

Day 1: Kathmandu to Khartali

Barahbise is a 10 minute drive beyond Lamosangu on the east bank of the Bhote Kosi. Just south of Barahbise, the confluence of the Bhote Kosi (river from Tibet) forms a much larger river, the Sun Kosi. This river flows south, then east across Nepal to join the Arun River near Biratnagar. Barahbise is a crowded bazaar at 820 metres, inhabited mostly by Newars and Chhetris. The route begins on an unpretentious set of stone steps between two shops and begins a climb that will eventually be more than 2400 metres of uphill walking. Passing through a few scattered Gurung villages, the route soon enters country inhabited mostly by Tamangs. Most of the route is in open cultivated country with a few pipal trees, surrounded by stone chautaaras, providing welcome shade on hot days as the trail climbs to Parati, a small village at about 1300 metres. Beyond Parati the trail becomes less steep, and even has a few level stretches, as it continues through heavily cultivated country to the large Tamang village of Khartali at 1680 metres.

Day 2: Khartali to Thulo Tingsang

Beyond Khartali the trail continues to traverse eastward along the ridge, high above the Sun Kosi. Few villagers use this trail except porters carrying rice, wood and slate for roofing down to Barahbise. The trail climbs a ridge to a small bhatti and a rushing stream at 2290 metres. After the ridge, the trail enters deep rhododendron forests and makes some short climbs and descents as it traverses in and out of wooded side valleys. Below the trail and across the valley houses are splashed across the hillside, but above the trail there is mostly forest. Rounding a ridge, the trail offers a view of the large spread out village of Dolangsa, a Sherpa village with clean whitewashed houses, each surrounded by fields of corn, potatoes, wheat and barley. From the ridge, the trail enters another side canyon (watch for stinging nettles) and crosses a stream on a bridge hewn from a huge tree – a reminder of what the forests of this region must have been like before a rising population forced the cutting of large amounts of firewood. A short distance beyond the bridge, take the left trail which makes a steep uphill climb to the Sherpa village of Dolangsa, at about 2380 metres. There is no hotel here, but you can probably find accommodation in a private home. High above the village is a gompa.

Beyond Dolangsa the trail climbs through rhododendron forests past a few kharkas used during summer as pastures for herds of cattle. The pastures are uninhabited during the trekking season but are good camp sites if you have a tent. The trail then begins a steep climb to the pass, crossing the Tingsang La at 3320 metres. The pass affords good views in every direction. On a clear day Gauri Shankar (7145 metres) dominates the horizon and peaks are visible from Chhoba-Bhamare (6108 metres), a rock spire in the west, all the way to Pigpherago (6730 metres) and Numbur (6959 metres) in the east. A short distance below the pass is Thulo Tingsang, a large kharka at 3260 metres. The views from this camp are as good as from the pass. During summer, many people live in this high pasture and there is even a small shop and hotel. During winter, people remove the roofs from the stone huts and carry their household effects to lower permanent settlements. During the trekking season there is no food or accommodation here.

Day 3: Thulo Tingsang to Amatal

From Thulo Tingsang (big Tingsang) the trail descends through conifer and rhododendron forests to Sano Tingsang (small Tingsang), another kharka at 3000 metres. The trail continues a gradual descent (a very pleasant walk – most descents in Nepal are steep and rough) through forests and past small kharkas to a stream at 2230 metres. A small paper factory is here and you'll see frames with Nepalese paper drying in the sun. A few minutes below is another stream crossed by a covered bridge at about 2100 metres. From this point a rough steep trail

climbs 400 metres to Bigu at 2500 metres. Bigu is a Sherpa village with a large gompa and a nunnery. It is a strenuous side trip that involves a steep descent to rejoin the main trail. The direct route continues down the river valley through Tamang, Chhetri and Kami (blacksmith caste) villages with slate paved courtyards, to Amatal at 1680 metres.

Day 4: Amatal to Saunepani

It is a long but pleasant walk along the Sangawa Khola to its confluence with the Tamba Kosi. Stay on the south bank of the river, passing through Kopai and a few other small villages. Much of the route is in pine forest. Local people have cut off the lower branches of most trees for firewood – a traditional method of avoiding total deforestation. The trail ascends and descends over ridges and spurs and finally makes a steep descent to the Sangawa Khola, crossing it at 1220 metres. The trail continues along the north bank of the river, making a few ups and downs, but generally staying level and passing a few side streams, two of which flow from beautiful tropical waterfalls. Not only is the trail level, but the route is almost totally uninhabited during the afternoon's walk – two very unusual things in Nepal. Finally the route reaches the Tamba Kosi (here called the Bhote Kosi) at the village of Sigaati (1000 metres). The village has a few houses and a small shop.

Day 5: Saunepani to Serukapti

Walk south for about an hour along the west bank of the Tamba Kosi. This trail, if followed in the opposite direction, will lead to the Rolwaling Valley after a week of walking. The trail is level as it follows the river south to Biguti, across the Tamba Kosi on the east bank at 950 metres. A small shop is on the west bank and across the river there is a wonderful old chain link suspension bridge. These bridges are becoming rare in Nepal, being replaced by new cement and steel cable bridges, so the swinging bridge high above the river offers an exhilarating and unusual river crossing. About five minutes south of the bridge on the west bank is a new trading centre, Gumbu Khola. The ground floor of every house here is either a shop or hotel. If you are looking for an excuse to delay crossing the chain bridge, reinforce your courage with a glass of rakshi from this village.

At Biguti, turn north and cross a small stream, then climb the ridge to the north-east. The trail climbs a bit and turns east as it passes through the Tamang villages of Jaku (1460 metres) and Yarsa. Unlike the brief walk along the Tamba Kosi, which is a main trade thoroughfare, the trail is now on a rarely used route that climbs through forests and small villages towards the head of the valley. Because this is an out of the way trail, there are places where it is steep and narrow. Route finding is also a problem. Ask for the trail to Serukapti when you reach a dead end in someone's front yard. The trail becomes better and more defined as it passes through Sarsepti, a large Tamang village at 1760 metres, then continues to climb through beautiful forests of oak and rhododendron with an abundance of ferns and orchids. After more climbing, you will reach the Sherpa village of Serukapti at 2300 metres.

Day 6: Serukapti to Mali

From Serukapti the trail continues up into forests. A trail junction is about 15 minutes beyond the village. The lower (right-hand) trail goes to Jiri and the upper (left-hand) trail crosses Hanumante Danda and bypasses Jiri. Since one of the purposes of all this uphill climbing is to avoid the motor road, there is no good reason at this point to go to Jiri, so continue up the valley to a large kharka, a beautiful high altitude meadow surrounded by big trees, at 2300 metres. Climbing through a forest of large moss covered pines, the trail finally emerges at the top of the ridge at 2900 metres, high above Jiri. There are many trails here. One trail descends to a cheese factory and then climbs back to the ridge above Mali. The most direct trail runs along the ridge to the east for a while, then drops slowly as it traverses below the ridgetop, making another easy descent past a few slate mines before reaching the Patashe Danda and descending on a broad trail (stay on the ridge) to Mali, a Sherpa village at 2200 metres. Here the route joins the trail from Jiri and continues to Shivalaya and Bhandar.

Annapurna Region

Central Nepal is dominated by the Annapurna himal and the village of Pokhara. There are three major trekking routes in central Nepal: to Jomsom, to Annapurna Sanctuary, and a circuit of the Annapurna himal itself. Pokhara is also a good starting place for short treks of one to four days, including the 'Royal Trek', which I have described in this chapter.

INFORMATION
Annapurna Conservation Area Project

ACAP was established in 1986 under the guidance of the King Mahendra Trust for Nature Conservation. The project encompasses the entire Annapurna range, more than 2600 sqkm. In an innovative approach to environmental protection, it was declared a 'conservation area' instead of a national park . A large number of people live within the protected region, but traditional national park practices dictate that few, if any, people reside within park boundaries. In an effort to avoid any conflicts of interest, ACAP has sought the involvement of local people and has emphasised environmental education.

Projects include the training of lodge owners, with an emphasis on sanitation, deforestation and cultural pride. They have provided cook training and encouraged hoteliers to charge a fair price for food and accommodation. ACAP encourages the use of kerosene for cooking throughout the region, and requires its use above Chhomrong in the Annapurna Sanctuary. ACAP is supported by a conservation fee of Rs 200 that is collected from all trekkers who obtain trekking permits for the Annapurna region.

ACAP has encouraged the construction of toilets throughout the area; use them. The project has also made provision for the supply of kerosene in the Annapurna Sanctuary area.

Maps

ACAP has produced a contour map of the entire Annapurna region with detailed advice on the back. These maps are available in Kathmandu book shops for Rs 100 each.

There are no recently produced, detailed, topographic maps of this region like the Schneider maps of Everest and Langtang. The US Army maps that cover the region are NH 44-16, *Pokhara* and NH 45-13, *Jongkha Dzong*.

There are many locally produced maps available in Nepal, some printed and some blueprints; most are titled *Around Annapurna*.

PLACES TO STAY
Pokhara

All treks in the Annapurna region either start or end at Pokhara, the main city in central Nepal.

Accommodation in Pokhara includes the fashionable and peaceful *Fish Tail Lodge* located on the lake. The Western-style *New Hotel Crystal*, the *Mount Annapurna Hotel* and the *Himalayan Hotel* are all across from the airport. At the latter, you have a choice of setting up your own tent or using their bungalows. The *Tragopan* and *Dragon* hotels are a short distance south of the airport; the *Base Camp Lodge* is the best of the lakeside hotels. You can also find excellent accommodation among the many small hotels along the shore of Phewa Tal, or camp in the government camp site near the lake, at about 900 metres elevation.

Among the lakeside restaurants, try the *Hungry Eye* and the *Yak & Yuppie*.

Trekking Lodges

There are numerous trekkers hotels throughout the region; most are adequate and some are outstanding. You can assume that you can find a room and food wherever you go on the main routes on the Annapurna region. During the busy October and November season, it might be prudent to bring a mattress in case everything is full and you are forced to sleep on a floor. Bedding is often available, but you should not rely on this at high elevations, eg Thorung La and Annapurna Sanctuary.

GETTING THERE & AWAY

Air

To/From Pokhara Pokhara is a 30 minute flight from Kathmandu. RNAC operates a network here that serves Manang, Jomsom, Dolpo and Jumla with early morning flights.

To/From Jomsom Jomsom is located in the upper Kali Gandaki Valley and is served by frequent flights from both Kathmandu and Pokhara. Don't fly to Jomsom; if your time is limited, walk up the spectacular Kali Gandaki Valley to Jomsom, trek up to Muktinath, then fly from Jomsom back to Pokhara.

Jomsom flights are notoriously unreliable, because the wind makes flying impossible after 10 or 11 am. Kathmandu is often fogbound until 10 am during the winter, and this delays flight departures. When the combination of unfavourable weather conditions at both Kathmandu and Jomsom causes several days of flight cancellations, the crush of local people and trekkers waiting for planes in Jomsom can become intolerable.

There are usually one or two flights each day from Pokhara to Jomsom; because there is no fog problem in Pokhara, these flights operate far more regularly than Kathmandu flights. If you do get stuck in Jomsom it is possible – though not particularly pleasant – to walk to Pokhara in 4 days or less.

To/From Manang At the upper end of the Marsyandi Valley is Manang, just across the pass from Jomsom. There is a severe risk of altitude sickness if you fly to Manang and try to cross the Thorung La pass. You should view Manang as an emergency airport; it is not a sensible starting point for an Annapurna trek.

Airfares RNAC fares in 1990 are:

Kathmandu to Pokhara	US$61
Kathmandu to Jomsom	US$83
Pokhara to Jomsom	US$50
Kathmandu to Manang	US$88
Pokhara to Manang	US$50

Bus

To/From Pokhara There is frequent service by both day and night buses to Pokhara. Fares are Rs 56 to Rs 74, or Rs 120 for a more comfortable 'tourist bus'. Road conditions are appalling for the first 100 km, so it takes 8 to 9 hours for the 200 km trip. There are also special tourist buses that operate between Kathmandu and Pokhara, including the famous 'Swiss Bus'. They are more expensive, about Rs 200, but they are more comfortable and hopefully faster than public buses.

The trek to Jomsom begins in Pokhara and the Around Annapurna trek ends there. The town is known for its lake, Phewa Tal, and its large collection of inexpensive hotels and restaurants. A spectacular panorama of Nepal's central Himalaya, the Annapurnas, Machhapuchhare and Manaslu, dominates the skyline. A new road is under construction between Pokhara and Baglung, a village on the Kali Gandaki. As this road is completed, the actual trailhead for the Jomsom trek will shift to Betrawati and possibly to Baglung itself.

To/From Dumre Dumre is 135 km from Kathmandu and is the starting place for the trek around Annapurna. There is no service that specifically serves Dumre, so you should take a Pokhara bus and jump ship at kilometre 135.

To/From Gorkha An alternative starting point for the trek around Annapurna is Gorkha. The Gorkha road starts near Mugling and provides access to a route that avoids the dusty Besi Sahar road, joining the trek in the Marsyandi Valley near Tarkughat. Gorkha is served by two buses daily; the cost

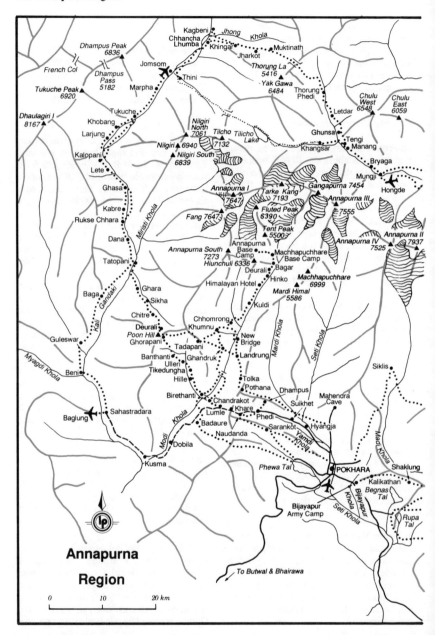

Annapurna

Region

0   10   20 km

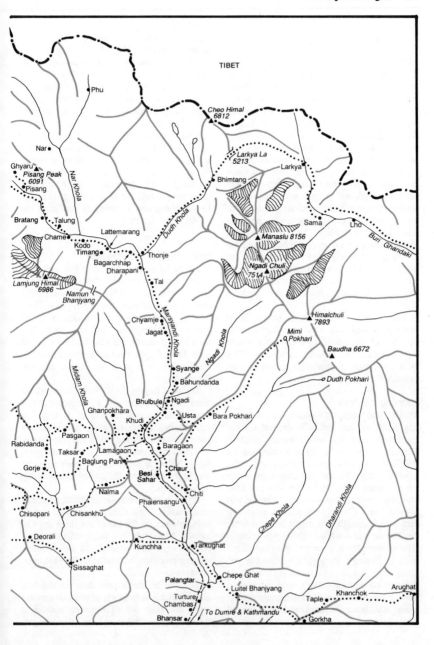

is Rs 35 for the 7 hour ride. There is no night bus service.

JOMSOM TREK

The trek to Jomsom is the classic tea house trek and boasts some of the best trekking hotels in Nepal. You can trek to Jomsom and back in 14 days, and you will share the trail with trains of burros and ponies travelling to Mustang and other areas closed to foreigners. This is a major trade and trekking route, so there are facilities for trekkers almost every hour all along the trek. Many of these are surprisingly well-equipped hotels operated by Thakalis, people who inhabit the valley between Annapurna and Dhaulagiri. From the Kali Gandaki Valley, you can make side trips to either the 1950 French Annapurna base camp or the base camp for Dhaulagiri. The views of the mountains are spectacular, and the route actually crosses to the other side of the main Himalayan range for some unusual views of the northern flanks.

The entire route remains below 3000 metres, though the trek is still strenuous enough to be stimulating (see the Route Profile for the trek around Annapurna). This is a good trek if you wish to avoid high altitudes.

Starting the Trek

Pokhara to Baglung Road The actual starting point of the trek will depend on the completion of the new Chinese road to Baglung. This road is already complete (in 1990)almost to Kusma, but it is not officially open to traffic. You may be able to get a ride on a Chinese truck or, by the time you read this, there might be bus services. Ideally, you would like to be able to travel almost to Birethanti, though you might have to settle for Lumle and walk downhill to Birethanti. The master plan is to extend the road all the way to Jomsom, through Lo Mantang and into Tibet, but the people of Jomsom have announced that they don't need, or want, a road. Now that the road exists, there is little point in walking the first few days of the old trek route.

Mustang

Jomsom is the district headquarters for the Mustang region of Nepal. To many people, however, Mustang implies the area of Nepal that extends like a thumb into Tibet. This is the region described in Michel Piessel's book *Mustang*, and includes the walled capital city of Mustang, Lo Mantang. This part of Mustang, however, is on the list of restricted areas. Despite the reassuring and optimistic brochures printed by many trekking agents, there are no signs that the Home Ministry will open the area soon. Parts of the Mustang district are open, but the area that most people refer to as 'Mustang' is really Lo Mantang and is certainly not open (in 1990) to foreigners.

Day 1: Pokhara to Birethanti

From the lake or the airport in Pokhara, you can either take a taxi (for about Rs 20) or the city bus (for Rs 1) to Bagar, elevation 1060 metres, the roadhead near the Shining Hospital at the north end of Pokhara. You can also walk through the Pokhara Bazaar, but it's a long distance and all uphill on a paved road. From Bagar there are frequent buses to Phedi, and perhaps on to Lumle or even Birethanti.

The road passes the Tibetan camp, where there is a carpet factory, a monastery and a few hotels, then continues to Hyangja at 1070 metres. In the morning, there is often a good view up the valley to Machhapuchhare. The road then emerges into the broad Yamdi Khola Valley at Suikhet, then goes on to the foot of the Dhampus hill and switchbacks up to Naudanda.

If you only drive as far as Phedi, go uphill on a broad trail that climbs gently (for Nepal) to Naudanda, on the top of the ridge at 1430 metres. Naudanda is a large village with a police check post, school and several inns, varying from tiny bhattis to well-developed, Western-style hotels.

The police check post here is insistent about looking at trekking permits. If you are on a day hike out of Pokhara without a trekking permit, this may be as far as you get.

By Road If the road is open, you will zigzag up the ridge and then wind down in a billow of dust into the Modi Khola Valley. At about km 42,near the settlement of Naya Pool, you can leave the road and start walking. Go behind a ridge and walk upstream on a level trail to a suspension bridge. On the far side of the bridge is Birethanti, a large and prosperous town with a winding street paved with large stones. Birethanti boasts many well-stocked shops, hotels, sidewalk cafés, a bank, a bakery and a police check post. A trail up the Modi Khola to Ghandruk begins at Birethanti, behind the first house of the village.

Walking If you are walking, add an extra day to the trek. Climb from Naudanda to Kaski, then further to Khare, a large strung-out village situated at the head of the Yamdi Khola Valley at 1710 metres. The Jomsom route descends from Khare on a muddy trail through deep forests, down a set of wide, stone stairs below the British project, and continues to the village of Lumle. There are several hotels and even a medical hall among the slate-roofed houses of the village, elevation 1585 metres. The trail follows the Lumle's flagstone-paved main street, exiting the village only a bit lower in elevation than when it entered. If you find yourself heading steeply downhill, ask directions; the downhill trail goes to Dhorpatan, Baglung and Beni, not to Jomsom.

Beyond Lumle, you leave the road and walk along the side of the ridge, finally rounding a bend and descending to Chandrakot, which is perched on the end of a ridge at an elevation of 1550 metres. The views of Annapurna South and Machhapuchhare, the 'fish tail' mountain, are excellent from this point, except that from this angle it looks more like the Matterhorn than a fish tail. To see the mountain in its proper perspective you must go into the Annapurna Sanctuary, several days to the north – but that's another trek. There are several hotels here with English signboards and menus – it's a good place for lunch.

From Chandrakot, the trail descends a

steep, dusty (muddy when wet) trail that switchbacks down to the Modi Khola. Passing a few houses near the river, the route crosses a suspension bridge to Birethanti at 1065 metres.

Day 2: Birethanti to Tikedungha
The hotels in Birethanti are excellent, but if you spend a night here, it is a long, 1700 metre climb the next day to Ghorapani. It's more comfortable to break the climb into two stages by continuing to Hille or Tikedungha for the night. (If you are coming from Jomsom and are reading this backwards, then Ghorapani to Birethanti is an easy, though knee-cracking, descent and Birethanti makes a good stopping place.) The trail follows the main street of Birethanti, going through bamboo forests and past a large waterfall and swimming hole. A small tea shop here provides cold drinks after your swim. The trail stays on the north bank of the Bhurungdi Khola to Baajgara – don't cross the large, inviting-looking suspension bridge.

Beyond a pasture that the pony caravans use, the trail reaches Sudami, then climbs steadily up the side of the valley, reaching Hille at 1495 metres. There are several hotels alongside the wide stone trail here and others in Tikedungha, about 15 minutes (and 30 metres) above Hille. There is a large campsite just beyond Tikedungha near two suspension bridges.

Day 3: Tikedungha to Ghorapani
The trail crosses a stream on a suspension bridge near the campsite at Tikedungha, then drops and crosses the Bhurungdi Khola itself on a large bridge at 1410 metres. The trail climbs very steeply on a stone staircase; there are no tourist hotels from the bridge to Ulleri, just a few bhattis that have only tea. As you climb, the tops of Annapurna South (7273 metres) and Hiunchuli begin to emerge from behind the hills. The climb continues steeply to the large Magar village of Ulleri at 2070 metres. There are hotels in the centre of the village, and others above the village where the trail climbs gently through

pastures and cultivated fields. The fields soon give way to deep forests as the trail climbs to Banthanti, a settlement of hotels in a forest clearing at 2250 metres.

Beyond Banthanti, there are magnificent oak and rhododendron forests. The trail crosses two sparkling clear streams, a small ridge and another stream before making a short, final climb to Nangathanti, a hotel complex in a forest clearing at 2460 metres. *Thanti* is a Magar word meaning 'rest house' or 'dharamsala'. In the winter the trail can be covered with snow, and in many places it is sloppy mud, so all sorts of short detours are necessary in this section.

Ghorapani is about an hour past Nangathanti, at 2775 metres elevation. There are several hotels in Ghorapani, but most people walk on to the pass, Deurali (which means 'pass'), at 2834 metres, about 10 minutes beyond the village. There is a large collection of hotels, shops and camping places and the requisite police check post at Deurali.

There is a map in the village that shows the location of 11 lodges; the *Annapurna Hotel* and the *Snow View Hotel* are among the largest. In 1990 the *Super View* was supposed to be the best, but all the hoteliers have standardised their prices, so don't waste your time looking for the cheapest food and accommodation. It is worth staying at the pass to see the spectacular panorama of Dhaulagiri I, Tukuche, Nilgiri, Annapurna I, Annapurna South, Hiunchuli and Glacier Dome. An early morning excursion to Poon Hill (3193 metres), about an hour's climb, provides an even better, unobstructed view of the high Himalaya.

Ghorapani means 'horse water', and it is no doubt a welcome watering stop for the teams of horses, mules and ponies that carry loads between Pokhara and Jomsom. The exotic horse caravans, with melodious bells that echo over great distances, and wondrous plumes and headdresses on the lead horses, are reminiscent of ancient Tibet. Herded by Tibetan men who shout up and down the trail, they lend a unique touch to the Jomsom trek. The ponies also grind the trail into dust and slippery mud with their tiny sharp hooves and careen downhill, frightening trekkers into jumping into the bushes, but the colourful photographic possibilities and the harmonious tinkle of bells almost make it worth the trouble.

Some people, almost overcome by the ammoniatic stench of horse urine on the trail, suggest a different derivation of the name Ghorapani. On a typical day, you will encounter 200 to 300 pack animals, travelling in large trains and ranging in size from huge mules to tiny burros no bigger than a large dog.

Day 4: Ghorapani to Tatopani

From the pass at Deurali, the trail makes a muddy, steep descent through rhododendron and magnolia forests, interspersed with a few shepherds' goths, bhattis and pastures, to Chitre at 2390 metres. The *New Annapurna* is the dominant lodge here. There are several trail junctions along this part of the trip. The correct trail almost invariably leads downhill. The country opens up into a region of extensive terracing. At one point the trail crosses a huge landslide. Observe the way the slick mica soil has slid off the underlying rock.

The trail descends towards Sikha, a large and prosperous Magar village at 1980 metres, that has many shops and hotels; *Shanti & Someone's Bar and Grill* (the owner's name keeps changing) is near the top of the village, above the British Army training centre. From Sikha, the trail makes a gentle descent across another slide area to Ghara at 1705 metres, then climbs to the top of a rocky spur where there are some bhattis. The trail makes a steep descent of about 500 metres to the Ghar Khola, crossing it on a suspension bridge. The trail then makes a short climb above the Kali Gandaki and crosses the river on a large suspension bridge at 1180 metres elevation. An older version of this bridge appeared on the cover of Toni Hagen's *Nepal, The Kingdom of the Himalayas*. The peak in the background is Nilgiri South (6839 metres). On the opposite side of the river, the trail turns north; it is a short distance upstream to Tatopani.

Tatopani means 'hot water' in Nepali; the village gains its name from the hot springs near the river below the village. There are two cement pools on the banks of the river. Don't pollute these pools by using soap in them. Tatopani is the epitome of the Thakali inn system; the extensive choice of hotels and garden restaurants rivals Thamel in Kathmandu and the lakeside in Pokhara. Some hotels have installed gobar gas generators to produce fuel for light and cooking. It is intriguing to see these facilities in daily use; it is good progress in the alternate energy field. Many people who are making only a short trek come here from Pokhara and spend their time relaxing in the hot springs and enjoying the hospitality of this small village. Try the *Kamala Lodge* at the north end of town for Italian and Mexican food. This is citrus fruit country, so you can stock up on small mandarin oranges.

The Kali Gandaki Valley was the focus of an American aid project named RCUP, the Resource Conservation and Utilisation Project. From the mid '70s until 1985, a vast amount of money was spent here on an integrated approach to rural development. The primary legacy of this effort is a collection of Western-style buildings, both offices and residences, that you will encounter on your journey up the valley. When you see a facility that looks totally out of place in Tatopani, Kalopani, Ghasa, Marpha and Jharkot, it's probably an RCUP leftover.

Day 5: Tatopani to Kalopani

Register with the Tatopani police check post and head up the Kali Gandaki gorge, said to be the deepest in the world. The rationale for this is that between the top of Annapurna I and the top of Dhaulagiri I (both above 8000 metres and only 38 km apart) the terrain drops to below 2200 metres. From Tatopani, the route ascends gently, passing through a small tunnel carved out of the rocky hillside, to Dana at 1400 metres. Dana consists of three separate settlements of buildings with

elaborately carved windows and balconies. The hotels in Dana are near the post office at the south end of the village. Most of the people of Dana are Magars, though there are also a few Brahmins and Thakalis. The large peak across the valley is Annapurna South (7273 metres); the large village high on the hillside across the valley is Nerchang.

From Dana, a trail leads across the Kali Gandaki. After several days of rough climbing in bamboo jungle above the Miristi Khola, this trail reaches the base camp used by Herzog's Annapurna expedition in 1950. At the time of this first ascent, Annapurna was the highest mountain ever climbed. The base camp is also accessible by an equally difficult trail from Lete. Maurice Herzog's book *Annapurna* provides essential background reading for the trek up the Kali Gandaki. There are no hotels on this difficult side trip.

Above Dana, the trail continues to the hamlet of Rukse Chhara, elevation 1550 metres. It is situated at the foot of a high waterfall that tumbles into a series of cataracts near the village after passing through some water-driven mills. Stop a moment and look at the wooden turbine that powers the rotating stone; these home-made mills are found throughout Nepal and are a very unusual design.

The next stretch of trail is through the steepest and narrowest part of the canyon; the way is cut through solid rock. This portion of the trail is subject to frequent landslides and from year to year the preferred route moves from one side of the river to the other, depending on which side has the less severe landslide. Beyond Rukse Chhara, the 1990 version of the trail follows the west bank, descending to the river where the water rushes through a steep rocky canyon, then climbs across a landslide to join a rough rocky trail near Kabre, at 1800 metres. The route climbs along a spectacular stretch of narrow, cliffhanging trail, then descends to the river at 1935 metres.

The east bank trail was the favoured route from about 1982 to 1989, and may be repaired by the time you read this. The east

Dasain Ferris Wheel

vegetation changes from subtropical trees and shrubs, including stinging nettles and cannabis, to mountain types such as pine and birch. You might spot grey langur monkeys in this area.

The trail ascends steeply through forests to the Lete Khola. There are a few bhattis here, near the long suspension bridge. This bridge, as with many in Nepal, has a steep descent on the approach and a similar ascent at the exit, so there is an alternate trail that drops to the stream, crosses it on a log, and rejoins the trail on the opposite side. The trail then climbs through Lete itself, which is a spread-out town with three clusters of buildings at 2470 metres. The *Namaste Fooding & Lodging* is the place to patronise.

It is a steep 20 minute walk from Lete to Kalopani, elevation 2560 metres, another town that is prospering from the influx of trekkers. There is an enclosed campground among the whitewashed houses of the village; hotels include the Westernised *Kalopani Guest House*, the *Thak Lodge*, the *See You Lodge*, and the *Annapurna Coffee Shop*. The *Kalopani Lodge* in upper Kalopani has Western toilets and solar-heated showers. There is a 360° panorama of peaks here: Dhaulagiri, the three Nilgiris, Fang and Annapurna I.

Day 6: Kalopani to Jomsom
Beyond Kalopani, the trail goes up the east bank a short distance, then crosses to the west bank on a large bridge where the river races through a narrow cleft, climbs over a wooded ridge past some small lodges and bhattis, then descends to a new suspension bridge. Here there are two trails to choose from.

The West Side By crossing the suspension bridge, you can take the west bank trail that climbs to Sukung, then descends through pine, juniper and cypress forests to Larjung (2560 metres), an architecturally exotic town with narrow alleyways and tunnels connecting houses which are built around enclosed courtyards. This is a complex and pictur-esque system that provides protection from

bank trail crosses the river just beyond Rukse Chhara, then climbs on the east bank to Kopchepani, pops over a ridge and descends again to the riverbank. The trail on this side was also blasted out of the rock face and has a short section that is a three-sided tunnel. Beyond the steepest part of the gorge, the trail descends to the river, then crosses to the west side of the Kali Gandaki on a suspension bridge at 1935 metres.

Either route ends with a short climb to Ghasa, which has three settlements, at about 2000 metres elevation. This is the first Thakali village on the trek and the southern-most limit of Lama Buddhism in the valley. The *Eagle's Nest Hotel* is at the south end of the village. Other good facilities are in middle Ghasa; these include the *Kali Gandaki*, the *Lekahli* and the *Mustang* guest houses. There are fine kanis in upper Ghasa and there is a large locally-supported refor-estation project behind the school. Here the

the winds of the Kali Gandaki gorge. A bit beyond Larjung is Khobang, also called Kanti, at 2560 metres elevation. This trail also provides access to the gompa just above Khobang. There are good views of Dhaulagiri (8167 metres) and Nilgiri (7061 metres) along this part of the trail. At the south end of Larjung are three or four hotels. On the roof of the northernmost house of the village you may be able to see the remains of the hovercraft in which Michel Peissel travelled from Lete to Marpha in 1972.

A trail to the Dhaulagiri icefall begins just south of Khobang and climbs the south bank of the Ghatte Khola. Herzog's expedition explored this route in 1950 and abandoned it because it was too dangerous. In 1969, an avalanche killed seven members of the American Dhaulagiri expedition in this area. You might take a side trip to a meadow near the foot of the icefall at an elevation of about 4000 metres. It's a long, long climb on very steep grassy slopes, so it is wise to make an additional camp at Tal, a lake at about 3100 metres elevation above the village of Naurkot. From this camp you can make a day trip to the icefall area and return to Tal for the night.

The East Side The east bank trail makes a long but easy traverse along the gravel bars alongside the riverbed, then crosses the river on a series of temporary bridges just before Tukuche. Here in its upper reaches, people call the Kali Gandaki the Thak Khola, thus the name Thakali for those who live in this region.

The Kali Gandaki/Thak Khola Valley has been a major trade route for centuries. Until 1959, traders exchanged salt collected from salt lakes in Tibet for rice and barley from the middle hills of Nepal. They also traded wool, livestock and butter for sugar, tea, spices, tobacco and manufactured goods from India, but the salt-for-grain trade dominated the economy. This trade has diminished, not only because of the political and economic changes in Tibet, but also because Indian salt is now available through

Nepal at a much lower price than Tibetan salt.

Indian salt, from the sea, contains iodine. Many people in Nepal once suffered from goitres because of the total absence of iodine in their diet. Indian aid programmes distributed sea salt in a successful programme to prevent goitres, but the Tibetan salt trade suffered because of the artificially low prices of Indian salt.

The Thakali people of the Kali Gandaki Valley had a monopoly on the salt trade of this region. They are now turning to agriculture, tourism and other forms of trade for their livelihood. There are few mani walls or religious monuments along the Kali Gandaki, although there are large gompas in Tukuche and Khobang.

Tukuche, elevation 2590 metres, was once the most important Thakali village. Tukuche (*tuk*, 'grain' and *che* 'flat place') was the meeting place where traders coming with salt and wool from Tibet and the upper Thak Khola Valley bartered with traders carrying grain from the south. The hotels in Tukuche are in beautiful old Thakali homes; the *Himali, Usha, Laxmi* and *Sunil* lodges are all good. At the north end of town the *Yak Hotel* advertises a 'real yak on display inside' – it's worth a look. Tourism has not totally offset the economic effect of the loss of the grain trade, so many people have moved from Tukuche to Pokhara, Kathmandu and the Terai. A walk along the back streets of the village, particularly close to the river, will reveal many abandoned and crumbling buildings behind the prosperous facade of the main street.

A dramatic change in the vegetation, from pine and conifer forests to dry, arid desert-like country, takes place during this stretch of trail. The flow of air between the peaks of Annapurna and Dhaulagiri creates strong winds that howl up the valley. The breezes blow gently from the north during the early hours of the day, then shift to powerful gusts from the south throughout the late morning and afternoon. From here to Jomsom, these strong winds will be blowing dust and sand at your back after about 11 am.

As the trail proceeds north, it passes an agricultural project set up in 1966 by the Ministry of Agriculture to introduce new types of produce into the region. The motivating force behind this project has always been Passang Khambache Sherpa who accompanied David Snellgrove during his studies throughout Nepal. It may be possible to purchase fresh fruits, vegetables and almonds here. Local apple cider and fruit preserves are available in Marpha and Tukuche, and there is also, of course, excellent apple, apricot and peach rakshi. Try the bottled *Tukuche Brandy*.

Between the agricultural project and Marpha is *Om's Home*, a very clean hotel that has excellent food, and facilities ranging from rooms with attached baths to dormitories. The village of Marpha is huddled behind a ridge for protection from the wind and dust. This is a large Thakali village, at 2665 metres elevation, which exhibits the typical Thak Khola architecture of flat roofs and narrow paved alleys and passageways. The very limited rainfall in this region makes these flat roofs practical; they also serve as a drying place for grains and vegetables.

In Marpha, the Thakali inn system has reached its highest level of development. Hotels have private rooms, menus, room service and indoor toilets. In this clean and pleasant village, there is an extensive drainage system that flows under the flagstone-paved street and there is even a library in the centre of the town. There are impressive kanis at both ends of Marpha and the gompa has recently been totally refurbished and painted. The *Dhaulagiri Lodge* and *Baba's Lodge* have elaborate carved windows, comfortable inner courtyards and good toilet facilities. A plastic signboard advertises *Bhakti's Lodge*, and the *Miami* has a solar-heated shower.

Across the river from Marpha is the village of Chaira, a Tibetan settlement with a carpet factory. Traders from Chaira often sit along the trail near Marpha selling their wares. Pause a minute along this part of the trail and look at the scenery – high snow peaks, brown and yellow cliffs, splashes of bright green irrigated fields and flat-roofed mud houses clustered here and there. Except for the height of the peaks, this country looks the same as central Afghanistan; it is eerie to find such similarity in a place so distant both physically and culturally.

Marpha may be a better choice than Jomsom for a night stop, or you can take it easy and spend a night at Tukuche and then go on to Jomsom. It is a bit far, but not unreasonable to reach Muktinath in a single day from Marpha, though it is more interesting to break the trip up with a stop at Kagbeni. From Marpha, the trail continues along the side of the valley, climbing imperceptibly, to Jomsom.

Jomsom (or more correctly Dzongsam or 'new fort'), the administrative headquarters for the region, straddles the Kali Gandaki at an elevation of 2713 metres. It is an administrative and trading centre. The major inhabitants are government officials, and merchants engaged in the distribution of goods brought in by plane and by pony caravans. From Jomsom, you can make an easy side trip to the gompa at Thini, about an hour from Jomsom on the east bank of the Kali Gandaki.

Jomsom is in three separate parts. The section on the east bank of the river is the main part of the town, with dwellings, the *Nilgiri Lodge*, a bank and the post office. On the west bank are shops, bhattis, the telegraph office and a bakery, and to the south, near the airport, are large hotels, restaurants and the RNAC office. The *Lali Guras*, the *Moonlight* and the *Alaka* hotels are all near the airport. Just north of the airport is an army post and the mandatory police check post. If you have come from Manang, it is important to obtain the endorsement of this station on your trekking permit, because all police posts to the south will want to see it. The power lines, electric lights and the military people jogging in the mornings are a bit incongruous in this remote location.

Day 7: Jomsom to Muktinath

From Jomsom, the trail follows the broad river valley, sometimes above the river, but mostly along the rocky bank of the river itself as it passes beneath vertical rock cliffs. The trail eventually crosses to the east bank of the Kali Gandaki and proceeds up the valley to Chhancha Lhumba, the site of the *Eklai Bhatti* ('alone hotel') at 2370 metres.

Unless you are in a tremendous rush, you should take a side trip to Kagbeni. From Chhancha Lhumba, the trail follows the river to Kagbeni at 2810 metres, a green oasis at the junction of the Jhong Khola and the Kali Gandaki. Kagbeni looks like a town out of the medieval past, with closely packed mud houses, dark alleys, imposing chortens and a large, ochre-coloured gompa perched above the town. The people dress in typical Tibetan clothing, though the children have, even in this faraway village, learned to beg, rather insistently, for sweets.

Kagbeni is the northernmost village in this valley that foreigners may visit; the police check post here fastidiously prevents tourists from proceeding towards Lo Mantang, the walled city of Mustang. The *New Annapurna Lodge*, in the centre of Kagbeni, has inexpensive dormitory accommodation and also apple pie, mustang coffee and a sun terrace. Another popular establishment is the *Red House*.

The trail from Kagbeni makes a steep climb up the Jhong Khola Valley, joining the direct trail to Muktinath below Khingar. Along the way you will see hundreds of small piles of rocks erected by pilgrims to honour their departed ancestors.

The direct route to Muktinath climbs immediately upon leaving Chhancha Lhumba, to a plateau above the Kali Gandaki, and then turns east up the Jhong Khola Valley. The trail ascends to Khingar through country that is arid and desert-like, in the same geographical and climatic zone as Tibet. The striking yellows of the bare hillsides contrast dramatically with the blue sky, white peaks, and splashes of green where streams allow cultivation. The views of Dhaulagiri and Nilgiri are tremendous.

The walk from Khingar at 3200 metres to Jharkot is a delightful walk amongst meadows, streams and poplar and fruit trees.

There are often flocks of cranes in the area. The trail is here high above the Jhong Khola as it climbs to Jharkot, an impressive Tibetan village at 3500 metres. One of the hotels here offers solar-heated rooms. The village itself, with its picturesque kani, is well worth exploring. There are some peach trees nearby; local people grind the peach seeds to make oil. Across the valley you can see the ruins of Dzong, the ancient capital of this region.

The first part of Muktinath that you reach is Ranipauwa at 3710 metres, the site of a large rest house for pilgrims and a host of hotels, bhattis and camping places. This area is often crowded with both pilgrims and foreign tourists. The *North Pole Lodge* is good, but the *Shree Muktinath Hotel* is reported to have the best food in town.

The Tibetan traders here are unrelenting in their efforts to convince you to buy their wares. One item that is unique in this region is *saligram*. These are black stones that, when broken open, reveal the fossilised remains of prehistoric ammonites. You might find some yourself between here and Jomsom, but you can always buy them, at inflated prices, from these traders – and then curse yourself all the way back to Pokhara for carrying a backpack full of rocks. Hindu pilgrims also purchase these ammonites because they represent the god Vishnu. They were formed about 130 million years ago.

The most colourful pilgrims to Muktinath are the ascetic *sadhus*, whom you must have seen many times between Pokhara and here. They travel in various stages of undress, smear themselves with ash and often carry a three-pronged spear called a *trisul*. A rupee or two donation to these holy men is not out of place. They are Shaivite mystics on a pilgrimage that, more often than not, began in the heat of southern India.

The temple and the religious shrines of Muktinath are about 90 metres above Ranipauwa. There are no hotels, and the temple committee does not allow camping here. Muktinath is an important pilgrimage place for both Hindus and Buddhists. Situated in a grove of trees, the holy shrines at

Muktinath include a Buddhist gompa and the pagoda-style temple of Jiwala Mayi, containing an image of Vishnu. Around the temple is a wall from which 108 waterspouts, cast in the shape of cows' heads, pour forth sacred water. Even more sacred is the water that issues from a rock inside an ancient temple a short distance below the pagoda. Inside this gompa, behind a tattered curtain, are small natural gas jets that produce a perpetual holy flame alongside a spring that is the source of the sacred water. This auspicious combination of earth, fire and water is responsible for the religious importance of Muktinath. It is often possible to see Tibetan women, with elaborate headdresses, embedded with priceless turquoise stones engaged in devotions at these shrines.

The most charming description of Muktinath is the one on the signboard erected by the Ministry of Tourism at Jomsom:

Muktinath is beautiful, calm and quiet,
great and mysterious for pilgrims,
decorated with god and goddess.
Although you are kindly requested not to snap them.

ANNAPURNA SANCTUARY

The route to Annapurna Sanctuary (Annapurna Deuthali in Nepali), the site of the Annapurna South Face base camp, is a spectacular short trek. Though it has some steep climbs the trek is not difficult, but it can become impassable because of snow and avalanches in winter and early spring. It is the only major trekking route in Nepal that has significant avalanche danger, so you must inquire locally whether the trail is safe. Some trekkers have died because of avalanches, and others have been stranded in the Sanctuary for days. The Sanctuary trek traverses a variety of terrain, from lowland villages and rice terraces to glaciers, and offers outstanding high mountain views. This trek is a fine opportunity to surround yourself with Himalayan peaks in a short time, without having to contend with the altitude and flight problems of the Everest region.

You can make the trek, from Pokhara to Annapurna base camp and back, in as few as ten or eleven days, but it is best to allow two weeks to fully appreciate the high-altitude scenery. A diversion to Ghorapani on the return route provides a view of Dhaulagiri from Poon Hill. There are frequent tea shops along the entire trek, sometimes five or ten minutes apart, and you will rarely walk for as long as an hour without finding some source of refreshment.

Day 1: Pokhara to Tolka
The most direct approach to the Annapurna Sanctuary is via the trail from Dhampus to Chhomrong that uses a 'new bridge', built in about 1985. Take a taxi, jeep or bus from Pokhara to Phedi, then continue a short distance along the road to a trail that climbs steeply up the hill to the right. You can spot the Dhampus trail coming down the hill and easily find it where it reaches the valley floor.

Starting at an elevation of 1080 metres, in a forest that is so overgrazed that it looks like a manicured municipal park, the trail climbs steeply past some scattered houses to the ridge at Dhampus, at 1580 metres. At Dhampus, you are rewarded with great views of the mountains that continue to improve as you ascend along the ridge. There are a few hotels at this end of Dhampus, but it is a large village strung out along the ridge over several km and you will pass several other hotels, including the upmarket *Dhaulagiri View Hotel*, during the next half-hour of walking.

Dhampus is the centre of the theft racket in central Nepal. Thieves often cut the tents of trekkers and remove valuable items during the night, so it's not a good idea to camp alone here. Trekking groups circle their tents like an old-time wagon train and post a guard with a lighted lantern throughout the night. If you stay in a hotel, be sure that you know who is sharing the room with you and lock the door whenever you go out – even for a moment. The thieves do watch everyone, in order to decide who has something worth taking or is likely to be careless.

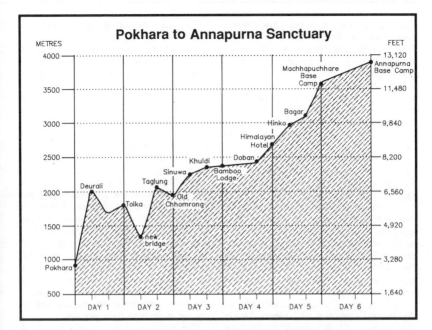

Pokhara to Annapurna Sanctuary

METRES / FEET

They will wait patiently all night to make their move if necessary.

The trail climbs through Dhampus, past a police check post, then gradually ascends a forested trail paved with stones. There is a short steep climb to Pothana, a bunch of hotels that grew up around a new water pipe, at 1870 metres. Just before Pothana is an inconspicuous trail junction; this is a trail that leads to the 'Australian Camp' and a route back to the road at Khare.

The trail climbs through forests to a clearing on top of the hill at 2010 metres, where there are views of Annapurna South and Hiunchuli. From there make a steep descent, through forests alive with birds, ferns and orchids, into a huge side canyon of the Modi Khola. The trail descends past several tea houses at Bichok (also known as Bheri Kharka), then descends further to the head of the canyon. After crossing a stream on a suspension bridge at 1690 metres, the trail climbs gently out of the side canyon. There

are frequent tea shops as the trail emerges into the main Modi Khola Valley and descends to Tolka, a small settlement at 1710 metres, with several lodges scattered along the trail. In this region, men hunt birds and wild goats with ancient muzzle-loading guns that look like leftovers from the American revolution.

Day 2: Tolka to Chhomrong

From Tolka, the trail descends to a stream at 1620 metres, then climbs through forests to a tea shop on a ridge. It's an easy walk, past fields, a school and some unusual oval-shaped houses, before the trail drops a bit to the flagstone streets of Landrung, a Gurung village at 1550 metres. There are many hotels here; the best ones are either above or below the village. The hotels in the village itself are in old houses, so they are small and a bit crummy. Along the trail you will probably meet people collecting money for schools. They will produce a ledger book showing the donations of other trekkers and enter your contribution into their records. They are legitimate, but it is an adult version of the creative begging that tourists have encouraged.

Descend through the paved courtyards of Landrung to the small *Himalaya Hotel*, below the village at 1480 metres. The trail to the Sanctuary leads to the right, just behind the hotel. There may be an orange sign pointing the way.

The downhill trail leads to the river and then climbs to Ghandruk. You can see Ghandruk village high above you on the opposite side of the river.

The trail to the Sanctuary turns north up the Modi Khola Valley on a narrow trail, alongside rice terraces then through forests, to the rustic *Namaste Lodge*. A short walk up the river bed leads to Shiuli, better known as New Bridge, or *Naya Pool* in Nepali, at 1340 metres elevation. There are several substantial hotels on both sides of the suspension bridge. The trail climbs steeply to Samrung, then crosses a stream at 1430 metres. This is the lower part of the Khumnu Khola, but here it is known as the Kladi Khola.

A stiff climb leads to Jhinu Danda, where there are two hotels on a ridge at 1600 metres. There is a hot spring with cement bathing pools about 25 minutes up the valley from here; ask the lodge owner about them. You can see houses on the top of the ridge far above; this is your next destination. It is a long, steep climb along a treeless ridge to a few tea shops at Taglung at 2050 metres. The route now joins the Ghandruk to Chhomrong route, so the trail is wider and better from here to Chhomrong.

A short distance from Taglung is the isolated *Himalayan View Lodge*, then the trail rounds a bend and enters the upper part of Chhomrong. This Gurung village has evolved into two separate parts. New Chhomrong is the upper part, at an elevation of 2040 metres, with resort hotels, the school and a helicopter pad; old Chhomrong, at 1950 metres, is the main part of the village with shops, offices and lodges. The fancy hotels in New Chhomrong have slate patios,

private rooms and dining rooms with picture windows.

Down a long staircase in the centre of the village is a kerosene depot, the ACAP office and several shops. *Captain's Lodge* is Chhomrong's most popular inn, though the captain himself is a strong personality. The *Chhomrong Guest House* is also near the centre of town. All the hotels have provision shops at which you can stock up on food for the trip into the Sanctuary. The ACAP regulations prohibit the use of firewood beyond Chhomrong, so all trekkers and hotels must cook with kerosene. If you are camping, you can buy kerosene and rent Indian pressure stoves and plastic jerrycans here. Stoves rent from Rs 10 to 20 per day and jerrycans from Rs 1 to Rs 3 depending on the size. In 1990, kerosene cost Rs 13 per litre; the operator of the depot can give advice on the quantity that you will need. If you are staying in hotels, the hotelier will take care of the kerosene problem. The ACAP office also maintains a check-in, check-out system for the Sanctuary and inspects trekking permits.

The houses and hotels in old Chhomrong have electric lighting thanks to Mr Hayashi, popularly known as *Bijuli Japani*, the 'electric Japanese' who installed a small hydroelectric plant and equipped the houses with miniature light bulbs. The hotels and lodges in this area have formed a committee to fix prices in all lodges. They have prepared printed menus for each locale – with increasing prices the further you go from Chhomrong. This is a positive move because trekkers used to bargain and stay in the cheapest hotel. Now everyone quotes the same rate, so you can choose a hotel according to quality, not price. Dhal bhaat is Rs 20 per plate, tea is Rs 2. The price increases dramatically from here on, and the menu gets very limited because of the kerosene restriction. Chhomrong is the northern limit of pies, cakes and bread.

This the highest permanent settlement in the valley, but herders take sheep and goats to upper pastures in the Sanctuary during the summer. There is a tremendous view of Annapurna South, which seems to tower above the village, and there are good views of Machhapuchhare (*machha*, 'fish', and *puchhare*, tail) across the valley. It is from this point onwards that the reason for the name of this peak becomes apparent. In 1957, Wilfred Noyce and David Cox climbed Machhapuchhare to within 50 metres of its summit. After this attempt, the government prohibited further climbing on the mountain, so technically the peak remains unclimbed. A lower peak to the south, Mardi Himal, elevation 5586 metres, is open to trekking parties.

Day 3: Chhomrong to Bamboo Lodge

Leaving Chhomrong, the trail descends on a stone staircase and crosses the Chhomrong Khola on a swaying suspension bridge, then climbs out of the side valley. Climbing high above the Modi Khola on its west bank, the trail passes through the tiny settlement of Tilche in forests of bamboo, rhododendron and oak. Climbing further on a rocky trail (beware of the stinging nettles) you reach three hotels at Sinuwa, 2250 metres.

The trail continues in rhododendron forests, climbing to Kuldi, 2350 metres. This was once a British sheep-breeding project; now the stone houses are occupied by an ACAP visitor centre and lodge. In winter, it is common to find snow anywhere from this point on. From Kuldi, the trail descends a long, steep stone staircase into deep bamboo and rhododendron forests. It is then a short distance on a muddy trail to Bamboo Lodge (2190 metres), a collection of four hotels, none of which is built of bamboo. In early autumn and late spring, this part of the trail is crawling with leeches.

Day 4: Bamboo Lodge to Himalayan Hotel

The trail climbs steeply through stands of bamboo, then through rhododendron forest up the side of the canyon, occasionally dropping slightly to cross tributary streams, but ascending continuously. When there is snow this stretch of trail is particularly difficult, because the bamboo lying on the trail, hidden beneath the snow, provides an excellent start

to a slide downhill. Local people hack down the dense bamboo forests beyond Kuldi to make mats for floors and roofs, and for dokos, the baskets that porters carry. The isolated *Tip Top Lodge* is about an hour from Kuldi.

At Doban (2430 metres), about 1½ hours beyond Kuldi, there is also a good hotel. Beyond Doban the trail traverses several avalanche chutes, to upper Doban and the *Annapurna Approach Lodge*, at 2470 metres. The trail is muddy and high above the river, but it is no problem for those who suffer vertigo, because thick stands of bamboo block the view of the rushing river and waterfall. The trail then crosses a landslide and another avalanche track, to *Himalayan Hotel* at 2680 metres. Just before the hotel you can see the debris left from an avalanche that killed a Sherpa kitchen crew in the spring of 1989.

Day 5: Himalayan Hotel to Machhapuchhare Base Camp

From the Himalayan Hotel it is about a 1 hour walk, first on a rocky trail through forests then up a steep ravine, to Hinko at 2960 metres. This is called 'Hinko Cave' because a huge overhanging rock provides some protection against rain and avalanches. There is a funny hotel built into the cave that can accommodate 12 or 13 people.

The trail crosses a ravine and a major avalanche track just beyond Hinko, then climbs through large boulders. About a half-hour beyond Hinko is (yet another) Deurali, at 3000 metres, where two hotels offer an alternative to the crowded conditions at Hinko. Above Deurali, the valley widens and becomes less steep and you can see the 'gates' to the sanctuary. Avalanches from Hiunchuli and Annapurna South, peaks which are above, but not visible from this point, come crashing into the valley with frightening speed and frequency.

As the trail continues into the Sanctuary, it crosses two wide avalanche tracks on a narrow trail that huddles up against the cliffs. The trail then descends to meet the Modi Khola and follows the river to Bagar, two lodges at 3110 metres. The normal trail follows the left side of the valley, but when an avalanche has blocked the trail it may be necessary to take an alternate route. There is a trail that crosses the river, climbs along the east side of the river and then recrosses on a log bridge just before Bagar. The local people will know when to take this diversion. The normal trail will probably be open in October and November and late spring.

From Bagar, climb across more avalanche paths, cross a moraine and a stream, then climb towards a two-storey building. This is a German meteorological project office. There is a hotel here, and several others five minutes beyond in an area known as Machhapuchhare base camp, elevation 3480 metres. These hotels may or may not be open, depending on whether the innkeeper – and the supplies – have been able to reach the hotel through the avalanche area. Most of the inns in the Sanctuary close during the winter. All are operated by people from Ghandruk or Chhomrong, so you can easily find out in advance which, if any, are open. Prices have been raised again; dhal bhaat is Rs 35, tea Rs 5 and eggs Rs 10 each.

The mountain views are stupendous; the panorama includes Hiunchuli, Annapurna I (8091 metres), Annapurna III (7555 metres), Gangapurna (7454 metres) and Machhapuchhare (6997 metres).

Day 6: Machhapuchhare Base Camp to Annapurna Base Camp

It's about a 2 hour climb to Annapurna base camp, elevation 3900 metres. The trail passes a few roofless herders' huts alongside a moraine to three hotels situated on a knoll. These hotels are often ridiculously crowded. The *Paradise Hotel* is the upmarket establishment; the *Mount Annapurna* advertises 'quick and civilise service'. The price of dhal bhaat has increased again – to Rs 45 per plate. The area is often snowbound. When I was here one April the snow reached the roofs of the hotels.

There are tremendous views of the near-vertical South Face of Annapurna that towers above the sanctuary to the north-west. This face was climbed in 1970 by an expedition led by Chris Bonington, and still remains as one of the most spectacular ascents of an 8000 metre peak.

Several peaks that are accessible from the Sanctuary are on the trekking peak list. Tent Peak (5500 metres) offers a commanding 360° view of the entire Sanctuary. Its higher neighbour, Fluted Peak *(Singu Chuli*, 6390 metres), offers a mountaineering challenge. Hiunchuli (6441 metres) to the south is also open to trekking parties. All three of these peaks are significant mountaineering challenges and require skill, equipment and planning.

There are few birds in the sanctuary, but there are ghoral, Himalayan weasel and pika.

Chhomrong to Ghorapani

To reach Ghorapani from Chhomrong, follow the route back to Taglung, at the junction of the trail from Landrung and New Bridge. Stay on the wide main trail, walking west above the prosperous-looking houses and potato and wheat fields of Taglung, then descend gently through forests to a single tea shop, the *Hilcross Lodge* at 2020 metres. From here, the trail drops steeply on switchbacks to Khumnu (also called Kimrong) village, situated above the Khumnu Khola at 1720 metres. There are hotels in the village, and a very funky tea shop near the bridge.

To reach Ghorapani, cross the river on a new suspension bridge and then walk about 100 metres upstream to the site of the old bridge, where a faint trail leads steeply uphill. The trail becomes more distinct as it switchbacks up through wheat fields to the Brahmin village of Melanche at 2050 metres. Above Melanche, the trail becomes less steep as it climbs steadily through rhododendron forests to Tadapani at 2540 metres. Here the route joins the main Ghorapani to Ghandruk trail.

Chhomrong to Ghandruk

Follow the trail described above to Khumnu, then cross the suspension bridge and stay on the main trail as it climbs out of the Khumnu Valley. The trail makes a steep climb to some tea houses at Uri, situated on a pass at 2220 metres. The trail then descends through huge boulders to a small creek and descends gently into the maze of trails of Ghandruk, at 1940 metres.

Ghorapani to Ghandruk

It is a long, though not difficult, day (except when the trail is snow-covered) from Ghorapani to Ghandruk. Local people rarely use this trail, but it is becoming an increasingly important trekking route, and there has been overwhelming and uncontrolled development of the area in the past few years. Villagers have chopped down large parts of what used to be an unbroken stretch of rhododendron forest wilderness to build hotels.

From the Ghorapani pass, known as Deurali, the trail climbs south on a muddy path through deep forests. It finally emerges on a grassy knoll which offers good mountain views, including a view of Machhapuchhare (not visible from the Ghorapani pass), and a panorama all the way south to the plains of India. It is a similar view to Poon Hill. Keep climbing along the ridge in pine and rhododendron forests to a crest at 3030 metres, then descend to two inns at a second pass, also called Deurali, at 2960 metres.

There is a trail junction here with a route that leads down to Chitre and Tatopani. The Ghandruk trail descends to the *Lali Guras Lodge* in a rhododendron forest, then follows a dry stream bed. A ridge hides the mountains as the trail makes a steep, sometimes treacherous, descent on a narrow path alongside the stream, which becomes larger as the descent continues. The stream has some clear pools alongside the trail (remember Nepal's disapproval of skinny-dipping) and finally becomes a series of waterfalls over a jumble of boulders and logs that were washed down when this harmless-looking stream ran amok during the monsoon rains.

The steep descent becomes more gentle as the route reaches Banthanti, six hotels in the shadow of a huge rock face. The tables and benches outside the lodges here present a scene reminiscent of a ski lodge – especially when there is snow. (This is not the same Banthanti that is between Ulleri and Ghorapani.) Follow the stream down to a bridge, where a tiny trail leads off to a rock quarry; porters carry slabs of slate from here to make roofs for the homes of Ghandruk and Melanche. The trail starts climbing, leaving the moist, high mountain forests and entering a field of cane, making some ups and downs past the *Tranquillity Lodge*, to a vantage point that offers a brief view of the mountains. The trail then descends steeply to a stream before climbing again through forests to Tadapani, a clutter of hotels with a dramatic view at 2540 metres. Not content with the view from ground level, one hotel has built a stone lookout tower. Tadapani means 'far water'. The village water supply is a long distance below the village, and it takes porters more than half an hour to fetch a load of water.

From Tadapani, there is a trail to the left that descends through forests, then through terraced fields, to the Khumnu Khola. This direct route to the Annapurna Sanctuary is described, in reverse, in the previous section.

The Ghandruk trail descends steeply from Tadapani, through forests to a clearing with two hotels. (This is yet another spot called Deurali!) A short, steep descent among rocks leads to a stream crossing, then the descent continues gently past other streams, finally leading out on a ridge towards Ghandruk. The trail enters the village near the tin-roofed handicraft factory, then descends on stone steps into the maze of the village itself. The first hotels that you come across from this direction are the *Himalayan Hotel* and the *Gorkha Lodge*. Both are very heavy advertisers along the trail – you can't miss them. There are other hotels at the south end of the village where the trail to Landrung begins.

Ghandruk, a huge Gurung village at 1940 metres, is the second largest Gurung village in Nepal (the largest is Siklis), and is a confusing cluster of closely-spaced, slate-roofed houses. There are neatly terraced fields situated both above and below the town. Older maps spell the village name 'Ghandrung',

Ghandruk Village

but Ghandruk is the currently accepted spelling. Ghandruk is the Nepali name, but the village's real name is Kond; each Gurung village in Nepal is known locally by its own Gurung name.

It is wonderfully easy to get lost in the network of narrow alleyways while trying to trek through the village. As you enter Ghandruk, either from above or below, you will find a set of signs that describe the town's many facilities. The largest hotels are near the top of the village; the rest of the inns are at the bottom of Ghandruk, not among the houses of the village itself.

Ghandruk has an extensive water supply system with tanks, pipes and taps throughout the village. There is a large handicraft factory at the top of Ghandruk, near the Himalayan Hotel. The views of Annapurna South (Annapurna Dakshin) from here are outstanding. Machhapuchhare, seen from here in its fish tail aspect, peeps over a forested ridge. ACAP has a visitor centre and an office in Ghandruk and provides offers information about its activities.

AROUND ANNAPURNA

It takes a minimum of 18 days to trek around the entire Annapurna massif, visiting the Tibet-like country on the north slopes of the Himalaya and the dramatic Kali Gandaki gorge. Nepal opened Manang to trekkers in April 1977, although a few expeditions and scientific parties visited the region in the 1950s.

The last seven days of this trek are the reverse of the popular trek from Pokhara to Jomsom; you will have to read that section of this book backwards from Muktinath onwards. There are tea shops and hotels about every hour all along the route from Dumre to Pokhara, except on the pass between Thorung Phedi and Muktinath.

It is easiest and safest to cross Thorung pass, 5416 metres, from east to west, as

Top: Danphe Lagna, en route to Rara Lake (SA)
Bottom: Spinning a prayer wheel (SA)

Top: Chorten at Ringmo village, Phoksumdo Lake (SA)
Left: A carved effigy called dok-pa (SA)
Right: The narrow trail to Phoksumdo Lake (SA)

shown in this route description. Here's why: if you travel from west to east, there are no camping spots or water sources on the west side of the pass from a meadow above Muktinath, at 4100 metres, to a spot 2 to 3 hours beyond the pass on the Manang side, at 4510 metres. This means that you have to make a 1300 metre climb, plus at least a 900 metre descent, in a single day. This is an impossible feat for many people, especially those who have not yet acclimatised to high elevation. From Manang to Muktinath, the pass is not difficult, but it is a long way at high elevation. You should be aware of the chance that you might have to return to Dumre if it is impossible or dangerous to cross Thorung La because of snow or altitude sickness. There are years where the weather allows it to stay open, but Thorung La is usually snowbound and closed from mid-December to mid-April.

Clothing and equipment for porters must be a prime consideration if you are taking them over the Thorung La. Many lowland porters from Dumre have suffered frostbite or snow blindness on this pass because trekkers (and/or their sherpas) have not provided the proper footwear, clothing and, most importantly, sunglasses for the pass. Porters from near-tropical villages like Dumre have no idea what to expect on a snow-covered pass, or they hope that the pass crossing will be in warm weather, and they join a trekking party clad only in cotton clothing. If you employ porters for a crossing of Thorung La, you incur both a moral and legal obligation for their safety and well-being.

Getting There & Away

To Dumre

An express bus takes about 5 hours from Kathmandu to Dumre. Leaving the Kathmandu Valley, the road descends from the Chandragiri pass on a wild series of steep switchbacks along the narrow Indian-built Tribhuvan Rajpath. It then continues south through cultivated fields to Naubise, 26 km from Kathmandu. Naubise is the beginning of the Ariniko Rajpath, completed in 1971 with Chinese aid. The Tribhuvan Rajpath continues south from this point and winds its way to the Indian border at Birganj. The Chinese road heads east along the Mahesh Khola to its confluence with the Trisuli River. It then follows the Trisuli Valley to Mugling, elevation 220 metres, at the confluence of the Trisuli and Marsyandi rivers, 110 km from Kathmandu. The large river thus formed flows south to become the Narayani River, one of the major tributaries of the Ganges. Most rafting in Nepal is done on this part of the river, finally emerging at one of the game parks in Royal Chitwan National Park. A new road follows the Narayani Valley south from Mugling to join the East-West Highway at Narayanghat in the Terai.

Beyond Mugling, the road follows the Marsyandi River, passing the road to Gorkha and the huge Marsyandi power project, actually going across the dam in front of the powerhouse. Dumre is 25 km beyond Mugling at an elevation of 440 metres. This is a new village, settled by Newars from the nearby town of Bandipur after the completion of the road from Kathmandu to Pokhara. Dumre exists because it used to be at the beginning of trails that lead both to Gorkha, a day's walk away, and to the Marsyandi Valley and Manang. Most of the village consists of warehouses, shops and bhattis that serve the porters who carry loads from the roadhead to remote villages. In Dumre there are also a few hotels, including the *Annapurna* and the *Dhaulagiri* that cater to trekkers.

A 41 km motor road is under construction from Dumre to Besi Sahar (also called Lamjung), the headquarters of the Lamjung district. In 1990, the road had been under construction for at least seven years and it is muddy and sometimes impassable when it rains. There is a daily minibus to Besi Sahar, a 4 to 5 hour trip when the road is dry. A better choice is to get a ride in a tractor or 4WD truck. A bumpy, dusty ride in one of these decrepit army surplus trucks costs Rs 40 to Rs 50, plus an extra charge for luggage; trucks leave from Dumre whenever they have a full load of passengers and baggage.

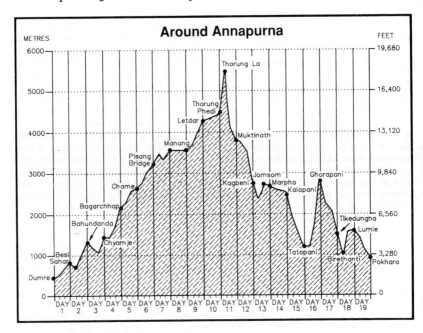

Around Annapurna

Day 1: Dumre to Besi Sahar

The hotel facilities along the road above Dumre are mediocre because most trekkers bypass them and drive to Besi Sahar. The road passes through terraced rice fields and small villages, inhabited by Newars, Brahmins and Chhetris, to Bhansar at 530 metres. It then follows the west bank of the Marsyandi upstream through a region dotted with gigantic banyan and pipal trees.

A short distance on, from the town of Chambas at 500 metres elevation, there are good views of the high Himalaya, especially Baudha (6672 metres) and Himalchuli (7893 metres). From Turture at 530 metres you can see Palangtar, the site of the defunct Gorkha airport. Gorkha is the major town in the central hills and is the site of the ancient palace of King Prithvi Narayan Shah, the founder of modern Nepal. Palangtar airport is no longer served by any flights because the new road to Gorkha has made flying unnecessary.

Tarkughat is a fair-sized bazaar on the east bank of the Marsyandi, across a large suspension bridge at 490 metres elevation. The route to Manang does not cross the bridge, but stays on the west bank of the river through fairly level country, passing through Shurebas, and Bhote Odar at 550 metres. There is a police check post here and the *Star Hotel* offers accommodation. The road climbs over a ridge, passing Udipu at 730 metres and descends to the Thakali bazaar of Phalensangu, situated below the road at 670 metres.

At Phalensangu, there is a bridge perched high above a narrow wooded gorge. If you cross the Marsyandi on this bridge, you can make a side trip to Bara Pokhari. This is a high-altitude lake (elevation 3100 metres) that offers outstanding views of Manaslu, Himalchuli and Baudha. The trip involves a long, steep climb, but you can make a trek to Bara Pokhari in as few as three days, leaving the main trail at Phalensangu and rejoining the trail to Manang below Usta on Day 2.

The bridge at Phalensangu also provides access to an alternative route that avoids the motor road. From the east side of the bridge at Phalensangu, a trail climbs to Chiti, then follows the river valley north. The trail passes through sal forests and rice terraces to Chaur at an elevation of 760 metres, then enters a sugar cane-growing region. From Chaur (also called Simbachaur), the trail stays near the river, crosses the Bhachok Khola, and climbs through Baragaon, elevation 910 metres, and over a ridge before descending to Bhulbule, where it joins the route described below.

From Phalensangu, the road makes a few small ascents and descents and fords a lot of small streams before reaching Besi Sahar, situated on a plateau at 820 metres. Here is the first of many police check posts, radio and watch repair facilities, shops selling Chinese and Japanese goods, and some trekkers' hotels, including the *Hotel Tukuche Peak*, which advertises that it is able to supply porters.

Above and to the west of Besi Sahar is Gaonsahar, elevation 1370 metres, where there are the remains of an old fortress and palace. From the 15th to 18th centuries, this region was a collection of independent kingdoms that continually waged war on each other. In 1782 the kingdom of Gorkha absorbed Lamjung, the principality ruled from this palace.

The trail to Manang has been renovated, graded and widened to allow horse and mule caravans to transport supplies to these remote villages – though you may not believe this as you walk the rough trails. The mules travel from Besi Sahar to Manang village, though they stop at Chame when there is snow in the higher regions of the Manang Valley.

Day 2: Besi Sahar to Bahundanda

From Besi Sahar, the trail makes a steep descent of about 150 metres followed by an equally steep climb through the deep river gorge. It is a long walk with several ups and downs, through rice fields, subtropical forests and small hamlets, to Khudi at 825 metres elevation. Khudi is a mixture of tin and thatch-roofed houses, hotels and shops clustered around the anchors of a long, sagging suspension bridge that crosses a side stream. The old bridge is precarious, but the new one is about 10 minutes upstream. Khudi is the first Gurung village on the trek. Most of the people in the wide river valley below Khudi are Brahmins and Chhetris, although there are a few Gurung villages in the side valleys and slopes above the river.

The trail continues northward up the Marsyandi Valley, with Himalchuli and Ngadi Chuli (also known as Manaslu II and formerly known as Peak 29), 7879 metres, dominating the horizon. The trail then crosses the Marsyandi River on a suspension bridge at Bhulbule, elevation 830 metres. The *Hotel Arjun*, which looks like a Spanish hacienda, is just across the bridge on the right; the other major hotel here is the *Manang Hotel*. There are shops, and even a tailor, near the bridge. The trail now travels up the east bank of the river, past a majestic waterfall 60 metres high that is surrounded by a type of tropical tree called a pandanus, or screwpine. The path then wanders through small villages scattered amongst extensive rice terraces.

Beyond Bhulbule, there are good views of Manaslu (8162 metres) and Ngadi Chuli. The small settlement of Ngadi used to be only a winter settlement before trekkers proliferated, but now there are several hotels run by Manangis. The *Himalayan Lodge* offers 'clean and friendly service'. Beyond Ngadi, the trail crosses the Ngadi Khola on a long suspension bridge at 880 metres elevation.

It is fascinating to see the extensive public works programme in the hills of Nepal. To build this bridge, porters had to carry the steel cables and towers for several days. There are thousands of bridges throughout the country in unbelievably remote locations that have required huge expenditures of time and money for their construction. It is all too easy to see only the undeveloped aspect of Nepal and ignore the extensive expenditure of labour and money over the last 30 years that has developed an extensive network of trails and bridges. There is an excellent campsite just after the bridge.

Above the Ngadi Khola is the village of Usta, where the trail from Bara Pokhari rejoins the route to Manang. After the bridge, there is a trail junction marked by a pipal tree on the left and a stone dharamsala, or rest house, on the right. Just beyond these landmarks, take the trail to the left; the right trail goes up the Ngadi Khola, not to Manang. The Department of Tourism has erected signs saying 'Manang' at many trail junctions along the route, and there should be one here to aim you in the right direction.

The trail climbs gradually, then makes a steep climb in scrub forests to Bahundanda, an attractive village situated at 1310 metres in a saddle on a long ridge. The school nestles in a grove of bamboo, and there are a few shops, bhattis and several hotels nearby. Bahundanda ('Hill of the Brahmins') is the northernmost Brahmin settlement in the Marsyandi Valley. If you are camping, try the school; they have built an excellent campsite with good toilet facilities. They expect a donation to the school in addition to a camping fee. There is, of course, also a police check post here.

Day 3: Bahundanda to Chyamje

Descend on a steep, slippery trail past amphitheatre-shaped rice terraces, and cross a stream and a large slide area to Khane, high above the river at 1180 metres. The flocks of birds in the rice fields are slaty-headed parakeets. Continuing in and out of side canyons, the trail climbs, then drops to cross the Marsyandi on a long suspension bridge at 1190 metres. There are shops and two hotels, the *Sonam* and the *Karma*, along the stone streets of Syange on the west bank of the river. Beyond Syange, the trail stays near the river for a while, then climbs quite high on an exposed trail carved into near-vertical cliffs, which are forested with rhododendron and pine and garnished with healthy crops of stinging nettles and marijuana.

Because of the steep terrain, the villages in this region are small and infrequent. In 1950, when Tilman visited Manang, this portion of the trail did not exist. Instead, the route followed a series of wooden galleries tied to the face of the rock cliffs alongside the river. At 1250 metres is the village of Jagat, inhabited, as are most villages in this region, by people of Tibetan heritage. The stone village has a medieval atmosphere and the shops and hotels are small and not very clean. From Jagat, the trail climbs through forests to Chyamje, at 1430 metres. The *Tibetan Hotel* in Chyamje has bins of roasted soybeans, chiuraa (beaten rice) and popcorn, and is a good place to load up on trail snacks. There is a place to camp, just across the suspension bridge on the west side of the river, at Sattale, 1430 metres elevation.

Day 4: Chyamje to Bagarchhap

The path is rough as it passes through stands of bamboo and climbs along the steep riverbank to a single tea shop. The trail makes a short descent, then the valley suddenly opens into a large plateau. In this dramatic setting, at the foot of a large waterfall, is the village of Tal, 1675 metres elevation. There are many good hotels in Tal, arranged so they look like an old American pony express outpost. The Buddhist influence is apparent from the small white chorten on a nearby hill; the trek has now entered the Manang district.

Tal is the southernmost village in Manang and is in a region called Gyasumdo, one of three distinct divisions within Manang. Gyasumdo was once highly dependent on trade with Tibet. Since the disruption of this trade in 1959, herding and agriculture assumed greater importance. Corn, barley, wheat, buckwheat and potatoes are grown in Gyasumdo, which has enough warm weather and rainfall to produce two crops a year. The people of Gyasumdo used to hunt musk deer, and the sale of musk was once an important source of income and trade. Although they are Buddhists, the people throughout Manang slaughter animals and hunt in the nearby hills, unlike other Buddhists who have strict taboos against the taking of life.

The trail crosses the broad, flat valley that

was once a lake (*tal* means 'lake'), through fields of corn, barley and potatoes, then crosses a small stream on a wooden bridge near two tea shops. There is a short climb, then the trail makes a few small ups and downs high above the river, finally descending on a staircase-like trail to some tea shops in Orad. A short distance beyond is a suspension bridge across the Marsyandi at 1850 metres. Just after the bridge is a tiny, dirty hot spring that flows from a fissure near the trail; you need a cup to collect the hot water.

The trail climbs from the bridge to an unpainted stone kani that marks the entrance to Dharapani, elevation 1890 metres. All the old villages from here to Kagbeni have these entrance chortens at both ends of the village; the kanis get more elaborate and picturesque as the Tibetan influence becomes stronger in each successive village. Go through the village, then 10 minutes beyond to a police check post and the large *Dharapani Hotel*. Beyond Dharapani, the trail passes a school and climbs over a spur before descending to Bagarchhap. Across the Marsyandi, just beyond Dharapani, is a long, covered bridge. This leads to Thonje, an important village at the junction of the Marsyandi and the Dudh Khola. It is not necessary to go to Thonje en route to Manang. There is a police check post in Thonje that controls the route up the valley that leads to the Larkya La.

The trail continues into the east-west Manang Valley in a forest of blue pine, spruce, hemlock, maple and oak. The jay-like bird that you see is the nutcracker; it eats the seeds from the blue pine cones. Bagarchhap, at 2160 metres, is the first village on the trek with typical Tibetan architecture: closely-spaced stone houses, with flat roofs piled high with firewood. The village is in a transition zone between the dry upper Marsyandi and the wet regions of the lower valley, so there are also many sloping wooden shingle roofs. Higher in the Marsyandi and Kali Gandaki valleys, where there is little rainfall, the shingle roofs disappear, the houses are packed even closer together, and all have flat roofs.

The well-maintained, whitewashed Diki Gompa in Bagarchhap contains many Tibetan Buddhist paintings and statues. The *Pearly Gates* hotel offers 'heavenly food and lodging', and there is a well-stocked shop nearby. The trail now travels west up the Manang Valley with the high Himalayan peaks to the south; there are occasional glimpses of Lamjung Himal and Annapurna II (7937 metres) through the trees. To the east, Manaslu provides a dramatic backdrop at the foot of the tree-filled valley.

Day 5: Bagarchhap to Chame

Much of the Manang Valley is virgin forest of pine and fir, but construction of new houses and hotels, and the constant requirements for firewood are causing people to cut down many of these fine trees. On the trail to Manang there is much evidence of this cutting. People have stacked huge piles of firewood alongside the path and have hauled great timbers to home sites.

The trail climbs along the mule track through forests to Dhanakyu (also called Syal Khola, 'the river of jackals', and sometimes called Timang Phedi, 'lower Timang'), a settlement at 2290 metres with several hotels run by people from Bagarchhap. Stop a moment at the Gurung Furniture Factory and the local distillery. On the hill to the south of this village a trail leads to upper Timang, 2600 metres, and climbs over Namun Bhanjyang (5784 metres) en route to Ghanpokhara in the south. This was the old route to Manang; few people, other than herders, use it now. Namun Bhanjyang is a difficult pass because there is often snow, and there is no food or shelter for four days.

Climbing further, the trail continues to be rough and rocky. Suddenly a broad level stretch of trail appears. There is a fine wooden bridge near a waterfall, and outstanding stonework supports the trail. Climbing further, the route reaches Tyanja, also called Lattemarang, elevation 2360 metres. There are four or five small but comfortable hotels here. There is a tiny hot spring across the river, but it is hard to get to.

The track stays near the Marsyandi in forests of oak and maple, climbing and descending amongst river-worn boulders, then crosses a large stream before reaching Kodo, also known as Kyupar (2590 metres), situated in a meadow surrounded by huge pine and spruce trees. This is a police check post that controls access to the Nar-Phu Valley to the north. That remote valley, populated by only 850 people, is one of the three regions of Manang. It has a heritage and traditions different from that of other parts of the district. The restricted area regulations prohibit foreigners from the entire Nar-Phu Valley.

The next village is Chame (2630 metres), the administrative headquarters for the Manang district. There is electricity here, and also a wireless station, a school, many shops, a health post, post office, police check post and a bank among the closely-spaced stone dwellings. The incongruity of a shotgun-toting guard in front of the bank is almost worth a picture. There are many hotels in Chame, and also beyond the village on the other side of the river; the *Kamala Lodge* is the most popular trekkers' hotel. Across the river, there are two small hot springs; they are not big enough for swimming however. Throughout the day there are views of Lamjung Himal (6986 metres), Annapurna II (7937 metres) and Annapurna IV (7525 metres).

Day 6: Chame to Pisang

From Chame, the trail crosses a side stream, and then the Marsyandi itself on a large suspension bridge, passes by a few houses, the *Kesang Lodge* and *Chhiring Lodge* on the north side of the river, and proceeds through fields of barley to Talung at 2775 metres. The large *New Tibetan Lodge* is downstream from the bridge on the way to the hot spring.

After climbing past a huge apple orchard surrounded by a stone wall (apples and peaches are available everywhere in the region during the autumn), the trail descends to a bridge at 2840 metres. The village just across this bridge, Bratang, used to be a Khampa settlement, although it is now largely abandoned. The Khampas had

installed a gate on the bridge, thus controlling the traffic up and down the Manang Valley; you can still see the remnants of the gate. In Bratang, there is a small carved stone that is a memorial to a Japanese climber who died in an avalanche while trekking across the Thorung La – a grisly reminder to wait several days after any heavy snowstorm before trying to cross the pass.

Don't cross the bridge to Bratang; stay on the north side of the river and follow a new trail that was blasted out of the side of the cliff.

The valley is steep and narrow here, and the trail goes through deep forests. When the trail crosses to the south side of the river on a long suspension bridge at 3040 metres, there is the first view of the dramatic Paungda Danda rock face, a tremendous curved slab of rock rising more than 1500 metres from the river. There are also views of Annapurna II to the south and Pisang Peak to the north-east. Climbing over a ridge marked with a stone cairn and prayer flags, the trail continues the steep ascent to the upper Marsyandi Valley.

The lower portion of Pisang, a cluster of houses and a long mani wall near the bridge, is at an elevation of 3190 metres. Note the wooden canals for water to drive the two mills in this village. There are many hotels bunched together at the bridge here, including the *Annapurna Lodge*, the *Ghalung Gurung* and the *Himali Hotel*. The main village of Pisang is across the bridge and 100 metres uphill, but there are no hotels in that part of the village. There are excellent camping places in the forest on the south bank of the river.

Day 7: Pisang to Manang

The trek is now in the region known as Nyesyang, the upper portion of the Manang district, which has about 5000 inhabitants in six major villages. The region is much drier than the Gyasumdo region down the valley. There is only a small amount of rainfall here during the monsoon because the Annapurna range to the south alters the climate significantly from that of the rest of Nepal south of the Himalaya. The people of Nyesyang raise wheat, barley, buckwheat, potatoes and beans, but the cold, almost arid, climate limits them to a single crop annually. They keep herds of yaks, goats, cows and horses. Horses are an important means of transportation in the relatively flat upper portion of Manang Valley. People often ride them, or use horses as pack animals to altitudes as high as 5416 metres, over the Thorung La between Manang and Jomsom.

Many people in Nyesyang villages speak fluent English and dress in trendy western clothing they have bought during overseas trading excursions. This presents an incongruous picture as they herd yaks and plough the fields of these remote villages. Their exposure to the West also makes them shrewd and eager businesspeople, so the traders and shops of Manang are all expensive. There are few bargains to be had here. If you travelled to Kathmandu from Hong Kong or Bangkok, perhaps you were aware of the Tibetan-looking people all dressed in identical jackets or jogging suits and carrying identical luggage; these people were Manangis returning from a shopping expedition.

A short distance beyond Pisang, the trail climbs a steep ridge that extends across the valley. At the top of this spur is an excellent view of Manang Valley, with Tilicho Peak (7132 metres) at its head and a view back to Pisang Peak, one of the trekking peaks. After a short descent from the ridge, the trail reaches the broad, forested valley floor. Most of the valley is used as grazing land for sheep, goats, horses and yaks. Across the river, high on the opposite bank, is the village of Ghyaru.

There is a an alternate high route from upper Pisang along the north bank of the river that passes through Ghyaru and Ngawal and rejoins the main trail at Mungji. The trail is steep and takes about 1½ hours longer than the direct route along the south bank, but provides spectacular views of the Annapurna range to the south, and is a worthwhile side trip. This is also the start of the climbing route to Pisang Peak, Chulu East and Chulu West, and all are visible from the trail. You can also make a diversion to Ser Gompa, located on a plateau high above the river on the north side.

The southern trail avoids all this climbing and follows the valley past Manang's airstrip at Hongde, elevation 3325 metres. The last police check post in the valley is at the airport. A few bhattis and hotels have grown up around Hongde; the largest is the *Marsyandi Hotel*. Several curio shops nearby sell 'real Tibetan things' made in India, Hong Kong and Kathmandu.

There are scheduled flights from Hongde to Pokhara, and occasional direct flights to Kathmandu. They are usually booked by rich Manangis en route to and from trading excursions, so there is little chance of obtaining a seat except in an emergency.

Half an hour beyond the airport is the huge Sabje Khola Valley, with Annapurna III and IV at the head. Just south of the trail, in this spectacular setting, is the building that houses the mountaineering school funded by the Yugoslav Mountaineering Federation, and operated since 1980 by the Nepal Mountaineering Association in cooperation with UIAA, the Union of International Alpine Associations. They offer a six-week course for climbers from Nepal and neighbouring countries during August each year.

The trail crosses the Marsyandi again on a big wooden bridge near Mungji at 3360 metres, then traverses to Bryaga at 3475 metres. The largest part of this Tibetan-style village of about 200 houses hides behind a large rock outcrop. The houses are stacked one atop another, each with an open veranda formed by a neighbour's rooftop. The gompa, perched on a high crag overlooking the village, is the largest in the district and has an outstanding display of statues, thankas (ornate Tibetan paintings) and manuscripts estimated to be 400 to 500 years old. The kanis over the trail that mark the entrance and exit from Bryaga are particularly impressive.

There is a good place to camp in the meadow below the village. Bryaga was one of the last villages to join the trekking bandwagon. For years there were no hotels here, but now there are several establishments, including the large *New Yak Hotel* near the trail. There are also hotels half an hour away in Manang. Be careful when you enter the village of Bryaga, especially at night; the dogs are vicious.

The country here is very arid, dominated by weird cliffs of yellow rock, eroded into dramatic pillars alongside the trail, and by the towering heights of the Himalaya across the valley to the south. It is only a short walk, past mani walls and across a stream where several mills grind wheat and barley, to the plateau of Manang village at 3535 metres elevation. The *Annapurna Himal Hotel* adjoins the entrance kani to Manang village, and has Tibetan gloves, hats and sweaters for sale, as well as food and lodging. The walls are decorated with pictures from Chinese and Hindi film magazines. There are other hotels before the main part of Manang; the

Karma Hotel, in the centre of the village, is the most popular facility. Manang has electricity and the villagers have a very western outlook; hot showers and videos are the speciality here.

The Himalayan Rescue Association operates a post here, with a doctor in attendance throughout the trekking season. The HRA post occupies a new building and provides daily lectures on altitude sickness, usually at 3 pm. The doctors are available for consultation and treatment. Their services are not free; ask to see the schedule of charges before you request a diagnosis. There are shops where you can stock up on medical supplies, food, clothing and equipment for the pass crossing. If you or your porters do not have warm socks, hats and gloves, this is the time and place to buy them.

Day 8: Manang

You should spend the day in Manang village and the vicinity to acclimatise to the higher elevations you will encounter towards Thorung La. There are many opportunities for both easy and strenuous day excursions from Manang. It is possible to climb the ridge to the north of the village for excellent views of Annapurna IV, Annapurna II, and Tarke Kang (formerly known as Glacier Dome), 7193 metres; or to descend from the village to the glacial lake at the foot of the huge icefall that drops from the northern slopes of Gangapurna, 7454 metres. From the village of Khangsar, the last settlement in the valley en route to Tilicho Lake, there are splendid views of the 'Great Barrier', a name given by Herzog to the high ridge between Roc Noir and Nilgiri North. Another choice would be a walk to visit the Bhojo Gompa, the red edifice perched on the ridge between Bryaga and Manang, and the most active monastery in the region.

Before the first trekkers came to Manang in 1977, the region saw few outsiders. The only traders were the people of Manang themselves, and the population was intolerant of outsiders. There was little need of inns and other facilities. In 1950, Maurice Herzog came to Manang village in a futile search for food for his party, only to return nearly starving to his camp at Tilicho Lake. With the advent of tourism, however, there has been extensive hotel construction, and the Manangis warmly welcome tourists – particularly those with lots of rupees. The resourceful Manangbhot people have been quick to adapt to this new source of income, selling semiprecious stones, (from Tibet, they claim, but more likely from Bangkok), foodstuffs, Tibetan jewellery and other items of interest to tourists. An alternative to a day hike is a bargaining session with these skilful traders.

The village itself is a compact collection of 500 flat-roofed houses separated by narrow alleyways. To reach a doorway you must ascend a steep log notched with steps. The setting of the village is most dramatic, with the summits of Annapurna and Gangapurna less than 8 km away, and a huge icefall rumbling and crashing on the flanks of the peaks.

The route to Tilicho Lake is closed to trekkers; there are army training exercises in the region west of Tilicho Lake, so it's not wise to try to subvert this regulation.

Day 9: Manang to Letdar

The trek now begins an ascent of almost 2000 metres to Thorung La. From Manang village, the trail crosses a stream, climbs to Tengi, 120 metres above Manang, then continues to climb out of the Marsyandi Valley, turning north-west up the valley of the Jarsang Khola. The trail follows this valley north, passing a few goths as it steadily gains elevation. You have left the large trees below; here the vegetation consists of scrub juniper and alpine grasses.

The trail passes near the small village of Ghunsa, a cluster of flat mud roofs just below the trail at 3960 metres. The *Marsyandi Hotel & Lodge*, alongside the trail, specialises in Tibetan bread and chhang. The route is now through meadows, where horses and yaks graze, and sparse forests of juniper, rose and barberry. After crossing a large stream that flows from Chulu Peak and

Gundang, the trail passes an ancient mani wall in a pleasant meadow at 4000 metres.

Beyond here is Yak Kharka, where there is a good hotel that offers an alternative to staying at Letdar. Villagers from Manang collect firewood from the slopes above. An hour further, at 4250 metres, on is a single two-storey house, now rapidly deteriorating – the stone walls are falling down and the biscuit-tin roof is both rusting and blowing away. This is Letdar, the next-to-last shelter before the pass. A very westernised young Manangi operates *Jimmy's Home*, where you can get almost anything – including granola, chocolate and beer. Less popular is the *Lathair Guest House*.

Day 10: Letdar to Thorung Phedi

From Letdar (some spell it Lathar), the trail continues to climb along the east bank of the Jarsang Khola, then descends and crosses the stream on a covered bridge at 4310 metres. After a short ascent on a good trail built in connection with the bridge, the route follows a narrow trail across a high, unstable, scree slope, then descends to Thorung Phedi, a dirty rock-strewn meadow surrounded by vertical cliffs at 4420 metres. This is the best camp site on this side of the pass, although camping is possible on a shelf about 10 minutes above, and at another small flat spot about an hour beyond that.

Local traders ride horses from Manang to Muktinath in a single day, but the large elevation gain, the need for acclimatisation, and the high altitudes all make it imperative to take at least two days to do the trip on foot. There is only one hotel in Thorung Phedi, on the first shelf, about 10 minutes above the valley. This hotel can be very, very crowded, especially if there is snow. There are two buildings; one for dining and one for sleeping. Forget about sitting around a pleasant fire here; in the busy season, you buy a meal coupon from a faceless person behind a window and are handed a cup of tea (Rs 6) or a plate of dal bhaat (Rs 45) through another window. A hundred people or more cram into the hotel each night, except when snow has blocked the pass for a few days –

at those times, several hundred irritable trekkers pack themselves into every corner of the hotel.

Nights are even more miserable because of the 3 am departure that many people schedule. It really isn't necessary to start that early. In fact it can be dangerous because it is quite cold until the sun rises and this can lead to hypothermia and frostbite. A reasonable departure time is just before daybreak, at 4 am or 5 am. The hotel operator at Thorung Phedi has a horse that you can ride over the pass for an exorbitant price (last quotation was Rs 1500) if you are not well. Blue sheep, and even snow leopards, sometimes magically appear in this valley; the crow-like birds are choughs and the large birds that circle overhead are lammergeiers and Himalayan griffons, not eagles. Be sure to boil or treat water here; the sanitation in Thorung Phedi and Letdar is terrible, and giardia is rampant.

Day 11: Thorung Phedi to Muktinath

Phedi, which means 'foot of the hill' is a common Nepali name for any settlement at the bottom of a long climb. The trail becomes steep immediately after leaving Thorung Phedi, switchbacking up moraines and following rocky ridges as it ascends to the pass. Local people have used this trail for hundreds of years to bring herds of sheep and yaks in and out of Manang. Thus the trail, while often steep, is well defined and easy to follow.

The only complications to the crossing are the high elevation and the chance of snow. When snow blocks the pass, usually in late December and during January, the crossing becomes difficult – often impossible. It then becomes necessary to retreat back to Dumre, or to wait until the snow has consolidated and local people have forged a trail. The only shelters between here and Muktinath are the tiny facilities at 4100 metres, far down the other side of the pass. An overnight stop in the snow, unless well planned in advance, can be treacherous and deadly, especially for porters.

The trail climbs and climbs, traversing in and out of many canyons formed by interminable moraines. It is a reasonably good trail unless there is snow, in which case the route may traverse scree slopes and ascend steep snow. It takes from 4 to 6 hours from Thorung Phedi to the pass, but the many false summits make the climb seem to go on forever. The pass, with its traditional chorten, prayer flags and stone cairn built by travellers, is at an elevation of 5416 metres. The views from the trail, and from the pass itself, are outstanding high Himalayan scenes: the entire Great Divide with the Annapurnas and Gangapurna to the south, the barren Kali Gandaki Valley far below to the west, the rock peak of Thorungtse (6482 metres) to the north, and Yak Gawa (6484 metres), a heavily glaciated peak, to the south. Well-acclimatised, technically proficient and well-equipped trekkers have climbed high on Yak Gawa during a crossing of the pass.

The descent is steep and rough on the knees – a loss of more than 1600 metres in less than 3 hours. The descent often begins in snow, which soon gives way to switchbacks down another series of moraines. Sometimes the correct route is not obvious; just remember that you are headed downhill and that Muktinath is on the left side of the valley. During the descent there are excellent views of Dhaulagiri (8167 metres) standing alone in the distance across the valley. Eventually the moraines yield to grassy slopes and the final descent to Muktinath is a pleasant walk along the upper part of the Jhong Khola Valley.

There is a hotel at 4100 metres elevation where the grassy slopes begin. It's run by a Tibetan man from Jharkot, and offers drinks, food and even souvenirs. It is better to rely on this hotel only for refreshment, not for accommodation, though you could stay here if you were crossing the pass in the opposite direction. It is also possible to camp here if the tiny stream nearby is flowing.

The trail crosses meadows, drops into a ravine that is the start of the Jhong Khola, climbs out of the ravine and enters Muktinath at 3800 metres, near the temple.

There is no accommodation here, but it is only a five to 10 minute walk to Ranipauwa where there is a large choice of accommodation. The *Muktinath Guest House* is the best, charging Rs 25 for a room with twin beds and hot baths from a bucket. The young couple who run the hotel serve good food (and good apple rakshi). There is a police check post at Ranipauwa.

Days 12 to 18: Muktinath to Pokhara

The route to Pokhara follows the Jomsom trek described earlier, but you must read this part backwards. Kagbeni is worth a visit, as is the Dhaulagiri icefall above Larjung, so schedule an extra three days on this route. The winds in the Kali Gandaki are powerful and can drive sand and dust into your face. A scarf and sunglasses provide good protection as you trek down the valley.

THE ROYAL TREK

This is an easy, short trek that starts near Pokhara and offers good mountain views. It gained its name because Prince Charles and an entourage of 90 guests, camp followers and staff trekked here. The trek has also seen the likes of such luminaries as Mick Jagger. The route is not a popular one, so you will see few other trekkers, but this also means that the hotel facilities are mediocre.

Day 1: Pokhara to Kalikathan

It is about 5 km, a 20 minute drive by taxi, to the Bijayapur Army Camp just east of the Bijayapur Khola. A broad trail starts in rice fields, then ascends through the village of Rakhigaun to a chautaara, a resting place under a large pipal tree.

These trees, planted centuries ago, have broad leaves and branches that extend outwards for a long distance in mushroom fashion, offering welcome shade to travellers. It was under a banyan tree (also called a Bodi tree) that Buddha attained enlightenment in India, over 2000 years ago. You can differentiate the banyan from the pipal tree (a related species) by the long roots that droop down from the limbs, a peculiarity of the banyan. Around these shade trees, people

have built walls and chautaaras, stone benches, for porters to rest their loads upon as they pause during the hot, steep climbs. Many people build a chautaara in the name of a deceased relative.

The trail climbs gently along a ridgetop through Brahmin and Chhetri villages towards Kalikathan at 1370 metres. The children along this part of the trail are particularly persistent about asking for money, balloons or pens. Depending on the time that you start walking, you can camp either before or after the village of Kalikathan. Both campsites are on ridge tops with good mountain views, including Machhapuchhare and Annapurna.

Day 2: Kalikathan to Shaklung

The trail continues along the forested ridge top through Thulokot to Mati Thana, where there are a few tea shops. There is a short climb, then the trek reaches Naudanda (not to be confused with the Naudanda west of Pokhara). Continue along the ridge to a school at Lipini village, then make a steep but shortclimb through forests to the Gurung village of Shaklung at 1730 metres.

Day 3: Shaklung to Chisopani

The Himalayan skyline continues to change as the route comes abreast of Annapurna II, Lamjung Himal, Manaslu and Himalchuli. From Shaklung, the trail drops steeply down the south side of the hill to a large tree, a chautaara, several tea shops and a police check post. This is a trail junction; trails lead from here west to Begnas Tal and east to the Marsyandi Khola. The Royal Trek route climbs towards Chisopani, winding around the back of the hill to the village. A short distance above Chisopani village is a high knoll where there is a small temple. This is Chisopani Danda, meaning 'Chisopani ridgetop'; the camp here has splendid mountain views.

Day 4: Chisopani to Pokhara

From Chisopani Danda, descend along the ridge for an hour or so, then descend steeply on the stone steps, into a small valley and a stream that feeds Rupa Tal. Continue for a short distance through the rice fields, then make a final ascent, to the ridge that separates Begnas Tal and Rupa Tal, on a wide path that you will share with many local people. From the ridge, descend into the Pokhara Valley, joining the road at the crowded, dirty and noisy Begnas Bazaar. Take a taxi or a bus for the 12 km, 30 minute drive back to Pokhara.

Langtang & Helambu

The region north of Kathmandu offers a multitude of trekking destinations, all accessible without flights. The three major areas are Langtang, Gosainkund and Helambu, which can be combined in many different ways to make a trek from seven to 16 days long.

Langtang is a narrow valley that lies just south of the Tibetan border. It is sandwiched between the main Himalayan range to the north and a slightly lower range of snowy peaks to the south. Langtang Lirung (7246 metres) dominates the valley to the north; Gang Chhenpo (6388 metres) and Naya Kangri (5846 metres) lie to the south; and Dorje Lakpa (6975 metres) protects the east end of the valley. The area was designated Nepal's first Himalayan National Park in 1971.

This high and isolated region is inhabited by Tamangs whose religious practices, language and dress are much more similar to those of Tibet than to the traditions of their cousins in the middle hills. A visit to the Langtang Valley offers an opportunity to explore villages, to climb small peaks and to visit glaciers at a comfortably low elevation. According to legend, a lama following a runaway yak discovered the valley. Hence the name – lang is Tibetan for 'yak' and teng (more correctly dhang) means 'to follow'. Yaks still live in the valley, but they now share it with trekkers who make a seven to 11 day round trip from Kathmandu. Because there are good opportunities for moderate climbing excursions here, you should allow a few extra days for exploration of the extensive glacier system.

You can vary the trek by returning to Kathmandu via the holy lakes of Gosainkund at 4300 metres, or you can make a short trek from Dhunche to Gosainkund. Thousands of Hindu pilgrims visit the lakes during a full moon festival in August. The lake is also sacred to Buddhists.

Helambu is an area inhabited by Sherpas, about 75 km north of Kathmandu. You can include Helambu in a Langtang trek, either via Gosainkund or across the 5106 metre Ganja La. In winter, both of the high routes from Langtang are usually snow-covered and dangerous, difficult or impossible. The Helambu trek is popular because it is short, stays below 3500 metres and is feasible all winter. It is an easy trek to organise because transportation from Kathmandu to Sundarijal, the starting point of the trek, is readily available and inexpensive.

The language, culture and dress of the Helambu Sherpas are very different from the Solu Khumbu Sherpas. The accessibility of Helambu has created an influx of tourists who have encouraged begging, the sale of 'genuine antiques' aged over the family fireplace, and several incidents of thievery. It takes eight days to trek from Kathmandu to Helambu and back, or 12 to 14 days to include both Langtang and Helambu in a single trek without any backtracking.

INFORMATION
Maps
The fanciest map of Langtang and Helambu is the German *Helambu-Langtang* 1:100,000 map. The Mandala *Helambu Langtang* 1:150,000 map is a two-colour job printed in Kathmandu. The US Army Maps of the region are sheets 45-1, *Kathmandu*; 45-13, *Jongka Dzong*; and 45-2 *Mount Everest*. All are based on the Survey of India maps that were published in the early 1960s, so all show the trails as they existed then – not now. Beware especially of the area from Dhunche to Langtang village as shown on any of these maps.

GETTING THERE & AWAY
Air
Langtang The airstrip is about an hour beyond Kyanjin Gompa, but it has no scheduled service. Charter flights are irregular, and are only in six-passenger Pilatus Porter aircraft, so don't count on finding a seat back

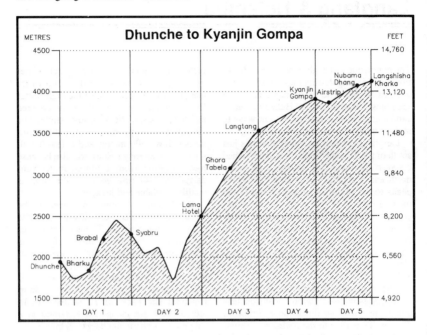

Dhunche to Kyanjin Gompa

METRES / FEET

Labels on chart: Nubama Dhang, Langshisha Kharka, Kyanjin Gompa, Airstrip, Langtang, Ghora Tabela, Lama Hotel, Brabal, Syabru, Bharku, Dhunche

DAY 1, DAY 2, DAY 3, DAY 4, DAY 5

to Kathmandu unless you have made prior arrangements. The airstrip is notorious for becoming snowbound in December, January and February.

Bus

Dhunche The starting place for Langtang treks is Dhunche (pronounced doon-chay), 112 km from Kathmandu. Buses to Dhunche leave from Ghora Khute, near the intersection where the Balaju road enters Kathmandu, close to the Malla Hotel. The first bus leaves at 7 am, costs Rs 55 and takes all day to reach Dhunche. You can also take a bus to Trisuli Bazaar and walk to Dhunche, but the trail is steep and has nothing to offer except physical exertion. It is better to take a bus all the way to Dhunche in order to let the bus do all the initial climbing on your behalf at the beginning of the trek.

The bus from Dhunche to Kathmandu leaves at 7:30 am. Make reservations the day before at the Thakali Hotel in Dhunche.

Sundarijal At elevation 1265 metres, Sundarijal is the best place to start a Helambu trek. You can get to Sundarijal by minibus, or even a taxi, on an unpaved road from Bodhanath. You can also begin the trek from Bodhanath, taking a few hours to walk to Sundarijal along the level roadway.

Panchkal This is an alternate starting point for a trek to Helambu. Panchkal (the name of the settlement where the trail meets the road is actually Lamidanda) is on the road to the Chinese border. Take a bus to Barahbise or Lamosangu, bang on the roof of the bus just after the army camp and jump off.

The Helambu road joins the Kathmandu to Kodari road at Lamidanda, near Panchkal; here you can catch one of the rickety local buses that ply between Barahbise and Kathmandu.

Indrawati Valley You can finish the Helambu trek by flagging down a jeep, truck or bus from the road in the Indrawati Valley. Minibuses are available in Sipa Ghat, and seats are negotiable on vehicles further up the valley.

LANGTANG TREK

This section suggests a five day approach to the heart of the Langtang Valley. From Langtang village or Kyanjin Gompa there are several alternatives for returning to Kathmandu. It is possible to make the trek back to Dhunche in only three days from Langtang village because much of it is downhill. If you have basic mountaineering skill, you can cross the high route over the Ganja La into Helambu. A third alternative is to trek back to Syabru from Langtang, then cross into Helambu via Gosainkund.

Day 1: Kathmandu to Dhunche via Trisuli

It is about a 4 hour drive (6 hours by local bus) on a paved highway that twists and climbs over ridges to the Trisuli Valley. Passing Balaju and Nagarjun, the road climbs over Kakani pass (2145 metres), which offers excellent views of Annapurna II, Manaslu and Ganesh Himal, and descends into the broad Trisuli Valley. The bus usually makes a tea stop at Rani Pauwa, the only large village on the route, at km 27. After a long descent through terraced fields, the road crosses the Tadi Khola at km 60, then climbs onto a plateau and passes fields of mustard, corn and rice planted in bright red soil. There is a police check post 2 km before Trisuli where the police examine trekking permits and record details in a register. The road then passes an army camp just before Trisuli Bazaar at 548 metres, 72 km from Kathmandu.

Trisuli is the site of a dam and hydroelectric project built by the Indian Technical Mission. A large bridge dominates the town; most shops are before the bridge, and most restaurants are on the opposite side, near the hydroelectric plant. Hotel facilities here are spartan and the restaurants are pretty grim. Try the *Ranjit Lodge* for dhal bhaat. If you must spend the night here, take a look at the

Pratistha Lodge near the power plant or the *Shakyar Lodge* near the beginning of the Betrawati road. Otherwise, continue 8 km to Betrawati for a better selection of hotels.

The road to Betrawati and Dhunche is a Nepal Army project, and is still under construction in its upper reaches. This unpaved road reached Dhunche in June 1984, and now continues for a total of 105 km to Somdang, at the foot of Ganesh Himal, where there are lead and zinc mines. If you are travelling in a private vehicle, you must obtain a special permit from the army headquarters in Kathmandu before your vehicle is allowed to pass the barrier at Betrawati. The army normally allows foreigners and buses only as far as Dhunche.

The Dhunche road starts at a police check post just before the bridge and follows the east bank of the Trisuli River. The road passes two bridges carrying massive pipes that feed the hydro project and climbs slightly to the village of Betrawati at 620 metres. Betrawati is at the junction of the Trisuli River and the Phalangu Khola, at the foot of a steep ridge that rises towards Langtang and Gosainkund. It's 42 km of steep switchbacks on a wild road to Dhunche; at some points it hangs on to a steep cliff 1000 metres above the river. The road is subject to continual landslides – especially when it rains – so a bus trip to Dhunche can be an adventure.

There is another police check post at Betrawati, then the road crosses a bridge and switchbacks back and forth up the end of the ridge for 15 km, through Brahmin and Chhetri villages, to Kalikhastan at 1390 metres. This is the entrance to Langtang National Park; the police again examine trek permits. The villages now become more spread out, and the intense cultivation of the lowland rice-growing country gives way to herding and small fields of corn, millet and vegetables as the elevation increases. The road reaches its high point on the ridge at 1980 metres, then makes a long contour, with a few ups and downs through oak and rhododendron forests, passing above Ramche at km 33, and then through Thare at km 37. The

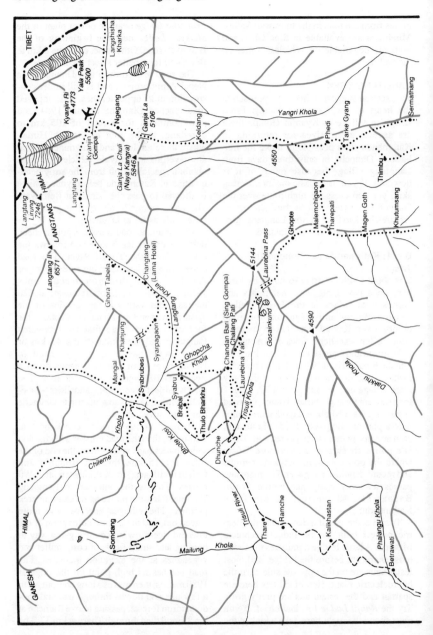

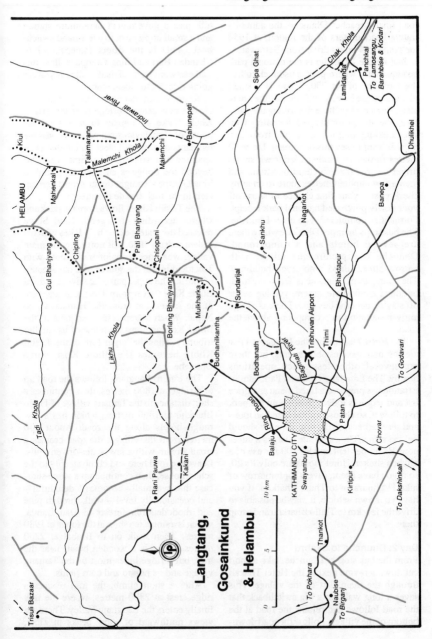

Langtang, Gosainkund & Helambu

road finally reaches Dhunche, the administrative headquarters of the region, at 1950 metres, 3 to 4 hours drive from Betrawati.

Just before Dhunche is the national park headquarters, where park personnel collect the park fee of Rs 250. There is a small visitors'centre here, and if you ask, they may also produce a brochure describing the park. Keep the receipt for the park fee safely with your trekking permit – everyone from here on will want to see this document. Drive 50 metres further to another barrier where the driver records the vehicle information, and then a few hundred metres more to an army check post – your first chance to show off your newly purchased national park receipt. Formalities completed, you enter Dhunche. The bus stops in upper Dhunche where there are several hotels and a campground. Dhunche is a picturesque village with narrow streets lined with stone buildings. The main part of Dhunche is below the road, but there are no hotels there; you are better off staying near the bus stop. There is a large army installation in a compound above the road.

The *Hotel Thakali* and the *Langtang View* are the upmarket establishments, but there are several other less fancy operations nearby. The Langtang National Park administration has prepared a fixed menu and price list and requires lodges throughout the park to follow it, so choose a hotel based on looks and service because the prices are (or should be) the same. The camp site charges a larcenous Rs 50 per tent and Rs 100 for use of a kitchen shelter. Hotel rooms are only Rs 20, so if you have a tent, save it for tomorrow or hike 1½ hours on to Thulo Bharkhu. If you have your own vehicle, it may be possible to drive the few km to Thulo Bharkhu and camp there.

Day 2: Dhunche to Syabru

From the bus stop at Dhunche, take a short cut down a ravine next to the Hotel Thakali through the main part of the village. This saves a long walk on a big switchback that the road follows and rejoins the road at the bottom of the village. Follow the road down-

hill, past a government agriculture station and a small army post, to a left-hand switchback. This is the direct (steep) trail to Chandan Bari and Sing Gompa; follow this trail eastward up the Trisuli Valley if you are going directly to Gosainkund.

To go to Langtang, stay on the road and cross a new cement bridge over the Trisuli Khola. Take a moment to reflect on the power of Himalayan streams as you pass the remnants of a twisted steel bridge that once spanned the stream. The first waterfall beyond the bridge is an alternative trail to Sing Gompa – straight up an almost vertical cleft in the rock beside the stream.

The Trisuli Khola flows from Gosainkund where, according to legend, Lord Shiva released the waters of the holy lakes with his trident (trisul). The trail north, up the main valley, was once a major trade route with Tibet and is still the source of a fair amount of traffic. The upper part of the river is named Bhote Kosi ('river from Tibet'), as are most of the rivers that cross the Himalaya into Nepal. When a Nepalese river joins it, the Bhote Kosi assumes the name of its smaller tributary. Thus the larger fork of the Trisuli Khola becomes the Bhote Kosi above Dhunche.

The trail to Langtang follows the road up to a ridge at 1800 metres, then continues a short distance to the Tamang village of Thulo Bharkhu at 1860 metres, which has a few rough hotels along the road. About 100 metres from the village, the road crosses a small stream with a few water-driven mills. Leave the road here and climb steeply to the schoolhouse, then continue up a stone staircase that eventually becomes a delightful – and occasionally level – walk through pine and rhododendron forests to Dau Danda, which is a single tea shop in the forest at 1980 metres. Then walk on to Brabal at 2200 metres. There is a wooden bhatti near the trail, but a ridge hides most of the Tamang village and its potato and corn fields.

After a short climb, the trail reaches a ridge crest at 2300 metres, where the trek finally enters the Langtang Valley. There are views northward of snow peaks in Tibet, west to Ganesh Himal and east to Naya Kangri, the 5846 metre peak above Ganja La. A short, steep descent through bamboo forests leads to Syabru at 2100 metres, a pleasant village of about 70 houses, many with elaborately carved wooden windows, strung out along a ridge. There are many hotels at the upper end of the village where the trail enters it. There is no need to suggest a hotel here; a bevy of very aggressive English-speaking Tamang women will accost you as you enter the village to extol the virtues of their establishments. Before you settle in for the night, consider the implications of the sign at the camp site before the village that advertises 'no dogs here'. There are camp sites before Syabru and in corn and millet fields far below the village.

Day 3: Syabru to Changtang (Lama Hotel)

The trail to Langtang descends along the ridge on Syabru's main street, then drops to the Ghopcha Khola, first through terraced fields, then through forests of oak, maple, alder and finally bamboo. The trail crosses the stream on a stone and cement bridge, then begins a climb across a ridge dotted with a few bhattis. The route descends on a steep, slippery path to the foot of a huge landslide at 1550 metres. A trail junction here is marked with signs painted on a rock directing you either to Langtang or back to the road at Syabrubesi. Just beyond the slide, the *Landslide Lodge* provides a chance for a short rest, before climbing back along the southern banks of the Langtang Khola as the trail very quickly gains elevation.

For the rest of this day and the following morning, there is very little habitation, but the forest abounds with bird life. There is also a variety of wildlife in these forests: yellow throated martin, wild boar, langur monkey, red panda and Himalayan black bear. The trail climbs to *Bamboo Lodge*, a jungly hotel at 1850 metres that is not as exotic as its name implies; 10 minutes farther is its cousin, *New Bamboo Lodge*. This region specialises in the sale of colourful

woollen socks and belts. The ascent continues to a steel suspension bridge at 2000 metres; there is a small bhatti on the south (shady) side, and the *Hotel Bridge Side* on the opposite bank in the sun.

The route crosses to the north bank of the Langtang Khola, then climbs alongside a series of waterfalls. The forest is sparser and drier on this side of the river, consisting mainly of scrub oak, as opposed to the damp forest of large pines on the shady southern bank. The climb is steep, and continues to a landslide and the *Langtang View & Lodge* at 2250 metres, the *Namaste Tibetan Lodge* at 2330 metres, and the *Tibetan Lodge* 10 minutes beyond. There is a trail junction here that connects to a high route back to Syarpagaon and Syabrubesi; this was the old trail to Langtang before the bridge was built across the Langtang Khola. You have now finished most of the day's climbing; descend gently to the settlement of Changtang, popularly known as Lama Hotel, at 2380 metres elevation. There are at least five hotels here, including the *Lama Hotel* itself, and a few camping spots. The next accommodation is about 1½ hours beyond at *Riverside Lodge*.

Day 4: Changtang to Langtang Village

The day starts with a gentle climb, but it soon becomes steeper, climbing high above the Langtang Khola. In places it is so steep that the trail is on logs anchored to the valley wall. Tantalising glimpses of Langtang Lirung, 7246 metres, appear through the trees. The settlement of Gumnachok consists of *Riverside Lodge*, on the banks of the river, and another *Riverside Lodge*, in a clearing 15 minutes beyond. The trail crosses a stream on a log bridge, then climbs through meadows to Ghora Tabela at 3000 metres. Once a Tibetan resettlement project, this is now a Nepalese Army and national park post and has no permanent inhabitants.

The national park lodge is operated on contract and is now named *Lovely Lodge*. There is another police check post where they check, yet again, to be sure that you paid the national park entrance fee. If you somehow slipped past the station at

Dhunche, they will collect the fee – and possibly a fine – here. The trail ascends gradually, as the valley becomes wider and wider, past yak pastures, *Thangshyap Lodge*, some mani stones and scattered Tamang villages to the *Langtang Gompa Hotel*. You can see the village gompa just above the hotel; if you want to visit the temple, ask the hotel for information and assistance. The trail then descends into a valley to cross a stream and climbs past several water-driven mills and prayer wheels to the large settlement of Langtang at 3500 metres.

This village is the headquarters for Langtang National Park; the park buildings are those with green metal roofs below the village. The best hotel is the *Village View Lodge* at the entrance to the town; most other hotels in Langtang are in rooms of private homes, which are heated and scented by yak-dung fires. The park administration allows an increase in hotel prices at Langtang village and above, so everything suddenly becomes more costly. The houses of Langtang and the surrounding communities have Tibetan-style flat roofs and are surrounded by stone walls enclosing fields of buckwheat, potatoes, wheat, turnips and barley. The villagers keep herds of yaks and cattle here and in pastures above the village.

Day 5: Langtang Village to Kyanjin Gompa

The trail winds through the village and climbs onto a ridge dominated by a large square chorten and a long row of mani walls. It then climbs gradually past the small villages of Muna and Singdum, where there is a small lodge. Continuing through yak pastures as the valley becomes broader, the path crosses a wooden cantilever bridge, then climbs a moraine where you can finally see Kyanjin Gompa. It is a short descent to lodges, a cheese factory and an almost defunct gompa. The Swiss Association for Technical Assistance started the cheese factory in 1955. It now produces about 7,000 kg of cheese annually, all of it hauled by porters to the dairy in Kathmandu. It is easy to reach Kyanjin Gompa, elevation 3800

metres, before lunch, allowing time to acclimatise and explore the surroundings. The best place in town is the *Hotel Yala Peak*; the *National Park Lodge*, with its fancy solar heating, has been leased by a local person and has gone to seed – probably because of the park's price controls.

Day 6: In Langtang Valley

Spend a day here and take a hike up the moraine north of Kyanjin Gompa to an elevation of 4300 metres or more. From the moraine, there is a spectacular view of Langtang Lirung and the foot of one of its major glaciers.

There are two good viewpoints in the area that you can climb. The peak to the north of Kyanjin Gompa is Kyanjin Ri, elevation 4773 metres; it is about a 2 hour climb. Do not head directly up the ridge behind the gompa; there is a trail of sorts that starts on the opposite side of a stream beyond the national park lodge. The views are superb. A longer excursion is to Tsergo Ri ('Tserko' on the German map), 4984 metres, a 4 hour climb from Kyanjin Gompa. Both of these peaks are visible from Kyanjin Gompa and prayer flags mark their tops.

There are also two possible climbing projects: Yala Peak, 5500 metres (not to be confused with Yala Kharka on Tsergo Ri), and Tsergo Peak, 5749 metres (which is different from Tsergo Ri). Both are two-day expeditions that involve glacier climbing and a high camp on a saddle above the trail near Nubama Dhang.

Day 7: Day Trip to Langshisha Kharka

You should take an extra day or two to continue further up the Langtang Valley itself to Langshisha Kharka for views of Langshisha Ri (6310 metres), Gang Chhenpo (6387 metres), Urkeinmang (6151 metres), and Penthang Karpo Ri (6830 metres). There are no hotels beyond Kyanjin Gompa, but you can make a day trip and return to Kyanjin Gompa for the night. If you have a tent and food you can camp at Langshisha Kharka or another of the summer pastures high in the valley.

Return to Kathmandu

You can return to Kathmandu by the same route, or you might be lucky enough to find a plane at the Langtang airstrip above Kyanjin Gompa at 3960 metres.

Alternative routes to Kathmandu are either over Ganja La or via Gosainkund when conditions are suitable on these high altitude routes.

ACROSS GANJA LA

The route from Kyanjin Gompa in Langtang to Tarke Gyang in Helambu requires crossing the 5106 metre high Ganja La. This pass is difficult and dangerous when covered by snow, so local inquiries about its condition, good equipment and some mountaineering experience are necessary for a safe crossing. You can assume the pass will be open from April to November, though unusual weather can alter its condition at any time. A guide who knows the trail, a tent, food and fuel are imperative on a crossing of Ganja La.

Kathmandu to Kyanjin Gompa

For the first five days, follow the route described in the preceding section. An extra day in Langtang Valley for acclimatisation is essential before beginning the ascent to Ganja La.

Day 7: Kyanjin Gompa to Ngegang

This is a short day from Kyanjin Gompa, but Ngegang is the last good place to camp before beginning the final climb to the pass, and you should minimise the elevation gain today to aid acclimatisation. Crossing the Langtang Khola below Kyanjin Gompa, the trail makes a steep climb along the ridge on the south side of the valley through a forest of rhododendron and juniper. Finally becoming more gentle, the trail reaches the yak pasture of Ngegang about 4000 metres elevation. There are goths here and on the other side of the pass, but they have no roofs during the winter, so a tent is very handy on this trek. During the monsoon, herders carry bamboo mats to provide roofs for the stone goths here, and live the entire summer in high meadows with herds of yaks and goats.

Day 8: Ngegang to Keldang

The trail continues south, following streams and moraines, and climbing steeply towards the pass. As the trail climbs higher, and comes under the shadow of the 5800 metre peaks to the south, you will find more and more snow. Turning south-west, the trail makes the final steep ascent to the pass at 5200 metres. The last 100 metres of the climb is a tricky balancing act on a snow slope above some steep rocks.

The pass itself is flanked by gendarmes (pinnacles) and topped by prayer flags on a large cairn of rocks. The views to the north, of Langtang Lirung and the snow peaks in Tibet, are outstanding from the pass, and on a clear day there are views to the south of many ranges of hills. To the west of the pass is Naya Kangri, previously named Ganja La Chuli, at 5846 metres. This is one of the trekking peaks that you can climb with a permit from the Nepal Mountaineering Association. A base camp in this region provides a good starting point for this reasonably easy climb.

The descent from the pass is steep and dangerous, as it follows a loose scree slope for about 1200 metres before emerging onto a snow slope. Somehow, the descent from Ganja La, like most mountain descents, seems more treacherous than the ascent, no matter which direction one crosses the pass. However, Ganja La is one of the steeper and more difficult of the major passes in Nepal. After the initial descent, the trail descends gradually in a huge basin surrounded by glaciated peaks.

The route descends through the basin along an indistinct trail, marked occasionally by rock cairns, to a small stream at 4400 metres. If you are travelling in the reverse direction, from Helambu to Langtang, it will require a full day to reach this point from Keldang, and you should schedule two days from Keldang to the pass.

From this camp site, the trail enters the steep Yangri Khola Valley and drops quickly down a rough scree slope to the stream. Following the stream for some distance through grassy meadows, the trail reaches a

few goths (again without roofs) at Keldang, about 4270 metres elevation.

Day 9: Keldang to Dukpu

This is a long and tiring day as the trail descends along a ridge, making many ups and downs. In winter, there is no water from Keldang to the bottom of the ridge, near Phedi, so you should plan food accordingly for this stretch of the trail. In October and November, there is usually no water problem because the monsoon rains leave an ample groundwater supply in several small springs.

The route heads down the valley, but stays high above the river, finally meeting the ridge itself, then follows the ridge line to the small summer settlement of Dukpu at 4080 metres.

Day 10: Dukpu to Tarke Gyang

From Dukpu, the trail descends further along the ridge, then makes a 180 metre climb to a pass at 4020 metres. The pass offers a commanding view of the Himalaya, from Dorje Lakpa east almost to Everest, and a panorama of the first part of the Everest trek from Lamosangu to Khumbu. From the pass, the trail descends through pine and rhododendron forests past tiny herders' settlements to a ridge high above Tarke

Gyang. It then drops steeply to Gekye Gompa at 3020 metres, a small monastic community, and the first permanent habitation since Kyanjin Gompa. The trail continues its steep drop to Tarke Gyang, a large Sherpa village at 2560 metres.

Days 11 to 13: Tarke Gyang to Kathmandu

For the return to Kathmandu, follow the route described below for days 5, 6 and 7 of the Helambu circuit.

HELAMBU CIRCUIT

This is the description of a seven day trek that makes a circuit of the Helambu region. The easiest starting point for this trek is Sundarijal because of its proximity to Kathmandu. You can make the trek in either direction, because it closes a loop from Pati Bhanjyang, the first night stop of the trek. The preferred route is clockwise as I have described here; visit the high ridge to the west of Helambu Valley first, then go to Tarke Gyang and descend the Malemchi Khola before climbing back to Pati Bhanjyang. There are all kinds of other possible variations, including a direct route to Tarke Gyang from Pati Bhanjyang, then down the ridge through Sermathang, ending at Panchkal on the Chinese Road.

The Helambu trek is an easy trek to organise. The transportation to and from Sundarijal, the starting point of the trek, is fast and cheap, and the trek is at a low elevation, so you do not usually need any fancy warm clothing. There are fewer trekkers here than either the Everest or Annapurna regions and hotels are abundant, good and uncrowded.

Day 1: Kathmandu to Pati Bhanjyang

At Sundarijal, elevation 1350 metres, there is a large water project that supplies much of Kathmandu's drinking water in an immense pipe. The unpaved road from Bodhanath turns into a trail near a small hydroelectric plant and starts up concrete steps alongside the water pipe. Beyond the trailside village of Sundarijal, the trail climbs continuously

in forests beside the pipe and alongside a small stream to a medieval-looking reservoir, dam and water works. Crossing the dam, the trail leaves the water supply system and climbs steeply to a road at 1550 metres. Cross the road and continue the climb to the top of the Shivapuri ridge.

The road is an unfinished (in 1990) project that will eventually lead from Budhanilkantha to Chisopani and beyond, on the north side of the Shivapuri ridge. The first village on the trail is the sprawling Tamang settlement of Mulkharka, at an elevation of 1895 metres. There are a few small tea shops here, where you can sit and enjoy a spectacular panoramic view of Kathmandu Valley and watch planes taking off from Tribhuvan Airport. If you start the trek early in the morning, you will meet hundreds of people walking uphill to gather wood that will be used as fuel in Kathmandu.

Beyond Mulkharka, the trail continues to climb steadily, is sometimes almost level, and sometimes climbs steeply in deep, eroded chasms. After passing through an army camp, the trail enters the Shivapuri Watershed & Wildlife Reserve, a 112 square km walled area. You can see the remnants of the village of Chaurabas as you climb on a heavily eroded trail to the top of the ridge at 2440 metres. Most of the Shivapuri ridge is a dense forest of pine, oak and rhododendron trees.

Just below the ridge on the north side is the village of Borlang Bhanjyang. A night stop in one of the hotels in this village, or 45 minutes further in Chisopani, will afford excellent mountain views the following morning. The sunrise on the Himalaya, from Annapurna to Everest, is particularly outstanding from this point.

The route continues down the ridge through a forest of oak and rhododendron to Chisopani at 2300 metres. There is an unfinished tourist resort here, and you can see the ongoing construction of the road you crossed early this morning. The trail continues to drop from Chisopani on a good, sometimes level, trail that crosses meadows and fields. The final descent to Pati Bhanjyang is on a trail that has eroded into a ridiculous, steep, slippery slide.

Pati Bhanjyang is on a saddle at the bottom of the ridge at 1770 metres elevation. This is a Brahmin and Chhetri village with a few shops and hotels and a police check post, though the police here are usually not interested in trekking permits. There is a big hotel here, the tatty-looking *Shivapuri Lodge*; the *Pati Lodge* advertises a Chinese restaurant. When I was here, the old lady who ran the downmarket *Sewa Sadan Lodge* insisted in a very friendly way that I really should spend the night at her establishment. I didn't, so I cannot vouch for anything except the cardamom-flavoured tea that she prepared.

Day 2: Pati Bhanjyang to Khutumsang

The trail heads north out of Pati Bhanjyang. If you want to do the Helambu circuit backwards, turn right and climb the ridge, then descend into the Malemchi Khola Valley. To go to Langtang, or to make the normal Helambu circuit, bear left and follow a long stretch of level trail to the foot of a steep hill. Make a very steep ascent up switchbacks to Chipling at 2170 metres. There are a few tea shops in shacks at the entrance to the village, but Chipling does not have much else to offer. At the upper end of the village, the trail makes another steep, 200 metre climb on a stone staircase to a pass at 2470 metres, the top of the Jhogin Danda ridge, then descends through forests to Thodang Betini, a long strung-out village at 2100 metres. The *Tasi Lodge* is the last house at the north end of the village.

Continuing along the forested ridge, the trail descends to a large chorten overlooking the Tamang village of Gul Bhanjyang, 2130 metres. This is a delightful, classic hill village with a pleasant main street. There are several shops and a few lodges, but it has not yet converted itself into a trekkers' town. The trail climbs the ridge from Gul Bhanjyang to another pass at 2620 metres, then descends to Khutumsang, 2470 metres, in a saddle atop the ridge. This village has completely adapted itself to trekkers; every house in town is a hotel. The national park office is located here. Pay Rs 250 if you started at Sundarijal; show your receipt again if you are headed in the opposite direction.

Day 3: Khutumsang to Tharepati

The route continues due north up the Yurin Danda ridge and affords views of the peaks above Langtang and of the Gosainkund peaks. The trail climbs above Khutumsang on a steep, eroded trail, mostly through fir and rhododendron forests where there are no permanent settlements, although there are few small herders' huts. There are two bhattis at the settlement of Pambu, then the route climbs to a large cairn at the top of the Panghu Danda, 3285 metres. This is herding country, and there are many goths along the way; in season you may be able to buy milk or curd from the herders.

The trail descends to Magen Goth at 3150 metres. There is a hotel here and a fancy-looking army check post – again they check your national park entry ticket. Continuing to climb, steeply at first, then more gradually, the trail makes some ups and downs and finally reaches Tharepati, which consists of a few goths and hotels at 3490 metres. The trail to Gosainkund turns north-west from this point, and the trail that completes the Helambu circuit turns east just after Tharepati. The region is now truly alpine, with meadows and shrubs typical of high elevations.

Day 4: Tharepati to Tarke Gyang

Turn east from a lodge at the north end of the settlement and descend steeply down a ravine. The vegetation changes rapidly to large firs, then to oaks and rhododendrons, as you rapidly lose all the altitude you gained during the last two days. Crossing a stream, the trail reaches the prosperous Sherpa village of Malemchigaon at 2530 metres.

The Sherpas of Helambu are very different from their cousins in Solu Khumbu. Instead of the Tibetan-style black dress and colourful apron, the Sherpa women of Helambu wear a dress of red printed cotton.

Their language is also quite distinct from the Sherpa language of Solu Khumbu; in addition to being grammatically different, Helambu Sherpas speak much more rapidly than other Sherpas. Helambu women have a reputation for being very beautiful, and many Helambu Sherpa girls were once employed in aristocratic Rana households in Kathmandu during the Rana regime. Many of their benefactors gave gifts of land to these girls, so many Helambu families now own large tracts of farmland in the river valley far below.

From Malemchigaon, the trail descends further to the Malemchi Khola, crossing it on a bridge at 1890 metres, and immediately begins the ascent up the other side of the valley towards Tarke Gyang. Sometimes hoteliers from Tarke Gyang come all the way down to the river to try to induce you to patronise their establishments. It is a long climb to this picturesque village at 2600 metres, situated on a shelf high above the river.

Tarke Gyang is the largest village in Helambu and the destination for most trekkers in this region. There is a large new hotel at the southern end of the village and many other hotels to choose from. In 1949, Tilman described the gompa here, with its impressive array of prayer flags, in a sorry state of disrepair. It now has new paintings and a huge brass prayer wheel. The stone houses of Tarke Gyang are close together with narrow alleyways separating them. Inside, the homes are large, clean and often elaborately decorated, and furnished with elegant brassware and traditional Tibetan carpets on highly polished wooden floors.

The people of Helambu do a lot of trading in India during the winter. Many of the people are quite well-to-do, and own cultivated fields in the lower Malemchi Khola Valley. A special racket among the people of Helambu is the sale of antiques, usually manufactured in Kathmandu and aged over smoky fires in the homes of Tarke Gyang. Beware of any such bargain here. It is illegal to export any item over 100 years old from Nepal, so it is better to purchase well-made handicrafts in Kathmandu or Patan, rather than try to beat the system by purchasing a phoney antique in the hills.

Day 5: Tarke Gyang to Kiul

From Tarke Gyang, there is a choice of trails back to Kathmandu. The trail south along the ridge through Sermathang, down to the river at Malemchi, and down the road to Panchkal, requires two days. The first part of the trail, along the ridge through forests and Sherpa villages, is quite delightful. The later part of the route, on the dusty road along the Indrawati River is boring. You can probably get a ride in one of the jeeps or trucks that ply this stretch of road. There are hotels all along the road and there is a regular minibus service from Sipa Ghat. The route meets the Chinese road at Panchkal and it is a 3 hour ride back to Kathmandu by bus.

It is more worthwhile to take an extra day in the hills and walk back to Sundarijal, where it is easy, cheap and fast to catch transport back to Kathmandu.

The route to Sundarijal passes the hotel in Tarke Gyang, then drops off the west side of the ridge in a rhododendron forest, along a broad, well-travelled path. The trail passes several chortens, mani walls (walk to the left) and kanis. Passing through the Sherpa villages of Kakani at 2070 metres and Thimbu at 1580 metres, the trail enters the hot rice-growing country of the Malemchi and Indrawati valleys, and leaves the highland ethnic groups for the Brahmin, Chhetri and Newar people who inhabit the lower regions.

The steep descent continues to Kiul, 1280 metres, strung out on terraces above the Malemchi Khola. The trail is now in semitropical banana and monkey country at an elevation below that of Kathmandu.

Day 6: Kiul to Pati Bhanjyang

From Kiul, the trail follows the river, descending slightly, then crosses the river on a suspension bridge (do not take the first bridge the trail reaches, take the second one a bit further downstream), at 1190 metres elevation. A short distance beyond the bridge, the trail reaches Mahenkal (1130 metres) and joins the road. As the road descends the valley, it passes through the village of Gheltum, the site of an imposing two storey schoolhouse and a post office. You can follow a trail that cuts across some large road switchbacks as you descend into Talamarang, a pleasant village on the banks of the river at 940 metres. There are some small shops here, and you can probably find a jeep or truck here if you decide to drive back to Kathmandu.

Crossing the Talamarang Khola on a long, rather precarious suspension bridge, the trail leaves the road and proceeds west up the south bank of the stream. The trail starts along rice terraces and fields, then deteriorates into a boulder-strewn route up the river valley. The same monsoon flood that destroyed the road at Talamarang also destroyed this portion of the trail, and washed many fertile fields downstream in the process. After following the stream for a long distance, the trail begins a steep climb towards the top of the ridge on a wide, well-constructed trail. From the uninhabited valley floor, the trail soon enters a densely populated region, passing through the village of Batache en route to the top of the ridge, which it reaches near the village of Thakani at 1890 metres. Following the ridge through meadows and terraced fields, the trail crosses over to its south side and descends to Pati Bhanjyang at 1770 metres, completing the circuit through Helambu.

Day 7: Pati Bhanjyang to Kathmandu
Retrace the route back to Sundarijal, as described on the first day of the trek.

GOSAINKUND
You can make the trek through Gosainkund in either direction combined with a trek to Helambu or Langtang. It is also a worthwhile seven or eight day trek in its own right. There are lodges all along the route except during the winter (late December to early March). The national park enforces the ban on use of firewood in Gosainkund, so if you are camping, be sure to bring kerosene for fuel. The route I have described here is from

Dhunche or Syabru to Tharepati. From Tharepati, you can either continue to Helambu or go directly back to Kathmandu. You can also make the trek in the opposite direction, starting from Sundarijal or Helambu.

Day 1: Syabru or Dhunche to Sing Gompa
From Dhunche From Dhunche, at 1950 metres, follow the road to the first switchback. There is a sign marking a level trail that follows the south bank of the Trisuli Khola through fields and pastures to a few houses. Cross the river on a wooden bridge just before the valley narrows and becomes steeper. The trail follows the north side of the river for a short while, then begins the steep climb towards the ridge. After the initial climb, the trail levels a bit, passes through a village, then continues up to a ridge. Climb through a forest of firs and rhododendrons for about an hour to a small clearing, then another hour to a very basic tea house where there are views back down the valley. The trail continues to climb to the ridge and a trail junction. Turn right and continue up past an army camp, then up through scrub and oaks to Sing Gompa, near the top of the ridge in an area of dead trees. Do not take the inviting-looking trail that descends steeply to an apple farm.

From Syabru There are at least three routes from Syabru to Gosainkund. Two of these bypass Sing Gompa and head directly to two tea shops at Chalang Pati. The route I have described here is a more circuitous trail via Sing Gompa. This trail is easier to follow and breaks the climb into more manageable segments. The direct route from Chalang Pati to Syabru is a good choice if you are coming down from Gosainkund, because the trail is easy to see from above. A guide who knows the way will be very helpful, perhaps essential, if you plan to climb up this route, otherwise you will probably follow a lot of useless yak trails.

Once you evade the pushy Syabru hoteliers, climb past the gompa, school and army

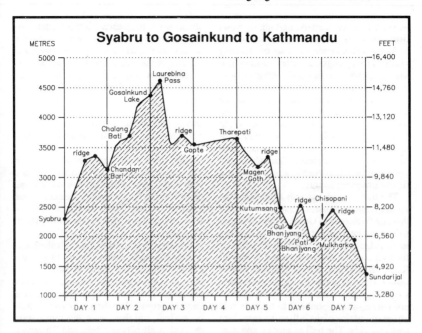

Syabru to Gosainkund to Kathmandu

post, and switchback up the steep hill above the village. There are a few houses and potato fields, but always take the upper, steep trail and you will eventually find yourself at two pleasant tea shops in the settlement of Dursagang at 2550 metres. The trail continues less steeply, now mostly in forests, past an old chorten to the top of the ridge and two shoddy tea shops at 3000 metres.

This is also a trail junction; the right hand trail leads downhill to Brabal and the Dhunche road, and the left trail is a short cut to Chalang Pati. The Sing Gompa trail climbs, then cuts across the ridge top, staying fairly level in forests as it crosses the head of a valley. Take the uphill trail at each junction and cross another forested ridge. There is a view of Dhunche far below in the valley. The trail continues across the head of a second valley, then reaches a final ridge at 3260 metres. Sing Gompa is about 100 metres along the trail to the left.

Sing Gompa is the main attraction at Chandan Bari, elevation 3250 metres, which also has several hotels and a small cheese factory. The gompa is not well cared-for; the caretaker will unlock it for you for a small fee. The hillside near Chandan Bari is bare and scorched through a combination of logging, fire and wind storms.

Day 2: Sing Gompa to Gosainkund

The trail climbs steeply up the ridge, at several points on top of the ridge itself. The ridge is a transition zone between rich, moist mountain forests to the north and dry scrub vegetation on the southern slopes. The trail crosses behind the ridge and stays in deep forests for a while, then emerges onto a saddle at Chalang Pati, 3380 metres, where the *Chalang Pati Hotel* offers a welcome cup of tea. When you start walking again, you will see a sign in Nepali. It says that you are now entering the Gosainkund protected area where killing of animals, lighting of wood fires, and grazing of goats is prohibited.

As the trail ascends, there are outstanding views across Langtang Valley to Langtang Lirung. There are a few goths along the way to the tea shops at Laurebina, elevation 3930, known locally as Laurebina Yak. There are three hotels here; one advertises 'astounding mountain views' as you eat 'breakfast on top of the world'. The views here are truly magnificent – you can see the Annapurnas, Manaslu (8156 metres), Ganesh Himal (7406 metres), unnamed peaks in Tibet and finally Langtang Lirung.

The trail ascends, now in alpine country, up the ridge to a pair of small stone pillars that say 'Welcome to Gosainkund' – but you still have a lot more climbing to do. Continue to the ridge at 4100 metres and climb further for a view of the first of the lakes, Saraswati Kund, in a valley several hundred metres below. The trail leaves the ridge and follows a trail high above the Trisuli Valley. This is not a trail for acrophobics; fortunately it is on the sunny side of the hill, so the snow here melts quickly. The trail is spooky and dangerous if it is snow-covered. If there has been a lot of snow recently, it may not be possible to cross into Gosainkund. People have perished floundering in the deep snow in this region; return to Dhunche if conditions are not good.

After the trail crosses a spur, the second lake in the chain, Bhairav Kund, comes into view. The trail climbs gently but continuously to a ridge and drops about 20 metres to the third and largest lake, Gosainkund, at an elevation of 4380 metres. There are two small hotels, a shrine and several small stone shelters for pilgrims on the north-west side of the lake. Hundreds of people come here to worship and bathe in the lake during the full moon festival each August.

Gosainkund lake has a black rock in the middle, said to be the head of Lord Shiva. There is also a legend about a white rock under the water that is the remnants of an ancient shrine of Shiva. According to legend, Shiva himself created this high altitude lake, when he pierced a glacier with his trident to

obtain water to quench his thirst after consuming some poison. It is also said that the water from this lake disappears underground via a subterranean channel and surfaces in Kumbeshwar pool, next to the five storey Shiva Temple in Patan, more than 60 km away.

Day 3: Gosainkund to Ghopte
The trail passes the north side of Gosainkund Lake and climbs further through rugged country towards the pass. The trail is rough and crosses moraines, but it is well marked with rock cairns. Passing three more small lakes, the trail finally reaches Laurebina pass at 4610 metres. There is a small hillock above the trail that offers good views in both directions.

From the pass, the trail descends alongside a stream through alpine country to a single hut at 4100 metres. Here, at Bhera Goth, there is a choice of trails. The upper trail is a new, high and direct trail to Tharepati. It is very dangerous when there is any snow at all on the trail, and there is no accommodation or food at all between here and Tharepati. Get advice from other trekkers or from the man who lives at Bhera Goth before you take this trail. The low, old, safer trail descends along the middle of the valley to Phedi, which comprises two hotels (the *Taj Mel* is one) by a stream and wooden bridge, at 3500 metres.

Across the valley, you can see a ridge with a steep trail across its face at an angle of almost 45°. Yes, this is where you are going. The route continues across the head of the valley on an extremely rough trail, across moraines and past two goths that have minimal hotel facilities – just tea and Pepsi – to the bottom of the 160 metre climb to the ridge. The ascent is just as steep as it looks, but it is not as exposed (and therefore not as frightening) as it looked from across the valley.

I climbed this trail in the snow, following steps that the trek cook had cut with his kitchen knife. Another sherpa led the way tossing gravel onto the snow and into the steps to provide a footing on the hard and slippery surface. As I sat at the top of the ridge taking photographs, I was thinking how to describe this particular stretch of trail. Was it dangerous or impassable in winter? My musing was interrupted by a sadhu in bare feet and loincloth who carried only a blanket, a brass bowl and an iron trisul. He was on his way to Gosainkund for a day and would return two days hence. Off he went down the trail, followed in quick succession by a Nepali in gum boots striding along listening to a football match on a radio – the only item he was carrying. These apparitions add a bit of perspective to the trail. Just be careful, go slowly and travel with reliable companions.

From this infamous ridge, the trail descends through forests, climbing in and out of ravines across the head of the valley. Giant cliffs tower far above, forming the top of the Thare Danda. On one of the ridges there are some prayer flags; just beyond these flags is the settlement of Ghopte at 3260 metres. There are two tea shops here and a cave that offers some shelter. This is a long and rough day of trekking. The hotels of Tharepati are visible on the far ridge; at night you can see the lights of Trisuli Bazaar far below and the glow of Kathmandu to the south-east.

Day 4: Ghopte to Tharepati

Descending from the ridge at Ghopte, the trail continues up ravines and across the boulders of old moraines, then makes a final ascent to Tharepati, on the ridge at 3490 metres. There are several hotels below the

ridge, and two more on the ridge itself. Take a moment to climb the hill to the east of the ridge for views of Dorje Lakpa, Xixapangama and peaks all the way to Khumbu. Here, the trail joins the Helambu circuit; see Day 3 of that description in this chapter. You can travel 2 hours downhill to Malemchigaon and on to Tarke Gyang, or go directly down the ridge to Kathmandu via Pati Bhanjyang.

The 'new' trail from Bhera Goth rejoins the trail here. If you are walking from Sundarijal to Gosainkund, be sure to ask the people of Tharepati if this trail is safe. The dangerous snow-covered parts of this high trail are on the north-west slopes, and not visible from here.

If you want to return directly to Kathmandu, the days work out as follows:

Day 5: Tharepati to Khutumsang

Day 6: Khutumsang to Chisopani

You might be able to get all the way to Kathmandu from Khutumsang, but the view of the Himalaya from Chisopani is spectacular enough to justify a night here. Beware of thieves in Chisopani, especially if you are camping in tents.

Day 7: Chisopani to Kathmandu

Follow Day 1 of the Helambu trek in reverse, back to the Borlang Bhanjyang, then down the Shivapuri ridge to the road at Sundarijel, from where you can get a bus back to Kathmandu.

Eastern Nepal

Most treks in eastern Nepal begin from the village of Dharan, where the flat Terai ends at the foot of the Siwalik Hills. Destinations include Makalu base camp, an eastern approach to Everest, and the area near Kanchenjunga. There is endless variety in this part of the country. Most ethnic groups are represented and many villages, such as Dhankuta and Bhojpur, are large, prosperous and clean. The area has hot, rice-growing districts and the cooler tea-growing region of Ilam. The heavily populated middle hills are gouged by the mighty Arun River which has cut through at an elevation of less than 400 metres. The Himalayan here includes the major mountain massifs of Kanchenjunga and Makalu.

Treks here tend to be more expensive, since you and your gear must travel to the east of Nepal by bus or plane. The treks are longer because it requires two weeks to travel from Dharan to the high mountains. Flying to STOL airstrips at Tumlingtar and Taplejung can shorten the time, but increases the expense. Inhabitants of this part of Nepal have not seen many westerners in their villages. If you travel in eastern Nepal, you should take great care to avoid the mistakes that trekkers have made in the more popular regions; mistakes which have contributed to theft, over-reliance on the whims of tourists to support the economy, and to problems of garbage, pollution, begging by both adults and children and unnecessary hotel construction.

Kanchenjunga, elevation 8586 metres, is the world's third-highest mountain. The peak is on the border of Nepal and Sikkim and has several distinct summits. It is visible from Darjeeling, so many expeditions explored this region and tried to climb the mountain during the British rule in India. A British team led by Charles Evans made the first ascent of Kanchenjunga in 1953. They trekked from the south of Nepal and climbed the south face of the peak.

One of the most spectacular peaks in the region is Jannu, 7710 metres. The Nepalese renamed this peak Khumbakarna in the 1970s when they Nepalised the names of many peaks. Jannu was also called 'Mystery Peak' and 'Peak of Terror' by early expeditions. A French team made the first ascent of Jannu in 1962.

INFORMATION

Eastern Nepal has not received the attention that the Everest and Annapurna areas have, so the information about this part of the country is sparse. The Arun Valley is described in E W Cronin's *The Arun*, which concentrates on natural history.

There is not a lot of recent literature describing the Kanchenjunga region. The definitive book is *Round Kanchenjunga* by Douglas Freshfield, published in 1903. Reprints of this book are available in Kathmandu. Another good reference is F S Smythe's *The Kanchenjunga Adventure*, published in 1930.

The British colonial names of other peaks near Kanchenjunga were changed during the Nepalising process. Tent Peak (7365 metres) became Kirant Chuli, the Twins (7350 metres) became Givigela Chula, White Wave (6960 metres) is now Andesh Chuli, Wedge Peak (6750 metres) was renamed Chang Himal and Pyramid Peak (7168 metres) became Pathi Bhara. Most of the literature about Kanchenjunga refers to Jannu and uses other Anglicised names, so I have used these names throughout the text. Newer maps that are published in Kathmandu all use the Nepali names.

Maps

Army Map Service sheets NG 45-3 *Kanchenjunga*, and NG 45-2 *Mount Everest* cover eastern Nepal, as do Mandala Maps *Kanchenjunga* and *Arun Valley*.

PLACES TO STAY

Because eastern Nepal is not swarming with trekkers, there is not the abundance of trekking hotels that there is in central Nepal. The region is, however, well served by local bhattis that cater to the unbelievably large number of porters carrying goods throughout the region. The facilities tend to be primitive and unsanitary, and the food dreadful, but if you can handle this, you can make your way through much of eastern Nepal using local accommodation.

GETTING THERE & AWAY

Air

Biratnagar This airport is served by daily RNAC flights and is the centre of RNAC's eastern Nepal hub. There are early morning flights from Biratnagar to Taplejung, Tumlingtar, Lukla and Lamidanda. Biratnagar airport is a fancy new facility built by a South Korean contractor. The airport is quite a distance from the city and the most reliable transport into town is by rickshaw.

Unlike Lukla, the flights to Biratnagar are regular because there is rarely a weather problem. There are instrument-landing facilities and a paved runway, so RNAC can use larger planes that have enough capacity to meet the demand for flights. A flight to Kathmandu takes 50 minutes. In clear weather, it provides an excellent overview of the entire trek and good views of the Himalaya from Kanchenjunga to Langtang.

Taplejung This is the focal point for Kanchenjunga treks. At present it is accessible only by air, but there is a road nearing completion that will provide more reliable access to the region. There is a weekly direct flight from Taplejung to Kathmandu and several services each week to Biratnagar. The airport is in Suketar, a village high on a hill about a 1½ hour walk above Taplejung; reservations are controlled from the city office, not at the airport.

Tumlingtar This airport is located on a flat plateau in the Arun Valley and provides an access to, and from, treks to Makalu, and an early bail-out from the Lukla to Dhankuta trek. The runway is long and will accommodate 44-seat Avro aircraft, so seats to Tumlingtar may be available when all other destinations are fully booked. For some strange reason, the airfare from Kathmandu to Tumlingtar is one of the lowest in Nepal.

Bhojpur On a ridge above the west bank of the Arun River is Bhojpur. It is a possible emergency airstrip if you are walking from Khumbu to Dhankuta.

Lukla Read about Lukla in the Everest region chapter. Avoid this airport if you can.

Airfares These are the current fares between Kathmandu and airports in eastern Nepal:

Kathmandu to Taplejung	US$110
Kathmandu to Tumlingtar	US$44
Kathmandu to Biratnagar	US$77
Kathmandu to Bhojpur	US$77
Biratnagar to Taplejung	US$50
Biratnagar to Tumlingtar	US$33
Biratnagar to Lukla	US$66

Bus

Biratnagar There are night buses from Kathmandu to Biratnagar. It costs Rs 150 for the 540 km, 13 hour journey.

Biratnagar is Nepal's second largest city and the kingdom's industrial centre. The largest factories here process jute into carpets, bags and rope. There are also many smaller factories making matches, cigarettes, tinned fruit, jam and other items. For trekkers, Biratnagar is strictly a transit point and the hotels are abominable. If possible, move on immediately to Dharan, Dhankuta or Basantpur.

A good road connects Biratnagar and Dharan, passing through villages and cultivated fields for most of the distance between the two cities. Originally this was all jungle and fine sal forest, but over the years logging and development have cut it back drastically. There is little to remind one now of the extensive malarial jungle that once blan-

Yak

keted this region – although there are still glimpses of this jungle in Royal Chitwan National Park.

Biratnagar is a typical Terai town, with noisy bazaars, inhabited mainly by plains people. There is nothing of interest in Biratnagar and the chaos of rickshaws and trucks makes it pointless to spend much time there as a tourist. The 45 km drive from Biratnagar to Dharan requires about an hour.

Dharan This trailhead is north of Biratnagar at the foot of the hills. A road connects Dharan with Dhankuta and Basantpur, starting places for treks to Kanchenjunga and the Arun Valley. Dharan is 540 km from Kathmandu and is served by night buses for Rs 150, and day buses for Rs 120. The night bus takes about 14 hours. You can also reach Dharan from Biratnagar and from Itahari on the east-west highway. Much of the Dharan bazaar was severely damaged by an earthquake in 1988.

You can return to Kathmandu by night bus directly from Dharan to Kathmandu. A more costly but less tedious route is by bus to Biratnagar, then a flight back to Kathmandu.

Dhankuta This is the starting point for treks up the Arun Valley. If possible, you should go about 10 km beyond Dhankuta to Hile and start walking from there. There is no direct bus service from Kathmandu to Dhankuta, so you must take a local bus from Dharan; it costs Rs 25 to Rs 30 for the 50 km trip. There is a good hotel in Dhankuta and there are several Tibetan-operated hotels in Hile.

Basantpur About 2 hours drive beyond Dhankuta is Basantpur, a starting point for treks to Kanchenjunga. The bus service to Basantpur is irregular; if you have trouble, hire your own vehicle or try for a ride in a truck from Dhankuta or Dharan.

Ilam Another possible starting point for Kanchenjunga treks is Ilam. There is no direct bus service; take the bus from Kathmandu to Kharkavita and get off in Charsli, just east of Birtamod, then take a 6 hour local bus ride on the winding road to Ilam. The road to Taplejung passes through Ilam; when this road is completed, this will be the best way into the Kanchenjunga region.

Getting to India An alternative to the return to Kathmandu is to take a bus from Itahari to Kharkavita, cross into India and take a taxi to Siliguri. From Siliguri, it is about a 3 hour drive by taxi (or a 7 hour ride on the famous 'toy train') to Darjeeling, a pleasant Indian hill station.

SOLU KHUMBU TO DHANKUTA

This section describes an alternative to the Jiri to Everest base camp trek. Though I have shown it as a route from Solu Khumbu (the Mt Everest region) to Hile, you can also use it as an approach route to the Everest region. The first foreign visitor to Everest base camp, Tilman in 1950, used this route and described it in some detail in *Nepal Himalaya*.

By walking from Jiri to Everest, and then walking via the route described here to Hile, you can make a rewarding 32 day trek. Walking to Hile avoids the flight complications at Lukla and lends a sense of continuity

Top left: Chobar Gorge Bridge(TW)
Top right: Covered bridge at Bratang (SA)
Bottom left: Bridge over the Tamba Kosi, Biguti (SA)
Bottom right: Bridge near Pangboche (SA)

Mt Everest - 8848 metres (SA)
Dhaulagiri - 8167 metres (GA)
Fluted Peak - 6390 metres (SA)
Annapurna South - 7273 metres (SB)

Lhotse - 8511 metres (PS)
Ama Dablam - 6856 metres (SA)
Machhapuchhare - 6997 metres (SA)
Ganja La Chuli - 5846 metres (SA)

to the trek that you will not feel when you fly back from Lukla.

Though it's possible to make this walk as a tea house trek, it is not easy. The first six days, from Lukla to Phedi, are through country that sees few travellers, so there are almost no hotels and local people are not used to cooking meals for trekkers in their homes. It is most important to carry food for the nights at Gaikharka, Bung and Sanam, because facilities in these villages are poor or nonexistent.

Day 1: Lukla to Puiyan

Instead of flying from Lukla, take a leisurely stroll down the 550 metre long runway, continue down to Surkhe, then climb back up to Puiyan at 2730 metres. If you are travelling from Namche Bazaar it is not necessary to go to Lukla; you can walk from Jorsale to Chaunrikharka, then from Chaunrikharka to Puiyan.

Day 2: Puiyan to Pangum

The trail follows the same route as the Lamosangu to Namche Bazaar trail as far as Bupsa, then heads into new trekking country. From Bupsa, climb on the old trail to the large white house at the top of Kharte, then climb over a fence and turn south-east up the broad Khari Khola Valley. The beginning of this trail is not obvious. Ask people for the trail to Pangum (pronounced 'Pankoma' locally); *kun baarto Pankoma jaanchha?* There are some ups and downs as the trail gradually gains elevation up the forested valley, passing isolated Sherpa houses and small streams, to the village of Pangum, at about 2850 metres. Here is yet another Hillary school (there are 12 such schools in the region), a gompa and a paper factory.

The Nepali paper produced here is used for all official government transactions and is carried to Kathmandu in huge loads by porters. We call it rice paper, but actually it contains no rice; it is made from the inner bark of the daphne bush, known in Nepali as *lokta*.

Day 3: Pangum to Gaikharka

From Pangum, it is a short climb to the 3173 metre Pangum La (also called the Satu La), the pass between the watersheds of the Dudh Kosi and the Inukhu Khola. From the pass, there is a great view, not only of the Khumbu Himalaya, but also of the peaks at the head of the Inukhu (also called Hinku) Valley, including Mera Peak, one of the easiest but least accessible of Nepal's trekking peaks. The trail descends gradually to Chatuk, a small Sherpa settlement, then drops almost vertically in a series of short switchbacks to the river at 1855 metres. The trail crosses an exciting bridge suspended high above the river on two steel cables. A Himalayan Trust team built this bridge in 1971. When I asked one of the volunteers about the fantastic engineering that must be required for the construction of a bridge in such a remote location, he replied: 'We don't engineer them, we just build them.'

The trail climbs a short distance, alongside a picturesque waterfall that widens into a pool just above the river; this is a good place to take a bath after the cold of Khumbu. The trail then ascends the side of the wild, sparsely inhabited Inukhu Valley to the Sherpa hamlet of Gaikharka ('cow pasture'), at about 2300 metres. Although the only permanent settlements in this valley are those of Sherpas, the neighbouring Rais graze their cattle here. Gurungs also graze large herds of sheep which they bring up from the south during the summer.

Day 4: Gaikharka to Bung

The route continues to climb, past the roofless goths of Najidingma in a large meadow at 2650 metres, then makes a steep ascent in forests towards Sipki (or Surkie) pass at 3085 metres. Beyond the pass, the trail descends a short distance through forests, then the valley suddenly opens up above the village of Khiraule, at about 2400 metres. In the distance you can see Boksom Gompa surrounded by a large circle of trees. It is particularly sacred, but has fallen into disuse and disrepair. There are many crisscrossing trails here used by the people of Bung when

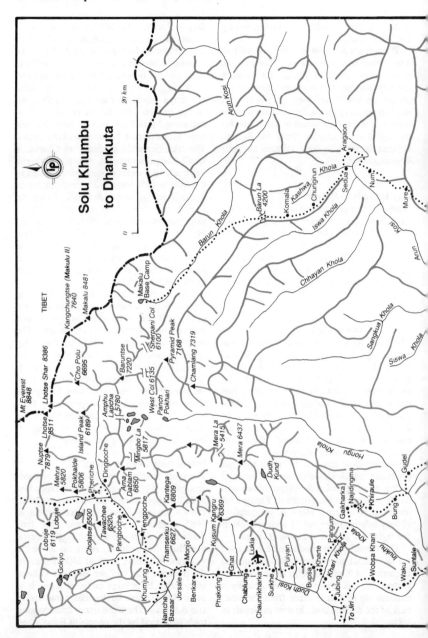

Solu Khumbu to Dhankuta

TIBET

Mt Everest 8848
Lhotse Shar 8386
Kangchungtse (Makulu II) 7640
Makalu 8481
Lhotse 8511
Nuptse 7879
Mehra 5820
Island Peak 6189
Cho Polu 6695
Baruntse 7220
Makalu Base Camp
Sherpani Col 6100
Pyramid Peak 7168
Chamlang 7319
Amphu Lapcha 5780
West Col 6135
Panch Pokhari
Mingbo La 5817
Barun Khola
Barun La 4200
Komala
Kashwa
Chungrirun
Kashwa Khola
Sedua
Aragaon
Num
Mure
Iswa Khola
Arun Kosi
Chhayan Khola
Sangkua Khola
Siswa Khola
Arun
Kosi
Mera La 5415
Mera 6437
Dudh Kund
Hongu Khola
Isoi Kosi
Gokyo
Lobuje 6119
Lobuje
Gokyo
Cholatse 6500
Tawachee 6520
Pokhalde 5806
Dingboche
Pheriche
Pangboche
Tengboche
Ama Dablam 6850
Kantega 6809
Thamserku 6623
Kusum Kangru 6369
Khumjung
Namche Bazaar
Jorsale
Monjo
Benkar
Phakding
Ghat
Chablung
Chaunrikharka
Surkhe
Lukla
Puiyan
Bupsa
Kharte
Khari Khola
Pangum
Najidingma
Gaikharka
Khiraule
Bung
Gudel
Inukhu Kola
Jubing
Wobsa Khani
Waku
Suntale
To Jiri
Dudh Kosi

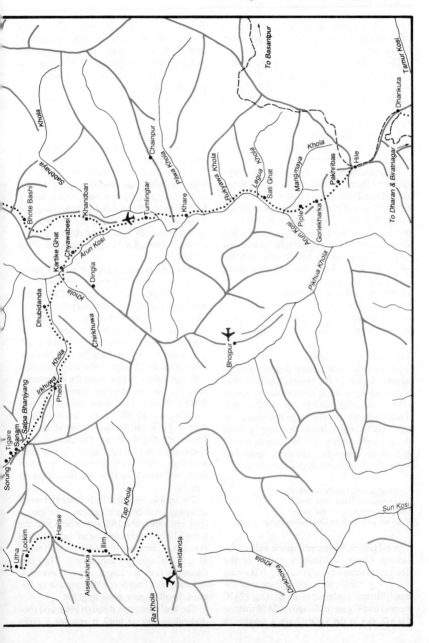

they collect wood, so it is easy to get lost; aim south and a bit east to the ridge above the gompa.

The trek is now in the great Hongu Valley, one of the most fertile regions of Nepal. Much of the rice for the Namche Bazaar market comes from this area and is carried back across three ridges to Khumbu. Except for some Sherpas living at higher elevations, and some Chhetris and Brahmins downstream near Sotang, the Hongu Valley population is exclusively Rai.

The trail descends a ridge crest to the large village of Bung, spread out over the hillside from about 1900 down to 1400 metres elevation. The most direct route through the village follows a ravine downhill, but soon gets lost wandering among the houses and fields in the lower part of this typical Rai village. There are no hotels here and the people of Bung are a bit unhappy about trekking groups camping in the village, so it's best to continue downhill and camp in fields below the village near the river. You are almost certain to hear the drum of a dhami, a local shaman, in the Hongu Valley.

Day 5: Bung to Sanam

From Bung, there is a steep descent through bamboo forests to the Hongu Khola, which is crossed by a large suspension bridge at 1316 metres, followed by an equally steep climb to Gudel, another large Rai village, at about 2000 metres. It was this long, useless descent and ascent that H W Tilman, travelling in the opposite direction, described poetically in his book *Nepal Himalaya*:

For dreadfulness, naught can excel
The prospect of Bung from Gudel;
And words die away on the tongue
When we look back on Gudel from Bung.

Beyond Gudel, the ascent up the side of the Lidung Khola, a tributary valley of the Hongu, continues more gradually. It is a long and tiring climb, through forests and the small Sherpa settlements of Sorung (2470 metres) and Tigare, to Sanam at 2850 metres. Rai villages in the valley have a maximum

elevation of about 2400 metres; Sherpa villages exploit different resources, so there is little economic competition between the two groups. Sanam is primarily dependent on herds of cattle, and there is often milk, yoghurt and excellent cottage cheese available in the village, a compact settlement of houses arranged in a single row.

Day 6: Sanam to Phedi

The route continues to climb through a totally uninhabited area. The trail drops slightly to the floor of the canyon that it has been ascending, crosses the Lidung Khola, which here is only a stream, and makes a final steep climb to the Salpa Bhanjyang, the 3349 metre pass between the Hongu and Arun watersheds. It is a long climb; the total distance from the Hongu Khola is 2033 metres.

This area is deep hemlock and fir forest abounding in bird and animal life, including Himalayan bear, barking deer and the lesser panda, a smaller, red-coloured relative of its more famous namesake. A large chorten marks the pass, and the final influence of Sherpa culture on the route. The first available water is about an hour beyond the pass, making the lunch stop on this day quite late.

It is possible, by following the ridge to the south, to take an alternate route to the one described here. This route passes through Bhojpur, a large hill bazaar, famous for its excellent kukhris, the curved Nepali knives. There are flights from Bhojpur to both Kathmandu and Biratnagar, or you can keep walking to the Arun, crossing it near Sati Ghat, and rejoin the trail described here on Day 10.

The trail to Hile descends through forests and past small herders' huts as it follows a spur separating the Irkhuwa Khola and the Sanu Khola. On this portion of the trail there is ample evidence of forest fires which occur in the dry season each spring. They are caused by fires in villages, careless smokers, lightning and shepherds burning the underbrush to allow new grass to grow.

The trail continues through birch and rhododendron forests until it reaches a large stone overlooking the Irkhuwa Khola Valley. The trail then drops almost vertically through bamboo forests into the Rai village of Phedi. There are many opportunities to get lost on the ridge; stay as high as possible and keep going east. Several trails drop off the ridge to the north and south; the trail to Phedi drops off the east end of the ridge. The best camp is below the village, at about 1680 metres, on the banks of the Irkhuwa Khola; or you can stay in the village at the *Sherpa Lodge*. This is one of the longest days and the longest downhill walk of the trek. The rakshi in Phedi is terrible.

Day 7: Phedi to Dhubidanda

The trek has now emerged into the fertile rice-growing valley of the Arun River. The route follows the Irkhuwa Khola, a tributary of the Arun, crossing and recrossing the stream on a series of bamboo bridges. Some of these are substantial and some very flimsy, but all are picturesque. After the continuous ups and downs of the last week, this is a particularly relaxing day. The trail loses elevation almost imperceptibly; yet by the end of the day you will have lost almost 900 metres. There are many pools large enough for swimming, and the water temperature – especially in comparison with streams higher up – is comfortable. A few hours below Phedi is Dotre Bazaar, which has the first real shops since Lukla. There is even a tailor shop that can outfit you with a new set of clothes while you wait.

The predominant ethnic groups in this part of the Arun basin are the Rais, Chhetris and Brahmins. Before the Gurkha conquest, about 200 years ago, the population of the middle hills region between the Dudh Kosi and Arun was almost entirely Rais. Following the conquest, when the Rais were defeated by the Gurkha army, considerable numbers of Hindus settled here, especially in the more fertile regions.

There is a good camping place on the banks of the Irkhuwa Khola near the village of Dhubidanda, at an elevation of about 760 metres.

Day 8: Dhubidanda to Chyawabesi

The trail makes a final crossing of the Irkhuwa Khola, this time on an excellent new bridge built by the local government. It soon begins to climb over a spur separating the Arun River from the Irkhuwa Khola. The main trail in this region climbs much higher, via the large village of Dingla at the top of the ridge. If you have a guide who knows the way or can ask local people, you can avoid this long, unnecessary climb and follow a circuitous route through the fields and back yards of a lower village. The trail is difficult to find as it crosses fields, doubles back on itself and traverses small irrigation canals and rice terraces.

From the ridge, you can finally see the mighty Arun River to the north. This river, which has its headwaters in Tibet, is one of the major rivers flowing into the Ganges in India.

The trail now turns south and descends to a small tributary of the Arun, the Chirkhuwa Khola, where there is a small shop and a fine swimming hole overlooked by a huge and noisy band of rhesus monkeys. This village, called Balawa Besi, makes an excellent spot to stop for lunch, though usually hot.

A short distance on, the route crosses the Arun River, here at an elevation of only 300 metres, on a large suspension bridge. There used to be a dugout canoe ferry here, but in 1984 the bridge replaced this exciting ride. From the bridge at Kartike Ghat, the trail follows the east side of the river southward for about a half hour to a good camp at Chyawabesi, at 280 metres elevation. Along the Arun Valley there are frequent bhattis, so finding food is no longer a problem, though both the quality and sanitation are marginal.

There is a huge hydroelectric project planned on the Arun River. A road up the Arun Valley is also planned, and several dams and generating stations will eventually be built along the Arun.

The character of this trek is changing rapidly, so the following days may be considerably changed by the time you trek in this area.

Day 9: Chyawabesi to Khare

The trail follows the Arun as it flows south, sometimes climbing high above the river and sometimes traversing the sandy riverbed. The climate, even during the winter, is hot and tropical. Houses sit atop stilts for ventilation and the people are darker-skinned than those seen so far on the trek. You will probably want to change your schedule to do most of the walking in the very early morning to avoid the heat. Many of the settlements along the bottom of the Arun Valley are inhabited only during the planting and harvesting seasons, by people who live higher in the hills above and own fertile farmlands in the valley.

It is a short climb to a huge plateau that provides almost 6 km of completely level trail to Tumlingtar, a small village with an airport served by regular RNAC flights. Many of the inhabitants of Tumlingtar are of the Kumal (potter) caste, and earn their livelihood from the manufacture of earthenware pots from the red clay of this region. There is very little water on the plateau, so you must continue a long distance in the morning before lunch. A cup of tea, and some oranges or bananas at the big shop under the banyan tree in Tumlingtar will provide the refreshment to keep moving under the hot sun.

The reward comes immediately after the short descent from the plateau when the trail crosses the Sabbhaya Khola, a tributary of the Arun. There is an excellent lunch spot beside a fine swimming hole in the warmest and most delightful stream along the entire trek route. There is a Rs 1 toll on the bridge, or you can swim or wade across the river, though the riverbed is rocky and slippery. The afternoon is short, involving a climb of only 100 metres over a ridge, then a descent to Khare, a tropical village on the banks of the Arun.

Day 10: Khare to Mangmaya Khola

The trail continues south along the east bank of the Arun. There are many porters on the trail from here to Dhankuta. These men carry goods from warehouses in Dhankuta to the bazaars of Bhojpur, Dingla and Chainpur;

they often walk at night with small kerosene lamps tied to their dokos (the bamboo baskets in which they carry their loads).

In another of his classic anecdotes, Tilman imagined these porters nose-to-doko along the trail. Each porter carries a T-shaped stick that he places under his doko whenever (and wherever) he wishes to rest, usually when he is standing in the middle of the trail. The entire trail then backs up, as each porter waits until the man ahead of him finishes his rest, thus halting a long line of porters. It presents a ludicrous picture, but a picture not totally removed from reality on this part of the trail. A short excursion into the villages here will often uncover such appealing items as papayas *(mewa* in Nepali), peanuts *(badam)* and pineapples *(bhui katahar)*.

The trail continues south, at no point climbing more than 100 metres above the river, until it crosses under a cable that supports a river gauging station. This is just before a small village named Sati Ghat, the site of another dugout canoe ferry. Herds of goats and sheep have devoured much of the vegetation along this part of the river. These animals, more than humans, are responsible for the extensive deforestation in Nepal, because they prevent any new saplings from growing into trees. After a short distance the trail comes to a large pipal tree and chautaara overlooking a huge side valley of the Arun. At the foot of this valley flows the Mangmaya Khola; the grassy banks of this stream, at 200 metres elevation, afford an excellent campsite.

Day 11: Mangmaya Khola to Hile

The trail crosses the broad valley, then climbs through hot tropical forests to the delightful village of Piple, which has two tea shops facing a small village square, at about 700 metres elevation. The upper portion of this town has several large shops. The trail continues to climb through villages inhabited by Limbus, relatives of the Rais, to Gorlekharka, at 1250 metres elevation. The trail finally gains the ridge and allows a fine view of Makalu (8463 metres) and Chamlang (7317 metres) almost 150 km away.

The route continues fairly level for some time to the British agricultural project at Pakhribas. This fantastic development presents a real contrast to the small gardens that surround every home throughout the trek. At Pakhribas, there are huge rows of vegetables, all neatly labelled with signs; there are walls, roads and irrigation canals, all paved with stone and cement. There are buildings of every description carefully labelled according to their function.

The trail then climbs a higher ridge crest to the roadhead at Hile. This is a very pleasant town situated high on a hill at 1850 metres; the elevation and cool breezes provide a welcome relief from the heat of the Arun Valley. The people who inhabit this village are primarily of Tibetan stock, who have resettled here. They came from Tibet and other parts of eastern Nepal, particularly from the village of Walunchung Gola, when the Chinese occupation disrupted trade with Tibet in 1959. There is often some genuine Tibetan jewellery for sale here, and many Chinese goods are available at prices below those in Kathmandu. The village is also famous for its ample supply of tongba. There is a weekly market (hat) in Hile on Thursdays.

Day 12: Hile to Kathmandu via Biratnagar

The road descends a spur to Dhankuta, at 1220 metres. The 10 km stretch of road from Hile to Dhankuta is not paved, so there are fewer buses here. You might have to walk part of the way to Dhankuta before you find a bus. From Dhankuta, there are hourly buses to Dharan (about a 1½ hour ride to cover the 50 km) or you might find direct service to Biratnagar. Take whatever is available; bus service is frequent in this region, especially once you reach Dharan.

The road does not pass through Dhankuta itself, but the town is worth a visit. It is a Limbu town; large, attractive and clean, with whitewashed houses and winding streets paved with stone. This is the largest town on the entire trek route. There is a police station flanked by polished brass cannon, a hospital,

a cold storage facility, bank, bakery, telegraph office and hundreds of shops. The region is famous for its wonderful oranges (suntala).

The road descends from Dhankuta and crosses the Tamur Kosi at Mulghat. The Tamur Kosi flows west to join the Arun at the same point where the Sun Kosi joins it after its long trip eastward across Nepal. Together these rivers form the Sapt Kosi ('seven rivers') that flows to the Ganges containing the waters of the Sun Kosi, Bhote Kosi, Tamba Kosi, Dudh Kosi, Arun Kosi, Likhu Kosi and Tamur Kosi.

The road turns south, following up a side valley of the Tamur Kosi until reaches the Churia Hills, the last range of hills before the plains. In India these hills are called the Siwalik range. The road climbs to a pass at 1300 metres. From some places on this ridge, there are views of Kanchenjunga (8598 metres) and its prominent neighbour Jannu (7710 metres), on the eastern border of Nepal.

At the pass is a most dramatic sight – to the south are nothing but plains. After weeks in the hills, it is unusual to see country that is absolutely flat as far as the eye can see. The road descends to Dharan at 370 metres. Dharan used to be the major trading centre serving the eastern hills region, and was the site of a British Gurkha recruiting centre, but its role has changed with the opening of the Dhankuta road and the closure of the British camp. Although Dharan is located in the plains, most of population consists of hill people who have resettled here.

KANCHENJUNGA TREK

Nepal opened the Kanchenjunga area to trekkers in 1988, though people have trekked in the area in connection with mountaineering expeditions since the turn of the century. Kanchenjunga is a long way from Kathmandu, and the nearest roads and airports are a long way from the mountain. You can trek either to the north or south Kanchenjunga base camp, but it takes luck, determination and a lot of time to visit both sides of the peak. The northern side is partic-

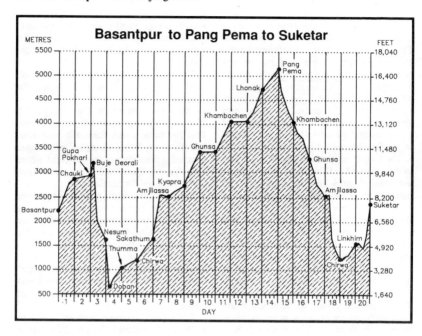

Basantpur to Pang Pema to Suketar

ularly remote; it takes almost two weeks of walking to get to the base camp at Pang Pema.

Kanchenjunga is on the border of Nepal and the Indian state of Sikkim, so a circuit of the mountain is politically impossible. The next best alternative is to visit both the north and south sides of the mountain from the Nepal side; you need to be equipped for a high pass crossing and have a minimum of four weeks. If the pass crossing does not work, then it's a long way around.

Since the region was opened, only a few groups have made successful crossings of either the Lapsang La or Mirgin La. Bad weather and snow is often to blame, but more often it is simply a lack of time. Many trekkers have wallowed around in the lowlands near Taplejung because they miscalculated the time required to reach the high country. Unless you have at least four weeks, and preferably five, you should plan to visit either the north or south base camp, not both.

If you can get to Taplejung by either road or air, the trek can be shortened by four days, making it a bit more reasonable.

The lowland portion of this region is culturally intriguing, but there are few good mountain views. The two treks that I have described here will probably need to be extended by a few days because of porter problems, weather, or the need for a rest day.

In the spring of 1990, the Immigration Office would only grant trekking permits for the Kanchenjunga region to groups, not to individual trekkers, and required a special US$10 per week trekking permit. The Kanchenjunga region remains technically restricted, but you can trek here if you get a trekking permit. Yamphudin, a village on the route to the south side of Kanchenjunga, is listed on both sides of the printed trekking permit form. It is included first as a village that is permitted, and on the reverse side as a village in the 'restricted area.'

There are a few tea houses in the lowlands,

but in the high country you must have food and a tent. If you are planning to take porters across the Lapsang La or Mirgin La, you will need to provide shoes, clothing and snow goggles for them.

The Kanchenjunga region is the home of the Limbus. Relatives of the Rais, Limbus dominate the region east of the Arun River and few live elsewhere. Limbu men wear a distinctive tall *topi*, a Nepalese cap that is much more colourful than that worn by other Nepalese.

A noteworthy contribution of Limbu culture is the drink *tongba*. They fill a wooden pot with fermented millet seeds and add boiling water. You sip the dangerously potent mixture through a special bamboo straw, with tiny filters to keep the seeds out of the drink, as the hotelier merrily adds more hot water. It goes down easily, as you might do yourself when you arise after a lengthy tongba session. Watch for this speciality anywhere north of Dharan. It is often served in a large plastic mug, but ethnically correct hotels serve it in a special wooden tongba pot, which has brass rings, and a wooden cap with a hole for the straw.

NORTH KANCHENJUNGA BASE CAMP
Day 1: Biratnagar to Basantpur

If you are travelling by air, fly to the Terai city of Biratnagar, at an elevation of only 70 metres. RNAC usually schedules the 50 minute Biratnagar flights at about noon, so if you have arranged for vehicles to meet you in Biratnagar, there may be time to drive to the trailhead at Basantpur before dark. If you are bussing it, take the direct night bus to Dharan, then transfer to a local bus to Dhankuta or Hile and then make your way on to Basantpur.

From Dharan, the road climbs over the Siwalik Hills to Dhankuta, then to Hile, a Tibetan settlement at 1850 metres elevation. The paved road ends here, but an unpaved road wends its way to Basantpur, a large bazaar at 2200 metres elevation on a ridge above the Tanmaya Khola, with a view of the entire Kanchenjunga massif. There are lots of shops and local-style hotels here, but it's a dirty, noisy road-head town. It's more pleasant to walk about 1 km up the trail and camp in a meadow beyond the village.

The road will eventually continue on from here to Tumlingtar in the Arun Valley as part of the Arun hydroelectric project.

Day 2: Basantpur to Chauki

The trek starts with a slow ascent on a wide trail through mossy rhododendron forests, with super views off both sides to the Arun Kosi and Tamur Kosi drainages and north to Makalu. This is a major trade route to Chainpur and the Arun Valley, as well as to Taplejung and the upper Tamur Valley, so you will travel in the company of droves of porters. At Tude Deorali the Chainpur trail turns off, so the horde of porters diminishes a bit as you approach Door Pani at 2780 metres. It's uphill to a tea shop at Panch Pokhari, then the trail drops gently to Tinjuri Danda and climbs through Phedi to a good campsite at Chauki, elevation 2700 metres.

Day 3: Chauki to Gupa Pokhari

Most of the day's hike is along the ridge of the Milke Danda, through pretty, grassy meadows with views of Chamlang, Mera, Makalu and Kanchenjunga. After some ups and downs through Manglebare, Srimani and Balukop, the trek reaches two small lakes at Lamo Pokhari. It's generally downhill past the bamboo huts at Koranghatar to more lakes at Gupa Pokhari, elevation 2930 metres.

Gupa Pokhari has several lodges and lots of places to buy food, biscuits, beer, rum and chhang. The shopkeepers are Tibetans who say they settled here two generations ago. Industrious women weave scarves and carpets alongside the trail. A large pond behind the village has a Buddhist shrine, and prayer flags in the trees surrounding it. The murky waters of the lakes are heavily polluted; treat the water carefully here. The area is subject to violent windstorms.

Day 4: Gupa Pokhari to Nesum

The route leaves the Milke Danda and heads out onto a ridge above the Tamur Kosi. The

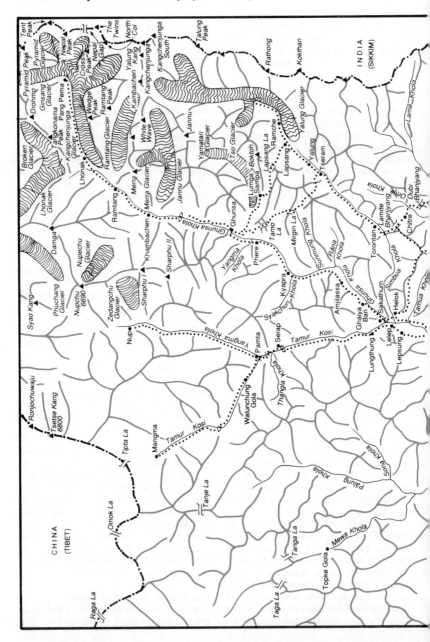

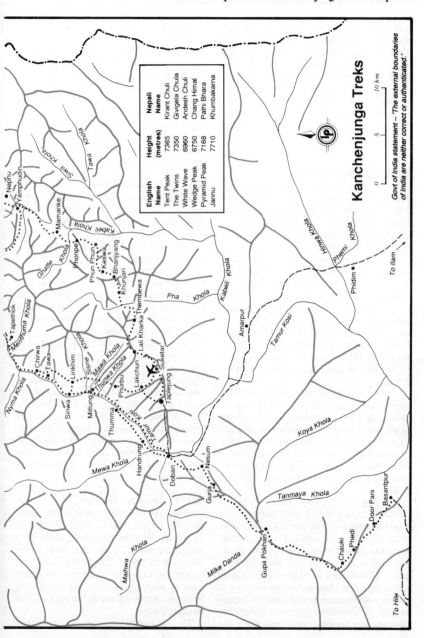

Kanchenjunga Treks

English Name	Height (metres)	Nepali Name
Tent Peak	7365	Kirant Chuli
The Twins	7350	Givigela Chula
White Wave	6960	Andesh Chuli
Wedge Peak	6750	Chang Himal
Pyramid Peak	7168	Pathi Bhara
Jannu	7710	Khumbakarna

Govt of India statement – 'The external boundaries of India are neither correct or authenticated.'

trail wanders uphill along the ridge through rhododendron forests, to Akhar Deorali at 3200 metres, then makes some ups and downs en route to Buje Deorali. Down to a kharka, up again to Mul Pokhari, then down through hazel and chestnut forests to Gurja at 2000 metres. Keep going down through cultivated country to Chatrapati, and then to Nesum at 1620 metres. There is a hotel in Chatrapati and two bhattis in Gurja.

Day 5: Nesum to Thumma

Make a long, zigzagging descent through scattered houses and the village of Banjoghjara to the Maihwa Khola. Deal with formalities at the police check post and cross the suspension bridge into the village of Doban at 640 metres.

The trail now meets the Tamur Kosi. There are trails up both sides of the river. Both are lousy and subject to landslides; it seems to make little difference which side of the river you start out on. There are frequent bridges across the Tamur Kosi in various stages of technological advancement and repair. Inquire locally and change your route to suit the current situation, though you need to end up on the east bank by the time you reach Sinwa.

At Doban, you can cross the Tamur Kosi and climb almost 1200 metres up to Taplejung. It is a long ascent and the village is not particularly lively, so there is no point in making a side trip unless you are trying to confirm flight reservations. Once the road is completed from Ilam to Taplejung it will be possible to drive to this point to begin the trek.

The population of the Tamur Valley is primarily Limbu, with a few Chhetris in the lower regions and Sherpas at higher elevations. Doban is a small, grubby Newar bazaar town with shops selling soap, toothpaste, cloth, thread, sandals, beer and rum. Many Tibetans live in flimsy bamboo shelters alongside the bazaar, and sell tongba and weave woollen scarves and aprons. Characteristic of misplaced priorities in getting development projects completed, there are electric lines and power poles here – but no electricity.

If you cross the suspension bridge at Doban and follow the east bank trail, you will travel up the Tamur in tropical forests, sometimes climbing above the river and sometimes on the riverbank itself. Thumma is on the west side of the river about 2 hours beyond Doban. If you followed the trail up the west bank through the village of Handrung, you can cross to the east side here on a reasonably safe suspension bridge.

Day 6: Thumma to Chirwa

From Thumma, stay on the east bank as the trail undulates along the riverside through rocky fields and across landslides to the Chhetri bazaar of Mitlung, elevation 800 metres, then climb over a ridge to Shisne. In 1990, most people crossed the river on a bamboo bridge here and followed the west bank for about 45 minutes before crossing back to the east side. This diversion may not be necessary if the trail on the east side is in good condition. Pass the settlements of Sinwa, Tawa and Porke. At Porke there is a flimsy bamboo and wire bridge which, fortunately, you do not have to cross. The valley narrows and the trail becomes worse as it climbs across landslides and boulder strewn river deposits to Chirwa, a pleasant bazaar with a few bhattis and shops at 1190 metres. Take a look at the village water supply system. It's an elaborate setup of bamboo chutes, pipes and channels that Rube Goldberg or Heath Robinson would have been proud of – if it has not been replaced with plastic pipe.

Day 7: Chirwa to Sakathum

Continue up the Tamur across big boulders, passing below the Chhetri village of Tapethok. Beyond Tapethok, there is a bridge across the Tamur that leads to the Sherpa settlements of Lepsung, Lelep and Lungthung. Lelep and the route up the Tamur Kosi to Walunchung Gola are specifically listed as restricted areas on the back of your trekking permit.

The trail makes more ups and downs, traverses a landslide, then crosses the Tamua Khola on a suspension bridge below the village of Helok. There is a tongba and tea shop near the junction where the trail to the Limbu village of Helok leaves the main Tamur Kosi route. To avoid Helok, climb over a spur and descend to the Simbua Khola, crossing it on a new suspension bridge. This river comes from the Yalung Glacier on the south side of Kanchenjunga; if you trek to the south base camp, you will reach the headwaters of this river.

A short climb over another ridge brings you into the steep and narrow Ghunsa Khola Valley. Cross the Ghunsa Khola on a rickety bridge and camp by the banks of the river near the Tibetan village of Sakathum, 1640 metres. If it's clear, you will have your first good close-up views of Jannu up the Ghunsa Khola Valley.

Day 8: Sakathum to Amjilassa

The hike is along a steep, narrow trail up the north bank of the Ghunsa Khola. Climb steeply for 100 metres, then drop back to the river and follow the riverbed for about 1 km. The trail them begins a sustained climb on stone steps to a waterfall and the settlement of Ghaiya Bari. Here the ascent becomes gentler, following an exhilarating, exposed, and potentially dangerous trail through arid country to a crest at 2530 metres, then descends a bit to the Tibetan settlement of Amjilassa at 2490 metres.

Day 9: Amjilassa to Kyapra

Ascend for 100 metres, then level off and round a bend of the river into lush bamboo, oak and rhododendron forests, with views of Nango Ma and the south west part of the Kanchenjunga massif. The trail makes many short climbs and descents and passes several waterfalls and pastures. Beyond a large waterfall in the Ghunsa Khola itself, start a steep climb to a campsite at Kyapra, called Chapla or Gyabla by the Tibetan inhabitants, at 2730 metres.

The Mandala map shows that the trail crosses the Ghunsa Khola at Kyapra; it does not. Kyapra is on the north bank and you stay on the north side of the river all the way to Ghunsa.

Day 10: Kyapra to Ghunsa

Descend steeply into a side ravine, then follow along the river through a fir and rhododendron forest. It takes all morning to trek past Killa and on to the yak pastures and potato fields of Phere. Both are Tibetan villages with pleasant gompas and friendly monks; you may find a better supply of food, especially potatoes, in Phere than in Ghunsa. The valley widens as you trek through fields and larch forests to a bridge across the Ghunsa Khola.

The prayer-flag bedecked houses of Ghunsa are on the south side of the river at 3430 metres. The police check post in Ghunsa takes itself very seriously; be sure your permit is in order before you pay them a visit. The high route to the south Kanchenjunga base camp via the Lapsang La begins here.

Day 11: Acclimatisation day at Ghunsa

The trek is now getting into high country; since you have been traipsing about in the lowlands for almost two weeks, you need to spend some time to allow your body to acclimatise to high altitude. You can use the day to reconnoitre the route over the Lapsang La by trekking to a small lake at the foot of the Yamatari Glacier, south of Ghunsa. The people of Ghunsa move their yaks over the Mirgin La to the high country south of Kanchenjunga in the summer, and take them down to Phere in the winter.

Day 12: Ghunsa to Khambachen

The trail makes a gradual ascent along the south bank of the Ghunsa Khola, then crosses a boulder-strewn flood plain and crosses back to Rambuk Kharka on the north side of the river. Once on the opposite side, the trail makes a short, steep ascent to a very unstable scree slope. Then it's a dangerous 250 metre passage across the slide, with loose footing, a steep fall to the river and lots of tumbling football-sized rocks. Beyond the slide, the trail drops to the single locked hut at Lakep, then climbs a bit to Khambachen, a Tibetan settlement of about a dozen houses at 4040 metres.

Day 13: Acclimatisation day in Khambachen

It's again time to stop and acclimatise. There are views of the high peaks near Kanchenjunga: Khabur, Phole, Nango Ma and the tip of Jannu. Climb a ridge above the village for more views, or take a day hike to the Jannu base camp. You might come across blue sheep grazing in the valley or on the slopes above.

Day 14: Khambachen to Lhonak

The trail climbs gradually through open rocky fields to Ramtang at 4240 metres, then across moraines northwest of the Kanchenjunga Glacier. Lhonak, at 4790 metres, is near a dry lake bed on an open sandy plain; water is scarce here. There are no houses, but you can camp among the large boulders here to get out of the wind. Terrific mountain views abound in all directions.

Day 15: Lhonak to Pang Pema

You cannot see the main Kanchenjunga peak from Lhonak; for a view of this peak you must go on to the base camp at Pang Pema at 5140 metres. You could make a day trip from Lhonak, but clouds often obscure the peak after about 9 am, and you could find yourself in Pang Pema without a view. It's really worth camping in Pang Pema in hopes of a cloudless vista just before sunset or in the early morning.

From Lhonak, the trail ascends gradually across the plain, then gets a bit steeper as it follows the moraine. The views are spectacular, but you cannot see Kanchenjunga or Wedge Peak until you almost reach Pang Pema. The spectacular main peak of Kanchenjunga, and a panorama of other peaks that make up one of the largest mountain masses in the world, tower over the single roofless hut at Pang Pema.

Day 16: Pang Pema to Khambachen

Take a morning hike up the ridge north of Pang Pema. A climb of 200 to 300 metres provides a vantage point with views of Kanchenjunga, Wedge Peak, the Twins, Pyramid Peak and Tent Peak.

As usual, the descent goes faster, so you can easily get back to Khambachen in a single day.

Day 17: Khambachen to Ghunsa

Day 18: Ghunsa to Amjilassa

Day 19: Amjilassa to Chirwa

Descend to Helok. If you are headed for the south side of Kanchenjunga, start climbing the stone stairs in Helok to the ridge. A local guide will probably save you a lot of energy on this route, because the trails here are used primarily by woodcutters and herders, not by trekkers.

The Mandala map shows a trail from Helok up the Simbua Khola towards Tseram. This trail, where it exists at all, is strictly for monkeys. There is a way through, but it is not a trail, it's a steep, slippery climb through thick bamboo forests up the side of the Deorali Danda. I came down this once; it was great fun, but it's not a sensible route. Everyone seems to agree that it's more practical to take an extra day and follow the woodcutters trail up the ridge from Helok to Yamphudin, then climb to the Lamite Bhanjyang from the south and re-enter the Simbua Valley.

If your destination is Taplejung, retrace your steps through the lower part of Helok and meander back down the Tamur Kosi to Chirwa.

Day 20: Chirwa to Linkhim

It's a straight shot down the Tamur Kosi to Taplejung. You can avoid the steep climb from Doban by contouring up the side of the valley. From Chirwa, start uphill, passing through Diwa village. Climb over a landslide and keep going up steeply, staying above Tawa. The trail drops into a large side canyon, then climbs back to the ridge before reaching Linkhim.

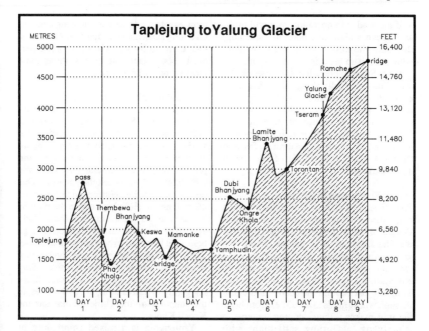

Taplejung to Yalung Glacier

Day 21: Linkhim to Suketar
Trek in and out of side canyons through the small Limbu villages of Helate, Pumbur and Phurbu to a ridge overlooking a monstrous slide area. Climb above the slide area to the Sherpa villages of Bung Kulung and Lakchun and you can get directly to the airport without going in to Taplejung.

Day 22: Fly to Kathmandu

SOUTH KANCHENJUNGA BASE CAMP
There are lots of ways to make this trek, but the way I have described here is the easiest – if you can arrange a flight in to Taplejung. Take a look at the route profile for this trek; there is an incredible amount climbing of up and down. When I trekked this route, I calculated that we climbed – and descended – more than 15,000 metres during two weeks of walking. Be sure you are ready for this kind of effort before you set out; there are no escape routes if you get sick, tired or bored.

If you cannot get a flight to Taplejung, consider driving to Phidim, two days walk to the south. The road is complete to this point and there is a bus or truck service from Ilam. From Phidim, you can bypass Taplejung and head over some ridges to the Kabeli Khola and Yamphudin. Be sure that Phidim is included on your trekking permit if you plan to use this option.

Day 1: Taplejung to Thembewa
A flight to Taplejung takes a half-hour from Biratnagar and 1½ hours from Kathmandu. To avoid clouds and wind, RNAC schedules its Taplejung flights for early morning, so you can probably accomplish a few hours of walking on the day you fly in. The airport is on the top of a ridge in Suketar village, far above Taplejung. Unless you need to confirm a flight back to Kathmandu or load up on supplies, it's not worth the long walk into Taplejung and the tedious steep climb back up to Suketar.

If the road is in operation, you will probably spend a night in a hotel in Taplejung, then start the trek to the South base camp with a climb up the ridge to the airport.

From Suketar, elevation 2300 metres, the trail climbs gradually along a rhododendron-covered ridge. The trail crosses the ridge and contours past the Deorali Khola and four more streams to a pass at 2570 metres. Descend through forests to Lali Kharka, two houses at 2220 metres, then through fields to the substantial Limbu village of Thembewa at 1880 metres.

Day 2: Thembewa to Keswa

From Thembewa, the trail ascends a bit to a ridge, then drops steeply through Shimu and Pokara villages to a suspension bridge across the Pha Khola at 1430 metres. There is a good swimming hole here and a possible campsite near the river. Climb steeply to Khunjari, a Limbu village at 1700 metres. Turn left just beyond the school and climb through wheat fields into a saddle. From here, the trail makes a long, looping traverse to Bhanjyang, a Gurung settlement with several bhattis, on a pass at 2120 metres. From Bhanjyang there are views of Kanchenjunga and Kyabru.

The trek has now entered the Kabeli Khola Valley, but you will spend the next two days climbing up and down, in and out of ravines and over ridges, only to end up in Yamphudin at the bottom of the valley. Turn left from Bhanjyang and head north just below the top of the ridge, descending to the scattered village of Keswa at 1960 metres.

Day 3: Keswa to Mamanke

Pass below waterfalls and cross several streams and a landslide to reach the village of Phun Phun, which is shown on some maps with the fanciful spelling *Fun Fun*. Cross a saddle, with a stately pipal tree offering a rest in the shade, and traverse to Yangpang, then head generally upwards through forests past a large waterfall. Descend through a series of side valleys to two shops on a ridge at 1850 metres, then drop a bit to Phonpe village at 1780 metres. Descend steeply through rice terraces into a side canyon, crossing a stream on a long suspension bridge at 1540 metres, then climb to back to Mamanke, a prosperous Limbu village with bhattis, shops and a large school at 1810 metres.

Day 4: Mamanke to Yamphudin

Climb to a ridge and then descend gradually to the Tenguwa Khola. Forego the decrepit bridge; cross the stream by jumping from stone to stone. Switchback steeply up to another ridge marked by a chorten and prayer flags, then descend across rubble and rockslides and cross another stream. This portion of the valley is steep, and portions of the trail are on cliffs high above the river as it makes its way down to the Kabeli Khola at 1640 metres. There is a lot of flood damage here, so it becomes a rock-hopping exercise, over boulders, tree roots and intersecting stream channels as you head upstream. Stay on the west side of the Kabeli Khola, climbing gently to Yamphudin, at 1690 metres, at the junction of the Omje Khola and the Kabeli Khola.

Yamphudin is a mixed community of Sherpas, Limbus, Rais and Gurungs. Among the corn and rice fields of the village there are a police post, a school, and some shops with minimal supplies. The 1989 monsoon produced floods that washed away portions of the village and many of its fields. A goat trail leads from Yamphudin up the ridge to the east, to Helok and the Tamur Kosi Valley.

Day 5: Yamphudin to Omje Khola

Beyond Yamphudin, you should plan to carry your own food and shelter. There are no tea shops or hotels beyond here, not even the local style ones that exist up to this point.

Cross the Omje Khola on a couple of bamboo poles and follow the Kabeli Khola upstream for a short distance, ignoring the suspension bridge. After you pass behind a ridge out of sight of Yamphudin, cross a small stream and take a trail that heads straight uphill. Zigzag up through fields of corn and barley to Darachuk, and keep climbing past meadows to Dubi Bhanjyang, a col (pass) at 2540 metres. Descend through ferns and big trees to the Omje Khola at 2340 metres and follow the stream uphill for a short distance. Cross the stream on a log bridge, and go a bit further upstream to a camp site.

It's a bit depressing to make the long climb over the Dubi Bhanjyang only to end up on the banks of the same stream that you camped beside last night. Unfortunately, there is no trail that follows the stream bed; besides, the Nepalese do not fret about steep trails as much as we do. This is a pretty short day, but the next part of the trek is steep and has few camp sites. If you are a small party you might keep going on to Chitre, but there isn't space there for a large camp.

Day 6: Omje Khola to Torontan

From the stream, the trail makes a steep climb through bamboo to a kharka at Chitre (2920 metres) and continues up to a notch. After a short descent, the ascent is less strenuous to a clearing, and then the trail passes through a forest of pines and rhododendrons to a pond at Lamite Bhanjyang, 3410 metres elevation. There is a water shortage here in the spring, otherwise it is a good place to camp. On a clear day this ridge provides views of Jannu and of the Taplejung road far to the south.

From the ridge, you can see a trail across a huge landslide scar; a better route is to stay on the ridge and follow it east along its top until you are well beyond the landslide, then follow a steep set of switchbacks leading downhill. Once the initial steep descent is finished, the trail becomes more gentle. The trail is generally level and wide, though there are some sharp drops along the way. It passes through damp, orchid-filled forests, crossing streams and isolated clearings used by herders and woodcutters.

The trail emerges into the open just above the Simbua Khola. A 1987 flood washed away large parts of the trail. Stay above the white silty river and follow it upstream, on a series of ascents and descents, to a temporary bridge built of stones and logs. There are campsites near the river, and also in a clear-

ing beyond Torontan, which is a few caves at 2990 metres.

Day 7: Torontan to Tseram

The hike starts in forests of several varieties of rhododendron, then crosses landslides to Tsento Kang, a goth at 3360 metres. The deeply forested valley is dotted with clearings, meadows and streams as it rises to another goth at Watha.

An hour beyond is a Buddhist shrine decorated with rock cairns, prayer flags and iron three-pronged trisuls. The shrine is in a cave that has a streak of dark stone along it, which is thought to be the image of a snake. This shrine marks the boundary of a sacred part of the valley, beyond which the killing of animals is prohibited. Peaks begin to appear in the distance as you climb further. There is a short stretch along the gravel bottom of the stream bed, then a climb to Tseram, a large, flat meadow with a single house at 3870 metres. The settlements in this valley are goths used by yak and cow herders from Ghunsa who cross the Mirgin La to graze their animals during the summer.

Day 8: Tseram to Ramche

Climb through forests to a slide area; near here is the junction of the trail to the Mirgin La, but the trail is hard to find. Stumble across a stream on a loose, rocky path and climb to some mani walls and a stone house near the tree line at 4040 metres. The peaks of Rathong and Kabru loom at the head of the valley; it's hard to believe they are both less than 6700 metres high. The trail climbs onto the moraine at the foot of the Yalung Glacier. The valley opens up as you approach Yalung, a pasture full of yaks at 4260 metres.

Climb alongside the moraine through scrub junipers up a stream to a lake at Lapsang, 4430 metres. Here you can see the start of the route to the Lapsang La headed off over the moraines in a valley to the north. Keep climbing to another lake and a big meadow at Ramche, elevation 4620 metres. There are two well-built stone houses here; one of them thinks it is a hotel, but the owner spends so much time away that it rarely fulfils its ambitions. The view is dominated by the spectacular Rathong Peak, elevation 6678 metres, situated on the Nepal/Sikkim border to the east. Herds of blue sheep live on the cliffs above.

Day 9: Day Trip to Yalung Glacier

Make a day trip to the Yalung Glacier. Follow a stream alongside the moraine for a long distance, then bear right to climb onto the moraine itself. From a chorten at about 4800 metres elevation there is a fine view of the Kanchenjunga south face. A short distance beyond the chorten is a view of Jannu. This is a good place to turn around. To go further, you must climb down the rough moraine onto the Yalung Glacier and pick your way through the boulder-strewn glacier towards Kanchenjunga. It's a one or two day project to reach the base camp itself.

Day 10: Ramche to Tseram

Day 11: Tseram to Lamite Bhanjyang

Day 12: Lamite Bhanjyang to Yamphudin

Day 13: Yamphudin to Phonpe

Day 14: Phonpe to Khunjari

Day 15: Khunjari to Suketar

There is a single tea shop at the airport that has one or two rooms for rent. Otherwise camp near the airfield and hope for clear weather for the flight in the morning. The hotel specialises in tongba, so you will have something to amuse you if the plane does not come.

Day 16: Fly to Kathmandu

Fly to Biratnagar or, if you are lucky, directly to Kathmandu.

North Side to South Side

There are two routes between Ghunsa and the Simbua Khola. The higher Lapsang La, elevation 5110 metres, is often snow-covered and may be difficult and dangerous for both trekkers and porters. This is a very remote area where help is a long way off, and evacuation is almost impossible. You will need to make a choice whether to cross the Lapsang La, or the lower and safer Mirgin La, or retreat down the Tamur Kosi Valley. Either of the high routes takes three days, with high camps on either side of the pass. The most critical factor on the high passes is snow. There is no regular traffic on these routes; if there is snow, you will have to break the trail yourself without any rock cairns or other landmarks to guide you.

The Mirgin La route actually crosses five passes: the Tamo La, 3900 metres; an unnamed, 4115 metre high pass; the Mirgin La, 4663 metres; Sinion La, 4660 metres; and a final, unnamed pass of 4724 metres elevation. It then makes a long, steep 1000 metre descent to the Simbua Khola. The route enters the Simbua Khola Valley above Tseram, at about 3900 metres, and you can probably make it on to Ramche the same day.

The Lapsang La route starts at Ghunsa and climbs across the foot of the Yamatari Glacier to a goth at Lumga Sampa. Cross the Lapsang La and make your way down through the large boulders of a moraine to a camp below the glacier. Descend further into the valley and meet the Simbua Khola trail at Lapsang, elevation 4430 metres. Then it's a short distance up the valley to Ramche at 4620 metres.

Western Nepal

Many people describe western Nepal as 'unexplored', but Westerners have a bad habit of assuming that what is unknown to them is unknown to everyone. Western Nepal has a large population of both Hindus and Buddhists, and the countryside is crisscrossed by trails in all directions. It is remote and unknown from the Western viewpoint because of its relative inaccessibility and its distance from Kathmandu. Regular flights to Jumla and several other airstrips in the west reduce this remoteness somewhat, but add considerably to the cost and to the logistic problems.

Another factor that discourages trekkers in western Nepal is that many of the culturally and scenically exotic regions are off-limits to foreigners. Many of the trails in the west continue to the northern side of the Himalayan ranges of Nampa, Saipal and Kanjiroba, making it easy for trekkers to zip up trails along river valleys and into Tibet – a practice that both the Nepalese and Chinese would like to discourage. Shey Gompa, to the north of Phoksumdo Lake, is closed. Humla to the north-west of Jumla is a restricted area, as is the Mugu Karnali Valley north of Mugu village.

The history and anthropology of western Nepal is complex and fascinating. The region is predominantly Hindu. Tibetans make up only a small part of the population, yet they have had a significant influence on the area through trading. Most of the homes are Tibetan style, their flat roofs covered with packed earth. They are well suited to the semiarid conditions of the region behind Dhaulagiri. In many villages the houses are packed closely together one atop another, climbing up the hillside and sharing common roofs. There are few stairs inside the dwellings. Instead, people climb from one level to another on carved log ladders outside the house. This is the only place in Nepal where Hindus live in such obviously Tibetan-style houses.

Cultural roots extend north into Tibet and west to Kumaon in India. Until Jumla was conquered by the army of Bahadur Shah in 1788, the people of western Nepal had very little reliance on Kathmandu. The Chhetris of western Nepal are categorised into three groups: Thakuris, who are the aristocracy; normal Chhetris as found throughout Nepal; and *Matwali* Chhetris, 'those who drink liquor'. The status of Matwali Chhetris is fascinating because many Tibetan immigrants long ago masqueraded as Chhetris. For many generations they have evolved their own form of religion that is a peculiar combination of Hinduism and Buddhism.

INFORMATION
Maps
Army Map service sheets 44-11 *Jumla*, 44-12 *Mustang* and 44-16 *Pokhara*, and Mandala Maps *Jomsom to Jumla & Surkhet*, *Dhaulagiri Himal* and *Api, Nampa & Saipal* cover western Nepal.

Elevations are difficult to confirm in this region. All the available maps were derived from the Survey of India maps which had little ground control in remote western Nepal. Most elevations I have indicated are based on altimeter readings related to the known elevations of Jumla and Dolpo airports, and to the Royal Geographical Society's *Kanjiroba Himal* map of 1967.

GETTING THERE & AWAY
Trailheads
Surkhet A night bus service goes to Surkhet (renamed Birendranagar), a roadhead in the hills north of Nepalgunj. It costs Rs 180 for the 600 km, 15 hour trip. It takes eight or nine days to walk from Surkhet to Jumla with porters, and there are no trekkers' hotels along the way. Local traders in Jumla bring most of their goods by horse caravan from Surkhet.

Sallyan This roadhead south of Chaurjhari is a four to five day walk from Dunai. There is no direct bus service from Kathmandu. Take a direct bus to Tulsipur or Nepalgunj, then a local bus to Sallyan. Porters from Sallyan and other villages in this region will probably refuse to go beyond Dunai.

Pokhara The trek from Pokhara to Dunai takes 13 days, or you can make a long trek from Pokhara all the way to Jumla via Dolpo.

Airports
Jumla There is a weekly flight from Kathmandu to Jumla, but seats are almost impossible to get. RNAC accepts reservations only 15 days before the flight and, the night before reservations are released, Jumli people camp in front of the RNAC domestic office to be first in line to get seats. The most reliable way to get to Jumla is to fly via Nepalgunj, or to try the new once weekly flight from Pokhara to Jumla.

Dolpo Dolpo Airport is at Juphal village, on a hill about 3 hours walk from Dunai. There are regular scheduled flights and also lots of charter flights that carry food into the region. Flying in is difficult because of heavy passenger and cargo traffic, but flying out is often easy, even without advance planning, because the cargo charters carry passengers on the return trip. There is no direct service from Kathmandu to Dolpo. All Dolpo flights originate in Nepalgunj except for a weekly Pokhara to Dolpo flight.

Chaurjhari This place is three days south of Dunai on the Bheri River. A good new trail from Chaurjhari to Dunai involves almost no climbing. It is an alternative to Dolpo Airport when winds or snow delay flights.

Nepalgunj This town is in the Terai near the Indian border. RNAC operates a western Nepal hub from here and has frequent flights to Jumla, Dolpo and many other destinations (some fascinating and others dreary) in western Nepal. The daily 1½ hour Nepalgunj flight is reasonably reliable because it operates in the afternoons when there is less demand for aeroplanes. Night buses from Kathmandu to Nepalgunj cost Rs 150 for the 16 hour, 540 km trip. Day buses are cheaper (Rs 120), but take longer.

Nepalgunj is not an exciting place, but because it is the largest city in a region that has a considerable number of development projects, it boasts two moderately good hotels. The *Sneha* and the *Batika* are both on the main road, 3 km from the main bazaar, 3 km from the Indian border and about 10 km from the airport. Costs are Rs 300 to Rs 350 a double room. There are cheaper hotels in the main bazaar, Birendra Chok. The *Shanti Shakya, Narayani, Karnali* and *Punam Guest House* all provide local-style accommodation. Food everywhere is basic dhal bhaat.

Jumla and Dolpo flights are scheduled at dawn. Transport from Nepalgunj to the airport is difficult to arrange, so be sure you have a firm commitment the night before. There are horse drawn tongas, bicycle rickshaws and a few motorised rickshaws in Nepalgunj. Allow an hour for the trip to the airport by tonga or rickshaw, and half that by motorised rickshaw.

Beware of baggage charges on Jumla and Dolpo flights. The allowance is 15 kg. The rate for excess baggage from Nepalgunj to Jumla is Rs 24 per kg. Many cargo charter flights are operated by businesspeople sending rice and other goods, so if you are having trouble sending all your gear, you may be able to freight it on one of these flights.

Airfares
	one way
Kathmandu to Jumla	US$127
Kathmandu to Nepalgunj	US$99
Nepalgunj to Jumla	US$44
Nepalgunj to Dolpo	US$77
Pokhara to Dolpo	US$87
Pokhara to Jumla	US$99

Jumla
The flight from Nepalgunj to Jumla takes 35 minutes, climbing from the plains over many

sets of hills, into the huge Tila Valley. Jumla Airport is one of the best of Nepal's remote airstrips – 900 metres long and an easy approach – so flights operate more regularly than at places such as Lukla. Upon arrival at Jumla Airport you must register with the police. An official sits in the security check booth and writes down the names of all passengers, both Nepalese and foreign, who arrive by air.

Jumla Bazaar is a 10 minute walk from the airport. There are shops, pharmacies, a bank, camps for both army and police, and a few restaurants along the stone paved main street. Accommodation is available at the *Rara Hotel* near the airport and also at the *Himalaya Trekking Hotel* in the western part of the bazaar, near the police post. Jumla has electricity, and one house sports a television satellite dish. The hotels are basic, food is limited to dhal bhaat and potatoes, and many goods are in short supply or are totally unavailable. There is a very limited supply of canned goods, jam and other packaged items, but you probably will not find speciality foods such as muesli.

Jumla, on the banks of the Tila River at 2370 metres, is one of the highest rice growing areas in the world. The entire Tila Valley is covered with paddy fields growing a unique red rice that is more tasty than white rice, but is scorned by most local people. Merchants fly white rice to Jumla and then transport it to more remote regions using trains of horses, mules, sheep and goats. The goat 'trucks' of western Nepal are fascinating. Traders equip herds of 100 or more sheep and goats with tiny woollen panniers that carry 10 kg of rice, then herd the animals through the countryside devouring grass as they travel. Hundreds of kg of rice and sugar are delivered throughout western Nepal in this manner.

The people in this region speak their own version of Nepali. When local people speak among themselves, Kathmandu Nepalese can barely understand them. They employ peculiar mannerisms in their speech. One porter told me that the hike to the next village was an easy one by saying that the trail was *sasto*, which translates as 'inexpensive'. He also said that one trail was *ek bhaat* shorter than another; this translates as 'one rice' or 'one meal' – a charming way to say half a day.

Despite the extensive rice cultivation, there is a chronic food shortage in this region. Most of the Nepalgunj to Jumla shuttle flights are cargo flights that carry rice and other staples, so it is difficult to purchase enough food for a trek in Jumla Bazaar. It is better to carry all your food from Kathmandu – if you can get it onto the plane.

There are a few porters available in Jumla, but they are expensive, they don't speak English, and they are not particularly eager to leave their homes. That being said, I was lucky enough in Jumla to hire two teams of excellent porters who, unlike porters in other parts of Nepal, were willing to carry loads long distances each day.

The people throughout the region are Thakuris, a Chhetri caste that has the highest social, political and ritual status. Westerners, who are considered low caste by high caste Hindus, are traditionally not welcome in Thakuri homes. For this reason hotels are scarce and cater mainly to locals. Consequently, do not plan a trek in the Jumla region as a tea house trek.

JUMLA TO RARA LAKE

Rara Lake (2980 metres) is the focal point of Lake Rara National Park and is a major destination for treks in western Nepal. The route is very much 'off the beaten track' and affords glimpses of cultures and scenery very different from that in the rest of Nepal. Rara is a clear, high altitude lake ringed with pine, spruce and juniper forests and snow-capped Himalayan peaks. In winter there is often snow on the ridges surrounding the lake. Nobody lives at the lake because the government resettled all the people of Rara and Chapra villages when the area was declared a national park.

The trek to Rara is somewhat strenuous and tends to be expensive because both food and labour are scarce and overpriced in this part of Nepal. If you are looking for wilder-

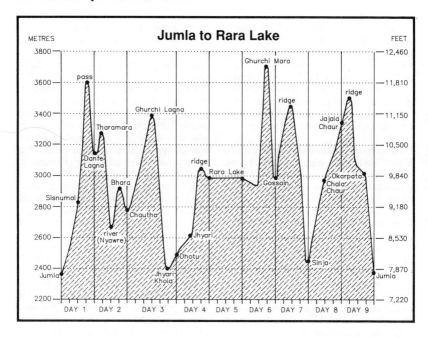

Jumla to Rara Lake

METRES / FEET

3800 — 12,460
3600 — 11,810 — pass
3400 — 11,150 — Ghurchi Lagna / Ghurchi Mara / ridge
3200 — 10,500 — Tharamara
3000 — 9,840 — Danfe Lagna / Bhara / ridge / Rara Lake / ridge / Jajala Chaur / Okarpata Chala Chaur
2800 — 9,180 — Sisnumal / Chautha / Gossain
2600 — 8,530 — river (Nyawre) / Jhyari / Dhotu
2400 — 7,870 — Jumla / Jhyari Khola / Sinja / Jumla
2200 — 7,220

DAY 1 DAY 2 DAY 3 DAY 4 DAY 5 DAY 6 DAY 7 DAY 8 DAY 9

ness solitude, and can overcome the logistical complications of the region, this trek is a good choice.

Day 1: Jumla to Danphe Lagna

There are two routes to Danphe Lagna. If there is snow, take the longer, lower route.

High Route Follow the main street of Jumla north up the river valley past the red-roofed hospital. The wide, level trail leads past college buildings to a settlement known as Campus. As the trail slowly gains elevation it passes a collection of very Western houses. They are the residences of teachers and administrators of the Karnali Technical Institute, a vocational school at Ghumurti, a short distance above. The school is a collection of more than 40 buildings at 2550 metres. It is operated by the United Mission to Nepal and has about 150 students studying agriculture, engineering and health.

After a long climb past the school, the trail passes through Sisnamul, at 2830 metres then enters a forest of big trees that soon gives way to meadows. Chere, at 2060 metres, is a large horse and sheep pasture with a few open herders' huts. Beyond Chere the trail becomes steeper and climbs through meadows on a route that is impassible in heavy snow. From the pass at 3600 metres there are views of Patrasi Himal (6860 metres) and Jagdula Himal (5785 metres) to the east. The trail descends gently in forests of spruce, birch and rhododendron to Danphe Lagna at 3130 metres. A single house stands in an attractive meadow beside a clear stream. It is usually possible to spot the Danphe (or Impeyan) pheasant, the colourful national bird of Nepal, in the nearby forests.

Low Route From Jumla the lower trail to Rara follows the north bank of the Tila River,

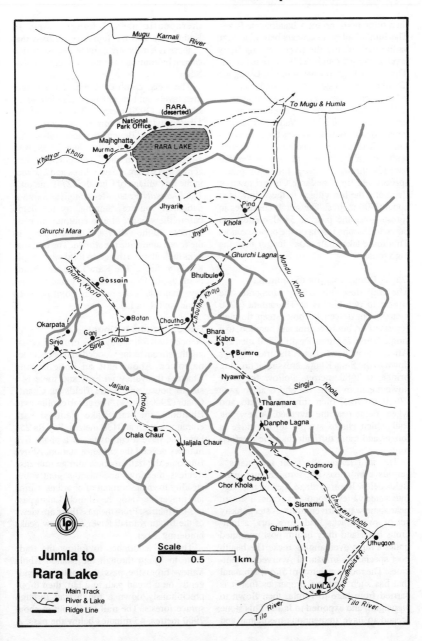

Jumla to Rara Lake

Scale

0   0.5   1km.

- - - - Main Track

River & Lake

Ridge Line

then turns north up the Chaudhabise River. The Jumla Valley disappears behind a ridge as the trail follows the river, keeping fairly level, passing through fields and pine forests. The first village on the route is Uthugaon (2530 metres). A good camp site is near the school, across the river from the village.

From Uthugaon the trail begins an ascent up the Ghurseni Khola Valley, beginning gently, but becoming steep as the climb continues. The canyon becomes very narrow with vertical cliffs on both sides as the trail ascends through a deep forest of pines, spruces and firs. The large Chhetri town of Padmora, the last village in the valley, is at about 2900 metres. The climb continues in forests over the pass at 3400 metres and down to Danphe Lagna on the opposite side. This route takes half a day longer than the high route.

Day 2: Danphe Lagna to Chautha

The trail descends gently alongside the stream to two bhattis at Tharamara (3280 metres). The descent becomes steep, through forests of fir, birch, walnut and bamboo, to a single house at Hiran Duski (2840 metres). After a short level stretch the trail zigzags down to the Sinja Khola, crossing it on a log bridge at 2680 metres. Follow the river downstream to some tea shops at Nyawre (2660 metres), then through potato and wheat fields near the riverbed. A new, big trail which climbs steeply up the ridge is longer and more difficult than the riverbed route.

The trail leaves the river and starts a serious climb, passing through marijuana fields below Bumra village, then over a ridge into a side valley, dropping to cross a stream near some water driven mills. A steep, nasty set of switchbacks leads to Kabra, a ludicrous hotel and dirty health post crammed under a huge overhanging rock. The health post specialises in natural Ayurvedic medicines. The rock is a source of *Silaji*, a mineral that has such amazing properties that it is carried from here to Jumla, then flown to Nepalgunj and exported to India. This stone is said to have tremendous medicinal and therapeutic uses. I bought some in Kathmandu and the literature claimed that '...there is hardly any curable disease which cannot be controlled or cured with the aid of Silaji'.

The steep climb continues for a while, then levels out before Bhara, also known as Bhadgaon (2920 metres). This is a classic Tibetan style village surrounded by splendid fields of wheat. Beyond this large village the trail turns into a big valley then descends to a tributary stream, the Chautha Khola. Just across this stream are two shops and a school in the tiny village of Chautha (2770 metres). The *Bhandari Hotel* offers rough accommodation. If you are camping, try the fields before the village, or else continue an hour or more up the valley and make a camp in the forest alongside the stream. The trail that exits the village to the south follows the Sinja Khola to Sinja. The Rara Lake trail heads north up the Chautha Khola. Local folklore says that this is the halfway point between Jumla and Rara Lake.

Day 3: Chautha to Dhotu

A rocky trail follows the stream uphill, crossing the stream as the wooded valley becomes narrower. About half an hour beyond Chautha the valley widens, and there is a single house and some fields at Chante Chaur (2940 metres). The climb continues to Bhulbule, the Rara Lake National Park entrance station at 3130 metres. Pay Rs 250 here and have a cup of tea at a bhatti five minutes beyond the entrance station. Above Bhulbule the trail emerges into an immense treeless meadow, and climbs gently but steadily to an assortment of chortens, cairns and prayer flags atop the Ghurchi Lagna pass at 3450 metres. From the pass there are views of the Mugu Karnali River and snow peaks bordering Tibet.

The trail continues to follow the trade route to Mugu through the Mandu Khola Valley. From the pass the route descends gently on a broad path to a hut, then drops precipitously down a rough trail through spruce forests. The trail levels out at about 2900 metres, 45 minutes below the pass. A trail junction is here. Perhaps it is still marked with a wooden post with 'Rara' painted in red. The inconspicuous trail to the left is a new direct route to Rara Lake. The broad trail that goes straight leads to the village of Pina (2400 metres),and then on to Mugu. The new trail stays more or less level through pine forests, then descends to the Jhyari Khola at 2400 metres. Another stretch of easy walking leads to the small settlement of Dhotu, an army camp and helipad.

Day 4: Dhotu to Rara Lake
Cross a stream and make a steep climb to the squalid Thakur village of Jhyari at 2630 metres, in a picturesque grove of giant cedars. Continue climbing through forests to a huge meadow atop a 3050 metre high ridge with a great view of Rara Lake. It is a short descent from here to the lake. There are no camping spots along the southern shore. The national park headquarters and camp ground are on the northern side of the lake. It will take 2 hours or more to walk around the lake to the camp ground. The ban on the use of firewood is strictly enforced, so cook on kerosene stoves.

Day 5: At Rara Lake
Rara Lake (3062 metres) is the largest lake in Nepal. It is almost 13 km around the lake, and a day devoted to making this circuit is well spent. Designated a national park in 1975, the region offers a remoteness and wilderness experience unlike any other in Nepal. There are a few park wardens' houses, and the remnants of the now deserted villages of Rara and Chapra on the northern side of the lake, but otherwise it is an isolated region where birds, flowers and wildlife thrive. Among the mammals in the region are Himalayan bear, Himalayan tahr, serow, goral, musk deer, red panda and both rhesus and langur monkeys. The 170 metre deep lake has otters and fish and is an important resting place for migrating water fowl.

Day 6: Rara Lake to Gossain
Although you can return to Jumla via the same route, it is more rewarding to make a

circuit via a different trail. From the bridge at the western end of Rara Lake the trail follows the Khatyar Khola (called the Nisa Khola in its upper reaches) to a small hotel in the settlement of Majhghatta, about 15 minutes from the bridge. A trail ascends from here to the village of Murma. To return to Jumla take a lower trail that descends gradually to the river, cross the river on a log bridge, and then cross another stream beside a decrepit mill that grinds away merrily. A small trail leads straight up the hill, climbing first through an area reforested with pine, then through spruce and rhododendron forests.

The ascent gets less steep through forests of pine and birch, then across meadows to a ridge at 3660 metres. There are views of Rara Lake far below as the trail skirts the head of a huge valley to the crest of the Ghurchi Mara at 3710 metres. If the weather is clear, there is an excellent view of the western Himalaya from the top of this ridge. The trail drops into the Ghatta Khola Valley, then heads towards Gossain, which the local people call 'the poster', referring to the police post there. An inconspicuous trail junction is at 3000 metres, about an hour below the pass, just before the main trail reaches the Ghatta Khola. This is yet another route to Sinja.

Day 7: Gossain to Sinja
There are two choices.

The Long Way This route heads down the Gatte Khola Valley, then follows the Sinja Khola downstream to the village of Sinja. There are several excellent camping places along the Ghatta Khola, both above and below Gossain. After working your way down the Ghatta Khola past Botan you will meet the Sinja Khola. It is a short walk down the fertile valley, on a newly renovated trail, through a very heavily populated region to Sinja itself.

The Short Steep Way Stay high on the side of the treeless Ghatta Khola Valley. From above, the police 'poster' at Gossain looks like a Hollywood movie producer's image of the classic American western ranch in a beautiful grassy vale. The trail descends to a stream, then climbs a big gully to a ridge at 3450 metres. It's easy to get lost between here and Sinja, so you'll be much better off with a local guide, if you can find one. From the ridge, follow the left trail and stay as high as possible on the ridge, looping in and out of side valleys and descending gradually to the village of Okarpata at 3070 metres. This is a big village of whitewashed, flat-roofed houses, with huge fields of wheat and barley and extensive apple orchards. The trail descends to a stream and then goes steeply down the ridge on a rough rocky trail to the Brahmin and Chhetri village of Sinja, on the banks of the Sinja Khola at 2440 metres.

From the 12th to 14th centuries, western Nepal was ruled by a Malla Dynasty that was different from the Malla rulers in Kathmandu. Sinja was the capital of the Malla kingdom. The ruins of the palace can be seen across the river. The large temple at the top of a promontory is the Bhagwati Than, a temple dedicated to Bhagwati, the goddess of justice who rides atop a tiger. The big buildings across the river from the village are government offices and a school.

Day 8: Sinja to Jaljala Chaur

It is very difficult to reach Jumla in a single day from Sinja, so it's best to break the trek with a night in the high meadows near the ridge. From Sinja, the trail crosses the Sinja Khola on a wooden cantilever bridge, then begins a long trip up the Jaljala Khola. After passing a few small villages and the trail to the temple, the trail crosses back and forth across the river on a series of quaint log bridges. Most of the trek is through forests of pine, birch and oak, though there are a few scattered houses and fields of barley and corn. From Chala Chaur, a meadow with a few herders' huts at 3270 metres, the trail makes a steep climb to Jaljala Chaur, a gigantic meadow full of horses at 3270 metres.

Day 9: Jaljala Chaur to Jumla

Keep climbing through forests to yet another meadow, just below the ridge at 3510 metres,

then descend to a few houses at Chor Khola (3090 metres). Cross a stream and contour across the head of the valley, staying high, eventually crossing another ridge to rejoin the upward 'high route' trail at Chere (3010 metres). The final descent to Jumla is the reverse of Day 1, through Sisnamul, past the school at Ghumurti, then from Campus village to Jumla Bazaar.

JUMLA TO DOLPO

Dolpo is the most remote and least developed district in Nepal. Although a few anthropologists and geographers hadexplored the region, the entire district was closed to trekkers until 1989 when the southern part of Dolpo was opened to organised trekking groups. In 1990 individual trekkers were allowed into the region if they obtained a special US$10 per week trekking permits and did a bit of a bureaucratic run-around. There are no tea houses along the route to Dolpo. I met a couple of trekkers who had trekked here and bought food in villages, but they had a rough time. You would be far better off in Dolpo with a fully equipped trek.

You can reach Dolpo from Jumla (6 days), Dhorpatan (10 to 12 days), Surkhet (9 days), Sallyan (5 days) and Jomsom (11 days, but not allowed). The Dolpo Airport is at Juphal, half a day from the district headquarters in Dunai. Another airstrip is in Chaurjhari, 4 days from Dunai.

Peter Matthiesen's *The Snow Leopard* and Snellgrove's *Himalayan Pilgrimage* have contributed to the mystique and attraction of Dolpo. Both writers visited Shey Gompa to the north of Phoksumdo Lake. As of 1990, Shey is still closed to foreigners. One story cites the reason for closure as the large-scale theft of statues from monasteries several years ago. It is possible to visit Tibetan-style 'inner Dolpo' villages in Tarap and at Phoksumdo Lake, but most of the southern part of Dolpo is a region of Hindu influence.

This section describes the trek from Jumla to Dunai, side trips to Phoksumdo Lake and Tarap, and an alternate high route over the Kagmara La to the Dolpo district. There's

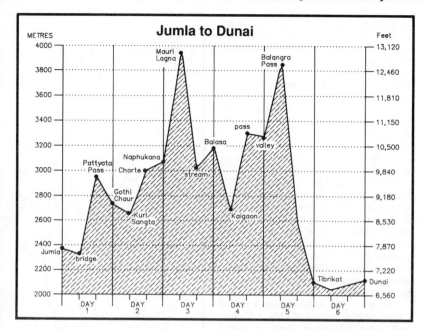

Jumla to Dunai

também an outline of a trek from Pokhara to Dolpo. All these trips could be combined into one long trek of 25 to 30 days, from Pokhara to Jumla via Dolpo.

Day 1: Jumla to Gothi Chaur

It's best to fly into Jumla and then spend the rest of the day hiring porters, buying last minute provisions and sorting loads. If you fly into Jumla and start walking the same day, you will probably have to alter the stopping places I have suggested, because it takes a full day to reach Gothi Chaur.

From Jumla (2370 metres) the trail leads past the airport to the eastern end of the runway, past several water-driven mills, then drops to the confluence of the Tila Khola and the Juwa Nadi at 2330 metres. Cross both rivers on cantilever bridges that look like they are held together by giant clothes pegs. A major logging operation is on the upper reaches of the Juwa Nadi. Loggers upstream dump logs into the river. They float down to

this point where they are snared and cut into timbers for use in Jumla and neighbouring villages. Unlike most rivers in Nepal, which are filled with silt, the Tila and the Juwa are clear because they are not glacier fed.

The trail climbs gently through a fertile valley of rice terraces along the southern side of the Tila to Depal Gaon. It crisscrosses irrigation canals to Jharjwala, then leaves the Tila Khola and climbs a ridge to the small villages of Bhajkati, Dugri Lagnu and finally Dochal Ghara at 2530 metres. Do not follow the steep trail that leads uphill here. Instead, take the lower trail that follows a stream to a meadow at 2830 metres.

Beyond the meadow the trail climbs to a rock cairn at Pattyata pass (2830 metres), then descends into a magnificent alpine amphitheatre that looks totally uninhabited from this point. Hidden behind a ridge is a huge government sheep breeding research project, but there are no villages in this isolated valley. The trail descends past the project buildings at Gothi Chaur, to a stream at the bottom of the valley. Some 13th century Malla Dynasty stone carvings are at the spring here.

Day 2: Gothi Chaur to Naphukana
Another trail junction is at Gothi Chaur. Do not take the trail that leads uphill out of the Gothi Chaur Valley. Instead, walk downstream through forests to a series of mills at Kuri Sangta (2660 metres). A good camp site is a short distance beyond where the Kuri Sangta Khola joins the Tila Khola.

The route has now re-entered the Tila Valley and over the next day you will follow the river to its source. The largish villages of Gothigaon and Khudigaon are visible high on the opposite side of the river. The trail crosses to the northern side of the Tila and passes corn and potato fields that belong to these villages, then climbs through fields of wheat and barley and attractive meadows full of grazing horses and cows.

The river forks at Munigaon, a village with a complex mixture of Chhetri, Thakali and Tibetan inhabitants. There are several houses and the beginnings of a hotel at the trail junction, Muni Sangu. Look both above and behind the houses for some peculiar carved wooden faces. You will see these effigies throughout the Thulo Bheri Valley. They are called *dok-pa* and are supposed to offer protection from evil. A police check post at Muni Sangu will want to see your trekking permits.

The trail follows the left fork, which is the main Tila Khola, as the valley narrows and enters a forest of spruce, poplar and maples. The trail stays on the southern side of the river, so don't cross any of the several bridges that you pass. A short distance beyond Changrikot, a series of four houses built into the hillside on the opposite side of the river at about 2900 metres, the trail finally crosses the river and climbs to the grey stone houses of Chotra at 3010 metres. The inhabitants of Chotra are Khampas, people from eastern Tibet who are traditionally Buddhists. The village has typical Tibetan trappings of mani walls and a kani

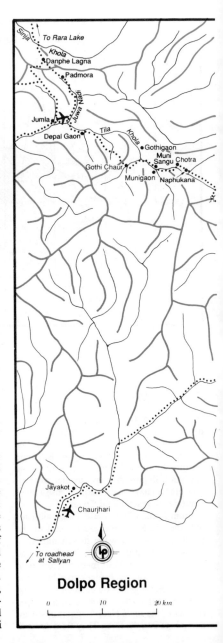

Dolpo Region

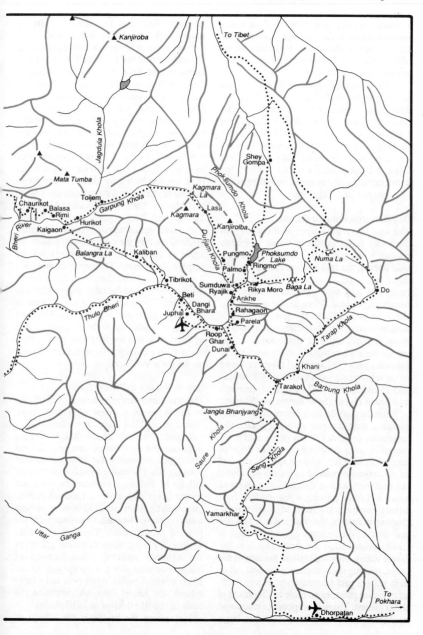

arching over the trail. Despite their background, these villagers long ago adopted Hindu names, dress and traditions in an effort to integrate themselves into mainstream Nepalese society.

A short distance beyond is the Tibetan settlement of Naphukana at 3080 metres. The large gompa above the village is Urgen Sanga Chorling where Tulku Tsewang Dorji Lama was recently installed as Rimpoche, or 'reincarnate lama'. The villagers of Naphukana keep large herds of yaks and horses. There are camp sites near the village, but better camping places are an hour further on, in a meadow at 3200 metres.

Day 3: Naphukana to Balasa

The trail becomes steeper as it climbs past the rocky fields of Rapati Chaur in forests tangled with Spanish moss. After crossing a side stream, the trail crosses the Tila Khola itself and starts a serious climb through birch, oak and rhododendron forests to the Mauri Lagna pass. When trekking in spring, the final approach to the pass is through meadows alive with blue lilies and stands of blooming azaleas and rhododendrons. In winter the trail is hidden under deep snow. From the pass (3820 metres) there are views of the snow peaks of Gutumba (5608 metres) and Mata Tumba (5767 metres) to the north and Bhalu Himal (5460 metres) to the east.

From the pass the trail descends a bit, then makes a long traverse across a potentially dangerous area. A Tibetan porter told me a tale of 20 yaks tumbling down this slope in an avalanche a few winters ago. At the end of the traverse, marked by cairns of stones, the trail starts a steep descent into a forest of pines and oaks, passing a few herders' huts before reaching a stream at 3110 metres. Staying in forests, the trail makes a few ups and downs, then climbs again to a ridge at 3140 metres. Here the trail turns into the Bheri Valley, keeping high on the side of the ridge, making short excursions in and out of side valleys past scattered houses and fields of corn and potatoes en route to Chaurikot at 3060 metres. There is no possible camp and no hotel – or even a shop – in this large

Khampa village, but the children are already trained in the ritual of asking for pens.

I met a man in Chaurikot who was 67 years old and insisted that his grandfather's grandfather settled here from Kham in eastern Tibet. He had the unlikely name of Pemba (a Tibetan first name) Budhathoki (a pure Hindu surname) and, like many men in this part of Nepal, wore an Afghan style turban.

Anthropologists categorise these people as matwali Chhetris and trace their heritage to Kumaon in India. Their religious practices have very little to do with Hinduism. Their rites are conducted by shamans known as *dhamis* or *jhakris* and their major deity is the god Mastha. There are shrines to Mastha in Tibrikot and Rahagaon.

From Chaurikot the trail drops to a stream at 2940 metres then climbs right back up again to an inviting looking notch on the ridge at 3080 metres. This would be an excellent camp except that there is no water. About 30 minutes beyond the ridge is the settlement of Balasa. There are several possible camp sites alongside the trail in the fields of Balasa, or further on in the fields of Jyakot or Rimi. You can see Kagmara peak on the horizon and Balangra La, the next obstacle on the route to Dolpo.

Day 4: Balasa to Forest Camp

The trail descends to a stream, then climbs to the ridge in a forest of walnut trees. Walnuts will be constant companions throughout the rest of the trek to Dolpo. Although the local people occasionally eat them, their primary value is as a source of cooking oil. The trail contours past the tiny village of Balasa, then past the corn and potato fields and apple orchards of Jyakot. Descend to Rimi at 2890 metres, where amusing carved wooden faces peek from the tops of most houses. The trail descends, steeply in places, through walnut groves to the closely spaced stone houses of Majagaon, then down a rocky trail to the Bheri River. A police check post and a large school and hostel complex dominate the bank of the Bheri River at 2610 metres.

Just across the bridge is the village of

Kaigaon, which boasts a veterinary station for cattle, a bhatti and the first real shop since Jumla. Stock up on the items for sale here – biscuits and cigarettes. The shopkeeper here told me a peculiar story about religious practices in Kaigaon, Chaurikot and Hurikot. The Hindu Chhetri people in these villages practice Lamaism (Tibetan Buddhism), hence the prayer flags that festoon the houses. The complication is that they also celebrate Hindu festivals, including Dasain, during which each house sacrifices an animal. It's all very complex and strange, especially when combined with Pemba Budhathoki's tale of the Chaurikot Khampa heritage.

Kaigaon is the departure point for a crossing of the Kagmara La. See the brief description of this crossing later in this chapter.

From Kaigaon the route climbs through pastures, then into a forest of birch and wild rose. Near the top of the ridge the climb rates the maximum scale for steepness. There are no stone steps, so you must either walk sideways in a crablike fashion or walk uphill on your toes. It's so steep that your heel cannot reach the ground unless you are double jointed. The trail crests at an elevation of 3230 metres, then levels out in a forest of rhododendron and oaks, the home of a band of black langur monkeys. A trail heads south from the pass and this is a route to Jajakot and Chaurjhari. The Dolpo trail continues east, and descends gently along the side of a large valley to a few small camp sites in forests of pines draped with Spanish moss.

Day 5: Forest Camp to Tibrikot

The trail makes many ups and downs as it contours out onto a ridge. Soon the downs become shorter and the ups longer, ending in a long climb to a false summit at 3660 metres. There is yet another false summit before the Balangra La itself, marked with cairns and prayer flags at 3760 metres. If it's clear, you'll see Dhaulagiri Himal to the east. You will also probably see herds of yaks grazing high on the grassy slopes above the pass.

There are two trails off the pass. The old

trail heads straight down into forests while a new trail contours around the ridge to the left. Both end at a government yak farm complex in a forest at 3160 metres. One trekker commented on the profusion of health facilities for animals along this trek, in contrast with the total lack of health care for people. Keep this in mind as you put together your medical supplies for a Dolpo trip.

From the yak farm, the trail heads out onto a ridge high above the Rimi Khola. There are a few camp sites along the route and there's even a primitive bhatti at Ghora Khola. Stay on the upper trail and beware of any steep drop towards the river. Beyond Bungtari, cross a stream and climb to Kaliban. Drop to a stream in a large side valley, then climb again to Dagin at 2930 metres. After passing Para and a few other small villages, the route reaches a treeless, waterless, uninhabited ridge, then makes a miserable 500 metre descent on a clutter of loose rocks to a stream just below Tibrikot at 2100 metres.

Day 6: Tibrikot to Dunai

From the stream, the trail climbs slightly to Tibrikot, a picturesque village on a promontory overlooking the Thulo Bheri Valley. This is an old fortress town and the police check post commands a view up and down the river. The houses have carved wooden windows and a large shrine and temple is dedicated to the goddess Tripura Sundari Devi. From the shrine, the trail descends past extensive rice terraces to a new, long suspension bridge at 2050 metres.

For the next day, you will follow the large, fast flowing, dark grey Thulo Bheri River, through arid country on the new trail that follows the Bheri all the way from Chaurjhari. Because of the heavy silting the Thulo Bheri is unfit to drink, so settlements in the valley occur only where there is a side stream. Passing the tiny settlement of Su Pani, the route passes over a low ridge and drops to Beti, several houses beside a small stream.

The trail to Dolpo Airport, above Juphal village, starts from Beti. If you want to confirm a flight, take the upper route and rejoin the river trail at Kala Gaura. The lower trail passes far below the airport. The stream leading from Juphal village creates a green oasis atmosphere in contrast to the barrenness of the valley. After more desolate country you will reach a few tea shops at Kala Gaura where the airport trail rejoins the route. The trail climbs a little over two ridges, then drops to a large side stream and three small bhattis at Roop Ghar. This is an excellent place to camp if you want to avoid staying in Dunai village. You can see the start of the trail to Phoksumdo Lake high on the opposite river bank.

From Roop Ghar the trail remains level, passing the national park and army offices at the confluence of the Phoksumdo Khola and the Thulo Bheri. The Ground Survey of India maps, and all others that have been derived from it, show the river named as the Suli Gaad, but most local people refer to it as the Phoksumdo Khola.

A few twists and turns of the trail lead to a view of Dunai and a large new hospital complex across the river. The trail enters the village through a fancy gate near the old health post, then passes through the old bazaar along a stone pavement. There are a few hotels and shops in this part of the town, but these cater mostly to traders. The larger facilities are in the eastern end of the village, past government offices, the police post and a statue of King Mahendra. No signs instruct you to visit the police post but, as this is the district headquarters, it's a good idea to seek out an official to fulfil bureaucratic formalities and gather the latest news on areas that are recently opened or closed to foreigners.

At the eastern end of the village is the *Phoksumdo Hotel* and the fancy new *Blue Sheep Trekkers Inn*, which has three private bedrooms and a separate restaurant facility. The large complex with turrets across the river is the district jail.

ACROSS THE KAGMARA LA

A high route to Dolpo leads across the 5115 metre high Kagmara La. It is not a difficult pass crossing, but you may have trouble finding porters willing to make the trip. The pass is snowbound, and potentially dangerous or impassable, from November to early May. A reasonable crossing takes four days from Kaigaon to Sumduwa.

Day 1: Kaigaon to Toijem

From the school at Kaigaon, stay on the west bank of the Bheri River, passing Hurikot, to a sign proclaiming the entrance to Shey Phoksundo National Park. The trail stays high above the river to the confluence where the Jagdula and Garpung kholas join to form the Bheri. Drop to the Jagdula Khola, crossing it on stones, and camp near the army post at Toijem (2920 metres).

Day 2: Toijem to Kagmara Phedi

Follow the trail up the western side of the Garpung Khola to about 3650 metres, then cross to the eastern side and continue upstream. The valley narrows and the river becomes a series of waterfalls as the trail climbs to a moraine at 3900 metres. Make a high camp in boulders at about 4000 metres.

Day 3: Kagmara Phedi to Lasa

Climb alongside the Kagmara Glacier to the Kagmara La pass, then descend about 900 metres alongside a stream to a camp on pastures in the Dorjam Khola Valley.

Day 4: Lasa to Sumduwa

The trail stays high above the stream, which eventually becomes the Dorjam Khola. The route enters forests and crosses the river on a wooden bridge, in the shadow of Kanjirolba peak to Pungmo village. Continue downstream to the national park headquarters at Sumduwa.

The following day, follow the trail up the Phoksumdo Khola to Phoksumdo Lake.

TO PHOKSUMDO LAKE

The trek to Phoksumdo Lake is steep and difficult. If you have the slightest fear of heights, don't even think about this trek. The trail is narrow and exposed in many places, and progress is limited by the small number of possible camping places. In 1990 there

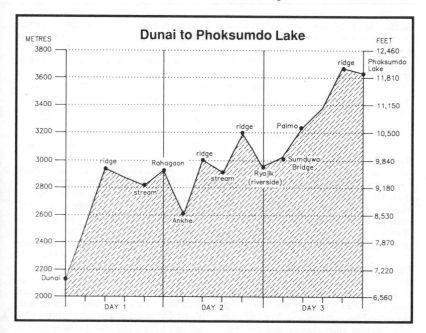

Dunai to Phoksumdo Lake

METRES / FEET chart showing elevation profile from Dunai to Phoksumdo Lake over Day 1, Day 2, Day 3, with labeled points: ridge, stream, Rahagaon, Ankhe, ridge, stream, ridge, Ryajik (riverside), Sumduwa Bridge, Palmo, ridge, Phoksumdo Lake, Dunai.

were no hotel facilities of any kind along the entire route. There is a plan to build a new trail following the river from its confluence with the Thulo Bheri to Sumduwa. Building is due to start in 1991 and a few people along the route are thinking about opening hotels. If these facilities exist, the character of the trek will change significantly.

The lake is within Shey Phoksundo National Park, established in 1981. The national park literature uses the spelling *Phoksundo*, but local informants believe that the correct transliteration is Phok, sum (three), do (stones), relating to the three arms of the lake. The park is said to abound in wildlife, though the most spectacular inhabitants, snow leopards and herds of blue sheep, are found primarily in the restricted regions of the park near Shey. The lake and trail are snowbound from mid-November to mid-May. Almost all the inhabitants of Ringmo village move to lower elevations at this time.

National park restrictions prohibit the use of firewood, so you must carry kerosene in addition to food. This requires some advance planning because there is no reliable kerosene supply in either Dunai or Jumla. Promoters in Dunai are talking of opening a kerosene depot which would simplify logistics for the trek.

Day 1: Dunai to Rahagaon

From the Mahendra statue, cross the new suspension bridge and turn left, following the trail past the hospital. The trail soon begins climbing up the side of the treeless Thulo Bheri Valley. The rocky trail crests a ridge and enters the Phoksumdo River Valley, finally reaching another ridge marked by cairns at 2500 metres. There is a view of Kagmara peak up the valley. The trek enters a large side canyon, making a long gentle descent past scattered houses and walnut groves to a stream at 2810 metres. High above the stream is the village of

Parela. The trail below the stream leads to Dhera, a winter settlement where people from higher villages keep herds of cows and goats. The camping opportunities here are very limited and the area is notorious for swarms of flies – worse in spring than in the fall. This region produces a lotuslike plant called *chuk* that is used to make vinegar and medicines. It is dried and flown from Dolpo to Nepalgunj and exported to India.

From the stream the trail climbs to Rahagaon, a Thakuri village at 2910 metres. In the fall it may be possible to camp in the village corn fields. In spring the only choice is the flat rooftops. Rahagaon has no water supply, so you must carry water from a stream about 15 minutes beyond the village. Above the village is a gompa dedicated to the local god Mastha.

Day 2: Rahagaon to Ryajik

The trail passes through the lower part of Rahagaon, then turns and descends to the village water supply. The route is now high above the Phoksumdo Khola. The trail turns into another side canyon and descends through deep dark forests to a large stream, then climbs to the Ankhe entrance station for Shey Phoksundo National Park. After paying the required entrance fee of Rs 250 you may be subjected to a baggage inspection – ostensibly for drugs and stolen art objects. It's a very peculiar formality in this remote locale. The three villages on the trail have a strange name connection: Parela *(parela* means eyelash), Rahagaon *(raha* means eyebrow) and Ankhe *(ankha* is eye).

There is no camp ground or accommodation at the entrance station, so proceed another 45 to 60 minutes to a good camp by the river. Climb to the ridge and stumble down a rocky trail to the river bank at 2650 metres. There is a single house at Chepka. Nothing was available here in 1990, but the Tibetan house owner had vague plans to build a camp site, toilet and shop, probably another addition to his already sprawling house. You can find another good camp site beside a huge rock in a walnut grove about 20 minutes beyond Chepka.

The trail makes some small ups and downs along the forested riverbed, then climbs steeply up to about 2900 metres. A small dangerous trail traverses under a huge cliff. Instead, it's far better to take the main trail that climbs another 90 metres over the top of the cliff, then descends under a huge overhanging rock. The ups and downs begin to be a bit tedious, but there are several streams along the way that offer a chance to cool off. The trail leaves the forests and traverses a grassy slope high above the river. Near a point where a stream enters from the west, the Phoksumdo Khola Valley turns right and becomes even steeper and narrower. The trail descends steeply through forests to a cliff, then makes a dizzying drop on a wobbly stone staircase to the river bank. You can almost look down between your toes to see the fast flowing river below. One slip and you are on your way back to Nepalgunj.

After reaching the river at 2950 metres, the trail becomes a collection of rocks and sticks that form a dike along the river bank. It's hard to imagine how people bring yaks and cows along this trail, but they do. Up, down, up, down; the trail continues upstream to a bridge near Ryajik village. A good camp is here and another is about five minutes further on.

Day 3: Ryajik to Phoksumdo Lake

The trail continues its ups and downs along the valley floor to the confluence of the Phoksumdo and the Dorjam kholas. Cross the wooden bridge to the western side. You can climb to the park headquarters at Sumduwa or take a lower trail that heads upstream. This is a major trail junction. The route to Kagmara La leads up the Dorjam Khola, the trail to Do and Tarap leads up the east bank of the Phoksumdo Khola and the trail to Phoksumdo Lake and Shey Gompa follows the west bank of the river. The village name reflects this. In Tibetan *sum* means 'three' and *duwa* is 'trail'.

Follow the trail up the western side of the river through forests to another bridge. Stay on the western side. There is a trail up the eastern side of the river, but it goes to the village of Rikya Moro and eventually to Tarap, not to Phoksumdo Lake. The Phoksumdo trail climbs though a forest of big cedars to a good camp site and then on to Palmo, a winter settlement used by the people of Ringmo village (3230 metres). The houses here are almost buried in the sandy soil. The route climbs steadily through open country to an elevation of 3370 metres, then starts up a steep set of switchbacks to a ridge at 3660 metres. From the ridge there are distant views of Phoksumdo Lake and a close view of a spectacular 330 metre high waterfall, the highest in Nepal. This is the source of the river that you have been following for several days. The trail makes a steep descent in birch forests to the upper reaches of the Phoksumdo Khola, then climbs gently to Ringmo village, a picturesque settlement with lots of mud-plastered chortens and mani walls.

Just below the village, cross a bridge and follow a trail north to the ranger station at Phoksumdo Lake. Continue to the shores of the lake near the point where the Phoksumdo Khola flows out of the lake. In 1990 it was possible to camp near the lake, but the park officials were discussing requiring trekkers to use an alternative camp site. Phoksumdo Lake is 4.8 km long, 1.8 km wide and is said to be 650 metres deep. A trail along its western side leads to Shey Gompa. However, access to this route is restricted for foreigners, so you are not allowed to go beyond the first wooden bridge on this trail. The lake is known for its aquamarine colour – a greenish blue similar to a special Tibetan turquoise. The large snow peak above the ridge on the western side of the lake is Kanchen Ruwa (6612 metres), also known as Kanjirolba.

A trail leads from the lakeside through juniper trees to an ancient gompa that overlooks the lake. In addition to the main temple, said to have been built 60 generations ago, there are four houses, each containing a private room for worship. These establishments are some of the few remaining facilities dedicated to the ancient shamanistic Bonpo religion, the antecedent of Tibetan Buddhism. The insides of the temples contain dusty Buddhist paintings and statues, but the trappings also reflect the animistic elements of the Bonpo religion, so some of the gompas are reminiscent of an ancient witch's cavern. Bonpo tradition dictates walking around mani walls to the right and uses the swastika symbol with the arms to the right, both exactly the opposite of Buddhist practice.

DO & TARAP

In 1990 there was a continuing discussion about whether the route between Phoksumdo Lake and Tarap was open or not. Check with the immigration office in Kathmandu and the ranger at Phoksumdo Lake for the latest decision. The route crosses two high passes. You would do well to have a guide who knows the route. Do not attempt the crossing if there is a lot of snow.

The following is a sketchy itinerary only. Several trekkers were allowed through the region in 1989 and early 1990, but by May 1990 both Tarap and the Baga La were closed and I had to return from Ringmo to Dunai. By autumn 1990, Tarap was open and there was an ongoing discussion between the national park and immigration authorities about the Baga La route.

Day 1: Phoksumdo Lake to Baga La Phedi

From Ringmo village, follow a trail through forests to a ridge and continue eastwards. There are two routes. One stays high and the other descends to the river and follows the main trail from Rikya Moro. The upper trail is more direct, but hard to find without a knowledgeable guide. The route continues up the valley to a waterfall and a camp site.

Day 2: Baga La Phedi to Numa La Phedi

Climb through alpine country to the Baga La at 5090 metres and descend to a stream, then continue up to the foot of the Numa La.

Be careful of the route between the two passes. A trail junction has routes leading to both Shey Gompa and the Baga La. Because the Nepal authorities are insistent about keeping Shey off limits to trekkers, it is this trail that is the incentive to keep the Baga La route closed.

Day 3: Numa La Phedi to Tokkyu

Continue through arid country to the Numa La, marked with mani stones at 5190 metres. The trail descends steeply to the Tarap Khola and meadows for camping.

Day 4: Tokkyu to Do

Continue down the Tarap Valley to Do, the largest settlement in Tarap.

Day 5: Do to Gorge Camp

The descent is easy, then becomes steep as the valley becomes very narrow and the trail crosses and recrosses the Tarap Khola. Camp in a large cave near the river.

Day 6: Gorge Camp to Khani Check Post

The trail continues to be steep, narrow and dangerous. The valley finally widens out and the route becomes easier. Camp in a cedar grove near the confluence of the Barbung Khola.

Day 7: Khani Check Post to Tarakot

Climb high above the river, eventually descending to the Thulo Bheri, crossing it just before Tarakot.

Day 8: Tarakot to Dunai

Follow the Thulo Bheri downstream along the south bank to Dunai.

DUNAI TO JUPHAL (DOLPO AIRPORT)

Dolpo flights are always early in the morning. This is because high winds in the Thulo Bheri Valley begin at about 10 am, making later flights impossible. It's at least 3 hours from Dunai to Juphal, so the only reasonable solution is to spend a night at the airport.

From Dunai, follow the river trail downstream to Roop Ghar and on to the small hotels at Kala Gaura (2090 metres). Take the uphill trail and climb through meadows past a few houses. Stay high and avoid the lower trail that leads to the large village of Dangi

Bhara, eventually reaching a large school just before the airport at 2500 metres. The airport is surrounded by a tangle of barbed wire. There are no sensible camp sites here but it is possible to camp below the airfield – or perhaps on the runway itself – if the airline people agree. Be sure you arrange an early wake-up call.

You should reconfirm your seats the day before the flight at the RNAC office in Juphal village, not at the airport. There are some basic shops in a complex of flat-roofed, mud buildings beside the airport. The *Parbat Hotel* has food and funky accommodation, and will also allow you to camp on their rooftop.

Take a walk down the runway, one of the most unusual airports in Nepal. The 490 metre runway is the minimum length required for Twin Otter landings at this elevation. To make matters even more frightening, the airport is on a slope and has a depression in the middle, reminiscent of a roller coaster. Also, there is a huge rock just at the end. Fares are high at US$77 for a 35 minute flight to Nepalgunj. Weight limits are strictly enforced and excess baggage is expensive. In 1990, the airline staff were enforcing a 10 kg free baggage allowance and leaving extra baggage behind. There is a lot of cargo traffic in and out of Dolpo. If you were a crate of apples you could fly at a subsidised rate of Rs 1.50 per kg.

POKHARA TO DUNAI

This is a long, remote, difficult trek with very few facilities along the way. The route is described in detail by George Schaller in *Stones of Silence* and by Peter Matthiesen in *The Snow Leopard*. There are no hotels beyond Beni, so you will be most comfortable if you take porters and food. With porters the trek takes 12 or 13 days. A rough itinerary follows.

Day 1: Pokhara to Kusma

Drive as far as possible – to the Birethanti junction, possibly to Kusma, or even to Beni if the road is completed. Kusma is at the confluence of the Modi Khola and the Kali Gandaki.

Day 2: Kusma to Beni
Trek up the Kali Gandaki to Beni, the last large village on the route to Dunai.

Day 3: Beni to Dabang

Day 4: Dabang to Dhara Khola
Camp at 1830 metres.

Day 5: Dhara Khola to Forest Camp
Camp at 2900 metres.

Day 6: Forest camp to Dhorpatan
Cross the Jalja La at 3350 metres and descend to Dhorpatan (2300 metres). An airport is at Dhorpatan, but there is no scheduled service.

Day 7: Dhorpatan to Forest Camp
Cross a pass at 4080 metres and descend to a camp in the forest.

Day 8: Forest Camp to Yamarkhar
Descend to the Ghustung Khola at 2800

metres, then climb to Yamarkhar at 2550 metres.

Day 9: Yamarkhar to Jagir
Continue up the ridge to a camp at Jagir (3350 metres).

Day 10: Jagir to Seng Khola
Cross the Nautala La at 3970 metres and descend into the Sang Khola Valley, camping at about 3600 metres.

Day 11: Seng Khola to Saure Khola
Climb a rock staircase leading to a pass at 4650 metres and descend to the Saure Khola. Camp at 4100 metres.

Day 12: Saure Khola to Tarakot
Cross the Jangla Bhanjyang (4500 metres) and descend through spruce and pine forests, then terraced fields, to Tarakot (2800 metres).

Day 13: Tarakot to Dunai
Follow the Thulo Bheri to Dunai.

Other Destinations

As scenic, interesting, culturally enriching and historic as the major treks may be, you should consider a trek to other regions. Although there are restrictions involved with the issuance of trekking permits, and some areas are still closed to foreigners, there are many places in Nepal that are both fascinating and accessible.

Many trekkers make the mistake of varying their route by attempting a 5500 to 6000 metre high pass. Upon reaching the pass they discover that they, their equipment or other members of the party are totally unfit for the cold, high elevation and the technical problems that the pass presents. Often the problems force the party to turn back, severely altering their schedule. In the end, they fail to reach their primary goal. It is best to plan a high pass crossing after achieving the major goal of the trek – usually on the return to Kathmandu.

You need not go to a particularly remote region to escape heavily travelled trails. The major trade and trekking routes are the shortest way to a particular destination, but if you allow another few days it is possible to follow less direct, often parallel, routes, through villages which are not even on the maps, in areas with less Western contact than the major trails.

In 1984 I visited an area less than a day's walk from an important trekking route. The local people insisted that I was the first trekker who had ever been there. Other foreigners had visited the region, of course, as engineers, doctors and teachers, but no foreigner had come there before simply to trek. There must be thousands of similar places in Nepal. In such places a guide is helpful, and it is almost imperative to carry your own food and the means with which to cook it. In areas that neither trekkers nor local porters frequent there are no bhattis. Food is available, but the time and effort necessary to scrounge out food and accommodation in homes can make progress almost impossible.

Some other possible trekking destinations are:

KATHMANDU TO POKHARA

Before the Pokhara road was completed in 1971, the only way to reach Pokhara from Kathmandu was to fly or to walk. The trek from Kathmandu is an easy nine or 10 day trek from Trisuli Bazaar to Begnas Tal, just outside Pokhara. This is the easiest trek in Nepal and has few uphill climbs of any significance. Trekking westwards there are many alternatives. A northern route presents a trek close to the mountains – Manaslu (7945 metres), Himalchuli, Baudha (6674 metres) and a side trip to Bara Pokhari, a fine high altitude lake. The more direct southern route to Pokhara allows a visit to the ancient town of Gorkha with its large bazaar and fort. This route has the attraction of lower altitudes and avoids the extreme elevation gains and losses common to other treks in Nepal. The views of the Himalaya are good on this trek, but the route never actually gets into the high mountains.

A lot of the interest and remoteness of this trek has vanished because the new road to Gorkha has totally changed the trading habits and culture of the region. Local people hardly ever walk this route now, so the facilities for food and accommodation have degenerated. A few Westerners travel the southern routes, but many parts of the northern regions are both remote and untrammelled by trekkers.

GANESH HIMAL

Between Kathmandu and Pokhara are three major groups of peaks: Ganesh Himal, Manaslu and Himalchuli, and the large Annapurna Himal. You can drive to Dhunche on the same road that leads to the start of the Langtang trek, then either continue driving (if the army lets you continue on the road to Somtang) or walk towards Ganesh Himal.

ROLWALING (Restricted)

Rolwaling is the east-west valley below Gauri Shankar (7145 metres), just south of the Tibetan border. This is an isolated and culturally diverse area, but most treks conclude their visit to Rolwaling by crossing the Tesi Lapcha pass (5755 metres) into Khumbu. It is better to cross Tesi Lapcha from Khumbu into Rolwaling, not by visiting Rolwaling first. There are two reasons for this: well-equipped, willing porters are easier to get in Khumbu than in Rolwaling; and in case of altitude sickness there are better facilities for help if you make your retreat on the Khumbu side rather than making a retreat back to the isolated villages of Beding or Na in Rolwaling. A second way to visit this region would be to forego Tesi Lapcha and go as far as Na, then retrace the route back to Kathmandu.

Tesi Lapcha is particularly dangerous because of frequent rockfall on its western side. The route through the icefall is becoming technically more and more difficult due to the movements of the glacier. The Rolwaling porters operate a Mafia-like system and will not allow outside porters to approach the pass from Rolwaling, forcing parties to accept people from Beding and Na as porters. The local porters either get frightened of the falling rocks and return without notice or demand exorbitant pay after the party is halfway up the pass. There are no facilities at all between Na and Thami. Tesi Lapcha is a true mountaineering project!

In 1990 Rolwaling and Tesi Lapcha were still closed to foreigners. It seems that different interpretations of the same rules rather than new regulations is what determines whether the immigration office will issue you a trekking permit or not.

MAKALU BASE CAMP

You can make an outstanding trek in eastern Nepal from either Hile or Tumlingtar by walking north up the Arun River to Sedua and Num, then crossing Barun La (4110 metres) into the upper Barun Khola Valley for a close look at Makalu (8463 metres) and Chamlang (7317 metres). The route is not particularly difficult but it becomes a long trek because of the long distance that you must walk up the Arun.

You can put together an even wilder trek by crossing Sherpani col and west col into the upper Hongu Basin. A few groups have tried this trek and it has proved itself difficult and potentially dangerous. It's better to travel from Lukla if you want to go into the upper Hongu Basin and the Panch Pokhari (five lakes), situated there.

TILICHO LAKE (Restricted)

There is another pass south of Thorung La between Manang and Jomsom. From Manang, the trail goes on to the village of Khangsar, then becomes a goat trail scrambling over moraines to Tilicho Lake (4120 metres) at the foot of Tilicho peak (7132 metres). Herzog's maps depicted Tilicho Lake as the 'great ice lake'. It is usually frozen (except when you decide to trust the ice and walk on it). From the lake, there are several alternative routes, including Meso Kanto pass (5330 metres) and another pass a little further north. The trail is difficult and hard to find. One very experienced trekker described the trail as only a figment of someone's imagination – he claimed there was no trail at all.

Thorung La is a good safe route between Manang and Jomsom. It's better to make a side trip to Tilicho Lake from Manang and not take all your equipment and porters on the Tilicho Lake trail. The route is currently on the list of restricted areas because of army training exercises in the valley east of Jomsom. Inquire at Kathmandu and again in Manang before making your plans. You might cross the pass only to have the army turn you back to Manang an hour before Jomsom.

JUGAL HIMAL

To the east of Kathmandu lies a chain of peaks called Jugal Himal, which includes Dorje Lakpa (6966 metres), Madiya (6257 metres) and Phurbi Chhyachu (6637 metres). From the south it is an easily accessible region, although it requires a long uphill climb. From Dolalghat on the Kodari road there is a jeep road to the large bazaar of Chautara (1410 metres). A trail from Chautara descends to the Balephi Khola, then follows a ridge to Bhairav Kund, a holy lake at 3500 metres.

You can return from there to Tatopani on the Kodari road or make a circuit around the head of the Balephi Khola Valley to Panch Pokhari (five lakes) at 3600 metres. From Panch Pokhari, trails lead to Tarke Gyang in Helambu or back down the ridge to Panchkal on the Kodari road. This is a remote and unfrequented region, despite its proximity to Kathmandu. Treks in this area involve a lot of climbing on narrow trails.

MANASLU & LARKYA LA (Restricted)

By crossing the Larkya La (5105 metres), the pass between the Buri Gandaki and the Marsyandi valleys, you can make a circuit of Manaslu (8162 metres) and Himalchuli (7893 metres). The opening of this area was announced in spring 1990, but by autumn 1990 it was still a restricted area. A trek completely around Manaslu will require three weeks. The trail that approaches the Larkya La is narrow, steep and slippery on the eastern side and no food or shelter is available near the pass. The Rupina La (4663 metres), a pass to the south, offers an alternative. It is a steep snow covered route with little to recommend it.

Mountaineering in Nepal

Although this is a book about trekking, a short discussion of mountaineering in Nepal is appropriate. The first trekkers in Nepal were, of course, mountaineers who were either on their way to climb peaks or were exploring routes up unclimbed peaks. There was furious mountaineering activity in Nepal from 1950 to the 1960s and all the 8000 metre peaks were climbed during this time.

By the early 1970s the emphasis had shifted to impossible feats such as the south face of Annapurna and finally Everest southwest face, both climbed by expeditions led by Chris Bonington. The expeditions in the '60s and '70s were often well equipped and sometimes lavish as governments, foundations, magazines, newspapers, film makers, television producers and even private companies sponsored expeditions to higher and more exotic peaks. Expeditions have become big business and climbers now approach the job with the appropriate degree of seriousness and dedication. It is not uncommon for expeditions to refuse trekkers admission into their base camps. The team members do not have the time or energy to entertain tourists and there have also been incidents of trekkers taking souvenirs from among the expensive and essential items that often lie around such camps.

There are three seasons for mountaineering in Nepal. The premonsoon season from April to early June was once the only season during which expeditions climbed major peaks. In the '50s all expeditions were in the 'lull before the storm' period that occurs between the end of the winter winds and the beginning of the monsoon snow. Cold and high winds drove back the Swiss expedition to Mt Everest in 1952 when they made an autumn expedition. It was not until 1973 that an expedition successfully climbed Everest in autumn. Now the autumn or postmonsoon season of September and October is a period of many successful expeditions.

In 1979 the Ministry of Tourism established a season for winter mountaineering. It is bitterly cold at high elevations from November to February, but recent advances in equipment technology have allowed several teams to accomplish what was thought before to be impossible – a winter ascent of a Himalayan peak. Climbing during the monsoon, from June to August, is not practical from the Nepalese side, though the north face of Everest has been climbed during August.

Two organisations control climbing in Nepal. The Ministry of Tourism is responsible for major expeditions and the Nepal Mountaineering Association issues permits for the peaks that are open to trekking groups. The type of climbing that appeals to most trekkers is encompassed by the regulations for small peaks.

TREKKING PEAKS

Since 1978 the Nepal Mountaineering Association (NMA) has had the authority to issue permission for small-scale attempts on 18 peaks. It is not necessary to go through a long application process, hire and equip a liaison officer or organise a huge assault on a major peak in order to try Himalayan mountaineering. The 18 'trekking peaks' provide a large range of difficulty and are situated throughout Nepal.

There is a minimum of formality, requiring only the payment of a fee and the preparation of a simple application. The fee is US$300 for peaks above 6100 metres and US$200 for peaks less than 6100 metres. The permit is valid for one month for a group of up to 10 people. An extra US$5 per person is payable if the group exceeds 10 climbers. Because the regulations for climbing a small peak also require an established liaison in Kathmandu (usually a trekking company), it is easiest to use a trekking agent to organise a climb rather than try to do the whole project yourself.

The designation 'trekking peak' is an unfortunate misnomer, because most of the peaks listed are significant mountaineering challenges. There are few 'walk-ups', and some peaks, such as Kusum Kangru and Lobuje, can be technically demanding and dangerous. As you think about these 'small' peaks, remember that all of them are higher than any mountain in North America. Before you consider climbing a trekking peak, reread some books on Himalayan expeditions. The weather is often bad and may force you to sit in your tent for days at a time. Usually a well-equipped base camp is necessary, and the ascent of a peak requires one or more high camps that must be established and stocked. Most of the trekking peaks require a minimum of four days and it can take as much as three weeks for an ascent.

Bill O'Connor's excellent and comprehensive guidebook, *The Trekking Peaks of Nepal*, is available in Kathmandu and in bookshops overseas. The book includes photographs, maps, trekking information and climbing routes on the 18 trekking peaks.

To get a climbing permit, go to the NMA office (tel 211596) in Kamal Pokhari, behind the Yak & Yeti Hotel. You must pay the peak fee in foreign currency cash or travellers' cheques. You must also employ a sirdar who is currently registered with the NMA, and if any Nepalese are to climb above base camp, you must insure them and supply them with climbing equipment. A climbing permit does not replace a trekking permit.

You can buy or rent climbing gear in Kathmandu, saving the expense of air freighting ironmongery around the world. Good mountain tents, stoves, sleeping bags, down clothing and most other expedition necessities are all available for rent. As with trekking gear, the items that might be in short supply are socks, clothing, large size boots and freeze dried food.

Peaks which can be climbed under the trekking peak regulations are:

Everest Region
Island Peak (Imja Tse) (6189 metres) One steep and exposed 100 metre ice or snow climb, otherwise a nontechnical snow climb.

Kwangde (6187 metres) The north face (seen from Namche) is a difficult climb. The southern side is a moderately technical climb (allow two to three weeks) from Lumding Kharka above Ghat.

Kusum Kangru (6369 metres) This is the most difficult of the trekking peaks.

Lobuje East (6119 metres) The top is exposed and often covered with rotten snow. There is an exposed knife ridge and some crevasses. Not a trivial climb.

Mehra Peak (Khongma Tse) (5820 metres) A rock and ice climb that is not difficult from either the Imja Valley or Lobuje.

Mera Peak (6476 metres) Easy snow climb from the Mera La, but sometimes crevasses complicate the route. No food at all on the approach from Lukla. Requires two weeks.

Pokhalde (5806 metres) A short steep snow climb from the Kongma La above Lobuje.

Rolwaling Region
Pharchamo (6187 metres) A steep snow climb on a route subject to avalanches. The peak is just above Tesi Lapcha.

Ramdung (5925 metres) The climb requires a long approach through Rolwaling Valley. Rolwaling is now closed, so you must either climb from the south or obtain special permission for Rolwaling.

Manang Region
Chulu East (6584 metres) The ascent starts after a long approach from Manang and needs one or two high camps.

Chulu West (6419 metres) Climbers must make at least two high camps. The route circles Gusang peak to climb Chulu West from the north.

Pisang Peak (6091 metres) Long snow slog above Pisang village. Steep snow at the top.

Langtang Region
Ganga La Chuli (Naya Kangri) (5846 metres) Snow and rock climb from a base camp either north or south of Ganja La.

Annapurna Region
Fluted Peak (Singu Chuli) (6501 metres) The peak is reached from the Annapurna Sanctuary. Its name comes from the steep ice slopes that make it difficult to climb.

Hiunchuli (6331 metres) Snow, ice and rock. Not easy.

Mardi Himal (5555 metres) Five day slog up the Mardi Khola to approach the peak, an outlier of Machhapuchhare.

Tent Peak (Tharpu Chuli) (5500 metres) Glaciers and crevasses; most people climb the easier 'Rakshi peak' to the south.

Ganesh Himal
Paldor Peak (5928 metres) A 10 day trek to base camp from Trisuli Bazaar.

MOUNTAINEERING EXPEDITIONS
The rules for mountaineering on major peaks require a minimum of six months advance application to the Ministry of Tourism, a liaison officer, a royalty of US$1000 to US$5000 depending on the elevation of the peak, and endorsement from the government or the national alpine club of the country organising the expedition. There are 87 peaks open for foreign expeditions and another 17 peaks open for joint Nepalese-foreign expeditions. Some peaks, such as Everest, are booked many years in advance, while other peaks remain untouched for several seasons.

Further information is usually available through alpine clubs in your own country. Even the most budget conscious expedition under these regulations would cost US$20,000 or more to cover a liaison officer's salary, insurance and equipment, peak fees, sherpa insurance, sherpa equipment and other compulsory expenses. If you want an inexpensive climb in Nepal, it is far more reasonable to set your sights on one of the trekking peaks.

CLIMBS ON EVEREST
Mountaineering and trekking in Nepal has relied heavily on the progress and inspiration developed by various expeditions to Everest. Much of the attraction of Nepal in the early days resulted from the discovery that the highest peak in the world lay within the forbidden and isolated kingdom. Though it was named Mt Everest by the Ground Survey of India in 1856 after Sir George Everest, retired Surveyor-General of India, the peak had been known by other names long before. The Nepalese call it Sagarmatha and the Sherpas call it Chomolungma. The Chinese now call it Qomolangma Feng.

The list of attempts and successes on Everest is one of the classics of mountaineering history. By 1989 there had been 274 ascents of Everest, including several by people who climbed it two or more times. The following section lists all the Everest expeditions until 1982. By 1983 both China and Nepal allowed several expeditions on the mountain at the same time, causing traffic jams, queues for the use of routes and fixed ropes, confusion, squabbling, crowded base camps and the inevitable trashing of the mountain. From 1983 onwards I have listed only the more spectacular or interesting expeditions. For a complete list of Everest ascents and an amazing set of statistics about climbs on the mountain, see the latest edition of *Everest* by Walt Unsworth (London, Oxford University Press, 1989).

1921 – British
The first expedition was a reconnaissance through Tibet from Darjeeling led by Lieutenant Colonel C K Howard Bury. They spent months mapping and exploring the Everest region and ran the first climbing school for Sherpas on the slopes leading to the north col. Though it was not an actual

attempt on the peak, they reached the north col at a height of 7000 metres.

1921 – British Reconnaissance
A team that included several surveyors and climbers travelled across Tibet with a portable darkroom and explored, photographed and mapped the mountain. On this expedition George Leigh Mallory named the Western Cwm and declared that Everest was probably unclimbable from the Nepalese side.

1922 – British
The first attempt on the mountain was led by Brigadier General C G Bruce. The expedition, as did all attempts until 1950, climbed the mountain from the north after a long approach march across the plains of Tibet. The highest point reached was 8320 metres. An avalanche killed seven Sherpas below the north col.

1924 – British
Again Bruce led a team of British gentlemen in their tweed suits to Everest. They didn't have crampons and had a furious argument about whether the use of oxygen was 'sporting'. On this expedition Mallory and Andrew Irvine climbed high on the mountain and never returned. Lieutenant Colonel E F Norton reached 8565 metres without oxygen.

1933 – British
This expedition, under the leadership of Hugh Ruttledge, reached a height of 8570 metres, just 275 metres short of the summit. Frank Smythe's book *Camp Six* is an excellent personal account of this expedition.

1934 – A Solo Attempt
Maurice Wilson flew alone in a small plane from the UK to India, then crossed Tibet to make a solo attempt on Everest. While usually dismissed as a crank, Wilson did accomplish a lot before he pushed himself too far and froze to death on the slopes below the north col.

1935 – British
A name to become associated with Everest first came into prominence when Eric Shipton led a small expedition as far as the north col. Tenzing Norgay accompanied this expedition as a porter.

1936 – British
Another British expedition led by Ruttledge reached a point only slightly above the north col.

1938 – British
Another famous name associated with Everest came to the forefront when H W Tilman led a small expedition in which Eric Shipton reached almost 8300 metres.

1947 – A Solo Attempt
Earl Denman, a Canadian, disguised himself as a Tibetan monk, travelled to Everest and made a solo attempt. He quit below the north col and returned immediately to Darjeeling.

1950 – British/American
After the war Tibet was closed, but Nepal had begun to open her borders. Tilman made a peripatetic trip all over Nepal, including a trek from Dharan to Namche Bazaar. This was the first party of Westerners to visit the Everest region. They made the first ascent of Kala Pattar and walked to the foot of the Khumbu Icefall.

1951 – Solo from Nepal
K Becker-Larson, a Dane, followed the same route as the Tilman party, then crossed into Tibet, reaching the north col before returning.

1951 – British Reconnaissance
Eric Shipton led another reconnaissance, reached the Western Cwm at the top of the Khumbu Icefall and proved that an expedition could climb Everest from the south.

1952 – Swiss
Leader Dr Wyss-Dunant organised an effort in which Raymond Lambert and Tenzing

Norgay reached a height of almost 8600 metres.

1952 – Swiss
Rushing to beat the British, the Swiss tried again in the autumn of 1952 but cold and high winds drove them back from a point just above the south col.

1953 – British Success
The huge British expedition, led by John Hunt, succeeded in placing Edmund Hillary and Tenzing Norgay on the summit on 29 May 1953.

1956 – Swiss
Albert Eggler led an expedition that placed four climbers on the summit of Everest and also made the first ascent of Lhotse.

1960 – Indian
The first Indian expedition reached a height of 8625 metres but bad weather forced them to retreat.

1960 – Chinese
This expedition made the first ascent from the north. The climb was discredited at first because three members of the team reached the summit at night, but mountaineering history now acknowledges the ascent.

1962 – Indian
The second Indian expedition was also unsuccessful, though they reached a height of 8700 metres.

1962 – An Unauthorised Attempt
Woodrow Wilson Sayre and three others obtained permission to climb Gyachung Kang, then crossed into Tibet and tried to climb Everest. They reached a point above the north col before returning.

1963 – American
The American Mount Everest Expedition, led by Norman Dyhrenfurth, was successful in placing six people on the summit, including two by the unclimbed west ridge.

1965 – Indian
Captain M S Kohli lead an Indian team that placed nine climbers on the summit of Everest.

1966 to 1968
Nepal was closed to mountaineers.

1969 – Japanese
The Japanese made a reconnaissance to look for a new route up the south-west face of Everest.

1970 – Japanese
A 38-member Japanese team placed four climbers on the summit. This was the expedition that included the famous 'ski descent' of Everest. Six Sherpas were killed in the Khumbu Icefall.

1971 – International
Norman Dyhrenfurth led an ambitious expedition with climbers from 13 nations attempting both the south-west face and the west ridge, finally retreating from a height of 8488 metres on the face route.

1971 – Argentine
An unsuccessful attempt led by H C Tolosa.

1972 – European
K M Herligkoffer led a team that attempted the south-west face, reaching a height of 8300 metres.

1972 – British South Face
Chris Bonington led an attempt on the south-west face.

1973 – Italian
The largest Everest expedition ever, under the leadership of Guido Monzino, placed eight climbers on the summit.

1973 – Japanese
Two members of a team led by M Yuasa reached the summit in the first successful ascent in autumn. The ascent was via the traditional south col route after the team made no progress on the south-west face.

1974 – Spanish
Financed by a Spanish battery company, the Spanish expedition was unsuccessful.

1974 – French
This expedition to the west ridge ended in disaster when an avalanche killed the leader and five sherpas.

1975 – Japanese
The Japanese Women's Everest Expedition was successful when Mrs Junko Tabei and Sherpa Ang Tsering reached the summit.

1975 – Chinese
A few days after the Japanese success, a Chinese team placed nine people, including one woman, on the summit. The large survey tripod they erected is still on the top of Everest.

1975 – British South Face
Bonington led a Barclays Bank financed expedition during which Dougal Haston and Doug Scott successfully climbed the difficult south-west face of Everest.

1976 – British/Royal Nepal Army
Two British members of a joint British-Royal Nepal Army Expedition reached the summit in spring.

1976 – American
The American Bicentennial Everest Expedition, led by Phil Trimble, placed two members on the summit during autumn.

1977 – New Zealand
Bad weather and heavy snow stopped this spring expedition.

1977 – South Korean
This expedition, in which two climbers reached the summit, was the earliest autumn success ever.

1978 – Austrian
In three separate teams, nine climbers reached the summit of Everest. Reinhold Messner and Peter Habler made the first ascent of the mountain without using oxygen.

1978 – German/French
Led by Dr Herligkoffer and Pierre Mazeaud, this gigantic expedition placed 16 climbers on the summit via the south col and made a live radio broadcast from the 'roof of the world'.

1979 – Yugoslav
Five climbers reached the summit via a new route – the west ridge all the way from the Lho La. Ang Phu Sherpa fell and was killed during the descent.

1979 – Swabian
Another international group placed 13 climbers on the summit under the leadership of Gerhard Schmatz. Mrs Schmatz and Ray Genet died during an overnight bivouac on the descent.

1980 – Polish Winter Expedition
The expedition made the first winter ascent via the south col after a long struggle. Two climbers reached the summit.

1980 – Polish
Another Polish expedition in spring, with many of the same climbers as the winter expedition, pioneered a new route via the south pillar, to the right of the British south face route. Two climbers reached the summit.

1980 – Basque
For the first time, Nepal allowed two teams on the mountain simultaneously, and two climbers reached the summit via the traditional south col route.

1980 – Japanese: from the North
After more than 40 years of closure, Tibet was once again accessible to mountaineers. A large and expensive expedition reached the summit by two different routes from Tibet. One climber reached the summit via the north-east ridge and two climbers via the north face.

1980 – Reinhold Messner (Solo)

On August 20, Reinhold Messner made his second oxygenless ascent of Everest, this time from the Tibetan side – and alone.

1980 – Nepal/Italian

A huge postmonsoon joint expedition of the Nepal Mountaineering Association and Club Alpino Italiano was forced back from the summit because of weather and logistic complications.

1981 – Japanese

A winter expedition was led by 1970 Everest summiteer Naomi Uemura. It ended without success after reaching the south col.

1981 – British

At the same time as the Japanese winter attempt, a British team led by Allan Rouse attempted the west ridge, but was not successful.

1981 – Japanese

Meiji University sponsored a spring attempt on the west ridge led by Sinichi Nakajimi.

1981 – American

Richard Blum led the first attempt on the Kangshung face in Tibet.

1981 – American

Three Americans and two Sherpas reached the summit via the south-east ridge during the American Medical Research Expedition.

1982 – Canadian

Two Canadians and four Sherpas reached the summit in a huge expedition that included live television transmissions from the mountain. Three sherpas and a Canadian were killed in the Khumbu Icefall.

1982 – British

During an attempt on the north-east ridge from Tibet, Joe Tasker and Peter Boardman were killed.

1982 – Soviet

Eleven climbers reached the summit via the south-west face.

1982 – French

A French Army expedition led by J C Marmier was unsuccessful.

1982 – Spanish

An attempt from Nepal led by L Belvis was unsuccessful.

1982 – American

An attempt on the north face from Tibet was led by Lou Whittaker.

1982 – Dutch

An attempt from Tibet.

1982 – French

An unsuccessful winter attempt from Nepal.

1982 – Japanese

Yasuo Kato made a solo winter ascent (his third ascent of Everest) and perished during the descent.

1982 – Belgian

A winter attempt via the west ridge during which one member fell into Tibet and eventually made his way back to Kathmandu by bus.

1983

From 1983 on, this list includes important or unusual expeditions only.

Three Japanese climbers reached the summit via the south col in autumn.

Six Americans made the first ascent of the difficult Kangshung face from Tibet on the same day that the Japanese climbed the peak from Nepal.

Six Japanese climbers reached the summit via the south-east ridge; two Japanese and a Sherpa died on the descent.

Gerard Lenser led an expedition that placed six Americans and two Sherpas on the summit via the south col.

Three Japanese and a Sherpa made a winter ascent from Nepal via the south col.

1984

There were 14 expeditions, five from Tibet and the rest from Nepal.

The first Indian woman and four other climbers reached the summit via the south col.

Five Bulgarians reached the summit via the west ridge; four climbers made a traverse and descended via the south-east ridge.

Climbing from Tibet, Greg Mortimer and Tim McCartney-Snape were the first Australians to reach the summit of Everest.

1985

Of 14 expedition attempts on Everest only three were successful.

A record 17 climbers from a Norwegian expedition reached the summit via the south col.

1986

Out of 13 expeditions, two were successful.

1987

Again, 14 teams attempted Everest and only one, a South Korean expedition, reached the summit.

1988

More than 250 climbers made up a joint Chinese, Nepalese, Japanese expedition that traversed the mountain in both directions. The teams met on the summit and made a prime time live TV broadcast.

On the Australian Bicentennial Expedition, three climbers reached the summit via the south col.

In autumn, three French teams, and American, Korean, Spanish, Czech and New Zealand teams all gathered at base camp. Latecomers were charged for the use of fixed ropes through the icefall. Four French climbers reached the summit and Jean-Marc Boivin jumped off by paraglider, landeding at Camp II 12 minutes later.

A total of 31 climbers reached the summit and nine people died.

Index

MAPS

ROUTE PROFILES

TEXT

Map references are in **bold** type.

TREKS

Guides to the Indian Subcontinent

Bangladesh - a travel survival kit
This practical guide – the only English-language guide to Bangladesh – encourages travellers to take another look at this often-neglected but beautiful land.

India - a travel survival kit
Widely regarded as _the_ guide to India, this award-winning book has all the information to help you make the most of the unforgettable experience that is India.

Karakoram Highway the high road to China - a travel survival kit
Travel in the footsteps of Alexander the Great and Marco Polo on the Karakoram Highway, following the ancient and fabled Silk Road. This comprehensive guide also covers villages and treks away from the highway.

Kashmir, Ladakh & Zanskar - a travel survival kit
Detailed information on three contrasting Himalayan regions in the Indian state of Jammu and Kashmir – the narrow valley of Zanskar, the isolated 'little Tibet' of Ladakh, and the stunningly beautiful Vale of Kashmir.

Nepal - a travel survival kit
Travel information on every road-accessible area in Nepal, including the Terai. This practical guidebook also includes introductions to trekking, white-water rafting and mountain biking.

Pakistan - a travel survival kit
Discover 'the unknown land of the Indus' with this informative guidebook
– from bustling Karachi to ancient cities and tranquil mountain valleys.

Sri Lanka - a travel survival kit
Some parts of Sri Lanka are off-limits to visitors, but this guidebook uses
the restriction as an incentive to explore other areas more closely – making
the most of friendly people, good food and pleasant places to stay – all at
reasonable cost.

Trekking in the Indian Himalaya
All the advice you'll need for planning and equipping a trek, including
detailed route descriptions for some of the world's most exciting treks.

Also available:
Hindi/Urdu phrasebook, **Nepal** phrasebook, **and Sri Lanka** phrasebook.

Lonely Planet Guidebooks

Lonely Planet guidebooks cover every accessible part of Asia as well as Australia, the Pacific, South America, Africa, the Middle East and parts of North America and Europe. There are four series: *travel survival kits*, covering a single country for a range of budgets; *shoestring guides* with compact information for low-budget travel in a major region; *walking guides*; and *phrasebooks*.

Australia & the Pacific
Australia
Bushwalking in Australia
Islands of Australia's Great Barrier Reef
Fiji
Micronesia
New Caledonia
New Zealand
Tramping in New Zealand
Papua New Guinea
Papua New Guinea phrasebook
Rarotonga & the Cook Islands
Samoa
Solomon Islands
Tahiti & French Polynesia
Tonga

South-East Asia
Bali & Lombok
Burma
Burmese phrasebook
Indonesia
Indonesia phrasebook
Malaysia, Singapore & Brunei
Philippines
Pilipino phrasebook
South-East Asia on a shoestring
Thailand
Thai phrasebook
Vietnam, Laos & Cambodia

North-East Asia
China
Chinese phrasebook
Hong Kong, Macau & Canton
Japan
Japanese phrasebook
Korea
Korean phrasebook
North-East Asia on a shoestring
Taiwan
Tibet
Tibet phrasebook

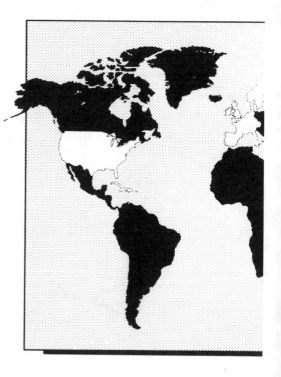

West Asia
Trekking in Turkey
Turkey
Turkish phrasebook
West Asia on a shoestring

Indian Ocean
Madagascar & Comoros
Maldives & Islands of the East Indian Ocean
Mauritius, Réunion & Seychelles

Mail Order

Lonely Planet guidebooks are distributed worldwide and are sold by good bookshops everywhere. They are also available by mail order from Lonely Planet, so if you have difficulty finding a title please write to us. US and Canadian residents should write to Embarcadero West, 112 Linden St, Oakland CA 94607, USA and residents of other countries to PO Box 617, Hawthorn, Victoria 3122, Australia.

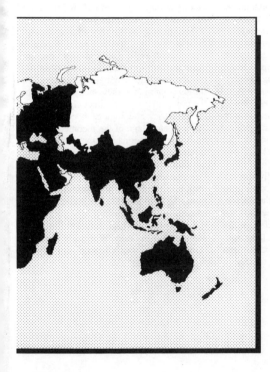

Europe
Eastern Europe on a shoestring
Iceland, Greenland & the Faroe Islands
Trekking in Spain

Indian Subcontinent
Bangladesh
India
Hindi/Urdu phrasebook
Trekking in the Indian Himalaya
Karakoram Highway
Kashmir, Ladakh & Zanskar
Nepal
Trekking in the Nepal Himalaya
Nepal phrasebook
Pakistan
Sri Lanka
Sri Lanka phrasebook

Africa
Africa on a shoestring
Central Africa
East Africa
Kenya
Swahili phrasebook
Morocco, Algeria & Tunisia
Moroccan Arabic phrasebook
West Africa

North America
Alaska
Canada
Hawaii

Mexico
Baja California
Mexico

South America
Argentina
Bolivia
Brazil
Brazilian phrasebook
Chile & Easter Island
Colombia
Ecuador & the Galápagos Islands
Latin American Spanish phrasebook
Peru
Quechua phrasebook
South America on a shoestring

Middle East
Egypt & the Sudan
Egyptian Arabic phrasebook
Israel
Jordan & Syria
Yemen

The Lonely Planet Story

Lonely Planet published its first book in 1973 in response to the numerous 'How did you do it?' questions Maureen and Tony Wheeler were asked after driving, bussing, hitching, sailing and railing their way from England to Australia.

Written at a kitchen table and hand collated, trimmed and stapled, *Across Asia on the Cheap* became an instant local bestseller, inspiring thoughts of another book.

Eighteen months in South-East Asia resulted in their second guide, *South-East Asia on a shoestring*, which they put together in a backstreet Chinese hotel in Singapore in 1975. The 'yellow bible' as it quickly became known to backpackers around the world, soon became *the* guide to the region. It has sold well over ½ million copies and is now in its 6th edition, still retaining its familiar yellow cover.

Today there are over 80 Lonely Planet titles – books that have that same adventurous approach to travel as those early guides; books that 'assume you know how to get your luggage off the carousel' as one reviewer put it.

Although Lonely Planet initially specialised in guides to Asia, they now cover most regions of the world, including the Pacific, South America, Africa, the Middle East and Eastern Europe. The list of *walking guides* and *phrasebooks* (for 'unusual' languages such as Quechua, Swahili, Nepalese and Egyptian Arabic) is also growing rapidly.

The emphasis continues to be on travel for independent travellers. Tony and Maureen still travel for several months of each year and play an active part in the writing, updating and quality control of Lonely Planet's guides.

They have been joined by over 50 authors, 40 staff – mainly editors, cartographers, & designers – at our office in Melbourne, Australia, and another 10 at our US office in Oakland, California. Travellers themselves also make a valuable contribution to the guides through the feedback we receive in thousands of letters each year.

The people at Lonely Planet strongly believe that travellers can make a positive contribution to the countries they visit, both through their appreciation of the countries' culture, wildlife and natural features, and through the money they spend. In addition, the company makes a direct contribution to the countries and regions it covers. Since 1986 a percentage of the income from each book has been donated to ventures such as famine relief in Africa; aid projects in India; agricultural projects in Central America; Greenpeace's efforts to halt French nuclear testing in the Pacific and Amnesty International. In 1990 $60,000 was donated to these causes.

Lonely Planet's basic travel philosophy is summed up in Tony Wheeler's comment, 'Don't worry about whether your trip will work out. Just go!'